D0621100

In the Company of Black Men

In the Company of Black Men

The African Influence on African American Culture in New York City

Craig Steven Wilder

NEW YORK UNIVERSITY PRESS
New York and London

NEW YORK UNIVERSITY PRESS
New York and London

© 2001 by New York University

Library of Congress Cataloging-in-Publication Data
Wilder, Craig Steven.
In the company of Black men : the African influence on African
American culture in New York City / Craig Steven Wilder.
p.   cm.
Includes bibliographical references (p.   ) and index.
ISBN 0-8147-9368-1 (cloth : alk. paper)
1. African American men—New York (State)—New York—Social
life and customs. 2. African American men—New York (State)—
New York—Societies, etc. 3. Voluntarism—New York (State)—
New York—History. 4. African American men—New York (State)—
New York—Religion. 5. Black nationalism—New York (State)—
New York—History. 6. African Americans—New York (State)—
New York—Relations with Africans. 7. Africa, West—Civilization.
8. Africa, West—Religious life and customs. 9. New York (N.Y.)—
Civilization. 10. United States—Civilization—African influences.
I. Title
F128.9.N4 W55 2001
305.38'8960730747—dc21   2001002836

New York University Press books are printed on acid-free paper,
and their binding materials are chosen for strength and durability.

Manufactured in the United States of America
10 9 8 7 6 5 4 3 2 1

For

Kenneth Terry Jackson,
Eric Foner,
Mark Naison,
Barbara Jeanne Fields,

and for

Terrie Diane Wilder
who taught me the meaning of "society"

Contents

All illustrations appear as a group following page 146.

Acknowledgments

I had some initial setbacks getting my first book to the public, and I am pleased to see that it has done well despite those early complications. I had left its final processing to its publishers while I dealt with an immediate personal concern: for a second time, a member of my family was suffering from schizophrenia. The loved ones of mentally ill people will wear some personal, emotional, and even professional scars, but these diseases reserve their greatest damage for those who directly suffer them. Over our lifetimes we will likely have a chance to realize a few of our dreams; however, mental illness will humble their endeavors and ambitions, distort their social lives, and threaten their personal bonds.

If fortunate, families like mine witness extraordinary exercises of human will. For instance, for the past several years, my oldest sister has struggled to control and conquer a disease that wants to destroy the basis of her person and erode the relationships that give life meaning. In a selfless expression of love, she has fought to maintain herself as a mother, sister, aunt, and friend. Her example has given us all the courage to confront the greater and lesser challenges of life.

Along the way, my family has enjoyed the support of many friends, and I have benefited from the generosity of many colleagues. My undergraduate and graduate mentors have been a well of comfort. Our relationships have evolved far beyond our professional ties. Writing this book has been a labor of pure enjoyment, and I think it appropriate that people who have so completely influenced my adult life share the dedication.

My romance with the African societies of Manhattan and Brooklyn began in the fall of 1991, when I rediscovered the New York African Society for Mutual Relief (NYASMR) papers while doing research in the library of Long Island University in Brooklyn. In 1945 the NYASMR folded and its records were abandoned in the Brooklyn Eagle Warehouse. A private collector took the papers after the facility was scheduled for demolition. They were later donated to LIU. I first used the collection to teach undergraduates to do primary research, and in the process I became quite familiar with the association and its members. I decided to write a history of the organization similar to one that Arthur Schomburg had proposed earlier this century. The structure of the book has changed significantly since then, but the desire to pay tribute to this important organization has remained. Following a lecture I gave on the NYASMR collection, the Schomburg Center for Research in Black Culture at the New York Public Library began microfilming the documents.

A few years ago, Niko Pfund, then editor-in-chief at New York University Press, contacted me about this work. His enthusiasm never waned. I also thank Eric Zinner, who inherited this undertaking, for his continued commitment to the project.

My colleagues at Williams College have formed a loud and much needed "Amen Corner."

The Ford Foundation funded the final revision of this book through the Schomburg Center for Research in Black Culture's Scholars-in-Residence Program. I extend my thanks to my Schomburg classmates—Leslie Maria Harris, Margaret Rose Vendryes, Martha Elizabeth Hodes, Jeffrey Stewart, Carolyn Anderson Brown, and Debra Walker King—for a raucous and productive tenure. Colin Palmer and Zita Nunes brought intellectual direction to the program and Diana Lachatanere and Aisha al-Adawiya administered it with care and enthusiasm.

A Rosenwald Fellowship at the New-York Historical Society allowed me to complete an important phase of this research.

Joan Maynard, Anna French, and Clement Scantlebury at the Society for the Preservation of Weeksville and Bedford-Stuyvesant History provided needed assistance in determining the significance of Brooklyn's African societies and the black women's associations. The staff of the New York State Library and Archives was a tremendous help. Craig Fisher and the librarians at Long Island University, Brooklyn, were patient and gracious. The Brooklyn Historical Society gave me generous access to its superb collection on the history of New York. I must also thank the Brooklyn Public Library, the New York Public Library, Sawyer Library at Williams College, Butler Library at Columbia University, Founder's Library at Howard University, and the Library of Congress.

My mother, Theresa Madeline Wilder, deserves a salute every time I turn on a computer. Terrie Diane Wilder and Gloria "Dr. Gloria" Wilder-brathwaite, M.D., my sisters, have shown unfailing confidence in me. My thanks to John Henry Wilder, Thoven L. E. Pearce, Travis Austin Wilderbrathwaite, Kai Maya Wilderbrathwaite, and Trent Dean Wilderbrathwaite, my nephews and niece, who inspire me to improve as a scholar and a person. Carlos Wilderbrathwaite certainly deserves my gratitude.

I also owe thanks to many friends and colleagues. Shanti Singham, Lester N. Wilson, Lynnette Virginia Diaz, Althea Spence, and the late Barbara Witenko all made countless contributions to this effort. One of my oldest friends, Kathryn Barrett-Gaines, regularly offered unsolicited advice on a manuscript that she never read, but I am fairly sure that she was trying to be helpful. Finally, friends like Doris Moreno, Elizabeth T. Rodriguez, and Dylan Goodrich shamelessly asked for mentions although they added absolutely nothing to this project.

In the Company of Black Men

"Some Little Tribute"
An Introduction

We feel that in the future some historian who may write the history of America and its progress, will be glad to add some little tribute to our work of benevolence.

—E. V. C. Eato, President, NYASMR, 1893

In her classic novel, *Brown Girl, Brownstones*, Paule Marshall describes the protagonist Selina's complicated relationship to the "Association of Barbadian Homeowners and Businessmen," a fictional Brooklyn benevolent society. For Selina, the association is a constant reminder of her mother's drive to "buy house," a determination that tore her family apart; but, the ABHB also sets the backdrop for the telling scene in which she emancipates herself from the burdens of her past. The organization meets in the basement of an old building on Fulton Street, where severe-looking men give inspirational speeches about community uplift. The walls of the meeting space are draped with yellow and red banners showing clasped black hands and the motto: "IT IS NOT THE DEPTHS FROM WHICH WE COME BUT THE HEIGHTS TO WHICH WE ASCEND." It exists to govern over a fund for loans, scholarships, political campaigns, and the like.[1] Marshall's society was modeled on the Paragon Progressive Community Association, a Barbadian-led organization formed in Depression-era Brooklyn. PPCA occupied an old Fulton Street building and operated an extraordinarily successful credit union and social outreach program.

Marshall took advantage of the Barbadian expression of a phenomenon that has repeated in New York's history. Paragon was just one of countless voluntary associations that local black communities have established over the last three centuries. Voluntary associations are discrete, interested, and self-regulated groups that function within the cleavages of more formal institutions to address the needs of their communities.[2] The roots of black voluntarism reach deep into the city's history. From their earliest arrival in the colony, Africans showed a particular talent for collective action through association, a phenomenon that laid the foundations for an African American culture. From the subaltern assemblies of the enslaved in colonial New York to the benevolent and spiritual New York African Society of the Early National era to the formation of the African Blood Brotherhood in twentieth-century Harlem, voluntary associations have been a fixture of African American communities.

The title and focus of this study reflect the greater availability of sources on antebellum men's organizations, which itself suggests that gender is a dominant variable in deciding the social place and public functions of voluntary associations. Darlene Clark Hine and Earnestine Jenkins assert that "the first generations of African men and women arrived on these shores with certain established notions about gender roles and identity" that were neither discarded nor erased. These gendered traditions influenced the emerging African American culture.[3] African heritage has contributed a unique voluntary tradition, and gender has set the contours of that influence.

Significantly, an increasingly broad literature on post–Civil War, African American women's associations—including examinations of local club movements, studies of national organizations, and histories of domestic and international church missions—has finally brought black voluntary associations into mainstream academic discourse. Women's associations have occupied the center of the institutional life of postbellum black communities. Women's organizations set the social agendas of black communities and provided a stage for challenging man-dominant politics over the past century.[4]

This scholarship also provides a template for interrogating the sometimes thin sources on antebellum black institutions in new ways, for lifting up new meanings, and for finding new connections. The origins of the distinctive African American voluntary tradition, the kinship and interplay of black secular and religious institutions, and black associations' role in forging a common African American identity and culture emerge as obvious themes for investigation. This literature begs a reconsideration of the idea that African American institutional culture is a deviation of Euro-American cultural forms, a notion that has cast black voluntarism as a learned rather than organic cultural response. "The reactive model," argues Robert L. Harris Jr. of this view of African American history, "impedes our appreciation of early black benevolent societies as voluntary associations and as the underpinning of black institutional life."[5]

Melville Herskovits writes that, in the United States, Africanisms—the survival "of African traditions and beliefs in the behavior of present-day Negroes in the United States and elsewhere in the New World"—were obvious in the benevolent and secret associations, which were "directly in line with the tradition underlying similar African organizations" and had an "Africanlike" blending of social, political, and spiritual interests through a cooperative model.[6] *In the Company of Black Men* begins there, with Herskovits's observation that the communitarian foundations of African American institutional life, when placed against similar patterns in West Africa and its Diaspora, appear to be the remnants of African sensibilities about social relations rather than deviations from a gross, white cultural standard.

Thomas Holt warns that the scholarly invocation of a Diaspora assumes that there is value in comparing "experiences that unfolded for *different* black peoples in *different* places and times." The danger of comparison rests in the need to hold constant sociocultural processes that are fluid.[7] Here, the goal is not to conflate or dissect the histories of peoples of African descent but to reveal a coherent pattern that can be detected across those experiences and over time. The universality of the voluntary tradition suggests that African American community has its basis in collectivism: a behavioral and rhetorical tendency to privilege the group over the individual. Collective cultures arose as enslaved Africans unleashed the potential for group action and mass resistance in familiar West African relationships. That does not mean that West African cultures were, by deduction or rule, collectivist, but rather that Africans entered the Americas equipped with intellectual traditions and sociological models that facilitated a communitarian response to oppression.

In the Company of Black Men explores that cultural expression within and through African societies: the antebellum voluntary associations that free and enslaved Africans organized to pursue public and covert goals and to provide leadership for emerging African American communities. It examines the New York African societies from their earliest appearance to the folding of the last such formal association, and argues that organizations forged out of necessity became the basis for three centuries of African American cultural development.

The axiom that black people united because they were oppressed is far too simplistic. It limits the investigation to what was happening to them and ignores what they were constructing for themselves. It suggests that they merely reacted from a common emotional place shaped by an external, vicious, and omnipotent oppressor. Rather, while collectivism responded to external forces, it was also the basis for intragroup relations. Persecution may have been a catalyst, but black culture still drew on sources that were independent of white forms and generated functions that were independent of white behavior. Collectivist notions were the organic product of real intellectual traditions and social relationships; they resonated because they were rooted in the African American institutional world.

The book is divided into three parts. Part One establishes a West African legacy in New York by examining the origins of the city's earliest black institutions and the ideology of enslaved and free black people. Of particular interest is the connection between the voluntary society and the church. Robert Gregg argues that historians' understandings of the black church have been driven by observation rather than analysis of "the way the churches operated and how they functioned within the larger community."[8] The church is generally considered the mother of African American institutional culture; however, voluntary associations preexisted the institutional church and played a critical role in the founding of black houses of worship. Long after the religious revolution that brought the conversion of thousands of black New Yorkers, voluntary societies continued to operate within and alongside churches, bridging the secular and spiritual worlds and creating a space for Christian social action. Part One offers a reinterpretation of the origins of African American religion by locating the voluntary association as a West African legacy and the source of the peculiar heredity of black institutional and philosophical Christianity.

Part Two explores the impact of voluntary associations on the public sphere in antebellum black New York. The black church was the symbolic center of the African American community, but the African association was the site of social action. In *Black Yankees*, William D. Piersen reshapes the image of African associations by noting their influence on religious and social life.[9] The argument can be pushed further. Societies were not simply the secular arm of the black church, they were an independent force that guided and nurtured political and social thought. *In the Company of Black Men* seeks to challenge the entrenched belief that the church was the nucleus of African American life. Voluntary associations claimed broader social functions than most churches and even rivaled churches as an institutional force in black communities.

Part Three examines the decline and transition of the voluntary tradition in the black metropolis. The rise of capitalist culture, a growing individualism, and the political revolution that followed the Civil War all worked to weaken the social role of African voluntary societies. This section uses the city's most prominent African society as a case study to argue that, while local African societies were shaken by the changing economic and political realities of postbellum America, the greatest crisis was ideological—the inability of the members to resolve their growing individualism with the organization's collectivist foundations. Finally, it explains how the rise of bourgeois culture increased the prominence of national and international black fraternities, unisex ethnic associations, and black women's organizations and brought the simultaneous decline of African societies.

PART I

African Voluntary Associations and the Rise of Black Spiritual Culture

1

A Taunt from the Oppressed

The West African Institutional Legacy in New York City, 1644–1783

You have seen the depth of their vengeance,
all their plots against me.
O Lord, you have heard their insults,
all their plots against me—
what my enemies whisper and mutter
against me all day long.
Look at them!
Sitting or Standing,
they mock me in their songs.
                    —Lamentations 3:60–63

The study of Africanisms—transplanted West African beliefs and traditions—in the United States has focused on linguistic and behavioral remnants, scattered cultural effects, divorced from their familial, political, and economic contexts, that disprove as much as they prove social continuity. In 1941 Melville J. Herskovits's *Myth of the Negro Past* sparked the modern debate by exposing West African influences in African American culture. Herskovits's examination does not disclose the mechanism of this perseverance. It is this shortcoming that E. Franklin Frazier exploits in refutation, arguing instead that for black people "in the New World, particularly in what became the United States . . . [the] new conditions of life destroyed the significance of their African heritage and caused new habits and attitudes to develop to meet new situations." Unimpressed with linguistic survivals or behavioral similarities, Frazier imposes a harsher standard, concluding that "there is scarcely any evidence that recognizable elements of the African social organization have survived in the United States. This has been especially true in regard to those phases of the African social organization which had a political character." Still, the need for more creative thinking about colonial society remains, Gary Nash writes, "unless we wish to continue picturing some one million Africans brought to or born in America before the Revolution as mindless and cultureless drones."[1]

It is easy to sympathize with Frazier's political concern that only those phenomena vulnerable to cultural criticism—such as instances of promiscuity or illegitimacy—will be examined as Africanisms, but his dismissal of possible connections is grounded in assumption. To assault the foundations for the belief in Africanisms, Frazier invokes an insidious product of racialism in American social science that has become axiomatic: "black culture" is imitative of, results from, or reacts to "white culture." Its central tenet is that in subjecting Africans to servitude, Europeans also achieved a cultural conquest. Beliefs and traditions were erased as persecution forced Africans to adapt to new, dominant institutions.[2] The effect is unilateral, for African American culture can be assumed to have Anglo-American origins, even when the links are unfounded or dubious and even when plausible alternatives are extant, but that supposition cannot be reversed without voluminous offers of proof.

The traditional approach casts African cultures as simple while European cultures are complex; thus, African social forms passively folded under the force of European organization. "There is no more theoretical support for an hypothesis that they [African Americans] have retained nothing of the culture of their African forbears, than in supposing that they have remained completely African in their behavior," Herskovits asserts. He is not alone in seeing cultural retention. "It ought not to be forgotten that each Negro slave brought to America during the four centuries of the African slave trade was taken from definite and long-formed habits of social, political, and religious life," reads W. E. B. Du Bois's Atlanta University publications. While their "blood relations" were broken, enslaved Africans did not have their minds swept of all experiences and ideas. Carter G. Woodson stresses similarities between African cultures and those encountered in Europe and America that created space for African retention. Joseph R. Washington Jr. adds that the habit of viewing African cultures as primitive leads naturally to the belief that enslaved Africans contributed nothing to the civilization of the Americas. A recent study more directly explodes many of these long-held myths. Sylviane A. Diouf argues that for centuries enslaved African Muslims maintained their religion, keeping its dietary laws, dress codes, spiritual routines, and even producing and smuggling copies of the Koran—all in the hostile cultural environment of the Caribbean and the United States. The evidence of Muslim cultural retention is abundant; however, many scholars do not recognize the features of the faith or they favor the idea that a dominant Christianity eradicated any traces of Islam.[3]

Assumptions about race and culture are so pervasive that the scholar interested in exploring African continuities needs to produce both the logical connections and the means of transfer; otherwise "the compelling force of Anglo-American culture," to quote Forrest G. Wood, cannot be overcome. "While others have focused on the differences between impalpable Africanisms in the United States and conspicuous Africanisms in much of the rest of the New World, they inadvertently called attention to a disturbing aspect of the American condition: Southern slaves lost most of the vestiges of their African heritage *because* the oppressive institutional forces of Protestant Anglo-American society easily smothered them." Wood rejects the cultural similarities that are the subject of the study of Africanisms and underscores the death of African philosophical and ideological traditions.[4]

The conjecture in Wood's assertion, hidden in the phrase "Anglo-American," is that white colonials were fairly good ambassadors of European cultures. Viewing "culture as some sort of undifferentiated whole," note Sidney Mintz and Richard Price, allows for the misguided assertion that two cultures—"'bodies' of belief and value, each coherent, functioning, and intact"—arrived and warred for dominance in Colonial America. The most identifiable European colonists, be they political and religious dissidents or profiteers, experienced revolutionary cultural change. Africans and, to a lesser extent, Europeans lacked the "personnel" to maintain the institutional foundations of their cultures.[5] Anglo-American culture was born out of the European encounter with the Americas and Africa. In the colonies, both Europeans and Africans confronted new situations and faced new demands, and Europeans differed only in that their social position allowed them to maintain their familial, legal, and political relationships. Those continuities should not mask the velocity of cultural transformation, for the culture that Wood identifies as dominant was not a fixed weapon of oppression but the fluid result of social intercourse.

Frazier and Wood are correct in arguing that bondage meant the destruction of most institutional attachments for individual Africans; nonetheless, accepting the harsh limitation to social relations and organization, the possibility of African continuity remains. The latter can be found in sociological and anthropological studies of West Africa. The corporate foundations of West African social life comprised groupings based on kinship, age, gender, labor, and ideology. Secret societies—defined by esoteric knowledge, structure, and ritual—are the foremost example of these. It is in these "nonrelationship groupings" that Herskovits finds a quality of "cooperative endeavor," or an example of an African heritage in African American social institutions. Carter G. Woodson, one of the first scholars to make this connection, notes that African American culture maintained the prominence of secret societies found in West African societies. John Thornton places secret societies among the indigenous West African institutions that enabled enslaved Africans to organize communities "without reference to kin or kinship groups" destroyed in the slave trade. Africans used these common institutions not to recapture something lost but to lay the foundations for something new. Following the logic of this connection, Michael A. Gomez concludes that, while even the major West African secret societies could not re-create their formal structures in the Americas, "informal arrangements would have continued and would have been, due to the clandestine nature of the societies, difficult to detect by outsiders."[6]

These influences did not constitute a transplantation of a culture because they were divorced from the rich institutional fabric of the West African civilizations that produced them; rather, they were part of a plausible African "heritage"—the social and intellectual material that can be roughly described as shared by West African peoples—in African American culture.[7] The societal connection offers the most provocative link between African and African American history, and the evidence suggests that clandestine voluntary associations also patterned early community life in black New York.

The nature of secret societies makes this line of argument risky. European societies were first formed among conquered peoples as a form of resistance that gave continuity to the old hierarchies. They took on various guises, from charitable to literary, to hide their purposes. However, the nature of these organizations encourages hyperbole; it, oddly, allows for the extremes that create secret societies as a superhistorical force or deny almost completely their existence. The tendency in European voluntary societies toward contrived secrets and traditions fuels this exaggeration. Scholars have largely abandoned this field to amateurs because of its conspiratorial emphases, writes J. M. Roberts in a call for serious academic study: "The result has been the mountain of rubbish—still growing, though now more slowly—which explains everything from the collapse of the Roman Empire to the Russian Revolution in terms of secret societies."[8]

West African societies are a very different set of institutions. They are not, in the European style, defined by contrived secrets from which non-members are excluded; rather, they are public associations that hoard special knowledge and skills, locate themselves between social beliefs and social behaviors, control ritual life, and protect the public interest. An early Mande association of enslaved people mediated disputes between servants and masters. In the Protectorate of Sierra Leone, the Poro society coordinated the 1898 uprising against British colonial rule. In a matter of days they executed the Englishmen in several districts and confiscated the property of British subjects. Poro held special meetings to plan the revolt, and it placed the greater community under an oath of secrecy. As late as the 1950s, Poro was still challenging British rule in Sierra Leone. Similarly, secret societies undermined English authority in Nigeria and were critical to establishing home rule after the fall of the colonial government. Secret societies also flourished in Central Africa. Christian missionaries targeted the Ubutwa society of Zambia as the primary barrier to conversion. The colonial government also opposed the association. Notwithstanding, Ubutwa remained a social force, infiltrated government institutions, and survived the colonial period.[9]

Such societies translate ideology into action, and enslaved Africans proved quite adept at reconstructing these traditions in the Americas. For example, the Gullah culture of the South Carolina Sea Islands evolved from West African secret societies, ancestral beliefs, and sacred medicines.[10] Through secret societies, African Americans re-created African social relationships in the United States and achieved power in the face of bondage. West Africans entered the Americas equipped with a model of community organization in the absence of legal authority and social power. Moreover, since their basis was ideological, societies insured that Africans entering the Americas did not simply stop *being* African.

During its reign in New Netherland, the Dutch West India Company immediately encountered West Africans' capacity for collective action. In 1644, eleven African men—Paulo Angola, Little Manuel, Big Manuel, Manuel de Gerrit de Reus, Simon Congo, Anthony Portugis, Peter Santomee, Jan Francisco, Little Anthony, Gracia, and Jan Fort Orange—petitioned West India for their liberty. The governor freed the African men and their wives under a set of harsh restrictions that included annual tributes and West India's continued ownership of their children. Within three years, five men and one woman acquired land in a small section of lower Manhattan and began the city's first free African community. By 1650 there were over a dozen black landowners. In describing the identity of this community, Graham Russell Hodges contends that it "best resembled the confraternities or brotherhoods found among Kongolese and Angolan blacks living in Brazil." The free Africans formed an informal association that governed their community and its relations with enslaved people.[11]

It is difficult to imagine that Africans could maintain any traditions in a colony premised upon their enslavement and subordination. In the seventeenth century, Africans were one-fifth of New York City's population. In the eighteenth century, the population of enslaved Africans in Manhattan came to rival Charleston, the nation's foremost slave city. By the 1790s, 10 percent of New York's population was African, and a majority of the Africans remained in servitude despite the Revolutionary discourse about liberty and justice. In Kings County, which included the town of Brooklyn, African bondspeople were one-third of the population, and more than 60 percent of all white families held at least one person in bondage. To control the enslaved, the legislature fashioned the harshest slave code outside the South. A history of crime in New York colony finds that Africans "were prevented by law from buying liquor, holding funerals after dark, going out at night without a candle or lantern, assembling in groups of more than three, belonging to the militia, or carrying a gun or other weapon of any kind, leaving their masters' houses on the sabbath, or even training a dog." New York City's white residents imposed elaborate regulations on the enslaved because of the concentration of Africans in that area. Manhattan masters were even given use of the local jail to punish recalcitrant servants.[12]

The slave code is a fairly good indicator of the African impact on the colony because—while it was influenced by Dutch experiences in the Caribbean and Brazil and English encounters in Virginia and the West Indies—the laws of bondage in New Netherland and New York typically reacted to the actions of the unfree. The code intended to force Africans to adhere to the socioeconomic culture of bondage; therefore, it specifically targeted African forms of resistance, particularly combinations of the unfree that sought to end or ameliorate their condition.

As lifetime hereditary bondage was being forged for Africans, Dutch colonists immediately faced the persistent problem of servants running away. In 1640 and 1642, the Dutch West India Company passed fugitive slave laws to control the damage that absconding did to the colonial economy and the social order. In 1654 Peter Stuyvesant revealed that residents of Amersfort (Flatlands), Kings County, were using enslaved Africans to hunt fugitive servants.[13]

The 1664 fall of New Netherland to England led to a rapid rise in the African population and more telling legislation. A New York act of 1684 confessed the problem of Africans' engagement in an illegal economy and their propensity to abscond. That law also created a limited machinery to deal with cruelty toward servants. By 1702 the problem of controlling enslaved Africans had worsened. Residents were forbidden to "Imploy, harbour, Conceal, or entertain other mens slaves at their house, out-house or Plantation" without consent. A similar concern guided the decision to make it illegal "for above three Slaves to meet together att any other time, nor att any other place, than when it shall happen they meet in some servile Imploym't for their Master's or Mistress's proffitt." The punishment, forty lashes on the "naked back, at [the] discretion of any Justice of the peace," underscored the severity of the crime. Cities and towns were given authority to tax slave owners in order to appoint public whippers and insure vigilance. (In 1694 Staten Island received its first whipping post, but within a few years the Islanders grew tired of paying the public whipper to come from New Amsterdam and the post was abandoned. In 1710 the free residents acquired a new whipping post to punish two men: one white man guilty of a minor offense, and one enslaved African convicted of burglary and the theft of "a number of choice and valuable fowl.") The African underground economy persisted, and the law prohibited all commerce with enslaved people not engaged in their owners' business. Justices received special procedures for cases in which Africans assaulted "any freeman or Woman professing Christianity." Perhaps a better glimpse at African behavior came from the limitations on enslaved people presenting evidence before courts. No bound African could testify in any procedure except in "Cases of Plotting or Confederacy amongst themselves, either to run away, kill or destroy their Master or Mistress, or burning of houses, or barnes or barracks of Corn, or the killing of their Master's or Mistress's Cattle."[14]

It is fantastic to conclude from such scanty evidence that seventeenth-century Africans joined into bands that facilitated the arming of the unfree, the establishment of maroon societies of fugitive Africans, flight, conspiracy, and rebellion through an illicit underground economy; however, the laws of New Netherland and New York identified these elements as the central concerns in the ordering of bondage. Dutch West India and Royal Africa erected defensive bulwarks that responded to and meant to eliminate African combination.

Both colonial enterprises encountered similar patterns of resistance when they attempted to enslave Africans in the Americas. In Brazil's Palmares, the great "Negro Republic," the West India Company battled an expansive maroon society, organized under an African system of rule, which sustained itself for a century through hunting, fishing, agriculture, and secret and open commerce with European colonials. The territory included several villages and thousands of residents. As R. K. Kent describes it,

> the most apparent significance of Palmares to African history is that an African political system could be transferred to a different continent; that it could come to govern not only individuals from a variety of ethnic groups in Africa but also those born in Brazil, pitch black or almost white, latinized or close to Amerindian roots; and that it could endure for almost a full century against two European powers, Holland and Portugal.

In eighteenth-century Jamaica, Royal Africa confronted two ancestral cults descended from West African secret societies. Maroon villages and cults exposed Africans' capacity for exploiting the West African heritage to establish their own institutions in the Americas.[15]

Although nothing on the scale of Palmares was ever constructed in their colony, Africans in New York responded to bondage by calling upon African forms. In the summer of 1706, white New Yorkers got a hint of that ability. On July 22, Edward Lord Viscount Cornbury, the provincial governor, armed justices of the peace in Kings County (today's Brooklyn), Long Island, with the death penalty in order to deal with African maroons who, after freeing themselves, were striking fear among the local colonists:

> Whereas, I am informed that several negroes in Kings County have *assembled themselves in a riotous manner*, which, if not prevented, may prove of ill consequence; you and every [one] of you are therefore hereby required and commanded to take all proper methods for seizing and apprehending all such negroes in the said county as shall be found to be assembled in such manner as aforesaid, or have run away or absconded from their masters or owners, whereby there may be reason to suspect them of *ill practices or designs*, and to secure them in safe custody, that their crimes and actions may be inquired into; and if any of them refuse to submit themselves, then to fire on them, kill or destroy them, if they cannot otherwise be taken; and for so doing this shall be your sufficient warrant.[16]

Free New Yorkers soon discovered the intent of this "riotous manner" and the substance of these "ill practices" and "designs." On the evening of January 24, 1708, an enslaved black woman and an enslaved Native American man named Sam sought revenge on their owner, William Hallet Jr., of New Town, Queens County. The servants reacted to Hallet's refusal to allow them to travel on the Sabbath. The bondswoman convinced Sam to kill Hallet, his pregnant wife, and their five children and to seize the estate, Hallet's Cove. After the revolt, the two conspirators and several other Africans were arrested. The *Boston News-Letter* reported evidence of a larger plot in which "several other Families were designed for the like slaughter." On February 2 the woman was burned to death and Sam was suspended in chains beside a blade that cut his flesh as he moved. They were "put to all the torment possible for a terror to others, of ever attempting the like wickedness." In the days that followed, two other Africans were executed. The legislature extended the death penalty to any human chattel who attempted to murder "her Majesties Leige [*sic*] People not being Negroes[,] Mulattos[,] or Slaves."[17]

New York's officials were concerned with the safety of the colonists, and their fears highlight the most easily ignored evidence of African influence: that web of interpersonal obligations and dependencies that can quickly be discarded as "slave unity." West African cultures were a complex of overlapping communities divided by age, gender, and lineage, grounded in ancestral and spiritual beliefs, and regulated by complicated ethical systems. Enslaved New Yorkers had West African models on which to pattern an African American collectivism. The legal and political machinery of eighteenth-century New York constantly reacted to such networks of the unfree.

Certainly every assemblage of black people did not constitute a borrowing on African tradition, but several did. Sometimes peaceful, sometimes not, these associations drew considerable official attention. The colonial administration repeatedly attempted to outlaw such public and private rendezvous, and for good reason. African uprisings always troubled those engaged in mastery, and their familiar pattern made white New Yorkers tremble at news of revolts in other places. European colonials spent little time trying to understand the West African heritage; rather, they attempted to punish it, control it, and curse it, but nonetheless Africanisms set the stage of their nightmares.

On New Year's Day 1712, "Cormantine" and "Pawpaw" bondservants, recently imported to New York, conspired to be free. The Reverend John

Sharpe, chaplain of the English garrison, wrote that the Africans tied "themselves to Secrecy by Sucking ye blood of each Others hands" and acquired invincibility from a "free negroe who pretends Sorcery [and] gave them a powder to rub on their Cloths which made them so confident." Several months later, Governor Robert Hunter recounted the events in a letter to the Lords of Trade. On March 25, these Africans drank and plotted further in a Manhattan tavern. Twenty-five to thirty enslaved Africans joined in a blood oath with two "Spanish Indians" and a free person of color. The *Boston News-Letter* claimed that most of Manhattan's Africans had prior knowledge of the plot. At about 2 A.M. on April 7, they met at an orchard in the middle of the city with guns, swords, knives, and hatchets. Cuffee and John, enslaved to Peter Van Tilborough, set fire to their owner's outhouse and then rejoined the larger band. The Africans freed the souls of neighbors who responded to the fire. Nine Christians were dispatched. They cut throats, stabbed chests, and lowered axes across necks. Hearing the gunfire and the screams, Hunter sounded the alarm. The rebels fled into the woods. The revolt ended. The governor ordered guards to secure all avenues of escape.[18]

The following morning, Hunter had the New York and West Chester militia "drive the Island, and by this means and strict searches in the town, we found all that put the design in execution." Six Africans took their own lives rather than surrender. Van Tilborough's Cuffee and Dick, an enslaved black boy, were the main witnesses in the trials that followed. The militia took seventy enslaved Africans into custody, the courts found twenty-five bondspeople guilty, and the government executed eighteen by methods that Hunter confidently declared "the most exemplary punishment inflicted that could be possibly thought of": one African was roasted slowly over a fire, two were burned to death, one was broken on the wheel, one was suspended in chains and left to starve, the others were hanged. The governor eventually ended the furor and the prosecutor's thirst for revenge by pardoning the remaining convicts. In particular, a pregnant woman, whose execution was postponed, "has suffer'd more than death by her long imprisonment" and deserved mercy; as did two prisoners who were among several men of mixed ancestry captured seven years earlier on a Spanish privateer and who, "by reason of their colour which is swarthy," were declared "to be slaves and as such were sold" although they claimed to be free citizens of Spain. Hunter "secretly pittyed their condition."[19]

The ethnicity of the participants in New York's 1712 revolt, the use of the blood oath, and the life-or-death struggle suggest African influence. The Reverend John Sharpe and many white Manhattanites wanted to believe that the Spanish Indians—"having [the] most understanding to carry on a plot and being Christians"—organized the insurrection. However, white colonials were too familiar with the pattern of African resistance to enslavement to sustain this delusion. It was not long before the Reverend Sharpe was encouraging the governor's mercy for the Spanish men. Only months before the New York plot, Manhattan received rumors and reports that "seven new Cormantine" servants rebelled in Port Royal, Jamaica. The Africans took a knife to their mistress's throat and "almost severed her head from her body." They then fell upon her sister, who "had her hand almost cut off," and a white boarder, who was stabbed in several places. Soldiers eventually captured and executed this band.[20]

White New Yorkers regularly confronted enslaved Africans' capacity to organize vengeance, and they knew the signs of that mischief. Blood oaths were significant in West African cultures and particularly important to Gold Coast ritual. Oaths and blood oaths confirmed both public and private ties and were sworn on ancestral lines. "No matter how widely scattered, rite participants remained brothers—'all of one blood,'" writes Michael Mullin in his history of African acculturation and resistance in the Americas.[21]

Slaving activities in the colony laid the foundations for the 1712 insurrection. In 1648 the directors of the West India Company empowered New Netherlanders to trade with Brazil and Angola, but ordered that private ships carrying goods to Angola "are to bring [back] Negroes to be employed in farming." For the sake of profit, the directors allowed the demographic homogeneity that other colonial authorities sought to avoid. In the decade before the uprising, the Royal Africa Company transported more than a hundred Guinea and Angolan men, women, and children. At the same time, two hundred African Caribbeans passed through the port of New York. Each year for the first quarter of the seventeenth century, private traders carried one hundred unfree Africans through New York's harbor.[22]

The combinations were volatile. Africans had the means to unite across ethnic lines for common goals. South Carolina planters feared the presence of Angolans among the enslaved and the militaristic Coromantee (Akan-speaking people from the Gold Coast) bedeviled the white people of the British Caribbean. Maroon societies, often organized along ethnic lines, appeared throughout the Americas. In 1545 colonial authorities in Peru were at war with a band of two hundred African maroons who elected their own king, kept a storehouse of weapons, and plotted to overthrow the Spanish settlement. Seventeenth-century colonists on Providence Island repeatedly warred with African maroons. Maroon villages peppered Brazil, and secret societies reorganized there virtually intact. Angolans provided much of Palmares's political and military strength. The maroon camps of Guyana were powerful enough to force the colonial authorities into negotiation. Africans in Jamaica used England's conquest of the Spanish colony to establish its earliest maroon society. English colonial policy jumped back and forth from appeasing to subduing the Jamaican maroons. In 1733 fugitive Africans outwitted, defeated, and then taunted a British military force sent to hunt them. Maroons compromised England's control of St. Vincent, Grenada, and Dominica. By the end of the eighteenth century, England was warring with the West Indian rebels. One maroon leader, Quashee, even offered a reward for the colonial governor's head. In Jamaica, writes Mavis C. Campbell, "most members of each [maroon] community were bound by the awesome Akan oath, where secrecy was enjoined." They quickly established village and communal relations and even coordinated resistance across the island. In eighteenth-century French San Domingo (Haiti), thousands of Africans populated the scattered maroon villages, many of which were ruled by chiefs. West African Muslims, regardless of their ethnic backgrounds, were a dangerous addition to the corps of the enslaved and conspicuous among the maroons. They organized the earliest rebellions in the Americas, had a hand in the Haitian Revolution, and were the central actors in the 1835 Bahian uprising. Through oaths, unity, and secrecy, maroons also converted the swampy areas of the United States into camps from which they raided plantations from Virginia and the Carolinas to Louisiana.[23]

West Africans were familiar with numerous intergenerational, international, and intertribal secret societies. In Africa these bands ranged from benevolent, burial, and religious associations to political, martial, criminal, and subversive societies. Some developed secret languages, adopted signs and rites, imposed ranks with insignia, and kept meetinghouses, shrines, and dormitories. Membership in the earliest associations was limited to men, with initiation at puberty, but unisex and women's organizations followed. The "Society of the Magicians" claimed its genesis around 1600 B.C. and spread from North Africa to West Africa in the following centuries. "Si'mo" and "Oro" were the oldest indigenous West African organizations. Their warrior-priests carried them from Guinea and Nigeria to Angola and multiplied their power by spawning kindred associations. From 1100 to 1500 A.D., Mande traders and smiths spread secret societies along the commercial routes of West Africa. In the Kpelle Chiefdom (Liberia), Poro was the foremost men's association, controlling ritual life over the region, and Sande was the primary women's organization. Poro and Sande descended from earlier societies. These collectives had far-reaching authority, and the dominant associations could even threaten or bolster secular power. Poro's spiritual prestige meant that it possessed an authority that transcended force, and it could thereby use its alliances to legitimize chiefdoms. By the seventeenth century, "societies [were] the repositories of the folklore, myths and history and the conceptions of art and culture and learning and wisdom the tribes possessed. Moreover, they became the teachers of these things. The only teachers," writes F. W. Butt-Thompson. In this way they consolidated their power wherever they operated and "when forced to migrate or when sold overseas, they planted the 'banner' of their society in the midst of their new homes."[24]

After 1712, the legislature passed successive laws to stop African confederacy, regulate the bound population, codify punishments, and mandate enforcement. Governor Hunter, in response to the "Late Hellish Attempt of yo[u]r Slaves," wished to put "that Sort of men under better Regulation" and suggested that the Assembly might "take away the Root of that Evill . . . [through] the Importation of White Servants." The 1712 "Act for preventing, suppressing punishing the conspiracy and insurrection of negroes and other slaves" tightened the law of 1702. It troubled the authors that Africans could get cash and goods, including weapons, through illicit trade, as did the laxity of colonists who entered into "Contracts and Bargains" with chattel. Confederacy continued to torment the colony, and the legislature restated its 1702 restrictions on African assemblies while warning of the "ill practices" that occurred during such gatherings. Most noticeable, however, was the growing fear of free people of color: "There are many Negroes, Indians or Mullattos, who have been formerly manumitted and made free within the Colony . . . and it is found by Experience, that they entertain, harbour, support and encourage Negro[,] Indian[,] and Mullatto Slaves, to the great detriment of the Masters of such Slaves." Declared members of "an Idle slothfull people," people of color freed thereafter were to be denied the right to hold or own land or houses and those who already had estates were to have their land transferred to "Her Majesty[,] Her Heirs and Successors" upon their death. The legislators made it more difficult to free the enslaved, extended the death penalty to cover a greater number of crimes, and imposed specific penalties on Africans who bore arms. Special powers were granted to the justices of the peace in New York City to facilitate the rebels' prosecution.[25]

As the first anniversary of the revolt approached, the Common Council of New York City published "A Law for Regulating Negro and Indian Slaves in the Night Time." After March 10, 1713, enslaved persons above the age of fourteen were forbidden from wandering in the city unless carrying a lighted lantern and candle sufficient to be seen from a distance. All free citizens were empowered to arrest any offenders and bring them to the mayor, recorder, or any alderman to be jailed. Masters and mistresses of the accused were fined, and the enslaved received forty lashes at the public whipping post. In 1722 the council struck at, and thereby admitted, the problem of Africans "Gaming or Playing in the Streets of this City, or in . . . Any House[,] Out House[,] or Yard." The question was not gambling; rather, the alderman feared that Africans acquired money through such sports. They detailed corporal punishments for bondservants and fines for their owners.[26]

On October 29, 1730, the legislature fortified the provincial code in an act that condemned the "too great Liberty allowed to Negro and other Slaves." To keep bondspeople from accumulating cash and to reduce their "Mischiefs," the lawmakers forbade trade with enslaved Africans without the permission of their respective owners. They then outlawed the sale of spirits to the unfree. The new act prohibited unsupervised gatherings of enslaved Manhattanites or meetings between enslaved and free people of color. It held masters liable for the actions of their chattel, appointed town whippers, and set compulsory punishments for Africans who "Shall presume to Assault or Strike any Christian or Jew." The legislature finally arranged for reimbursement to any masters who lost human property under the stronger code.[27]

However, the 1741 Manhattan slave conspiracy proved that enslaved Africans' capacity for collective action was greater than the vigilance of New York lawmakers. The facts of the plot are more easily separated from the exaggerations that followed its discovery when scrutinized against patterns in West Africa and the Diaspora. Historian T. J. Davis notes that a healthy sense of self-preservation and a belief in the inferiority of Africans kept white Manhattanites from the thought that black people had masterminded the scheme to set fire to the city and kill its free inhabitants. Instead, they stretched the logical scope of the conspiracy, conflating it with their other social phobias. They assigned blame to a great papal plot against the small Protestant colony and, then, found a core of Irish and Catholic malcontents to charge as corrupters. Some of the condemned Africans, who had been introduced to Catholicism in the West Indies, kissed crucifixes before going to their deaths and aggravated the fear of a religious conspiracy.[28]

The attorney general went so far as to rename the affair "Hughson's Plot," after the first white man put to death in its aftermath. However, Justice Daniel Horsmanden, who heard months of testimony, doubted that "an illiterate cob[b]ler" could devise such "a train of policy." The fact that Horsmanden believed John Hughson somewhat incapable but Africans even more inept pointed him to a greater conspiracy. Eventually, two white men and two white women were executed along with thirty black people from New York and Kings County, while scores of people were deported.[29]

White New Yorkers needed to accept that white men were behaving like Africans in order to reject the possibility that the enslaved were designing revolution, for the events of 1741 had a distinctly African pattern. Sarah, Hughson's daughter, and William Kane, an Irish soldier, both testified that Africans regularly came to the Hughson house where they often drew "a black ring" on the floor into which the participants placed their left feet. A bowl of liquor punch was held above their heads, vows were taken, and the drink was then consumed. The Hughsons and the Africans performed ring ceremonies more than once in the months before the plot was uncovered. African spiritual practices fortified the uprising. The participants could not be violent unless they were united; they could not be joined unless they were believers. "The circle ritual imported by Africans from the Congo region," in Sterling Stuckey's words, "was so powerful in its elaboration of a religious vision that it contributed disproportionately to the centrality of the circle in slavery. The use of the circle for religious purposes in slavery was so consistent and profound that one could argue that it was what gave form and meaning to black religion and art."[30]

The ring ceremonies reaffirmed the participants' oaths of secrecy and fidelity, oaths powerful enough to keep the plot undetected for months and to allow the conspirators time to gather, store, and distribute weapons. According to the testimony, several Africans and the Hughsons swore on a Bible, the Spanish (West Indian) Negroes on thunder and lightning, and others on blood and lineage. (Africans in nearby New England engaged in similar practices.) The thunder gods and ancestral worship were general aspects of West African religious cultures. "The obligation of that infernal oath, which had so often been administered to them by Hughson and the other principal conspirators, was the true reason for the backwardness and hesitancy of the criminals, and their alternately insisting upon the punctilio of the others opening first," cried Horsmanden. While Hughson engaged in illegal activity and conspiracy, his greatest crime was being the "fence" of a local African combination.[31]

At least three secret societies operated within the larger group of conspirators. Two of the chief plotters came from a criminal society, "a confederacy of negroes," that once sported the tag the "Free Masons," mocking the English association. (In 1730 the Duke of York and the Grand Lodge of England chartered the latter with Daniel Coxe as grand master of New York, New Jersey, and Pennsylvania, and it quickly spread throughout the colony.) The Free Masons were arrested and publicly whipped for stealing bottles of Geneva liquor from the cellar of a local tavern. Thereafter, they proudly wore their crime, renaming themselves the "Geneva Club." The enslaved Africans Caesar and Prince, the first two people executed in the plot, were leaders of Geneva, as was Cuffee, who was later put to death. The justices condemned Caesar and Prince for stealing—an event that, along with suspicious fires, precipitated the fears of conspiracy—before they could be tried for rebellion, although Caesar, Prince, and Cuffee bragged that they commanded New York's Africans. Caesar paid Hughson to purchase guns, pistols, and swords. Two African gangs at either end of Manhattan were to start the insurrection. As laid out, the "Smith's Fly Boys" were to burn the east side of town, while the "Long Bridge Boys" torched the west. Already mustered into companies with captains, the Africans were to take those fires as a signal to burn their owners' houses and kill their masters in the chaos. For all his paranoia, racism, and exaggeration, Horsmanden offered some interesting thoughts on the relationship between the chief African conspirators and the black community:

> It even appeared that these *head fellows* boasted of *their superiority* over the more harmless and inoffensive; that they held them in an inferiority and dependence, a kind of subjection, as if they had got such dominion over them, *that they durst not, at any time, or upon any occasion, but do as they would have them*; for whence it may be guessed, how likely the defection was to be general.[32]

Horsmanden's observations suggest something worth noting: West African worldviews could survive in New York. Following the trajectory of his fears and filling in that of which he was ignorant, it becomes more likely that it was the persistence of African traditions that allowed the 1741 conspirators to dominate so many people, white and black, and drag Manhattan to the brink of revolution.

A 1748 account restated Horsmanden's belief that the leaders of the 1741 conspiracy were conjurers who subordinated others with their fantastic claims and threats. The social authority of spiritualists, diviners, and priests was maintained among Africans in the Diaspora. Olaudah Equiano (or Gustavas Vassa)—who visited New York City in 1784 and whose *Narrative* was published there—remembered the "great reverence" afforded "priests and magicians, or wise men" during his childhood in West Africa. In the belief systems of many West African cultures the human community coexisted in time and space with the spirit and ancestral worlds in a way that has been disparagingly termed "superstition," but superstition is the lubricant of all religion. West African beliefs generally avoided the European natural-supernatural dichotomy; instead, the spiritual and material worlds interacted and cohabited. If a Christian could reach some other world through prayer, an African might turn to a person or a thing for intercession. Individuals and groups often achieved power through such knowledge and skill. For instance, the Mande blacksmiths acquired influence because their occupation placed them in control of religious ornaments. Since the talents of the craft were passed along family lines, blacksmiths constituted a "separate nation" of men who, by the nature of their work, also performed ritualistic and spiritual services.[33] The "head fellows" in the Manhattan conspiracy took advantage of an African survival.

Obviously, criminal societies like the Geneva Club are illicit and conspiratorial, but they can also achieve the societal definition of secrecy. In a study of nineteenth-century western European social movements, Eric Hobsbawm describes a basic and universal form of subversion: banditry. Bandits are criminalized by the power structure, not by local customs. They enjoy the support and protection of their community. The Geneva Club was engaged in banditry. The fact that they were enslaved criminalized the society, and thus they achieved secrecy before they ever engaged in an illegal act. Whatever the motivation, their crimes necessitated vengeance against and confrontations with an oppressive structure. Their misdeeds were simultaneously violations of property and acts of subversion. The local Africans were quite aware of this fact, as were white New Yorkers. During the investigation of the 1741 conspiracy, groups of militarized Africans were again menacing New York and Long Island, and

African gangs were active across the region. In the scholarship on West Africa, gangs and criminal associations are secret societies when they embody religious or political opposition to a ruling regime. Similarly, in an examination of Chinese secret societies, Jean Chesneaux includes gangs that invoked political justifications for their acts.[34] Whether or not the conspiracy was ever as broad or advanced as Horsmanden feared, the Geneva Club was a secret society.

In a recent collection of published essays, several Africanists debate the applicability of Hobsbawm's thesis to their field. Examining the Gold Coast, Ray A. Kea argues that by the latter half of the fifteenth century banditry was a visible phenomenon within the emerging mercantilist culture and that it became more pronounced during the militaristic seventeenth and eighteenth centuries. The period provided many opportunities and justifications for exploiting social change—land tenure, foreign intrusion, political realignments, and urbanization—by becoming outlaws. The contention here is not that Hobsbawm's model fits African history, but that it is quite reasonable to assert that African cultures armed enslaved New Yorkers with the ability to make basic and fundamental protests of their condition. Bandits, according to Hobsbawm, "are not so much men who right wrongs, but avengers, and exerters of power; their appeal is not that of the agents of justice, but of men who prove that even the poor and weak can be terrible." Such rogues can be turned into revolutionaries because "even those who accept exploitation, oppression and subjection as the norm of human life dream of a world without them: a world of equality, brotherhood and freedom, a totally *new* world without evil."[35]

The use of blood oaths, the invocation of African spirits, and the seduction of the greater community underscore the Geneva Club's self-conscious role as avenger. Secrecy produced special relationships between the actors, relationships that generated power from the possibility of betrayal. Once it becomes publicly known that a secret exists, the union and its actors are at once powerful and vulnerable, and the spectrum of human emotions can be reached. Through means both ritualistic and psychological, initiates are socialized to protect the association's confidence. The secret thus becomes the functional basis of intragroup relations as the holding of it alienates the union from the greater community. As J. M. Roberts postulates, "It may be that it was just here, in the illusions and fears they created, and in the dreams cherished about them, that the secret societies exercised their greatest power."[36] While Robert's definition best fits Western European associations formed around contrived secrets, societies exercise even greater power in cultures where secrets can have spiritual meaning.

In colonies with radical political and demographic differences, Africans were able to find comfortable and common mechanisms—ideological and sociological—when responding to enslavement; therefore, when placed in the history of organized African revolt, the Manhattan conspiracy's cultural pattern becomes clearer. John Thornton locates secret societies at the center of some of the earliest attempted revolts, arguing that they were the probable source of the 1537 and 1609 conspiracies in Mexico City and the 1675 plot in Barbados. Warning against ignoring even simple and informal associations, he continues:

> It should not be surprising that the sometimes inchoate agglomeration of secret societies (in the African sense), self-help groups, burial societies, or entertainment clubs organized on African national lines might also have engaged in more advanced political activities, including revolutionary ones. After all, they were one segment of slave society that was more or less under slave control, organized large numbers of people, had some leadership, and cut across other types of lines (family, estate, etc.).[37]

In New York during the French and Indian War (1754–1763), enslaved people took an "insolent" posture, and the legislature attempted to devise ways to keep Africans from conspiring with French colonials. On the eve of the American Revolution, a corps of Africans planned to torch the town of Kingston, New York, and kill its white citizens. The plot was uncovered. Three African organizations joined to carry out this conspiracy. A decade after the war, a small group of enslaved Africans in Albany, New York, were conspiring to burn the city and kill their masters. Executions followed.[38]

Quobna Ottobah Cugoano wrote that the Africans with whom he was transported to Grenada in 1770 plotted to burn the ship and die en masse. The plan was eventually betrayed. In 1789, African captives aboard the slaver *Ruby* revolted. They used blood oaths to solidify their compact. Blood oaths were common in such circumstances. Many of the *Ruby* Africans chose suicide over surrender, others fought to the death. The uprising ended.[39]

In the summer of 1791, Africans in San Domingo took advantage of the French Revolution and a conflict between the island's white and mulatto populations to cultivate their own rebellion. The majority of San Domingo's 500,000 bondspeople were born in West Africa. Under the leadership of Boukman, a high priest, who Diouf claims as one of many prominent Muslims, the Africans near Le Cap organized themselves. "Voodoo was the medium of the conspiracy," writes C. L. R. James, and West African blood oaths bound thousands of people to its purpose. The revolt began with the torching of the plantations outside Le Cap. The soldiers then marched into the town to destroy the white population. Here too, white residents believed Africans intellectually incapable of such machinations; however, the rebellion began a decade of revolution that resulted in the emancipation of Haiti.[40]

Plots with those same characteristics appeared in the British Caribbean. In 1801, enslaved Africans in Tobago formed into bands and communicated with free black people. The Africans then plotted to burn a town and kill its white inhabitants. The discovery of the conspiracy led to arrests, the establishment of a special court, trials, and executions. Four years later, the regiments of an African association in Trinidad organized a similar conspiracy.[41]

Brazil offers countless examples. The *maltas*—African dance and fighting brotherhoods—of nineteenth-century Rio de Janeiro employed secret rites, oaths, and greetings, and were influenced by the spread of Masonry. Colonial authorities feared their revolutionary potential. Organized on a neighborhood basis, the *maltas'* primary function was to safeguard the lives and interests of enslaved Africans within their territory. "Thus, in filling an institutional need—that of protection of their people—the *maltas* served to organize male slaves into a fraternal paramilitary organization that defended slaves in their neighborhoods," concludes Mary C. Karasch. Enslaved Africans in Bahia planned an uprising for the 1807 Corpus Christi observance. They were to burn the Customs House and a local church. Those fires were a signal to attack the white population. Enslaved and free Hausa Muslims were apparently at the center of the conspiracy, and "an elaborate clandestine organization appears to have existed, with a 'captain' in each parish of the city and a commander, known as the 'ambassador,'" notes João José Reis. The 1807 plot was betrayed. Two years later, ethnically varied African maroons attacked Nazaré. The campaign eventually failed, but the Africans' ability to unite and keep the plan secret shook Bahian masters. Africans conspired in Bahia again in 1814 and 1816. They rebelled during Brazil's 1822 War for Independence—as they had in New York during the Revolution—and white colonists repeatedly blamed Portugal for the bloodshed. In early 1835, African Muslims again took Bahia to violent crisis. As late as 1847,

Africans in Brazil used a secret society, consisting of multiple cells of five people with captains, to plan an uprising. This cabal joined under the protection of an African woman believed to have spiritual powers.[42]

African New Yorkers exploited the American Revolution to launch another campaign of intrigue. While Africans were not the intended beneficiaries of the Revolution, thousands of black people used the moment to free their families and destroy bondage. The African impact was felt at the onset of the war. On July 21, 1776, General Nathaniel Greene wrote General George Washington to inform him that the British Navy had arrived at New York Harbor, and he passed on a report, gathered by his underlings from an enslaved black man, that eight hundred Africans were formed into a regiment on Staten Island. "Among northern colonies, New York made extensive use of the Negro," writes Benjamin Quarles. Beginning in the spring of 1776, Africans from Manhattan and the surrounding area served under the United States and British flags. In March, all the free black men and bondsmen in New York City were ordered to report with tools to begin working on the city's fortifications. In August, after the swift defeat of the colonials, enslaved Africans flooded Manhattan seeking to gain their liberty under British decree. In the quartermaster's department most of the drivers were runaways. Fugitives provided a healthy supply of labor for the English, to the consternation of many white New Yorkers. A full century later, New York State Supreme Court justice Thomas Jones was still enraged at General Clinton's policy toward Africans. Some of the finer houses of Manhattan, Jones blasted, were "occupied by a pack of dirty, idle, thieving negroes. . . . These wretches were supplied with rations of all kinds, equally with the King's troops. They consisted of at least 2,000 men, women, and children." On March 20, 1781, Africans returned to the American cause when the legislature granted five hundred acres of land to any master who surrendered an able bondsman for military service. After England's surrender, the issue of slavery remained divisive. The British offered to reimburse American masters to keep the Africans free. In November 1783, at the completion of British evacuation from New York, three thousand black people were inspected and removed to freedom with the troops and, Quarles estimates, another thousand were removed illegally.[43]

L'Abondance left Staten Island on November 30, 1783, with the remainder of the "Black Brigade," which Graham Russell Hodges describes as a mixed crew of runaway and freeborn Africans united in "a conscious choice of alliance with the British who offered personal freedom and the potential for development of a black community." These soldiers came from almost every colony and went to war for England in Virginia, South Carolina, and the New York City region, where "they became a cohesive military force." Black loyalists worked as pilots, spies, guards, servants, interpreters, and executioners. White colonists feared the Black Brigade more than the regular British army because of the Africans' knowledge of the terrain and perceived penchant for revenge. Housed in New York, these soldiers led raiding missions into Westchester County, eastern New Jersey, and Long Island to fill their own purses and to benefit the Crown. The Africans helped the English hold New York City during the severe winter of 1779. The "Black Revolt," writes Hodges of Africans' struggle in Revolutionary New York, included eight years of conspiring, absconding, and taking up arms, and ended only when the British removed thousands of black men, women, and children to Nova Scotia.[44]

William Suttles Jr. argues that there is ample historical evidence of enslaved Africans' capacity for combining "religion and purposeful violence" in pursuit of community goals.[45] Spiritualism was the medium of all peaceful and violent expressions of community, and community was the context for all peaceful and violent expressions of religion. Thus, clandestine associations and collective action more frequently, if less dramatically, functioned to guide the evolution of African American religious culture. The most common manifestation of the societal tradition came as enslaved Africans fought to maintain their religious beliefs and practices.

It is generally accepted that black religion has enjoyed a significant African cultural retention. Du Bois credits the African priesthood with recreating religious ideas in the Americas and laying the foundations for the black church. Similarly, Nicholas C. Cooper-Lewter and Henry H. Mitchell explore oral traditions in West African cultures and African-American religious culture for continuities. Black religion in the United States and Africa shared experiential definitions of God. "There is little question that the most popular tales in African tradition were told for their usefulness and effectiveness. Likewise, the popularity of Moses, the emancipator, and Jesus, the suffering Son of God and link to heaven, were themes chosen by African-Americans in the crucible of need," they conclude. William D. Piersen notes that Colonial New England's small African American community maintained West African religious traditions. In his study of Jamaican society, Orlando Patterson utilizes anthropological work on West Africa to contextualize the culture of the enslaved. Patterson's work exposes the continuity of African belief systems. Sylvia R. Frey and Betty Wood argue that the religious cultures of West Africa were "neither casually forgotten nor discarded as unnecessary or irrelevant" by Africans enslaved in the Americas. "The ritualistic expressions of these convictions would be broadly similar to West and West Central African ones, but the local circumstances in which enslaved Africans found themselves dictated that they could never be identical." In a recent reexamination of the origins of black religion, Donald H. Matthews writes that cultural exchange allowed enslaved Africans to "adopt the manners but not necessarily the beliefs of their Anglo-European captors."[46]

Even in the realm of religion, the notion of African retention is not without its critics. In his classic study of American racial attitudes, Winthrop Jordan argues that Europeans' energy for proselytizing ultimately determined the pace of Africans' conversion to Christianity. In this construction, enslaved Africans were either never possessed of the capacity to resist a dominant European culture, or the very fact of bondage stripped them of that ability. In a recent synthesis of the scholarship on American bondage, Peter Kolchin harvests the same conclusion. He examines white Americans' inconsistent attempts to convert the unfree as the key to "Christianization" and limits black people's agency to indifference to that religious tradition. The latter decision is intended to counter a wave of recent scholarship fixed on establishing African agency that comes "dangerously close to replacing a mythical world in which slaves were objects of total control with an equally mythical world in which slaves were hardly slaves at all."[47]

However, the denial of the potency of African religious culture and intellectual heritage emerged first in defense of slavery, not in an attempt to achieve greater truth about the social order of slave societies. "Over and over again," writes Michael Gomez, "the sources repeat the fact that Africans and African Americans were cognizant of white ways of worship and consciously rejected them." "The myth of a people without a past holds forth the tradition that Africans were an empty (or emptied) reservoir into which an entirely alien religion was poured," Joseph R. Washington Jr. notes, and was fabricated by white colonists and missionaries who censured Africans for spiritual deviations from European norms. In the hands of sensitive historians, the idea that servitude destroyed the African ethos—that culture itself was a victim of bondage—eclipsed the image of a cultureless Africa. Writing for a popular audience in 1931, Carter G. Woodson personalized the results of that belief:

The thing about it all which vexes me most is that Negroes took over this nonsense from their ignorant oppressors. I inherited the Baptist faith from my father who learned it from his cruel master. My oldest sister inherited the Methodist faith through her husband which he obtained indirectly from his father's owner of antebellum times. Thus practically all Negroes embraced the religion of those who drove them behind the plow, lashed the blood from their backs when they would not willingly bear the yoke, and, if they survived the persecution, sold them to meet their doom in a more benighted part of the land of cotton.[48]

Christianization was never so simple a process. Slavery recorded its miseries in uprooted families, severed social relations, thwarted ambitions, scarred bodies, and shortened lives. Spiritualism provided the enslaved their only measure of security and continuity in a random and brutish society. African Christianity evolved through a dialogue in which Africans adapted the religious forms they encountered in America to those they contributed to its cultural milieu.[49]

The description of enslaved Africans as intellectually stunned and culturally stripped has unfortunately acted as a substitute for exposing the truly primitive nature of slave societies. The truth is not that Africans were perfectly prepared for victimization, but rather that white New Yorkers had the intent, capacity, and will to bring the extraordinary violence of their social apparatus against the enslaved, whatever their cultural and intellectual strengths. It was in the realm of culture, especially religious culture, that the African heritage had its greatest impact, and black people used traditional values to establish the conditions for and the meaning of their conversion to Christianity.

For instance, enslaved Africans' attempts to bury their dead and perform ancestral rites at funerals was a major point of contention between Africans and Europeans throughout the Diaspora. Enslaved black people in Colonial New England regularly held funerals that followed the ritual and spiritual traditions of Africa. "To the African tribesman, death and burial were perhaps the most important phase in a man's life cycle," Orlando Patterson writes. "On the funeral depended not only the prestige of those kin of the deceased surviving him, but the safe journey and status of the deceased in his new abode of the spirit world. It is not surprising then, that the funerary rites of the West African slaves in Jamaica survived more than most other cultural elements." Brazil's African brotherhoods—associations of black lay Catholic men—and African religious groups continued West African spiritual and burial rites. Attached to the churches of the elite, the black brotherhoods spread rapidly. In Rio, the Congolese organized the brotherhood of St. Philip and St. James around 1753, and Angolans united under Our Lady of Belem in 1765. Other African and native-born black Brazilians also formed associations.[50]

The struggle in Manhattan began early in the eighteenth century. Fearing large concentrations of the unfree, evening services, and unsupervised ceremonies, white New Yorkers repeatedly tried to govern African burials. Still, enslaved New Yorkers' most significant spiritual acts followed West African customs. Recent archaeological work on the African Burial Ground (1712–1794, originally established in the seventeenth century) has uncovered West African influences on the graves of enslaved eighteenth-century Manhattanites. The adornment of bodies and coffins, shrouding, and the orientation of corpses all establish the persistence of West African spiritual cultures in New York City. Mechal Sobel, in her history of eighteenth-century Virginia, confirms the survival of similar West African funerary customs, including the celebration of the souls of the deceased, the West African–style preparation of corpses and graves, and semiannual graveside feasts and reunions to respect the dead. "The direct parallel between black graves in the South and those on the West Coast of Africa is very strong," concludes Sobel, and that influence transformed the burial patterns of white Virginians. Similar, funerary rituals have been found among the Gullah of South Carolina. In fact, Eugene Genovese documents the endurance of such burial practices—especially African-Christian hybrids—in the southern United States well into the twentieth century.[51]

"Burying the dead in an east-west direction was a mechanical ritual that could be observed and repeated; it was a physical action, not a manifestation of a profound line of thought," retorts Forrest G. Wood; and, he would be correct if all that the evidence had uncovered was the peculiar orientation of corpses. Religious ideologies and social philosophies are not entombed at burials; however, graves provide physical evidence of a deeper social phenomenon, one that does have profound ideological meaning. The authors of the New York slave code acknowledged this when they attempted to regulate African funerary services but did not bother themselves with burial ritual. Legislators had little interest in the physical effects of funerals; they were consumed with the social results—especially conspiracies and uprisings. A disproportionate number of the acts in New York's slave code regulated African burials.[52] Thus, the code directly responded to the danger of Africans using funeral ceremonies to affirm and act upon the very ethical systems and social relations that Wood claimed were destroyed.

If a dominant European civilization simply overwhelmed the enslaved, African influences could be little more than the dregs of a pagan culture; however, what white New Yorkers persistently saw as heathenish residue is better understood as evidence of the African standards that enslaved people employed when judging Christianity. Throughout the colony, Africans continued traditional religious practices. In 1681, African gatherings on the Sabbath in Kings County brought an attempt to curb "rude and unlawful sports, to the dishonor of God and profanation of his holy day."[53] What Dutch and English farmers feared in this case is unclear, but, well into the eighteenth century, they were troubled by Africans' resistance to Christianity. The longevity of African spiritualism caused the difficulty that white New Yorkers encountered in converting the enslaved in the colonial era.

The indoctrination of New York's Africans stagnated despite the institutional rivalries of an abnormally heterogeneous religious colony. Prerevolutionary New York was home to Catholic, Jewish, and Protestant—Anglican, Baptist, Congregational, Dutch Reformed, French Protestant, German Reformed, Lutheran, Methodist, Moravian, Presbyterian, and Quaker—communities. As early as 1650, Holland censured Dutch West India for failing "to convert to Christianity either the Indians, or the Blacks or Slaves, owned by the Company" in New Netherland. Yet, by 1679 Gieran and Christine, a married couple, were the only African members of the Dutch Reformed Church of New Utrecht, Kings County. They also appear in the ledger of the church in Flatbush. In 1686 Domine Henricus Selyns recorded only five Africans—Franciscus Bastiaensz and his wife Barbara Emanuels, Claes Emanuels, Jan de Vries, and Susanna de Negrin, the widow of Thomas de Moor—as members of New York's Dutch Reformed Church, although there were well over five hundred Africans in Manhattan. That same year, James II ordered Governor Dongan and the council "to facilitate & encourage the Conversion of Negroes and Indians to the Christian Religion." In May 1688, the council began drawing an "act for instructing negroes in the Christian religion," which, when implemented, did little to increase the number of African converts.[54]

In the early eighteenth century, the Society for the Propagation of the Bible established two catechism schools open to Africans in New York City. In 1704 Elias Neau, a French convert to Anglicanism, began a school for all of the lax and unconverted Africans, Native Americans, and people of mixed ancestry in New York. Few black New Yorkers attended the school. Neau, who had himself been held captive under Louis XIV, proved fairly popular with some Africans, particularly because of his willingness to broaden the manner of instruction to include forms with which Africans were more familiar. In 1709 schoolmaster Huddlestone of Manhattan began instructing from Trinity Church's steeple with SPB funds. His regular students, children, and the unfree attended these public classes. At least two of the men arrested in the 1712 rebellion were from Neau's school, and many white Manhattanites blamed the instructor for the revolt. While only one of Neau's pupils was found to be involved in the conspiracy, the connection was firm in the public mind. After Neau's death in 1722, missionaries were assigned to labor among New York's Africans and Native Americans, but the belief in conversion as a method of control had waned. In the decades that followed, the growth of the European population stretched the resources of Protestant churches and sorely tested their ability and will to minister to Africans, and the tensions of Protestant pluralism made white colonials' commitment to spreading the Gospel among Africans and Natives even more volatile. African spiritualism stubbornly persisted. However, Revolutionary-era white New Yorkers were increasingly familiar with black preachers, because, as Joyce D. Goodfriend writes, Africans began "fusing elements of European and African culture in their everyday life."[55]

2

Raising Mother Zion

The Fusion of African and British Institutions in New York, 1784–1822

You will arise and have compassion on Zion,
for it is time to show favor to her;
the appointed time has come.
For her stones are dear to your servants;
her very dust moves them to pity.
The nations will fear the name of the Lord,
all the kings of the earth will revere
your glory.
For the Lord will rebuild Zion
and appear in his glory.
He will respond to the prayer of the destitute;
he will not despise their plea.
—Psalms 102:13–17

That the founding of African voluntary societies preceded the establishment of black churches is a fact now remembered with little interest; but, that relationship ties the first black Christian denominations to the covert alliances of the enslaved in Colonial America. In the aftermath of the Revolution, Africans organized benevolent societies in New York City and Philadelphia in objection to the inferior treatment of their deceased. "This extension to the dead of the racial inequalities among the living may have been especially grievous to Afro-Americans," Gary Nash writes, "whose African religious heritage stressed ancestor reverence and thus emphasized dignifying the dead." The institutional society—from which black churches and denominations arose—was an outgrowth of the surreptitious attempts of the enslaved to preserve African traditions by venerating and caring for the souls of the deceased.[1] African societies were the crucible of black people's Christianization, and they provide the unique ancestry of African American religion.

As a community of believers was the necessary precondition of an institutional assembly, so was the African spiritual society the prerequisite of the African church. The first black-American religious society was formed in Massachusetts in 1693 with the assistance of the Reverend Cotton Mather. In 1774 George Liele, a twenty-four-year-old enslaved African in Georgia, converted to the Baptist faith and began exhorting white and black people throughout the colony. Religious societies continued to meet on plantations around Savannah after Liele's visit, and, on January 20, 1788, an African church was constituted under the ministry of Andrew Bryan, an enslaved African whom Liele had baptized. In 1780 the Newport African Union Society was organized in Rhode Island. The Newport association later sired the city's first black house of worship, the Union Congregational Church. The spiritual and benevolent Free African Society (1787), under Absalom Jones and Richard Allen, founded Philadelphia's first African congregations (1794), a disagreement over affiliation producing Jones' St. Thomas Episcopal and Allen's Mother Bethel Methodist churches.[2]

While the Free Africans' role in establishing Philadelphia's black church is universally acknowledged, the relationship between African societies and African houses of worship elsewhere tends to be disregarded. According to historian John Daniels, the Boston African Society (1796) organized the African Meeting House (1805), the municipality's first black church, and correspondence between the Philadelphia and Boston societies supports that connection. The African Methodist Bethel Society (1815) founded the African Bethel Church of Baltimore. The charter members of the Brooklyn African Woolman Benevolent Society (1810) were also the first trustees of the local African Wesleyan Methodist Episcopal Church (1818), later named Bridge Street. The Colored Baptist Society (ca. 1826) established the African Baptist Church (1831) in the "Guinea" district of Newtown, Nantucket. In Hartford, the African Relief Society (ca. 1827) hosted religious services in its meeting hall. The spiritual community later split and began two churches, one Methodist and one Congregational; both continued to use the society building for some time. In the Gullah community of antebellum South Carolina, enslaved Africans came to the Baptist faith through a number of independent spiritual associations that were directly influenced by the Poro and Sande secret societies of Upper Guinea and Angola. Thus, the Sea Island's black community pursued Christianity without any considerable white interference, with its own priesthood and conjurers, guided by an "internal logic" based upon African Americans' definitions of community, authority, justice, and the divine. Through these spiritual associations, argues Margaret Washington Creel, "some adaptive concepts of community (and aspects of spirituality) inherited from [West African] secret societies fused with Gullah interpretations of Christianity, becoming part of folk religion in the slave quarters."[3]

Black religious culture evolved similarly in Manhattan. In 1784 Jupiter Hammon, the nearly seventy-year-old enslaved poet and preacher from Long Island, lectured before the New York African Society, a spiritual and benevolent organization of free and enslaved black men, and one of the nation's first independent African associations. The evidence suggests that the NYAS, whose members were meeting as early as 1780, organized Manhattan's Mother Zion Church (1796),[4] and that church's leadership continued to be closely tied to societies as bishops, ministers, and exhorters were drawn from African associations or founded new organizations.

Throughout the Diaspora, evangelical culture spread in this pattern. In 1783 the Reverend George Liele, who was freed under his master's will, emigrated to Jamaica with the assistance of British colonel Kirkland in order to escape attempts at his reenslavement. Liele preached to black and white people across the island, and he gained the spiritual fellowship of three black "refugees" from the United States: Moses Baker, T. N. Swingle, and George Givens. In 1784 the four men began the First Baptist Church and then constituted a second African church at Crooked Springs. To compensate for a scarcity of priests, the black brotherhoods of Rio de Janeiro provided religious space and spiritual services to enslaved and free Africans. Originally attached to elite churches, the brotherhoods built independent chapels and churches during the colonial period as their membership and wealth increased. As a result, other black brotherhoods moved to the African institutions. Having already expressed Africans' sensibilities about death and burial, the black brotherhoods now made African Catholicism institutionally independent.[5] While Portuguese customs influenced Brazil's black brotherhoods, Africans still adapted these institutions to their own spiritual goals.

It is easy to get so absorbed in the "Britishness" of evangelicalism that one loses the "Africanness" of its expression among black Americans—to focus on the churches and forget the associations that established them. African cultures generated numerous analogues to Christianity's blood imagery, iconoclasm, hierarchy, ritual, and mysticism. "It is the Africanization of the Christian faith, not its imposition by external forces, that accounts for its success in the African American community," argues Michael Gomez. Even E. Franklin Frazier, skeptical of such links, accepts that the prevalence of river cults in West Africa is a reasonable explanation for the dominance of Baptism in African American religiosity, although he prefers to blame Baptist proselytizing for the phenomenon. Herskovits sees similarities between European and African spiritual cultures that suggest a clear African influence on African American Christianity. Du Bois considers it a "historic fact that the Negro Church of to-day bases itself upon the sole surviving social institution of the African fatherland." European Americans viewed Christianity as an individualistic religion, while African Americans used the faith in communitarian and collectivist ways, notes Eugene Genovese. "The religion of the slaves manifested many African 'traits' and exhibited greater continuity with African ideas than has generally been appreciated," continues Genovese in a compromise position; however, the African contribution was "indirect, distorted, ambiguous, and even confused." Bishop William Walls's work does not question the African foundations of his denomination.[6]

The African society was the mechanism of the black conversion and the most direct link to the African past. While the drama of evangelicalism, its "demonstrative style,"[7] has been used to explain its appeal to Africans, full-bodied religious enthusiasm was already an aspect of African spiritualism and its rise within evangelical faith likely brought more white than black believers. Something greater than emotion catalyzed the black conversion. Africans reacted to evangelicalism's sociology, for there were ideological and sociological parallels between British evangelical and African spiritual cultures. Of particular importance was the votive community, or society.

Evangelicalism generated physical and emotional expressiveness at its foundations, in the intimacy of the spiritual association. In 1729 John Wesley and a handful of young Oxford men began the Holy Club, a religious society that engaged in benevolent work. That model of small spiritual communities and social outreach remained a fixture of Wesley's religious undertaking. On February 6, 1736, John Wesley and his brother Charles, clerics of the Church of England, "first set foot on American ground," arriving in Georgia to begin a ministry among Native Americans. Over the next two years a religious cross-fertilization occurred in North America as the Wesleys encountered Africans and slaveholders in

Georgia and South Carolina and left small communities of believers wherever they preached. John Wesley soon followed his brother back to England, but, as Sylvia R. Frey and Betty Wood note, "in less than two years he had made considerable progress toward the development of the Methodist system—the circuit, the society, the itinerant ministry, and lay leadership—that was destined to play a crucial part in the journey of African Americans to a new faith and, in general, in the making of Methodism."[8] It is difficult to sift the exact impact that enslaved Africans had on Wesley; however, Wesley's flirtation with the religious mechanism of the society and the spiritual medium of passion grew into a commitment during this sojourn in the Americas, and it was part of the apparatus of evangelicalism that black New Yorkers encountered during the Revolution.

Africans found in Methodist sociology a structure that paralleled and easily accommodated their traditional modes of spiritual expression. As the primary model of community organization, societies conducted the religious transformation in which black men and women used the spread of evangelical denominations to blend Christian and African spiritualism. Societies freed Africans to enjoy culturally specific ceremonies and to practice private or secret rites. "Africans and their descendants in Protestant America discovered analogues in revivalistic Evangelicalism to the religious beliefs and rituals of Africa, which turned out to be crucial for the process of reinterpretation that made Christianity intelligible and adaptable for large numbers of African-Americans," argues Albert Raboteau. Black men could become licensed preachers and exhorters in evangelical churches, which allowed Africans to control the style and substance of their Christianity.[9] The conversion of people of color awaited the appearance of a Christianity capable of institutionalizing an African American ethic.

Evangelical religion addressed the spiritual well-being of black communities, encouraged social philanthropy, and justified political activism. The rise of African Christianity in Jamaica came through the give and take of conversion and adaptation. There, African Christianity surfaced in the late eighteenth century after the Methodist and Baptist incursion, and prominent black ministers like George Liele and Moses Baker facilitated its spread. New York's first African church fully exploited the fabrications of Methodism—doctrinal looseness, lay preaching, class meetings, and revivals—to make the faith comfortable. Equally attractive was the personal involvement of John Wesley and the British Methodists in social work, including widow and orphan relief and charity to the poor. Methodism was especially adaptable to African Americans' collectivism. Capturing the social nature of black religion, Gary Nash writes that Philadelphia's "Free African Society soon began assuming a supervisory role over the moral life of the black community: it worked to forge a visionary black consciousness out of the disparate human material finding its way to Philadelphia."[10]

The origins of evangelism in New York City trace back to the 1740s,[11] but Africans' attraction to radical Christianity came later as its political and social potential increased. In a nation that not only contained fractures among the free classes but a dramatic gulf between the free and the unfree, emotional venting did not heal wounds. Black theology called for an earthly reawakening, announced by the end of slavery, as the precondition for the eternity of Christ. Slavery stood as a social barrier to individual, spiritual salvation. Black evangelists, therefore, shifted the focus from personal to group conversion while continuing to assert the necessity of prayer and the power of the Holy Spirit.

Africans also welcomed evangelicalism as an antislavery institution. Methodists came to Manhattan in 1760, and the Baptists established themselves about 1762. Revolutionary-era British soldiers exhorted the faith in the streets of New York and Brooklyn and wrapped their preaching in egalitarian and humanitarian rhetoric. In 1780, American Methodists pierced the silence of the major denominations with a strong repudiation of slavery, and the Baptists followed nine years later. Slaveholders and their allies eventually imposed the imagined biological boundaries between citizens and slaves upon American churches, and they did so precisely because that belief was not inherent to the faith.[12]

The fact that evangelical ministries were targets of proslavery intimidation was itself appealing; it, at least, advertised evangelicalism's abolitionist baggage. In 1771, the young Francis Asbury left England for North America. Asbury continued the Wesleys' effort to sow the seeds of religious excitement. Like the Wesleys, Asbury was antislavery. He presided over the 1780 Methodist conference at Baltimore that condemned slaveholding; but the power of Southern Methodists forced the cleric to compromise his antislavery beliefs, especially after the Revolution, when the American church achieved self-governance. Ultimately, writes Asbury's biographer, "he shifted from attempts to emancipate the Negroes to attempts to evangelize the Negroes." England's Thomas Coke also attacked slavery while in the South, and he joined with Asbury at a 1784 ministers' conference to pass another resolution denouncing bondage. Authorities indicted Coke for his words. He eventually retreated from his extreme antislavery position. George Whitefield, yet another English cleric who came to minister in America, underwent a personal decline from antislavery minister to defender of slavery to slaveholder. Planters in Jamaica jailed George Liele and his confederates and passed laws forbidding them to preach to the enslaved. After being beaten, Liele was tried, but acquitted, for his politics. One of his colleagues was hanged. David George, an enslaved African, was converted to Baptism with Liele in Georgia. At the end of the Revolution, he emigrated to Nova Scotia, where proslavery residents attempted to reenslave him to stop his ministry. In fact, as late as 1832, planters in Jamaica blamed an insurrection on "the Baptist and Wesleyan Missionaries, who, they allege, incited the negroes to revolt by inflammatory discourses from the pulpit, and otherwise. Churches belonging to those denominations had been demolished and their ministers obliged to fly for life."[13]

Peter Williams, probably a founder of the NYAS, was born enslaved. His birthplace was the Borite family's cow barn on Beekman Street, Manhattan. At the beginning of the Revolution, British captain Thomas Webb—a Wesley disciple who conducted classes in New York and Brooklyn during their occupation—converted Williams to Methodism. "In the revolutionary war, my father was a decided advocate of American Independence, and his life was repeatedly jeopardized in its cause," Peter Williams Jr. later wrote. Williams rescued Parson Chapman of New Jersey from a British manhunt. He rode horseback alerting parishioners to move the preacher's property to safety while he personally escorted the minister out of danger. During the war, James Aymar purchased Williams and had him trained as a tobacconist. Williams convinced the trustees of the John Street Church, where he was employed as sexton and where many Africans were helping to establish evangelicalism, to buy him with the promise that he would repay them. He handed the trustees a pocket watch as an initial payment, and on June 10, 1783, they purchased him from Aymar for forty pounds. On November 4, 1785, Williams made his final payment to the trustees. On October 20, 1796, the trustees gave Williams his emancipation papers:

TO ALL WHOM THESE PRESENTS SHALL COME OR MAY CONCERN.
Whereas, by a bill of sale made by James Aymar, of the city of New-York, tobacconist, and duly executed by him on the tenth day of June, in the year

of our Lord one thousand seven hundred and eighty-three, he, the said James Aymar, did, for and in consideration of the sum of forty pounds current money of the province of New-York, to him in hand paid at and before the ensealing and delivery of the said bill of sale, by the trustees of the Methodist meeting in the city of New-York, fully, clearly, and absolutely grant, bargain, sell, and release unto the said trustees his negro man, named Peter, to have and to hold the said negro man unto the said trustees and their assigns forever. Now know ye that we, John Staples, Abraham Russel, Henry Newton, John Sproson, and William Cooper, trustees for the time being of the said Methodist meeting, for and in consideration of services rendered and payments in money made to our predecessors, trustees of the said Methodist meeting, amounting in value to forty pounds, have manumitted, liberated and set free, and by these presents do manumit, liberate, and set free the said negro man, named Peter, now called Peter Williams, hereby giving and granting unto him, the said Peter Williams, all such sum or sums of money and property, of what nature or kind whatsoever, which he, the said Peter Williams, may, by his industry, have acquired, or which he may have purchased since the eighteenth day of November, in the year of our Lord one thousand seven hundred and eighty five. And we do also give and grant unto him, the said Peter Williams, full power and lawful authority to sue for and recover, in his own name and to his own use, all such sum or sums of money and other property acquired as aforesaid, which is now due, or which will hereafter become due, or which of right belongs to him by such purchase since the said eighteenth day of November, in the year of our Lord one thousand seven hundred and eighty-five. In testimony whereof we have hereunto set our hands and affixed our seals this twentieth day of October, in the year of our Lord one thousand seven hundred and ninety-six.

[signed] John Staples
          Henry Newton
          Abrm. Russel
          William Cooper
          John Sproson

Sealed and delivered in the presence of

          Nicholas Bayard
          Jacob Tabule

On January 16, 1797, the county clerk of New York recorded Williams's emancipation. The Reverend J. B. Wakeley claimed that after November 1785 Williams was free and that emancipation papers were unnecessary at that time; however, his emancipation papers establish that his freedom was bought for forty pounds and "services rendered," meaning that a term of service, a common feature of manumission agreements, was imposed in addition to repayment.[14] Moreover, in a city in which most Africans were enslaved or dogged by bounty hunters, neither Williams nor the trustees could be so naive as to believe that he needed no evidence of his manumission.

Before Williams's emancipation, the black men of John Street were already expressing their dissatisfaction with the connection. In describing Philadelphia's Free African Society, Joseph R. Washington Jr. captures the spirit of the moment: "The deepest desire of the movement was for interdependence and when this failed it grew into an independent freedom movement within religion." For Manhattan's Africans, the division was fully necessary because Christianity and antislavery were inseparable, while white New Yorkers increasingly disclaimed any friction between the faith and bondage. In a 1796 letter to New York governor John Jay, an author of the *Federalist Papers* and the first chief justice of the United States Supreme Court, William Hamilton refused to separate his political and religious philosophies. "How falsely & contradictory do the Americans speak when this land[,] a land of Liberty & equality[,] a christian country[,] when almost every part of it abounds with slavery and oppression," chided Hamilton, a central actor in the disconnection of New York's black Christians.[15]

The Africans' stride toward independence came rather quickly given that African evangelicalism was in its infancy, that in 1760 several immigrant Irish families organized the first Manhattan Methodist meeting, that it was only in 1784 that American Methodists achieved independence, that in 1788 the first annual conference was held in Manhattan, and that the evidence of the church's success was plentiful. It was a peculiar moment to separate; however, American Methodism's acquisition of self-governance made the African apostasy a necessity. "By a very uncommon train of providences, many of the provinces of North America are totally disjoined from their mother country and erected into independent states," John Wesley conceded while planning out the partition of his church and appointing Francis Asbury and Thomas Coke superintendents in the United States. "The English government has no authority over them, either civil or ecclesiastical, any more than over the States of Holland." By 1788 Wesley was already warning *Bishop* Asbury of the dangers of allowing prestige and status to intrude into the culture of the

American church. Under Captain Webb, John Street (1768) secured a building and the flock greatly expanded. By 1789 the fantastic increase at John Street had brought the congregation through two buildings. In a two-month period in the early 1790s, almost four hundred new members joined. That growth continued.[16] However, the rapid spread of the religion was shadowed by the creep of racial civilization, seen most clearly in repeated attempts to better serve white Methodists by neglecting black parishioners, a process that was tantamount to religious heresy given the clarity and stridency of the Wesleyan standards.

The African classes at the John Street Church were the source of defiance. Black Methodism was largely a women's movement, but its minority of men decided its politics. Among the African men drawn to the Methodist society was the group who directed the founding and incorporation of an independent African church. Probation, class assignments, services, and ceremonies were all segregated at John Street. That inequality bolstered the growing logic of complete separation, which was likely first discussed in the African classes. Black people, especially women, disproportionately supported the church. By 1794, 20 percent (133 of 689) of John Street's parishioners were Africans—only 13 percent (about 6,000 of 45,000) of Manhattan's residents were black—and more than two-thirds of the Africans were women. The following year, six of the eight black classes comprised women, many of whom brought their husbands and other male relatives into the men's classes. Class 31 combined William Hamilton, Thomas Sipkins, William Miller, James Varick, Jacob Jacobs, George Moore, George White, Thomas Cook, David Bias, and Abraham Thompson, while class 28 included Peter Williams Sr. and Thomas Miller.[17] Within those two classes were most of the leaders of the defection.

The African schism was intended to recapture Methodism from "un-Wesleyan innovations." Most troublesome was the growing hostility toward John Wesley's 1739 prohibitions against trading in slaves, a stricture that American Methodists voluntarily adopted in 1784 but that succumbed to white Southern Methodists' power and white Northern Methodists' moral ambivalence. Africans viewed antislavery as a critical tenet of the church, a stance that quickly eroded among its white disciples. (In fact, white Methodists in New York City did not form an Anti-Slavery Society until 1834, long after the racial division of the church.) Authority slowly shifted to those black men who doubted white New Yorkers' ability to embrace the social implications of the true faith; therefore, notes Bishop Walls, "several of the earliest leaders in the Zion Church movement were not members of the

John Street Church or [the] New York Circuit" but those whose conversion had occurred in a more uniformly African environment. Segregationist and proslavery sentiments homogenized the African religious experience and forged a resolution to separate. Bishop Asbury gave the black parishioners permission to hold independent prayer meetings that did not compete with those of the regular church. In 1796 Francis Jacobs, William Brown, Peter Williams, Abraham Thompson, June Scott, Samuel Pontier, Thomas Miller, James Varick, and William Hamilton opened an "African chapel" at Cross between Mulberry and Orange Streets in the shop of cabinetmaker William Miller. Hamilton, a house carpenter, outfitted the hall with chairs and a pulpit. They then secured African preachers and exhorters to conduct services: Abraham Thompson, June Scott, and Thomas Miller were the only licensed black preachers, and William Miller was the local exhorter. Services continued in Miller's shop for three years.[18]

The movement for independent black churches arose when integrated congregations took a decidedly proslavery turn or embellished the social barriers between black and white parishioners. The latter can be misleading because of the tendency to anticipate social disparity in unfree societies. In fact, evangelical religion was remarkable for the level of equality that it generated in practice. Part of the power of evangelical faith was the sight and experience of its universality. The model generated personal and passionate religious experiences between white and black, free and enslaved, men and women. Feverish conversions and celebrations within small, interracial societies defined the early evangelical experience. Such gatherings necessitated a rethinking of contemporary social relations. In a history of evangelical faith in eighteenth-century Virginia, Rhys Isaac emphasizes that white Baptists' "inclusion of slaves as 'brothers' and 'sisters'" constituted a revolutionary challenge to the social order.[19] Racial segregation in evangelical churches was intended to limit the emotional intercourse of black and white people and to thwart the social sympathies that such encounters necessitated.

In 1799 overcrowding in the Methodist Episcopal Church provided another justification for an African house of worship with a separate incorporation. African men met to consider the venture. They decided to accept the Methodist Episcopal government; named the church "African Methodist Episcopal Zion"; elected nine trustees including William Brown, Peter Williams, Thomas Sipkins, William Hamilton, Francis Jacobs (chair), Thomas Miller (treasurer), and George Collins (secretary); and agreed to fund a cemetery to lessen the hardship of burying their dead and further avoid the intrusion of white people into their religious ceremonies. Thomas Miller purchased a lot near the cabinet shop, but it was found to be unsuitable. On July 21, 1800, Francis Jacobs and William Brown leased two new lots. The members issued subscription books to buy the land, which was cleared of debt in 1806, and the trustees raised money for a building. By October 1800, the African Methodist Episcopal Church of the City of New York, commonly called African Zion or Mother Zion, opened in a wood building at Leonard and Church Streets. It was incorporated a year later. On July 30, 1800, Williams laid the cornerstone. Williams's mark appeared above Francis Jacobs's signature on Zion's charter. The trustees purchased a third adjoining lot and a small, wood dwelling house that they moved to the site. The additional land was used as a burial ground until August 17, 1807, when the church was allowed space in Pottersfield.[20]

The biblical promise that the city of Zion would be resurrected became a metaphor for the social and spiritual redemption of enslaved Africans, a usage that captured the depth of the black flight. "It is difficult to exaggerate the importance of the church as a cultural form in the American past," writes Forrest G. Wood in his study of race and religion. It is equally difficult to overemphasize the political and social message in Africans' departure from established denominations and the subsequent creation of independent African houses of worship. Raising Mother Zion was a boldly political act. James Varick and George Collins recalled the conditions:

When the Methodist Society in the United States was small, the Africans enjoyed comfortable privileges among their white brethren in the same meeting-house; but as the whites increased very fast the Africans were pressed back; therefore, it was thought essentially necessary for them to have meeting-houses of their own, in those places where they could obtain them, in order to have more room to invite their coloured brethren yet out of the ark of safety to come in; and it is well known that the Lord has greatly enlarged their number since that memorable time, by owning their endeavours in the conversion of many hundreds.[21]

Further evidence that the movement's leaders came from the NYAS appears in the fact that William Brown, Thomas Miller, George Collins, William Miller, James Varick, and William Hamilton later founded the NYASMR. Abraham Thompson and June Scott founded the African Marine Fund society for widows and orphans. Thomas Sipkins became a charter member and the first treasurer of the Wilberforce Philanthropic Association.

The trustees carefully negotiated "Articles of Agreement," placing Mother Zion under the discipline of the Methodist Episcopal Church of New York and displaying their trepidation about subjecting themselves to the governance of white men. Written on April 6, 1801, the agreement created a church to be forever held and regulated by black Manhattanites. All could attend services but no persons could be admitted to membership or enrolled in Zion's books unless they were "Africans and descendants of the African race"; moreover, "none but Africans or their descendants shall be chosen as Trustees of the said African Episcopal Zion Church, and such other church or churches as may or shall hereafter become the property of this Corporation." To perpetuate a man-dominant culture, voting was limited to "the regular male members of the said church, of at least twenty-one years of age, and one year's standing." The members of the African church tried associates for religious infractions, and anyone found guilty had a right to appeal to the elders, preachers, trustees, and exhorters of Zion. The trustees had corporate ownership of all current and future properties to use for the benefit of the conference and "likewise for our African brethren and the descendants of the African race." They also controlled the rents and income from real and personal estate. In turn, the trustees submitted to the discipline of the Methodist Episcopal Church of the City of New York. That denomination's elder directed Zion's spiritual concerns, including the nomination of its preacher and the administering of ordinances; however, even these regulations were not absolute, for the elder and his white preachers could only preach at Zion twice a week if there were African preachers available, and the agreement required that the elder license black preachers and exhorters who proved satisfactory.[22] Four of the nine African men whose names appear on the compact could not write, but they and their colleagues established the institutional foundations of black Christianity in New York City.

The Baptists followed. In June 1808 the Reverend Thomas Paul traveled from Boston to New York City, where he "organized a group of men and women who called themselves the Abyssinian Baptist Church." They first purchased property on Worth Street and later moved to Anthony Street. William Spelman, a barber who was once enslaved in the South, was pastor. Shortly after its founding, Abyssinian became the largest Baptist congregation in Manhattan. Here too, women were responsible for the success of black religion. By the 1830s, men filled the seven offices at Abyssinian Baptist, but 75 percent of its 245 members were women.[23]

White New Yorkers' hostility to black missions complicated the work of institutionalizing African Christianity. In 1807 George Collins appeared before the New York Common Council requesting and receiving police protection during Mother Zion's hours of worship. Unruly boys and adults regularly disturbed Sunday services. The city stationed a watchman and a watchbox outside the African church. Still, the following year Zion's trustees complained of riots in front of their church and accused the watchman of "abuse of his duty."[24]

Abraham Thompson, one of only three local black ministers, created a minor crisis by looking to become a professional preacher—the black pastors and exhorters of Zion having typically gone unpaid. John Edwards, a former Quaker, offered free residences for two pastors willing to found and serve a church on his property at 101 Greene Street. Thompson was tempted, and on March 27, 1812, the African Free Meeting Methodist Society, or the Union Society, was incorporated. June Scott joined Thompson. Under threat of expulsion from Zion, Thompson returned. Scott did not. He joined a third church after the Union Society suffered a financial collapse.[25]

The 1813 expulsion of Thomas Sipkins from the Zion Church resulted in the formation of yet another African spiritual society. The trustees accused Sipkins of being a "headstrong and rather ungovernable" sort, and he immediately proved his critics right. He formed a separate worship group and convinced Deacon William Miller of Zion to join him in procuring a church at Elizabeth between Walker and Hester Streets. The two then courted other Zion members to associate with their Asbury Church. There was apparently little hard feeling between the two churches; for, when Asbury's trustees applied for admission to the Methodist Episcopal Church of New York, Zion's trustees consented to have the Methodist elder receive them.[26]

Brooklyn's first African church also rose from the efforts of its local African society. Methodism attracted large numbers of Kings County's black residents, free and unfree. By 1798 Africans were one-third (26 of 76) of the members of the local Methodist society at the Sands Street Church, and half the Africans were women. In 1817 the leaders of the Brooklyn African Woolman Benevolent Society initiated a campaign to purchase a separate site and structure. The desire to split from the Sands Street Church had grown over the preceding decades. The church allowed African parishioners only inferior space in the rear gallery and attempted to tax them for that accommodation. The final break followed the installation of Alexander M'Caine—who had written proslavery tracts and continued to preach such views—as pastor. In 1818 the African Wesleyan Methodist Episcopal Church (originally the African Asbury M. E. Church) opened. On February 7, it was incorporated with Peter Croger, Benjamin Croger, and John Jackson, of the African Woolman Society, as trustees. Benjamin and Peter Croger also served as lay preachers.[27]

At about the same time, Zion's leaders were seeking total religious independence. The white Methodist Episcopal preachers' attempt to change the denomination's articles of incorporation was the pretense for the departure of the black congregation, but black members were more troubled by the Methodist Episcopal governance and the fact that white elders had threatened and berated the trustees of the African churches. They met at Peter Williams's home to discuss ways to "loosen Zion" from white authority. On July 21, 1820, the black men gathered at Rose Street Academy (an African school) and decided to use the "very grievous schism" among the white members to divorce themselves from the Methodist Episcopal discipline. Five nights later the congregation convened at the Academy and "unanimously sanctioned the foregoing resolutions."[28]

Some of the African pastors wanted to bring Zion under Richard Allen's African Methodist Episcopal church, but black Manhattanites were ambivalent toward the Philadelphia bishop. The New Yorkers believed that Allen had exploited their situation by forming a society and church on Mott Street while they were consumed with their reorganization. Yet, even James Varick was reverent enough toward Bishop Allen to open a prayer meeting for him in spite of a local ministerial agreement to have no exchange with the new Allenite church. Although many preachers favored joining Allen, when the official members of Zion met on August 11 they loudly responded "No" to the "two grand questions put and answered at that meeting": "Shall we join Bishop Allen?" and "Shall we return to the white people?" James Varick was appointed to a committee with George Collins, Charles Anderson, Christopher Rush, and William Miller to draft Zion's discipline. The 1820 "Founders' Address" stated that as a "consequence of the difference of color," African preachers did not enjoy the same privileges in the ministry as white men, although called by the same God. White ecclesiastical governance could not be allowed to operate as a barrier when God "raised up" preachers in the black community. The independent conference of African Methodist ministers was necessary to advance the black clergy and expand the limits of African

Christianity. (The whole affair was oddly reminiscent of the colonial struggle for greater independence from European churches, an autonomy intended to give underserved congregations better leadership by training a ministry in the Americas.) The organizers of the African denomination opted to keep the discipline of "our mother Church (with a little alteration)" as the "Doctrines and Discipline of our Church." Three ministers signed the covenant: James Varick, William Miller, and Abraham Thompson (all of them society members or founders). Christopher Rush and George Collins agreed to have twelve hundred copies of the discipline printed. On November 12, 1820, James Varick and Abraham Thompson, the elders, consecrated and administered the Lord's Supper at Zion. In 1822, Varick was elected bishop of the African Methodist Episcopal Zion denomination.[29]

Allenite pastors had spread across the Northeast, and their work seriously jeopardized the future of the new Manhattan denomination. George White, now under the Philadelphia bishop, even brought the African Methodist Church of nearby Flushing, Long Island, into that connection. White assured the Flushing society that virtually all the members of Manhattan's Zion Church were ready to unite with Allen. George Collins and William Miller visited Flushing to report Zion's independence but the local church remained loyal to Philadelphia. Revenge came quickly as a Philadelphia African society requested copies of the New York discipline to keep their new church separate from Allen. A New Haven society also came under the Zion church along with a Brooklyn congregation. Moreover, on November 30, 1820, Zion and Asbury approved "Articles of Agreement," a union that provided the institutional core of the denomination and served as a model for submitting other churches. Drawn by George Collins and approved by the official members of Zion and Asbury, the compact allowed the churches sovereignty over their internal affairs and property while bringing them under the same government. A quarterly conference was instituted so that mutual needs could be addressed. They regulated membership to avoid competition and made all financial business and transactions public. By the First Annual Conference in the summer of 1821, the church had experienced remarkable growth. Abraham Thompson was minister of Mother Zion, William Miller took the pulpit at Asbury, and Simon Murray pastored the Wesleyan Church in Philadelphia. Ten preachers were serving at Zion, four at Asbury, one in New Haven, two on Long Island, and five in Philadelphia and Easton, Pennsylvania. The denomination had over fourteen hundred members. Under Bishop Christopher Rush, who followed Varick, Zion churches were formed in Nantucket, Salem, and Boston, Massachusetts; Providence, Rhode Island; Hartford, Middletown, New Haven, and Bridgeport, Connecticut; Newark, Elizabeth, and Shrewsbury, New Jersey; Harrisburg, York, Carlisle, Shippinsburgh, Gettysburgh, Chambersburgh, Lewistown, Belleponte, Williamsport, Johnstown, and Pittsburgh, Pennsylvania; Wilmington, Delaware; Baltimore, Maryland; Washington, D.C., and across New York State. By 1843, Varick and Rush had brought forty-five churches into the denomination. In 1850, a Zion church (Rossville A.M.E.Z.) was founded at Sandy Ground, Staten Island, a community of black farmers and oystermen.[30]

Joseph R. Washington Jr. contends that Baptists and Methodists "not only prevented other communions from gaining hold upon Negroes after 1820 and completely sabotaged their endeavors, they granted Negroes a literal license to turn religion into a social concern supported by intense feeling." The power of the Methodist appeal could also be seen in the Caribbean. The Society for Mitigating and Gradually Abolishing the State of Slavery throughout the British Dominions described Methodist missionaries as one of the only successful forces at converting the enslaved. Africans in the West Indies disproportionately chose Methodism. By 1822, the British colonies reported 23,127 African and 847 white Methodists.[31]

In New York City a handful of black men, combined in two African associations—the New York African Society and the New York African Society for Mutual Relief—guided the African conversion. Arthur Schomburg claimed that the first association was the parent of the second, having undergone only the evolution of a more formal structure and a narrower focus, but the two were separate organizations. The difference was not just structural, it was ideological. The roll of the New York African Society was likely consistent with the names attached to the African Chapel and Zion Church. A few of these leaders became founders of Mutual Relief; however, the latter society was chartered by younger—with a few notable exceptions like Varick—and more militant black men. The NYAS founded the black church; the NYASMR protected the black church. Bishop Walls writes that the NYASMR was "composed chiefly of businessmen, many of them members of the A.M.E. Zion Church, and several preachers (practically all the black preachers of the city of that day)."[32]

The founders of the African Society for Mutual Relief chose the name of a Revolutionary-era association as a tribute to the daring men who established an independent black voice and free black community in New York

City. The choice also recognized the fact that the NYAS gave black Manhattan a unique claim within African American institutional and social history. Jupiter Hammon's "Address" at New York was circulated widely, and Philadelphia's black community even printed an edition. Richard Allen and Absalom Jones organized the Free African Society on April 12, 1787—three years after Hammon's lecture—as a benevolent, moral, and religious association. That month they wrote a preamble, and a month later they drew up a constitution. Samuel Baston, Joseph Johnson, Cato Freeman, Caesar Cranchell, James Potter, and William White joined Jones and Allen in founding the Philadelphia organization. Two years later, the FAS sent an emissary to study similar organizations in Boston and across the Northeast. The Free Africans eventually organized the African Methodist Episcopal denomination. By 1796 the black men of Boston had an African Society under the leadership of Prince Hall, who also established black Freemasonry. Initiation into the Boston African Society cost a quarter, and monthly dues were the same. The association offered sick and burial benefits to members and supported widows and orphans. It educated children and placed them in trades. The formation of the original New York African Society coincided with the establishment of the emigrationist Free African Union Society in Newport, Rhode Island, whose members organized the African Society of Providence in 1789. By 1807 black Newport founded the African Benevolent Society, a mutual aid association. In 1795 the black men of Philadelphia created the Friendly Society, an organization with the sole purpose of mutual relief. Within twenty years, there were eighty African relief organizations in Philadelphia with a combined membership of more than seven thousand. By 1849 the City of Brotherly Love housed more than a hundred African benevolent societies, and half of all black adults belonged to at least one.[33]

3

The Liberating Power of the Cross

The NYAS and the African Encounter with the Protestant Ethic, 1774–1796

> Your descendants will be strangers in a country not
> their own, and they will be enslaved and mistreated
> four hundred years.
> But I will punish the nation they serve as slaves.
> —Acts 7:6–7

The ideas that Africans held about their own enslavement and liberty remain elusive. The scholarship has largely concluded that unfree people prized freedom above all else. In this construction, Africans are singularly seen as slaves who possessed and acted upon a desire for liberty, a longing that was displayed in overt acts such as revolts and running away. Ultimately, the circle is closed as the master-slave hierarchy is complemented by a bipolar struggle to adjust that social arrangement. Yet this structure does not reveal the range and complexity of Africans' reactions to servitude. Enslaved Africans did not seek freedom as the only solution to bondage, and their resistance to enslavement was not simply behavioral. Brutality and emotion haunted the social space of the unfree, and enslaved people responded with physical rejections of servitude; however, they also lived and participated in a world of ideas. In *The Black Jacobins*, C. L. R. James explains Toussaint L'Ouverture's fidelity to the French Republic by disclosing the Haitian general's vision for bringing the Revolution to the colonies;[1] similarly, many African Americans embraced British evangelical religion as they encountered and invented the liberating power of the cross. An African-Christian fundamentalism, crafted during the Revolutionary era, was available to enslaved people who sought a thorough refutation of bondage but lived in a world that had not yet witnessed a national emancipation. Certainly, many Africans were ambivalent, at best, to the Christian tease that their fortune rested in the eternal tortured revelation of a divine plan. Still, hundreds of black New Yorkers saw an appeal in evangelical Christianity and they deserve a hearing.

Paradoxically, in their struggle to destroy slavery, Africans found a potent, if unlikely, weapon in the Protestant preoccupation with work. The question of whether human beings could affect their salvation or damnation tormented Christian theology and particularly concerned the Protestant sects. It generated a range of beliefs from fatalistic predestination to enthusiastic universal grace. Labor was a tangent of this fascination. For Calvinistic Puritans, industry and accumulation did not influence salvation but they could provide social evidence of divine election,[2] while for universalists thrift and work were among the individual behaviors that readied body and soul for a possible redemption.

The Protestant ethic—which Christopher Hill defines as "an emphasis on the religious duty of working hard in one's calling, of avoiding the sins of idleness, waste of time, over-indulgence in the pleasures of the flesh"— is most often examined for its impact upon free workers. Max Weber argues that Protestantism shifted the Christian focus from otherworldly monasticism to the earthly duty described in the "calling." The ascetic underpinnings of the Calvinist, Methodist, Pietist, and Baptist traditions elevated capitalistic values like work and prudence into moral obligations, creating the cultural context for the ascendance of bourgeois society. The advent of evangelical Protestantism compromised predestination with the promise that, if prepared, every person could achieve salvation. As E. P. Thompson writes, this salvation required sacrifice: "methodical discipline in every aspect of life." Methodism's "diabolic" effect on the late eighteenth-century English working class was that it guided them into labor drudgery during the British Industrial Revolution while directing their social anger into the innocuous space of religiosity. The reward came in the afterlife while the only earthly release came from "psychic masturbation": the chance for workers to unload their frustrations and angers in the socioemotional world of the revival.[3]

The Protestant ethic is best understood as an aspect of ideology, not a description of social behavior. To bridge that gap, Hill "assume[d] without argument that there is such a thing as the protestant ethic" before cataloguing its crimes against British labor.[4] Protestantism made a universal social act a measure of spiritualism. It created at least the illusion of extraordinary social engagement, a responsiveness to human affairs that has fueled speculation that it shaped history. The extent to which the ethic actually dictated social relations will likely always be debated, but it unarguably influenced social discourse.

For instance, the ethic drove the rhetoric and logic of Protestant antislavery as it arose in the eighteenth century. The "calling" shrouded work with divine dignity and brought all labor relations under intense religious scrutiny. Significantly, evangelical Protestantism's labor (or social) focus made the secular debates of the Enlightened Atlantic permeable to radical Christian thought. Bernard Semmel maintains that John Wesley's antislavery stance was peculiarly out of line with his political moderation: a thread of natural rights in a mind that feared revolution and treasured authority. John and Charles Wesley did object to the violence and caprice of the planters as simple political or social affronts, but they also philosophically objected to the damage that the social system did to spiritualism. "I had observed much, and heard more, of the cruelty of masters toward their negros," recalled Charles Wesley of their stay in South Carolina. In the political milieu of the eighteenth century, natural rights provided a vocabulary for human freedom, but it did not always furnish a path to antislavery. "The Enlightenment disseminated ideas that could serve the defender of slavery as well as the abolitionist," argues David Brion Davis, for rationalism was indifferent to the plight of unfree Africans. Evangelists were likely to turn rational philosophy against slavery. "The evangelical religious fundamentalism which flowed from the Great Awakening of the 1740s," writes Eric Foner of spiritual radicalism, "had become a potent source of egalitarian social and political ideology."[5]

Semmel correctly notes that John Wesley used the principles of natural law to attack slavery; however, Wesley's antislavery was more consistent with his theology. In 1774 he published his *Thoughts upon Slavery* in England and the United States. Wesley refused to condemn Africans for even violently "asserting their native Liberty, which they have as much right to as to the air they breathe." "And no human law can deprive him of that right, which he derives from the law of nature." Natural rights blended with his theology.

> But can law, human law, change the nature of things? Can it turn darkness into light, or evil into good? By no means. Notwithstanding ten thousand laws, right is right, and wrong is wrong still. There must still remain an essential difference between justice and injustice, cruelty and mercy....

Where is the justice in inflicting the severest evils, on those that have done us no wrong? Of depriving those that never injured us in word or deed, of every comfort of life? Of tearing them from their native country, and depriving them of liberty itself? To which an *Angolan* has the same natural right as an *Englishman*, and on which he sets as high a value? Yea where is the justice of taking away the lives of innocent, inoffensive men? Murdering thousands of them in their own land, by the hands of their own countrymen: Many thousands, year after year, on shipboard, and then casting them like dung into the sea! And tens of thousands in that cruel slavery, to which they are so unjustly reduced.

. . . I strike at the root of this complicated villainy. I absolutely deny all slave-holding to be consistent with any degree of even natural justice.[6]

That final line locates natural justice as the lesser of two standards, the greater being the Christian ethic. Wesley's natural rights principles were useful to the extent that they overlapped with Christian morality.

Wesley's public declaration set the radical standard for evangelical Christians on both sides of the Atlantic. He rejected all commercial, legal, political, religious, and historical justifications for bondage. He gleaned evidence from accounts of travelers in Africa and slave traders to defend the integrity of Africa and its people and to reply to those who shielded bondage with the claim of African inferiority. Servitude degraded the mind of the enslaved. As Wesley wrote, the people of Africa "were no way remarkable for stupidity." "The inhabitants of *Africa* where they have equal motives and equal means of improvement, are not inferior to the inhabitants of *Europe*: To some of them they are greatly superior." The accusation of inferiority cloaked guilt, for it was by force that "the christians[,] landing upon their coasts, seized as many as they found, men, women, and children, and transported them to *America*." The culture of barbarism increased as Christians cultivated intracontinental wars and waited like vultures for captives. "Till then they seldom had any wars: But were in general quiet and peaceable. But the white men first taught them drunkenness and avarice, and then hired them to sell one another," continued Wesley. The behavior of Europeans and Africans belied the labels Christian and heathen. It was, after all, Europeans who "procured" Africans through violence, debased them in an inhuman trade, branded and sold them, and let them die aboard trading ships. Once they had Africans enslaved, Christians resorted to violence, cruelty, and bloodshed to keep them bound. Castrations and other mutilations, whippings, beatings, and murder kept the order of a slave society. Summarizing his own spiritual politics, Wesley disclaimed England's profitable colonies:

> It were better that all those islands should remain uncultivated forever, yea, it were more desirable that they were all together sunk in the depth of the sea, than that they should be cultivated at so high a price, as the violation of justice, mercy, and truth.[7]

The wealth of the nation mattered only to the extent that it mirrored the godliness of its people. Stolen labor was evidence of ungodliness and inconsistent with radical religion.

Religious ideas did not evolve in a vacuum. Evangelicalism was in dialogue with Enlightened philosophy. "I believed that liberty was the natural right of all men equally," declared the Quaker minister John Woolman in 1757. Although expressed in political language, Woolman's antislavery was a tense reconciliation of religious fundamentalism, natural rights philosophy, and an abiding respect for the law. A year after the publication of Wesley's *Thoughts*, Thomas Paine, the Revolutionary propagandist and apostle of the Enlightenment, condemned American slavery in one of the first essays that he published in the colonies. Paine also used secular, rationalist language and logic to expose the hypocrisy of colonial bondage; however, he measured the threat that slavery posed by how far the society's behavior had ventured from the most basic Christian principles. "Is the barbarous enslaving of our inoffensive neighbours, and treating them like wild beasts subdued by force, reconcilable with all these *Divine precepts?*" he asked. Allowing his Quaker roots to captain his rationalism, Paine concluded that the danger of enslaving Africans lie not in white people's alienation from a political ideal but rather in "the punishment with which Providence threatens us."[8]

By making work a measure of devotion, evangelicalism may have conspired to tame free labor, but it also tended to elevate the unfree. That leveling predisposition is typically erased, or muted, in social histories of radical Protestantism that examine its relationship to capitalism alone. The habit is to cast evangelical antislavery as coincident—the vogue of its founders and early adherents—to its economic theology. In fact, the conviction behind Wesley's antislavery was a product of what Sylvia R. Frey and Betty Wood call "his special relationship with a handful of African women and men" whom he met in America, and his theology generated its syllogism. The roots of Wesleyan antislavery were in the Protestant ethic. It reflected a belief that moral people could demonstrate their spiritual submission in their daily labors. The free will that Christians needed to exercise to make labor an act of piety, the dignity of such work, and the moral discipline gained from personal responsibility made bondage abhorrent to evangelical thought. Wesley blasted slavery as "the scandal of religion, of England, and of human nature."[9]

The influence of British evangelists like Wesley over American Christians continued for some time, although English governance of American churches ended with the Revolution. "In moral even more than in literary matters, the United States was still a British province, and British devices in benevolence were eagerly imitated," asserts Gilbert Hobbs Barnes. Thus, on January 25, 1785, prominent white "free citizens and Christians" of Manhattan and Brooklyn—among them a significant number of slaveholders—formed a "society for promoting the Manumission of slaves, and protecting such of them as have been or may be Liberated," or the New York Manumission Society. In its founding document, the NYMS credited both "Providence" and natural law for its work, but the perceived spiritual threat from the religious impolicy of slavery, more than any genuine faith in the humanity of Africans, seems to have moved most of its members. Their subsequent domineering stance toward black New Yorkers confirms that it was fear of spiritual judgment that overwhelmed their doubts that natural laws and republican principles applied to Africans. The British evangelical attack upon slavery heightened the concerns of these New Yorkers. Shortly after the Manumission Society was founded, the young Thomas Clarkson won first prize at Cambridge for his dissertation against the slave trade. The Manumission Society purchased copies of Clarkson's essay for distribution in New York and other American cities. The Standing Committee also suggested that the association follow Cambridge's example and award a gold medal "to the person who shall deliver the best oration at the next annual commencement of the [Columbia] College in New York, exploring in the best manner, the injustice and cruelty of the slave trade, and the oppression, and ill policy of holding negroes in slavery."[10]

If the comfortable and secure men of the NYMS seriously considered the evangelical promise that slaveholding was a path to spiritual destruction then certainly black people could find the argument compelling. African Americans had already participated in the Methodist ferment in New York City, and the evidence shows that they were fully familiar with the evangelical critique of bondage. At the same time that Manhattan's black Methodists began holding separate meetings in the African Chapel,

William Hamilton—a founder of the chapel and later Mother Zion Church and the NYASMR—wrote to New York State governor John Jay, the first chairman of the NYMS.[11] Hamilton wrote in the jargon of radical Protestantism and included verse borrowed from a British evangelist.

William Cowper, the poet and the son of an Anglican minister, was born in England in 1731. In the summer of 1764 he began attending revivals and came under the tutelage of the Reverend John Newton, who, Hugh I'Anson Fausset wrote, "was the curate-in-charge of Olney, a little town in the north of Buckinghamshire, which was to earn the apt title of 'The Evangelical Mecca.'" In 1788 Cowper penned "The Negro's Complaint," a poem written in the voice of an African, containing traces of rational philosophy and influenced by Newton, Wesley, and, perhaps, the growing number of black evangelists in the Americas:

> Forced from home and all its pleasures,
> Afric's coast I left forlorn;
> to increase a stranger's treasurers,
> O'er the raging billows borne.
> Men from England bought and sold me,
> Paid my price in paltry gold;
> But, though slave they have enrolled me,
> Minds are never to be sold.
>
> Still in thought as free as ever,
> What are England's rights, I ask,
> Me from my delights to sever,
> Me to torture, me to task?
> Fleecy locks and black complexion
> Cannot forfeit Nature's claim;
> Skins may differ, but affection
> Dwells in white and black the same.
>
> Why did all-creating Nature
> Make the plant for which we toil?
> Sighs must fan it, tears must water,
> Sweat of ours must dress the soil.
> Think, ye masters iron-hearted,
> Lolling at your jovial boards,
> Think how many backs have smarted,
> For the sweets your cane affords.
>
> Is there, as ye sometimes tell us,
> Is there One who reigns on high?

Has He bid you buy and sell us,
Speaking from his throne, the sky?
Ask him, if your knotted scourges,
Matches, blood-extorting screws,
Are the means that duty urges
Agents of his will to use?

Hark! He answers—Wild tornadoes,
Strewing yonder sea with wrecks,
Wasting towns, plantations, meadows,
Are the voice with which He speaks.
He, forseeing what vexations
Afric's sons should undergo,
Fixed their tyrants' habitations
Where his whirlwinds answer–'No.'

By our blood in Afric wasted,
Ere our necks received the chain;
By the miseries that we tasted,
Crossing in your barks the main;
By our sufferings, since ye brought us
To the man-degrading mart;
All sustained by patience, taught us
Only by a broken heart;

Deem our nation brutes no longer,
Till some reason ye shall find
Worthier of regard, and stronger
Than the colour of our kind.
Slaves of gold, whose sordid dealings
Tarnish all your boasted powers,
Prove that you have human feelings,
Ere you proudly question ours![12]

Significantly, "The Negro's Complaint" presupposed the foundations of Protestant antislavery: that Africans were eligible for redemption, that slavery impeded their salvation journey, and that the wrath of God was impending.

Cowper followed his 1788 work with two brief antislavery poems, "Pity for Poor Africans" and "The Morning Dream." Four years earlier, he sharply condemned the slave trade in his classic poem "The Task." His London acquaintances published "The Negro's Complaint" under the title "A Subject for Conversation at the Tea-table." It was sold all over

England, and, according to the Reverend Thomas Clarkson, the little poem had extraordinary effect:

> Falling at length into the hands of the musician, it was set to music; and it then found its way into the streets, both of the metropolis and of the country, where it was sung as a ballad; and where it gave a plain account of the subject, with an appropriate feeling, to those who heard it.[13]

In two decades Wesley, Cowper, and Hamilton used natural rights language and Christian moralism to condemn slavery as unnatural, unjust, and ungodly; moreover, the actions of people across the Atlantic testified to the threat that evangelicalism posed to slavery. That menace could easily be unearthed from the Protestant ethic, and many black Americans saw the richness of that mine: emphasizing the spiritual meaning of work accentuated the immorality of bondage. Bishop Richard Allen, founder of the African Methodist Episcopal Church, experienced the social possibilities of evangelicalism in his own life. Born enslaved to Benjamin Chew of Philadelphia, Allen was later sold with his family to Delaware. A second sale separated the Allens. Richard Allen remained in Delaware and converted to Methodism. He attended secret class meetings in the woods. A remaining brother and sister also joined the Methodist society. When the meetings were discovered, neighbors warned Allen's master of the danger of African converts. "My brother and myself held council together, that we would attend more faithfully to your [*sic*] master's business, so that it should not be said that religion made us worse servants; we would work night and day to get our crops forward, so that they should not be disappointed," recalled Allen. The brothers even missed class, over their owner's objections, to tend to the field. Soon, their master "boasted of his slaves for their honesty and industry." He even allowed Allen to invite Methodist preachers onto his property. Among the guest ministers were Francis Asbury, future bishop of the Methodist Episcopal Church of the Unites States, and Freeborn Garrettson, a Maryland slaveholder, who, as a young man in 1775, freed his bondspeople after his emotional conversion. After hearing Garrettson, Allen's owner invited the Africans to join his family for regular prayer meetings in his parlor. He also offered to let the Allen brothers buy their freedom. They did.[14]

Evangelical culture advertised famous converts to Christianity and antislavery. England's John Newton, Cowper's mentor, entered the faith while commanding slaving vessels on the coast of West Africa. "For about the space of six years, the Lord was pleased to lead me in a secret way" to radical Christianity, and, following a seizure that he attributed to God's plan, he began training for the ministry. In 1792 a New Jersey college awarded Newton an honorary doctorate. He rejected the tribute. "My youthful years were spent in Africa and I ought to take my degrees (if I take any) from thence. Shall such a compound of misery and mischief[,] as I then was, be called a *Doctor*?" Newton explained. His salvation from heathenism and slavery remained defining elements until his death; in fact, both were the subjects of the epitaph that he wrote for himself:

> JOHN NEWTON, Clerk
> Once an Infidel and Libertine,
> A servant of slaves in Africa,
> Was, by the rich mercy of our Lord and Saviour
> JESUS CHRIST,
> Preserved, restored, pardoned,
> And appointed to preach the Faith,
> (He had long labored to destroy,)
> Near sixteen years at Olney, in Bucks,
> And . . . years in this church.

The Reverend Thomas Clarkson inspired James Stanfield, a crewman on slavers, to offer his own testimony against the commerce. In 1788 Clarkson published *An Essay on the Impolicy of the African Slave Trade*, which included a lengthy description of the economic costs and moral failure of the international slaving enterprise. Stanfield wrote Clarkson that same year hoping to "add a little to the mass of materials, your humanity has been at such labour to collect."[15]

Manhattanites knew the revolutionary potential of evangelicalism. In 1787 Freeborn Garretson brought his ministry to New York and bolstered the work of Thomas Webb and the British soldiers whose grassroots evangelizing converted white and black people on the streets of the Revolutionary city. By 1789 the former slave owner was the presiding elder of a region that included Long Island, and he spent the next four decades in New York and New England. In 1827, the year that hereditary slavery ended in New York and the year of his death, Garrettson came to Manhattan to preach his last sermon.[16]

Thus, two decades of tension between a feverish evangelicalism and a stubbornly unfree society set the backdrop for black New Yorkers' conversion. A powerful religious reawakening and an awareness of the damage that spiritual ideas could do to proslavery arguments were the context of the social transformation in the black community. In 1784 Jupiter Hammon delivered "An Address to the Negroes of the State of New York" before the New York African Society during this revival; in fact, it occurred just before the founding of the NYMS. It is most striking because it marks a step that many black people took on a greater religious pilgrimage, it offers an early example of the ideological governance of African-Christian associations, and it documents Africans' ability to manipulate Protestant thought; however, most scholars have been absorbed with what they see as Hammon's moderate politics. "It is easy to understand why whites were willing to print Hammon's *Address*," estimates one historian, "and it is surprising that it was not published in the South."[17] From a postemancipation or secular perspective, the "Address" appears a weak, apologetic, and visionless lecture.

Intellectual discomfort with Hammon's appeal focuses primarily on his insistence that enslaved Africans ignore their social status and concentrate on their spiritual salvation. The problem is not that scholars harshly judge the persecuted for succumbing to the awful temptation to hope, but that they would rather see optimism generated in the real sociopolitical world and not the surreal spiritual realm. Eugene Genovese eloquently captures the strain: "The truth of religion comes from its symbolic rendering of man's moral experience; it proceeds intuitively and imaginatively. Its falsehood comes from its attempt to substitute itself for science and to pretend that its poetic statements are information about reality." That is, of course, an application of Karl Marx's treatment of religion: "If Protestantism was not the true solution it was at least the true setting of the problem," wrote Marx, who viewed religion as the intellectual refraction of social suffering:

> Religious distress is at the same time the expression of real distress and also the protest against real distress. Religion is the sigh of the oppressed creature, the heart of a heartless world, just as it is the spirit of spiritless conditions. It is the opium of the people.

The challenge was to move the society from the consolation of religion to the radicalism of political philosophy. The struggle was not against the distraction of faith but against the real injustices of class. Religion was a perfectly human expression of social strife: the vessel of human sorrow. Politics were the means of channeling that sorrow into action.[18]

Hammon's failing was not evangelicalism's failing. He chose to view faith and social action as alternatives. Jupiter Hammon was not alone in surrendering to this enticement. In her short poem "On Being Brought from Africa to America" (ca. 1769), Phillis Wheatley came dangerously close to excusing the slave trade because it resulted in her conversion. She balanced that suggestion with a condemnation of racial hatred and an insistence that Africans were eligible for salvation. Hammon later celebrated Wheatley's devotion to Christian orthodoxy in verse. The New England minister Lemuel Haynes, the first black man ordained in the United States, offered little more than a vague promise that a godly republic might extend pity to enslaved Africans.[19]

Still, it is misleading to assume that a dominant culture imposed this spiritual optimism upon black Christians. The expression of a communitarian ethic was a peculiar feature of black culture, writes Donald H. Matthews, allowing for a "tragic sense of hope" to develop independent of Christianity. "In other words, the scholar need not 'blame' this feature of African American religion on the black community's adoption of a traditional orthodox Christian position," for this worldview probably descends from West African philosophy.[20]

The salvation theme in early African-Christian discourse causes historiographical mischief because of the conceit that centers social study around white actors and leads to the assumption that white people's thoughts and interests shaped such statements. Mechal Sobel, in her history of eighteenth-century Virginia, asserts that the evangelical celebration of the afterlife as a joyous spiritual and familial reunion—the basis of Christianity's social optimism—is itself an Africanism: a product of African ancestral values translated into the Christian paradigm. Encountering African religiosity at revivals, funerals, and deathbed sites, "white Virginians began to speak of preferring the after life death to the present one" and African familial and ancestral beliefs "now became 'white' ones as well."[21] If one can extrapolate, Hammon's confidence in the bounty of the afterlife was a particularly African contribution to Christianity. The fact that Hammon's "Address" is free of any direct concern for the souls of white folk strengthens that interpretation.

Hammon believed in freedom, but it did not dominate his vision of the world. "That liberty is a great thing we may know from our own feelings, and we may likewise judge so from the conduct of the white people, in the late war. How much money has been spent, and how many lives have been lost, to defend their liberty."[22] Oddly, Hammon did not ask the people of color in his audience to advance their freedom with the same zeal.

Rather, he greeted his audience of free and unfree black men with the obvious: that he was "one of your own nation and colour," that he was an old man who had earned the privilege of speaking, and that he had "no interest in deceiving you." He spoke out of concern, knowing that "I have had more advantages and privileges than most of you, who are slaves, have ever known, and I believe more than many white people have enjoyed." He asked them to hear his plea.[23]

Hammon turned to his fellow bondspeople and told them that they were in a "poor, despised and miserable" state, and that he was deeply troubled by the "ignorance and stupidity, and the great wickedness of the most of you." He instructed them to be obedient and respectful toward their masters. He offered biblical verse as proof that God intended each of them to obey his owner. "It may seem hard for us, if we think our masters wrong in holding us slaves, to obey in all things, but who of us dare dispute with God!" he warned. Then, he cautioned them not to steal from their masters. It was their duty to hold their masters' property sacred and to conduct their masters' business faithfully and efficiently. "I know that many of you endeavor to excuse yourselves, and say, that you have nothing that you can call your own, and that you are under great temptations to be unfaithful and take from your masters. But this will not do, God will certainly punish you for stealing and for being unfaithful," said Hammon. Do not be idle, do not cheat, do not take what is not yours, he implored. He then lashed out at profanity. "This you know is forbidden by God." Quoting the Bible, he told them to abstain from such acts and protect their salvation. "All those of you who are profane, are serving the Devil. You are doing what he tempts and desires you to do." Hammon even rejected the possibility of his becoming free. "I do not wish to be free: yet I should be *glad*, if others, especially the young negroes were to be free." He was not even especially desirous of a general emancipation: "This my dear brethren is by no means, the greatest thing we have to be concerned about. Getting our liberty in this world, is nothing to having the liberty of the children of God."[24]

Hammon offered his audience a set of solutions that wax equally moderate to the modern ear. Africans should read the Bible daily and lead their lives according to its codes. Those who could not read should have the Bible read to them or "let all the time you can get, be spent in trying to learn to read."[25] The Bible held answers to their predicament. It contained an offer of salvation that might give meaning to their time on earth and usher their souls to Heaven.

Hammon was not repeating the rhetoric of the master class. To assume that he was speaking to please white people or at their direction is to insult him, and to dismiss his message as warped extends the insult to his audience. He likely came to these opinions on his own and with careful consideration of his ideological terrain. If it now sounds sterile, it was potent at the moment that it was spoken. That element was not simply the visible break with history in which an enslaved man delivered an address to an audience of bondsmen and free men of color, nor was it delivered cryptically as Hammon implored his audience to read and congregate. It came through his profound faith that bondage and all human injustices were defenseless before God.

Eighteenth-century evangelical religion stressed obligation and instruction, gifts and punishments. Hammon accepted that social service, Christian discipline, and labor fidelity were the habits of the saved.[26] He was equally sure of the religious backwardness of humankind, but he was not insulting or demeaning the men seated before him. Hammon was lecturing under the structure of Christian humility through which all people come before God in wretchedness, sin, ignorance, and want. In spite of all his advantages, Hammon also described himself as unfit and unworthy.

He made his demand for obedience from slave to master, "whether it is right, and lawful, in the sight of God, for them to make slaves of us or not." Faithful service would bring spiritual and earthly benefits even if their masters did not deserve such attentiveness. Hammon's insistence that his listeners be honest and diligent was not intended to turn them into "men pleasers" but to protect them, for "the same God will judge both them and us." Theft and dishonesty did little to hurt masters as a class but it did much to impair Africans' salvation. Similarly, in warning against profanity, he sought not to make them better slaves but to make them better Christians. "If we are found among those who feared his name and trembled at his word, we shall be called good and faithful servants. Our slavery will be at an end, and though ever so mean, low, and despised in this world, we shall sit with God in his kingdom as Kings and Priests, and rejoice forever, and ever," proclaimed Hammon.[27]

Faith did not assure earthly freedom nor did it necessarily provide personal solace. Hammon carefully avoided promises of physical liberty and psychic comfort. Faith could bring rewards, but a Christian could not pursue rewards through faith. "The godliness which is profitable to all things becomes unprofitable when profit rather than God comes to be its interest," writes one scholar of the Protestant paradox.[28] The hunger of the godly was for Christ, and lesser ambitions threatened salvation. Hammon was a disciplined Protestant who urged a pure faith, a spiritualism that might carry Africans into the Kingdom.

In a sensitive critique, Elizabeth Rauh Bethel describes Hammon's views as a product of "the tension that many African Americans felt between civil and sacred authority." It was likely the absence of that division that guided the aged philosopher. Black Christians early embraced, what Lewis Perry terms, the anarchist possibilities of evangelicalism: as the government proved to be an agent of their persecution or a barrier to their emancipation, Africans became distrustful of civic institutions and substituted divine authority.[29] Bethel's separation is what allowed many white New Yorkers to conceive of themselves as slaveholders and good Christians—for instance, it solves the contradictions of the NYMS— while Hammon clearly accepted the transcendence of spiritual authority. For Hammon, the tension was not divine but social, it existed between the Africans and the white Americans, for the civil sins of the latter compromised the spiritual journey of the former.

Nonetheless, Hammon's lecture leaves today's reader uncomfortable. His impassioned offer of the Bible as a weapon against oppression and the essay's Christian draping do not erase the suggestion that each person make amends with servitude. As Hammon said: "If we should ever get to heaven, we shall find nobody to reproach us for being black, or for being slaves. Let me beg of you my dear African brethren, to think very little of your bondage in this life, for your thinking of it will do you no good." He repeated that message in a poem—"A Dialogue, Entitled, The Kind Master and Dutiful Servant"[30]—published a year earlier.

This discomfort, however, is not totally an eighteenth-century problem. Our ears have become accustomed to a conversation that is the luxury of free people, a conversation that assumes the absolute right and wrong of bondage, the reply of resistance to oppression, and, thus, the total incompatibility of the visions of slaves and masters. Liberty through salvation, or bliss after death, has grown weaker as a substitute for earthy joy. Hammon's question—"what is forty, fifty, or sixty years, when compared to eternity[?]"—is less easily answered.[31] Moreover, we suffer from the knowledge that American slavery had a beginning and an end, and we are seduced by the hope that its conception could have been retarded and its demise hastened.

Jupiter Hammon responded to his world. About 1720 he was born enslaved in Queens County, Long Island. He spent all his life there and in

New England. At his birth, the echo of the failed Manhattan rebellion of 1712 could still be heard. After that revolt, the governor ordered that more than a dozen African rebels be hanged, a handful were shot, one was torn apart on the wheel, one was "slow fire roasted" until dead, and two were burned at the stake. Hammon came of age as the 1741 conspiracy in New York City unfolded and its bloody aftermath played out. This time, seventeen Africans hanged and another thirteen met their end at the stake. He had, in fact, witnessed or heard of many major and minor conspiracies, insurrections, and revolts. He also understood absconding. Long Island had its share of runaways, and a village of maroons even survived there.[32] However, Hammon knew that every African could not run away, and it was unclear to him what they might run away to; he also knew of no rebellion that had resulted in the end of servitude. He rejected running away because Africans could not all abscond and it was an option primarily for the young and the skilled, and rebellion because his moral fiber would not permit him to propel his people toward their bloody end.

Hammon accepted that the security and unity of the spiritual family was greater than any individual's freedom.[33] He trusted the Bible because it documented his world's most successful emancipation. By following biblical codes of behavior they could create human space in an inhumane society. They did not have to accept that slavery was morally right or historically inevitable to behave in such a way as to earn greater rewards and privileges for themselves and their families. It was an ultimate act of sacrifice and a confirmation of their humanity for African men to rein their desires and emotions in order to manipulate their social system. By imploring them to be better Christians, Hammon begged them to create a community in which their families and neighbors could survive, improve, and multiply until slavery's destruction.

It was no act of weakness for the black men in his audience to forsake their individual liberty in order to preserve their collective humanity. Revolt is not, as the most earnest advocates style it, the logical outcome of social conflict and antagonism. People, even oppressed people, often choose life and its accouterments over righteous death for all its romance. They frequently balance the social things they cherish against those they despise and decide to compromise or even concede—and when they do, it is not a great cheating of the historical teleology, but simply another rational pattern of human affairs. Indeed, it is arrogant and misguided to impose standards of conduct on the past that make death the threshold to dignity and sell the lives of oppressed people so cheaply. The fact is that we tend to view enslaved people as *just* slaves, while they valued familial and social obligations and attachments that gave meaning to their lives in spite of their circumstances.

Again, the intellectual danger of dismissing Hammon is that he was not peculiar. In about 1810, sixteen men in Sierra Leone, West Africa, wrote an *Epistle* "to all Professors of all Christian denominations, who have not abolished the holding of Slaves." Blending African nationalism with evangelical antislavery, they condemned the practice of making "merchandize" of other Christians. Then, approaching Jupiter Hammon's words, they urged their "dearly beloved African Brethren" who remained enslaved to "be obedient unto your masters, with your prayers lifted up to God, whom we would recommend you to confide in, who is just as able in these days, to deliver you from the yoke of oppression, as he hath in time past brought your fore-fathers out of the Egyptian bondage."[34]

Bishop Richard Allen also addressed people of color in terms that approximated Jupiter Hammon's. During a lecture, he told the enslaved that he was once "a slave, and as desirous of freedom as any of you." He assured them that he had experienced the emotional pull of liberty and the torture of awaiting it patiently. He directed them to serve and trust in God "who sees your condition." Africans who lived by the dictates of the Bible could sway kind masters by their example, and God would defend them against cruel masters. Deliver a Christian love to your "so called" masters and mistresses and it "will be seen by them and tend to promote your liberty." More important, continued the bishop, such a course guaranteed a greater liberty. Live a good Christian life and "have a view of that freedom which the sons of God enjoy," he said, and upon your death "you will be admitted to the freedom which God hath prepared for those of all colors that love him. Here the power of the most cruel master ends, and all sorrow and tears are wiped away." Allen turned to the free people of color and reminded them that their behavior, condition, and progress were weapons in the struggle against slavery. "We who know how bitter the cup is which the slave hath to drink, O, how ought we to feel for those who yet remain in bondage! Will even our friends excuse—will God pardon us—for the part we act in making strong the hands of the enemies of our color," cautioned Allen.[35]

Perhaps still the lesson is better learned in reverse. Much of what Jupiter Hammon said in 1784 might have pleased the slave owners of New York, but there was also plenty to disturb them. As Hammon cried:

"Oh how glorious is an eternal life of happiness! and how dreadful, an eternity of misery."[36] Spiritual certainty attached to the enslaved and fled their masters. It would have unsettled most Manhattan slaveholders to know that so many evangelical Africans thought themselves destined for Heaven and that they were as sure that their owners would again be a class—in Hell.

There were already more radical philosophers closing on Hammon's heels; his was just one reading of African Christianity. Nonetheless, black New Yorkers took from Hammon's lecture what they needed. Had they thought of themselves only as slaves, they might have shunned his moderate critique of bondage; rather, in society, they admired his celebration of African humanity. The "Address to the Negroes" had an obvious appeal: Hammon appreciated Africans as people and parents and children and siblings and spouses and friends and families and communities. He understood the complexity of their personal and social ties, realities that typically determined the priority of physical freedom in an individual life. Hammon emphasized the humanity of the enslaved. While more militant messengers soon took the ring, for a brief moment Hammon stood at center and the Africans gave him honor.

Hammon should be criticized, but for the right reason. His failure is not his conversion or the requirements of that faith, but his personal limitations. It is not that Christianity weakened his resolve with its passionate idiom of hope, but that he did not exploit the social potential of evangelicalism. Hammon's deficiency is not in the "Address to the Negroes," rather he is culpable for what he did not say. Leading an industrious and honest individual life guided by the moral conscience was only half the duty of an ethical Christian. Hammon stopped there, ignoring an equally important tenet of Protestantism: the obligation to confront evil. The belief that the sanctified person could not be idle in the face of sin was an originating principle of Protestantism that was passed to all its branches. It was the wellspring of Protestant fanaticism, responsible for everything from separatism to witch hunts. George H. Williams argues that one of Protestantism's contributions to modern society is the notion of loyal opposition, which evolved as the theology refined critique and schism into religious, and eventually secular, duties. The principle is most identified with the Puritans. Historian Edmund S. Morgan calls it the Puritan dilemma, "the problem of doing right in a world that does wrong." In 1653 Puritan divine Michael Wigglesworth confided it to his diary: "I beg to walk with god in the world among a perverse generation." It was an assumption of Puritan "contractualism," the legalistic structure which, according to Perry Miller, ordered the culture of covenants within New England sociology.[37]

The burden fell with equal weight upon evangelical Christians. Bishop Richard Allen, who also believed that the rules of orthodox behavior applied to the unfree, thought himself compelled to bring the force of Christian prayer and moral protest against slavery. Phillis Wheatley's antislavery exploited this principle. John Wesley's missions to the irreligious, his involvement in charitable work, and the publication of his *Thoughts upon Slavery* resulted from this responsibility of faith. Hammon intentionally shunned the duty of dissent, fearing its effects, and in doing so he provided the Africans with a guide to becoming more, but not wholly, Christian.

4

"The Aristocracy of Character"

African Societies and the Moral Consequence of Nationalism, 1784–1845

And I will give you the keys of the kingdom of heaven;
whatever you bind on earth will be bound in heaven,
and whatever you loose on earth will be loosed in heaven.
—Matthew 16:19

By the end of the Revolution, black New Yorkers were publicly describing themselves and their institutions as African. That act was the signage of a nationalist culture forged in the early years of bondage. Black nationalism, write John Bracey Jr., August Meier, and Elliot Rudwick, constitutes "a body of social thought, attitudes, and actions ranging from the simplest expressions of ethnocentrism and racial solidarity to the comprehensive and sophisticated ideologies of Pan-Negroism or Pan-Africanism."[1] It advocates the physical and political self-determination of people of African ancestry and begins with the notion that African peoples remain a coherent historical, political, and cultural group. The rhetorical expressions of nationalism have been explored rather fully; however, its moral basis remains largely unexamined. There was a moral consequence to the assertion that black Americans were a nation, sharing a common history and destiny with other people of African ancestry. Some form of moral government was needed for that sense of interconnectedness to be more than rhetorical. The New York African Society for Mutual Relief (NYASMR) and its subsidiary associations (see table 4.1)—which included benevolent and secret societies—brought that moral discipline to the black metropolis. The ecumenicalism of African voluntary associations facilitated a political attack on slavery and civil inequality, and their proximity to established churches allowed them to expound the moral implications of black unity.

TABLE 4.1
Select African Voluntary Associations, 1784–1865

Society	Founded	Gender	Age	Leadership
New York African Society	ca. 1784	M	Adult	(Likely the same men who founded Mother Zion Church)[a]
New York African Society for Mutual Relief	1808	M		William Hamilton, president; John Teasman, vice president; Henry Sipkins, secretary; Adam Carman, assistant secretary; Daniel Berry, treasurer; Adam Ray, Daniel B. Brownhill, James M'Euen, Henry Rouse, Samuel Charley, Richard Tankard, Samuel Clause, Benjamin Sleighter, standing committee; James Varick, Peter Williams, Jr., chaplains
New York African Marine Fund	1810	M/W	Adult	Rev. June Scott, Rev. Abraham Thompson, Simon Hackett, Joseph Harman
Brooklyn African Woolman Benevolent Society	1810	M	Adult	Peter Croger, Benjamin Croger, Joseph Smith
Boyer Masonic Lodge	1812	M	Adult	Sandy Lattion, first Woshipful Master; probably *William Miller* and *James Varick*. Later: Patrick Reason, Charles Reason, *Alexander Elston*, Alfred Aldridge, Ransom Wake, *Thomas Downing*, Ira Aldridge, Joseph Gaston, Sr., *John Peterson*, *George Lawrence*, *John Brown*, *William Fenwick*, William C. H. Curtis, Henry Highland Garnet, Samuel Cornish, Jonas Townsend, Alexander Crummel, Dr. Peter Ray, *William H. Anthony*, E.V.C. Eato.
Wilberforce Philanthropic Society	1812	M	Adult	Robert Sidney, president; Thomas A. Francis, vice president; Stephen Ashaby, 2nd vice president; *William Miller*, secretary; James Stevens, Andrew Smith, Thomas Sanders, deputy secretaries; Thomas Sipkins, treasurer; *Thomas Miller*, librarian; Robert F. Williams, Scipio White, James Jackson, John J. Butler, Philip Ward, Philip Murray, James Hammond, John McPherson, *Benjamin Smith*, John Williams, Henry Scott, John J. Johnson, James William Wells, directors
New-York African Clarkson Association	1829	M	21–40	*Alexander Elston*, *William Hamilton*
New York Union African Society	1830	M	Adult	John Anin, Richard Augustus, James Miller, Lawrence Clous, *George L. Phillips*, James Williams
Phoenix Literary Society	1833	M/W	Open	*Boston Crummell*, *Rev. Christopher Rush*, *Thomas Jennings*, Rev. Samuel Cornish, Simeon Jocelyn, Thomas Van Rensellaer

TABLE 4.1
(continued)

Society	Founded	Gender	Age	Leadership
Garrison Literary and Benevolent Association, New-York	1834	M	4–20	*Rev. John Lewis*, president; Lucas Roe, vice president; Daniel Aldrich, 2nd vice president; Henry Highland Garnet, secretary; George D. Peterson, assistant secretary; *John Peterson*, treasurer; *Prince Loveridge*, librarian; William H. Day, assistant librarian; Robert Jones, runner; Thomas H. Tompkins, Joseph Murray, Edward J. Campbell, Christopher J. Huchington, Philip White, Samuel Johnson, William P. Jackson, George W. Francis, John Peterson, Thomas Oliver, Robert Jones, managers; James Williams, John J. Connor, Jr., *John Brown*, *William Thomas*, Thomas Bowers, directors; David Ruggles, Lewis H. Nelson, Henry Anderson, *John Crump*, Jacob Freeman, executive committee; William Smith, Henry C. Parker, William C. Loveridge, visiting committee; Silas Hicks, Samuel Aldrich, Richard Bird, marshals
Abyssinian Benevolent Daughters of Esther Association	1839	W	16–50	As of 1853: Susan Dawley, president; Caroline E. Williams, vice president; Frances Whitney, treasurer; Elizabeth Brown, banker; Sarah Van Clief, secretary; Lucett La Mar, assistant secretary; Mary Rix, Mary N. Wilson, Jane Valentine, Rosemond Dumps, Patience Congers, directresses; Margaret Griffin, Jemima Henry, marshals; Maria Derry, runner; Lewis Valentine, Jessey Dawley, guardians
Frères Réunis	1839	M		Michel Castor, A. Lambert, B. Duplessy, D. G. Cerci, Jean L. Chabert
Philomathean Odd Fellows	1843	M	Adult	*John Peterson, Timothy Seaman, Dr. James McCune Smith, William Fenwick, Thomas Hoffman, Edward V. Clark, George T. Downing*
New York Benevolent Branch of Bethel	ca. 1843	W	18–50	Unkown women
Brooklyn African Tompkins Association	1845	M		*Henry Brown*, John Sherred, Michael Thompson, Robert H. Cousins, *John Brown*, Robert Polston, Cornelius Williams, Henry White, Lewis Willett, Peter Brown, James Johnson, Anthony Johnson, William Abrams, Joseph Brown, James S. Brister, William Brown, William Williams, Abraham Brown, Benjamin Hampton, William

(continued)

TABLE 4.1
(continued)

Society	Founded	Gender	Age	Leadership
Coachmen's Union League	1864	M	Adult	Sherred, John Johnston, John A. Bomer, Enoch C. Harrington Unknown men

ᵃ See chapter 2.

NOTE: Names in italics indicate NYASMR members in other organizations.

SOURCE: *Constitution of the New York African Marine Fund, for the Relief of Distressed Orphans and Poor Members of This Fund* (New York: John C. Totten, 1810), collection of the New-York Historical Society; "An Act to Incorporate the New-York African Society for Mutual Relief. Passed March 23d, 1810," *Private Laws of the State of New-York, Passed at the Thirty-Third Session of the Legislature* (Albany, 1810), 107–9; "An Act to Incorporate the Brooklyn African Woolman Benevolent Society. Passed January 28, 1831," *Laws of the State of New-York, Passed at the Fifty-Fourth Session of the Legislature* (Albany, 1831), 12–13; William J. Walls, *The African Methodist Episcopal Zion Church: Reality of the Black Church* (Charlotte, NC: A.M.E. Zion Publishing House, 1974), 90; Harry A. Williamson, "Prince Hall Masonry in New York State," unpublished typescript, vol. I: 7–10, vol. II, part II:119–29; "An Act to Incorporate the Wilberforce Philanthropic Association. Passed June 8, 1812," *Laws of the State of New York, Passed at the Thirty-Fifth Session of the Legislature* (Albany, 1812), 189–90; "An Act to Incorporate the New-York African Clarkson Association. Passed April 23, 1829," *Laws of the State of New York, Passed at the Fifty-Second Session of the Legislature* (Albany, 1829), 380–81; "An Act to Incorporate the 'New-York Union African Society.' Passed February 23, 1830," *Laws of the State of New York, Passed at the Fifty-Third Session of the Legislature* (Albany, 1830), 38; "Constitution of the Garrison Literary and Benevolent Association, New-York," *The Liberator*, 19 April 1834; *Constitution and By-Laws of the Abyssinian Benevolent Daughters of Esther Association of the City of New York*. Adopted April 19th, 1839 (New York: Zuille & Leondard, 1853), collection of the Society for the Preservation of Weeksville and Bedford-Stuyvesant History; letter (written in French) from Michel Castor, A. Lambert, B. Duplessy, D. G. Cerci, and Jean L. Chabert to Monsieur [Pierre Toussaint], 19 November 1839, Pierre Toussaint Papers, Manuscripts Division, NYPL; James B. Browning, "The Beginnings of Insurance Enterprise among Negroes," *Journal of Negro History* (October 1937), 421–22; "An Act to Incorporate the Brooklyn African Tompkins Association. Passed May 13, 1845," *Laws of the State of New York, Passed at the Sixty-Eighth Session of the Legislature* (Albany, 1845), 242–43; *The Messenger* (September 1925), 320.

That black Manhattanites chose to label their institutions "African" is enlightening. More than a century and a half later, W. E. B. Du Bois examined black people's consistent choice of the designation "African" in the aftermath of the Revolution. Du Bois, on the verge of emigrating to Ghana, postulated that they "looked forward to a return to Africa as their logical end." Most of the people who founded voluntary societies and churches after the Revolution were not foreign born, so the possibility of a "return" was more daunting than the vision of a future in the United States, and the large minority of men born in Africa and the West Indies left no evidence of such a plan. Emigration schemes proved particularly unpopular among black New Yorkers. Even beloved figures like Peter Williams Jr. and Captain Paul Cuffe convinced few Manhattanites to relocate to West Africa. In an 1816 letter, Williams excitedly reported that "eight or nine" people were seeking to emigrate to Sierra Leone, although the fact that they were all "foreigners" dampened his enthusiasm.[2]

Africa was not a destination but a heritage. Africa was a balance to Europe. Given the hostility that greeted them, black people treated Africa as the physical source of their humanity and equality. The participation of black Caribbeans and continental Africans and the endurance of West African cultural expressions, however compromised, made the claim all the more informed and legitimate. Africa was the leveler between black and white New Yorkers and it subordinated cultural divisions between black people. For example, Juliet Gaston was part of an influx of enslaved black people brought to New York City during the Haitian Revolution, who, Shane White writes, "maintained a high profile throughout the 1790s and early 1800s, involving themselves in most of the black unrest in the city, and had a substantial impact on the mood and orientation of the black population." She married Pierre Toussaint, the well-to-do Manhattan hairdresser who came to New York from Haiti enslaved and earned his freedom and a fortune that made him one of the city's foremost Catholic philanthropists. In 1820 Juliet Toussaint donated money to the NYASMR to help it purchase land for a meeting house. Pierre Toussaint supported her decision, writes a biographer, because he "approved of this group as they were dedicated to . . . caring for widows and orphans of deceased members." Haitians were scattered throughout black Manhattan. The same year that the Toussaints donated to the NYASMR, the Society for the Prevention of Pauperism surveyed a section of Manhattan and found sixty-three black and three hundred white residents. Among the handful of black families living there were Mary Antoinette and her child and John Shoore's family—at 187 and 189 Church Street, respectively—Catholics and likely Haitian born.[3]

Africa was a unifying symbol for black people with very different ethnic and cultural backgrounds. As Africans, black New Yorkers acquired a history that predated America's, they could describe emancipation as a return to their rightful and natural condition, and they established an eternal justification for a social liberty that was yet realized. Africa gave them a past that transcended bondage and in doing so it allowed them to reject the idea that they were property or suspended property.

In a 1796 letter to New York State governor John Jay, William Hamilton located the great social struggle between two equal nations: "Africans" and "Americans." As Hamilton asked Jay: "What harm have they [the Africans] done the Americans[?]" "Have they ever injured them in the least[?]" Black people established a common nationality to link their somewhat independent claims to biological equality, economic freedom, and civil liberty. It gave them the fluidity to construct political unity in spite of their different economic and social circumstances. In describing themselves as Africans, they did not claim a linear culture; rather, Africa symbolized their self-determined Creolization. "I am dear Sir one of those whom the generality of men call Negroes," Hamilton explained to Governor Jay, "my forefathers or ancestors [were] from Africa but I am a native of New York." Hamilton instructed Jay that the "indisputable right of these Africans & their children is liberty & freedom" and that they are enslaved "against their will for none are willing to be slaves." He claimed the right to speak on behalf of the oppressed. "I plead the cause of the poor & needy," Hamilton insisted. A common ancestry and history permitted African men to assert a greater knowledge of and sensitivity to the plight of enslaved people, the potency of the claim being increased by Christianity's exaggerated virtue of suffering. They saw themselves as Africans, who by nature were vested with the same right to freedom and equality as other nations of men. "African I term it because . . . it makes no difference whether the man is born in Africa, Asia, Europe or America, so long as he is proginized from African parents," demanded Hamilton in an 1809 speech to the New York African Society for Mutual Relief. That use of Africa in black political ideology persisted for some time. At the close of the Civil War, Dr. James McCune Smith of the NYASMR wrote of the 1820s: "The people of those days rejoiced in their nationality, and hesitated not to call each other 'Africans,' or 'descendants of Africa.'"[4]

Unfortunately, some scholars have ignored and underestimated the associations that cultivated nationalist culture. African societies were "often little more than small-scale insurance cooperatives," writes John Rury, "narrow in scope and of limited effectiveness," their major impact being that membership in them "was an early sign of distinction among blacks." In a study of free black people's organizations in antebellum Manhattan, Daniel Perlman concludes much the same, adding only that relief associations marked a brief transition to more formal and complicated organizations. William Alan Muraskin takes the moral focus of early Prince Hall Masonry to define the Craft as the legacy of a "self-proclaimed" class of men seeking to create boundaries, "real and supposed," between themselves and the masses. He directly equates morality with white skin and, therefore, accused black associations of mimicking white society. "Blacks have from the beginning," continues Muraskin, "insisted upon copying the most important Euro-American fraternal organizations for a reason; they have wished to be identified with, and accepted as equals by, whites." Their material ambitions were, at least in part, intended "to truly impress the dominant race." Thus, for Muraskin, Prince

Hall Masonry "helped to psychologically bind the black Mason to white society by enabling him to identify with the Caucasian middle class" and it "created a haven within the larger black society where bourgeois Negroes have received protection from the values of the non-bourgeois blacks who surround them."[5]

To the contrary, it is difficult to overestimate the importance of voluntary organizations to antebellum black communities. Associations called and hosted public meetings, published lectures, sermons, and resolutions, and organized political campaigns. The charge of insignificance has typically come from scholars who devalue their social functions, exaggerate the importance of white philanthropy, and mistake religiosity for elitism. The latter is an important historiographical prejudice. The fact that white people have historically viewed black Christians as more civilized and refined has provided ample but untested evidence for historians who are predisposed to casting African Christians as an elite. There is little proof that adherence to Christian ethics alone was an avenue to material success and that linkage fails to explain the diversity of the people drawn into the voluntary associations that orbited the black church. Moreover, the idea that white patronage determined the success of black Christian social work is dubious, especially since white favoritism failed miserably at sustaining or spreading contemporaneous movements like colonization.

The prestige of these associations was not generated by white support or black elitism but by the fact that they possessed a viable social agenda. African societies were the instruments of social work because their spiritual but nondenominational basis permitted political organizing. Through societies, African Christians joined what they saw as the great social struggle against slavery and inequality.

The African reading of evangelicalism unfolded as Africans applied religious truths and lessons to social problems. It described enslavement as the original sin from which other degenerate and unnatural relations— particularly the political and social inequality of free people of color— were shaped. The prescription was moral reform: a broad ideology that included religious fundamentalism, individual elevation and responsibility, and civic activism toward a social reconstruction that would come of age with the end of slavery. Voluntary associations were the crucible of this movement. Samuel Cornish of the NYASMR was Manhattan's delegate to the first convention of the American Moral Reform Society, which pledged to bring spiritual weapons to the contest for African American freedom.[6] Moral reform began with the marriage of faith and social action. The ideology was dichotomous: the external message was that the nation needed to awaken to the social and spiritual danger of holding people as property while the internal message called upon the black community to struggle for moral perfection in order to usher in the death of bondage.

In an 1817 speech, the popular preacher Peter Williams Jr. utilized the principles of moral reform as he celebrated the life of Captain Paul Cuffe, a black Quaker merchant and Freemason who established a benevolent association in Manhattan to sponsor African emigration. Only two years earlier, Williams and Abraham Thompson organized and drafted a constitution for "the Society which you recommended [to] us," the New York African Institution, which funded emigrants to and encouraged trade with Sierra Leone. Now, speaking before that association, Williams stated that Cuffe should be esteemed not because he had wealth but because of the social distance he had climbed. Cuffe was the perfect example of moral reform's power: "one who, from a state of poverty, ignorance and obscurity, through a host of difficulties, and with an unsullied conscience, by the native energy of his mind, has elevated himself to wealth, to influence, to respectability and honour; and being thus elevated, conducts [himself] with meekness and moderation, and devotes his time and talents to pious and benevolent purposes." Among Cuffe's accomplishments, Williams first mentioned his refusal to deal in slaves and liquor, and then his philanthropy among the black population of Massachusetts and the people of Africa. Williams saluted Cuffe's support for emigration because it was a part of his personal vision of slavery's demise and the reunion of the African people. Cuffe's life and career became yet another reminder for black men to

> let a spirit of union and friendship prevail among us, and every facility in our power be given to all who are endeavoring to rise to wealth, to knowledge and respectability. Above all, let us endeavor to promote morality and the interests of the gospel of our Lord Jesus Christ. So shall we be the better prepared for whatever may be our future destinies; we shall pay the most suitable tribute of respect to the memory of our departed friend, we shall improve our condition in this life, and attain the felicities of God's kingdom when this scene shall close.[7]

The voluntary associations' attempt to impose a moral discipline on the community did invite criticism. In 1839 Peter Paul Simons charged that the singular focus on moral elevation made the black community timid, allowed white people to intrude into the community's affairs, and even created divisions among black New Yorkers; however, he offered this criticism during a lecture before the New York African Clarkson Association. Founded ten years earlier by William Hamilton and Alexander Elston of the NYASMR, the Clarkson Association was not Simons's target. Standing before his "Brother Clarksons," he attacked the inefficacy of the moral agenda. Simons supported benevolent societies. Their founders deserved "honor" and they had brought "virtue, benevolence, sympathy, brotherly affection, [and] unity" to black New York.[8]

Enforcing a moral code was one of the voluntary societies' most important functions. It was not intended to create a class system but to unfetter what Frances Harper, in a speech to the Brooklyn Literary Union, called "the aristocracy of character."[9] It has been misconstrued as the arrogant stamp of a tiny, elite class, when in reality the African societies' members were quite varied and their charges included the impoverished, fugitives, and orphans. That those who had material and social resources often became leaders is neither shocking nor profound. By definition, the societies were selective and, therefore, catered to an elite; however, the elect were not defined by wealth—or, its usual substitute, education—for fidelity to the community's political goals and obligations was an equally significant determinant of leadership. Fealty to a socially defined ethic decided which men exercised leadership over African societies and which young men came under their stewardship, and most of the people who combined in society were in no way elite. African society initiates saw their associations as instruments for personal uplift that by their very nature were group endeavors and, therefore, public with civic responsibilities.

Critics have therefore targeted the excessive moralism of these associations—their unforgiving Christian zeal—as evidence of their privilege and their coveting white approval. Ann DuCille, writing about a parallel perception of early-twentieth-century blues culture, describes this position as "an internally dysfunctional reading of the racial subject and the semiotics of the black body that categorizes moral value by color and class and defines 'authentic blackness' as the absence thereof. Such evaluations, in effect, make class, culture, and morality linear concepts in which the genuine, honest, authentic black experience is that of a unilaterally permissive rural peasantry or a homogeneously uninhibited urban proletariat."[10] The ritualistic equation of morality and whiteness creates the impression that African Americans lacked an indigenous ethical culture.

Black nationalism presupposed a common moral system. In a study of early-twentieth-century laborers in Texas, Emilio Zamora explains the importance of moral discourse to voluntarism. There, mutual aid societies faced both national and class boundaries but still created the intellectual and social environment for constructing Mexican unity, "consequently, even different and at times opposing groups adhered to the same legitimizing set of fundamentally unifying principles and values." Moralism facilitated this process, Zamora continues. It reflected the members' commitment to "such cultural values as fraternalism, reciprocity, and altruism," and the obsession with moral behavior protected the trust that made mutual endeavors possible.[11]

Voluntary associations were even more dominant among early-nineteenth-century black New Yorkers. African societies helped craft a shared worldview and narrate the common good; and, borrowing on Zamora's argument, there is no reason to suggest that the moralism that characterized their work existed to impress white people or divide black people when it primarily functioned to protect community trust. In fact, moralism was the least coercive means of enforcing the overlapping obligations that sustained social work in the black community. Nationalism assumed a basic moral pact and, through voluntary associations, African evangelicalism provided the language for its elaboration.

Moral stances should not be indiscriminately coded with race or class language. Class is especially impish when employed to analyze subgroup (i.e., intraracial or intraethnic) relations. It describes social relationships that are at once dependent and adversarial. Black Manhattanites had real divisions and disputes, but differences of strategy are not proof of distinct and opposed social positions, and all ideological conflicts do not flow from class antagonism. The connection between class and morality typically depends upon defining elitism as a social behavior, a set of affectations, rather than a social station. Here, class is a purely rhetorical creation. In 1839, when Peter Paul Simons criticized the existence of "classes of distinction" among black New Yorkers, he confessed that these divisions had no material basis. Simons was not attacking a social relationship but a social posture. Moreover, in *Uplifting the Race*, Kevin K. Gaines argues that the elaboration of a class-conscious uplift ideology came after the Civil War and contrasted sharply with antebellum moral discourse, which incorporated "collective social aspiration, advancement, and struggle."[12] Moral reformation was a political goal that dictated no single strategy for its accomplishment. No one class authored or owned the ideology, and scholars who have attempted to use moral discourse to establish the class fracture in antebellum black New York have actually only demonstrated the political diversity of black Gotham.

The nature of the voluntary associations' enterprise created an incentive for moral absolutism. Like the NYAS and the NYASMR, African associations throughout the Diaspora typically emerged in the public realm during the transition from slavery to freedom. People of African descent in Cuba established rather prominent *cabildos de nación*, mutual aid associations organized along African ethnic, kinship, and cultural lines. These societies initiated both the enslaved and the free and were particularly active during the process of gradual emancipation. They mixed spiritual, social, and political goals, and many associations were involved in antislavery from their founding. Muslims in Brazil established a *tontine* or *susu*, a collective fund to purchase members' freedom and to furnish religious apparel. Beginning in the 1850s, the Brazilian Mina used a common fund to free members and to arrange return transport to Africa. Brazil's black and mulatto Christian brotherhoods, besides offering mutual aid, burial assistance, and religious guidance, acted as savings and loan associations for enslaved Africans seeking to purchase their freedom. Keeping the community trust was key to the voluntary societies' campaign against bondage and their claim to that *social medicine* was the source of their influence.[13]

Mutual obligation and mutual dependence expressed through social combination—formal or informal, open or covert, peaceful or rebellious—was a part of Africans' adjustment to America. To that history belongs the June 6, 1808, convocation of black men in the Rose Street Academy, which was equally notable for the fact that it was conducted in a state that was twenty years from the full emancipation of Africans and a city that was a regional center for the selling and smuggling of the unfree. Earlier that year, William Hamilton and William Miller led a handful of black mechanics during several meetings to plan the organizational structure and codes.[14] They detailed a constitution, and they agreed to privacy and secrecy in the organization's affairs.

The June 6 meeting formalized the association, adopted a constitution, and elected officers. Hamilton was president, John Teasman was vice president, Daniel Berry was treasurer, Henry Sipkins was secretary and Adam Carman his assistant, while Daniel Brownhill, Adam Ray, James McEwen, Henry Rouse, Samuel Charley, Richard Tankard, Samuel Clause, Benjamin

Slighter, and Peter Vogelsang served on the first Standing Committee. With a clear sense of the uncertain future of black people in the northern states, they declared:

> We the undersigned subscribers, duly reflecting upon the various vicissitudes of life, to which menkind are continually exposed, and stimulated by the desire of improving our condition, do conclude that the most efficient method of securing ourselves from the extreme exigencies to which we are liable to be reduced is by uniting ourselves in a body, for the purpose of raising a fund for the relief of its members.

Thus, "we have formed ourselves into a society, with the pleasing hope of relieving the occasional distresses of each other by our mutual endeavors." The first act of the constitution stated that they were thereafter to be "distinguished by the name of the 'New York African Society for Mutual Relief'" and that membership was limited to men of "good moral character."[15]

The destruction of Mutual Relief's antebellum records makes it impossible to know if the association helped Africans finance their freedom; however, a significant number of enslaved men were members. John Teasman, Boston Crummell, John Maranda, Christopher Rush, George DeGrasse, and more than a dozen other members of the NYASMR were once bondsmen, a remarkable number given the chronic exclusion of black people, especially the enslaved and the recently manumitted, from the public record. John Anderson, Francis Cook, Thomas Johnson, and James Varick were bound when they signed the constitution. Anderson joined in 1809, but James Aymar owned him until 1813. In 1809 Francis Cook applied, although John Falconer enslaved him until 1817. Cook rose to become the proprietor of a Manhattan restaurant. Thomas Johnson was a founder of Mutual Relief in June 1808 and gained his freedom a month later. Thomas Thompson, William Thomas, and Charles Brown were only recently freed when they joined the African Society. In April 1802 Thomas Thompson was manumitted. He served as a director of the organization a few years after its founding. In November 1803, William Thomas was emancipated. Five years later he helped organize the NYASMR. He also became a successful Manhattan boot maker. In 1813 Charles Brown became free after James Aymar's death. He entered the NYASMR that same year.[16]

On January 10, 1768, James Varick, the innocent mastermind of the independent African church and denomination, was born enslaved outside Newburgh, New York. He was brought to New York City unfree and remained enslaved to Emma Miller. He was trained as a shoemaker. During the Revolution, Captain Thomas Webb and Philip Embury converted Varick to Methodism and he affiliated with the John Street Church. Although still enslaved, Varick was a charter member of the NYASMR and served as its first chaplain. On February 12, 1813, he was emancipated. He was well over forty years old. He served as a lay preacher and exhorter, prepared himself for the ministry, became the pastor of Mother Zion, and, after his fiftieth birthday, he became bishop of the church.[17]

In 1777 Christopher Rush came into the world enslaved in Craven County, North Carolina. In 1793, at the age of sixteen, he ran away. In 1798 he came to New York City. In 1803 Rush joined the Zion Church and began studies for the ministry. In 1815 he was licensed to preach and soon became an active member of the NYASMR. In 1822 Rush became a deacon and elder of Zion, and on May 18, 1828, he succeeded James Varick as general superintendent of the A.M.E. Zion denomination, becoming the nation's first fugitive bishop. (In 1840 William Miller succeeded Rush as bishop.) Rush organized and supported many of the lesser African mutual relief and education associations of New York. It was Rush who, in 1848, oversaw the drafting and approval of the constitution of the Preachers' Mutual Benefit Society of the African Methodist Episcopal Church in America. (As early as September 30, 1774, long before the racial division of the church, a Society for Relief of Widows and Children of Clergymen of the Episcopal Church had been organized in New York. In 1823, white Methodists in New York City established a Ministers' Mutual Assistance Society, which was incorporated in 1832. Each of these was influenced by John Wesley who, in the late 1760s, organized an English Preachers' Fund to support impoverished and elderly clerics.)[18]

On October 29, 1795, John Maranda[19] paid $200 to an intermediary, attorney Samuel Jones Jr., to purchase his liberty from John De Baan. A few months later Maranda freed his four-year-old daughter, Susan, from John Haring of New Jersey for $50. In May 1798 Maranda bought his wife Elizabeth from Dr. Gardner Jones for $150. Dr. Jones threw in Maranda's baby son John for $10 more. Within three years, John Maranda had purchased himself and his entire family out of bondage.[20] Ten years later he joined in founding the New York African Society for Mutual Relief.

Peter Williams Jr. became black Manhattan's leading Episcopal minister and a charter member of its most prominent African society. Peter and Mary Williams, his father and mother, adopted a daughter. On December 7, 1786, Peter Jr. was born. On April 8, 1787, the boy was baptized at John Street. Since his father could neither read nor write, young Peter was introduced to Methodism as a secretary and accountant. Williams converted to the Episcopal denomination, studied under Bishop Hobart, and was ordained in 1820. Williams was later installed as pastor of St. Philip's Church.[21] He joined the NYASMR and followed Varick as its chaplain.

Boston Crummell's freedom journey made him an institution in black Manhattan. Crummell was bold enough to reside as a fugitive from slavery in the same city as his former master. He was born in Sierra Leone, West Africa, and brought to New York City in bondage when he was approximately thirteen years old. Upon reaching adulthood, he informed his owner, Peter Schermerhorn, that he was emancipating himself. Crummell moved to a different section of Manhattan, became quite successful as an oyster dealer, and remained free in spite of Schermerhorn's attempts to reclaim him.[22] Crummell was also a founder of the NYASMR.

A similar pattern appears in the lesser associations. On June 8, 1812, three former bondsmen—Philip Ward, enslaved until 1804; James Jackson, freed in 1806; and James Hammond, liberated in 1809—founded the Wilberforce Philanthropic Society. The NYASMR provided the organizational skill, with the Reverend William Miller serving as vice president of Wilberforce, Thomas Miller Sr. acting as librarian, and Benjamin Smith sitting on the board. On May 13, 1845, Anthony Johnson and William Williams, both previously enslaved, became charter members of the Brooklyn African Tompkins Association. Mutual Relief contributed three charter members to this association.[23]

In short, many of the men of "good moral character" who sat atop the African societies had personally experienced the hardships of bondage. The moralistic language that saturates the constitutions, by-laws, and other publications of the NYASMR and its subsidiaries are not evidence of freeborn, elite rule, but a reflection of the ethical temperament of the people who joined in society. Association leaders came from the ranks of the religious and moral reformers, but they were also militant defenders of their own and their community's freedom. The fact that they found in radical Christianity justification for openly political acts hardly separates them from the larger black community, and their life experiences were not remarkably different from those who shunned Christianization. If they distinguished themselves, it was as divine soldiers joined in a social mission. "Worthy sir[,] when I behold many of the sons of Africa groaning under oppression[,] some laboring with difficulty to get free & others having to bear the yoke[,] I cannot help shed[d]ing a silent tear at the miserable fortune Providence hath brought upon them," wrote William Hamilton to Governor Jay in a letter draped with nationalist and Protestant imagery.[24] Hamilton and his generation used the African Society for Mutual Relief to unleash the antislavery potential of evangelicalism.

People who experienced slavery were the authors of the moralism that characterized African voluntary associations. In a study of antebellum Philadelphia, Theodore Hershberg reveals that "[voluntary] societies found ex-slaves more eager to join their ranks than freeborn blacks." Africans who gained their freedom were not more desperate for security; rather, people who were once enslaved were drawn to the personal and familial benefits of religious socialism and generally fared better than freeborn black Philadelphians. Black people acquired their freedom through industry, persistence, and craftiness, qualities that also guided their lives as free men and women.[25]

Moralism was organic to the culture of African voluntary associations. Influenced directly by the NYASMR, the Brooklyn African Woolman Benevolent Society (1810) limited membership to "free persons of moral character." A candidate for initiation had to apply to a member of the association who, once satisfied with his character, presented him to the larger body. Any member had the right to object to any candidate. The unisex African Marine Fund, founded in 1810 by Zion ministers June Scott and Abraham Thompson and two laymen, was the city's most philanthropic and moralistic association. The members submitted to the will of Mother Zion's clergy, agreed to irregular taxes and collections to meet its demands, and placed social welfare above their individual needs. In March 1834 the Garrison Literary and Benevolent Association was organized for boys and young men of "good moral character between the ages of four and twenty." It prohibited "*intemperance* and profane *swearing*." The Abyssinian Benevolent Daughters of Esther Association, founded on April 19, 1839, admitted women from ages sixteen to fifty who were not "addicted to inebriety," did not "have a plurality of husbands," and were not "guilty of improper conduct." Equally cautious about the character of its membership, the New York Benevolent Branch of Bethel (1843) initiated women from ages eighteen to fifty.[26]

It is as striking that a Manhattan benevolent association comprising foreign-born black men assumed this familiar structure. In November 1839 five Haitian New Yorkers wrote their countryman Pierre Toussaint. The five directors requested Toussaint's aid in establishing a mutual relief association. Toussaint and his wife Juliet Gaston were major benefactors to Catholic and African institutions in New York City. Calling their society Frères Réunis (Reunited Brothers), the founders hoped to relieve the hardships of a Haitian-born community already unable to respond to all of its adversities or meet all of its needs. To address this moral obligation, the founders turned to a traditional benevolent society with an active social outreach program. Toussaint funded Frères Réunis.[27]

Temperance offers equally compelling examples, for Africans had to some extent initiated a movement that is now primarily identified with white reformers. From 1800 to 1860, Africans established fifty temperance organizations in New York City. The Reverend Benjamin Croger of the Brooklyn African Woolman Society was president of the Brooklyn Temperance Association. Croger was typical of the religious folk whose political activity occurred through independent organizations. When Willis Augustus Hodges—who later published *The Ram's Horn* under the editorship of Thomas Van Rensselaer and Frederick Douglass—moved from Virginia to Williamsburg, Long Island, he joined the local African church and an antislavery society. Then, on October 2, 1841, he and several other black men organized the Williamsburg Union Temperance Benevolent Society, with Hodges as president.[28]

In 1847 the Independent Order of Good Samaritans and Daughters of Samaria, a biracial secret and benevolent society with segregated lodges, was established to spread the gospel of temperance. Black people were present at the founding of the Samaritans. At the first meeting, white delegates were surprised to find that black Samaritan lodges had already been organized, including two in New York, with three others being organized there, one operating in Brooklyn, and three Daughters of Samaria lodges in Manhattan. The black lodges' right to vote at Grand Lodge meetings was limited to matters concerning them; however, they received complete self-governance while promising only ceremonial and ritual uniformity. Of the black and white branches, the historian of the Samaritans writes, "they were simply two friendly bodies, having the same purpose in view, and maintaining correspondence for mutual benefit."[29]

Far from reflecting accommodation or subservience, moralism facilitated the spread of social work in the black community. It helped to fuse religious passion to African nationalism, two ideological currents that countered white New Yorkers' insistence that liberty was a function of biology by isolating the struggle as moral and civil. The institutional growth of black New York required the elaboration of an African-Christian ethical culture. The Zion Church, the NYAS, and the NYASMR recast

Africans' plight in America as part of the history of Christianity's evolution and prepared the community for the institutional revolution that brought the spread of voluntarism.

Nationalism cast Africans as a people, black evangelicalism provided a rhetoric for describing their mutual obligations, and voluntary societies offered a mechanism for policing those relationships and responsibilities. Speaking before the NYASMR, Peter Vogelsang asked, "When reflecting on the numberless incapacities to which we are subject, we naturally inquire, why should such unreasonable prejudice exist? Are we not of congenerous species with white men? Have we not hands and feet, formed for the same ends—governed by the same providence—and exist by the same sustenance as white men? Then why this distinction? Is it because we are of a different complexion?" African societies became the conduit through which the enslaved could express their natural right to liberty and white people could be forced to confront the horror and inhumanity of bondage. "Some [white people], by a kind of magical sophistry, would have us to believe that the Africans were created to be the slaves of Europeans and their descendants . . . as if it were possible to persuade us that the God of mercies 'can be a tyrant like themselves,'" chided Vogelsang.[30]

A resurrection of humankind's moral nature promised to return freedom to Africans and make everyone, even white people, eligible for deliverance. The end of the slave trade in the British dominions, the Haitian Revolution, the gradual emancipation law in New York State, and the pending abolition of the trade in the United States were evidence of an irresistible moral progress. Thus, in December 1807 Peter Williams, as chair of the Committee of Arrangements for the African celebration of the close of the slave trade, appeared before the New York Common Council to request "that they may be allowed to employ a sufficient number of peace officers to prevent any tumult that might otherwise happen on the occasion." The officers were assigned and two weeks later the Africans sent their thanks along with "tickets of admission to the Oration which is to be delivered by an African descendant at the African Church in Church Street corner of Leonard Street."[31]

The following month Peter Williams Jr. addressed the celebrants and historicized the moment through an extended metaphor between the Judeo-Christian fall from grace and African servitude. The Reverends Abraham Thompson and June Scott offered the opening and closing prayers. Young Henry Sipkins, the oldest son of Zion and Asbury founder Thomas Sipkins, gave the speaker a fiery introduction: the death of the slave trade proved "that justice has not yet forsaken her dominion in this sublunary scene; but that she still pleads with a tone of dignity, and in the spirit of truth, for the violated rights of humanity." Williams then took the stage and claimed the moment for black men: "We have felt, sensibly felt, the sad effects of this abominable traffic. It has made, if not ourselves, our forefathers and kinsmen its unhappy victims; and pronounced on them, and their posterity, the sentence of perpetual slavery." He offered a comparison between the fall of Eden and that of Africa, with which his audience was quite familiar, to charge the slave trade with destroying the tranquillity of African people, feeding the despotism of the Americas, and guaranteeing an economic system that left the people in his audience unbound but unfree. "Its baneful footsteps are marked with blood," he continued, "its infectious breath spresds [*sic*] war and desolation; and its train is composed of the complicated miseries, of the cruel and unceasing bondage."[32]

Williams continued the analogy with the Book of Genesis to denounce slavery. A tension traveled through his speech as he carefully balanced seemingly approving remarks about "European genius" at expansion and the spread of "civilized society" into the New World with their horrific results. On the scales of morality, the "innocent and amiable" people of Africa were easily the balance of the Europeans with their "diversified luxuries and amusements." It was, Williams argued, the temptation of material things that motivated Europe to upset the peace of Africa, to riot upon "the fair fields of our ancestors," and to drag an "indescribable misery" across the world:

> After Columbus unfolded to civilized man, the vast treasurers of this western world, the desire of gain, which had chiefly induced the first colonists of America, to cross the waters of the Atlantic, surpassing the bounds of reasonable acquisition, violated the sacred injunctions of the gospel.

Europe was the catalyst of Africa's fall from grace.[33]

In words that rang with the influence of John Wesley, Williams listed Africa with the ancient kingdoms of Greece and Rome before charging that it was invaded by the "seducer." Africans were the primary victims of Europe's work, for after the "aborigine" of the Americas had been destroyed through wars and purges, Europe turned to Africa as the source of its labor. Just as the serpent brought on the fall of Eden, Europe abused the "friendly countenance" of Africa's people to introduce greed and competition. Kings moved against their people and brother fell upon brother. "The prince who once delighted in the happiness of his people; who felt himself bound by a sacred contract to defend their persons and property; was turned into their tyrant and scourge," he lamented. There was a final and valiant struggle to save paradise from encroachment, "but, alas! overpowered by a superior foe; their force is broken; their ablest warriors fall; and the wretched remnant are taken captive." Africa was lost.

> Oh, Africa, Africa! to what horrid inhumanities have thy shores been witness; thy shores, which were once the garden of the world, the seat of almost paradisiacal joys, have been transformed into regions of wo[e]: thy sons, who were once the happiest of mortals, are reduced to slavery, and bound in weighty shackles, now fill the trader's ship.[34]

Africans suffered an unnatural separation from their motherland, the degradation of chattel slavery, and the insult of civil inequality—the price of humankind's fall from grace. Williams asked his audience to travel back to the moment when their forefathers were traded, "behold their dejected countenances; their streaming eyes; their fettered limbs: hear them, with piercing cries, and pitiful moans, deploring their wretched fate." Appreciate the horrors of the slave trade, then appreciate its demise, he instructed. "Oh, God! we thank the[e], that thou didst condescend to listen to the cries of Africa's wretched sons."[35]

Then Williams reminded the audience of the remaining struggle to destroy slavery, a statement that announced the African-Christian style, which made political activism a requirement of faith. He thanked the white people (particularly the Quakers and the manumission societies) who had the moral courage to oppose the trade. "Taught by preceding occu[r]rences, that the waves of oppression are ever ready to overwhelm the defenceless [sic], they became the vigilant guardians of all our reinstated joys," he said of white antislavery advocates. Williams then implored black men to sustain "a steady and upright deportment, by a strict obedience and respect to the laws of the land, form an invulnerable bulwark against the shafts of malice." By their labors, black men would determine the fate of their people, "when the sun of liberty shall beam resplendent on the whole African race."[36]

During the 1809 anniversary of the end of the slave trade, the NYASMR's Henry Sipkins took the podium at Mother Zion. Mutual Relief's Henry Johnson introduced the speaker by appealing to the audience of black men with the popular salute, "Africans and descendants of Africans," and by praying that "the whole world be a world of liberty." Sipkins picked up on the themes that Williams had expounded a year earlier. Wesley's influence came forth as he contrasted the barbarity of the procession of European nations engaged in the slave trade with the Edenlike innocence that once governed Africa.

> The harmless Africans, who had ever been strangers to the arts of deception, and unsuspicious of treachery in the bosoms of others, gratefully received the proffers of friendship from their cruel invaders, and consequently became an easy prey to European wiles.

Europeans incited the evils that destroyed the African people and carried the brutalities of European expansion into the Americas.[37]

Sipkins then fixed on the history of enslavement to reinforce the necessity of their mutual endeavor. Telling his audience of the savagery that awaited Africans on a slave ship, he reminded them that "once brought into port a new and unbounded field of oppression presents itself to their view." They are sold, and that act not only seals their fate but finally and forever separates them from their past and dissolves all friendship and familial bonds. They are rushed to the lands of a foreign man and thereafter "the plantation bell summonses [*sic*] them to the incessant fatigues of the day," and the scorching sun, whips, and deprivation decide their remaining days on earth. "In this state of hopeless servitude, do many yet remain, who look forward with pleasing expectation to the termination of their lives, as the only possible means of emancipating them from servile despotism," charged Sipkins.[38]

The men who held Africans in bondage were the rulers of a system that insulted and debased mankind. Sipkins contrasted them to the white men who opposed slavery and the slave trade. Focusing on the Quakers, he proclaimed:

> Oh, our most worthy advocates! . . . When we were under the iron hand of oppression, you did generously step forward to ease our burthen. . . . When sinking under the weighty shackles of slavery to the most consum[m]ate despondency, with unremitting zeal you flew to our relief.

To Sipkins and the free black men in his audience, the Quakers confirmed that moral justice could overwhelm profit and prejudice and penetrate the hearts of the nation's white majority, quickening the end of African bondage. Or, as Sipkins said, "They disdained the stimulous [*sic*] of pecuniary gains, and felt themselves amply compensated by the smiles of an approving conscience."[39]

It is not peculiar that these black Christians were the most consistent flatterers of those white people who espoused antislavery. Celebrating even modest antislavery efforts among white people was a feature of African politics that grew out of necessity, not awe. In his 1815 speech to the NYASMR, Secretary Peter Vogelsang admitted that white antislavery was a tool in the construction of a distinctly African response to bondage: "Our prospects in life would be gloomy indeed, did we not *persuade ourselves* that a majority of the white citizens of this country are opposed to the policy of degrading our colour."[40]

The names of the African institutions are instructive of this point. Black Manhattanites often attached the names of esteemed figures to their associations and churches in order to advertise the irresistibility of antislavery. The African Asbury Church had been named for Methodist Episcopal bishop Francis Asbury, a supporter of Manhattan's black churches and an antislavery minister. The Brooklyn African Woolman Benevolent Association honored John Woolman, the eighteenth-century Quaker who fought to abolish slaveholding among the Friends. The Wilberforce Philanthropic Association saluted William Wilberforce, who for decades authored and advocated laws in the British Parliament to end the slave trade, to emancipate Africans in the Canadian colonies, and to provide land for free black settlement. The New York African Clarkson Association recognized British abolitionist and pamphleteer the Reverend Thomas Clarkson, who wrote lengthy treatises against human bondage and the slave trade and traveled to Paris, on behalf of England's Quakers, to lobby against the traffic in people. (The tribute may have come indirectly from an earlier Clarkson Association, organized in 1811 by white Quaker women. It founded the city's first public school when it began holding classes for black women.) The Garrison Literary and Benevolent Association applauded the antislavery and anticolonization work of William Lloyd Garrison, editor of *The Liberator.* Daniel D. Tompkins, governor of New York when the NYASMR was chartered, pushed the legislature to accept the July 4, 1827, date for the completion of the state's gradual emancipation process and thereby became the honoree of the Brooklyn African Tompkins Association. Tompkins also served as a New York State Supreme Court justice and as vice president of the United States under James Monroe. Tompkins, like New York City mayor DeWitt Clinton, was a grand master of white Freemasonry in New York State, which might well have attracted the support of the black Freemasons who were active in Manhattan.[41]

Further evidence that these gestures were strategic appears in the fact that Africans simultaneously spoke of their serious doubts about the potential of white antislavery. For instance, they knew that Quaker antislavery intended to protect the Friends themselves. In 1837 the Reverend Theodore S. Wright of Manhattan's Shiloh Presbyterian Church explained that race prejudice limited the Quakers' attack on bondage to a concern for their own salvation. Africans applauded individual American Quakers who entered the public struggle against bondage, but when they saluted the Friends as a group they were typically referring to those British and American Quakers who formed the white antislavery vanguard. Therefore, Sipkins reminded his "beloved Africans" to walk carefully, for their actions would bring on the moment

> when slavery of every species shall be destroyed—when despotism and oppression shall forever cease—when the Africans shall be reinstated in their former joys—when the exulting shouts of Princes, embracing their long lost oppressed subjects, shall reverberate on our ears—when the bursting acclamations of approbation shall resound from the tombs of our worthy departed ancestors; and all find protection under the fostering wing of LIBERTY.[42]

Ultimately, that responsibility had to be theirs, for being free, black, and men their accomplishments would demonstrate that the subjection of Africans was immoral and unnatural.

As Sipkins and Johnson were addressing the black community at Zion, the other members of the NYASMR were holding a separate celebration of the end of the trade at the Universalist Church. Peter Williams Jr., who later served as vice president, wrote two hymns that were sung that day, each of which exposed black Manhattan's move to target slavery itself for destruction. The first hymn contained the familiar blend of religious and secular philosophy and concluded that *"All men are free* by right of Nature's laws." The second saluted "MUTUAL RELIEF" as a strategy for their improvement.[43]

President William Hamilton was the featured speaker, and he continued the metaphor of Satan in Paradise to underscore Europe's destruction of Africa. He began by attacking the slave trade and its impact on Africans. Having already called those Europeans who invaded Africa "foul fiends," Hamilton admitted that he was "confounded" that "there should be found any of the human family so lost to their nature and the fine feelings of man, as to commit, unprovokedly commit, such acts of cruelty on an unoffending part of the human family."[44]

He examined the prejudice and discrimination that fell upon free black men, particularly the charge of inferiority. Black men were constantly accused of having neither matched the achievements of white men nor of slaves in antiquity. Hamilton carefully laid out the differences between ancient and modern slavery to show the fallacy of the latter claim. To the former, he responded that servitude fettered African genius. Bondage meant that free black men could possess no "station above the common employment of craftsmen and labourers . . . did we possess both learning and abilities." The greatest evidence of free black men's capacity was their consistent performance within a social system that did not reward their talents. Turning the equation around, Hamilton asked why those who claimed superiority did not pull farther ahead although they are favored, and why "we do not fall far behind those who boast of superior judgment." Secretary Vogelsang put it more bluntly: "Let the European boast of his superior genius in the invention of the *mouth-piece*, the *crook*, the *stock*, the *pudden*, and a thousand other cruelties to which African slaves are subject."[45]

At only a year old, the New York African Society for Mutual Relief operated as a separate community of men and claimed a membership that "exceed[s] by three times the number of any civil institution yet attempted among us." Hamilton advised them that "many and repeated attempts have been made in this city, to establish societies of various kinds among the people of colour" but most had failed. Theirs was not a social organization; it had education, sick aid, widow relief, and the care of orphans as its goals, all under a formal and orderly structure. Each of them shared the task of building a society that would endure to receive "thousands of yet unborn members." Facing the governing bodies, he restated their responsibilities:

> To you, my Brethren, the Standing Committee, let me address myself. Your's [sic] is truly an exalted station in which there is much confidence and trust reposed; with you rests the credit of this society, her fame shall spread through your vigilance, it is for you to immortalize her name by your active attention to the duties imposed on you; be then attentive to the sick members, and the widows and orphans of deceased members. —If there should be found any one among you who should refuse this duty, let him be set aside as an unfit character, to have such high trust reposed in

him; but surely, my Brethren, there is [. . .] not one of you who would be so forgetful of his honor and the solemn pledge he has given of the strict performance of the duties assigned him.

The other Officers are no less bounden and no less responsible, and in them is reposed equal trust, and from them is expected an equal attention to their duty. Let us all be united, my Brethren, in rearing this edifice—steady to our several departments—and soon shall be raised a wide spreading dome that shall stand the admiration and praise of succeeding generations, and on its front shall be eternally engraven

MUTUAL INTEREST,

MUTUAL BENEFIT,

AND MUTUAL RELIEF.[46]

Hamilton laid out the ideological components of black New Yorkers' politics: the quest for physical and political freedom expressed through the language of moral reform.

By positioning Africa as Eden and Europe as the seducer, black men braided the history of ethical Christianity into the histories of African peoples. In fact, they positioned themselves as the moral agents of their society. The pursuit of earthly justice advanced the cause of Christianity, so that an aggressive attack on slavery did not require a rejection of the Bible-centered message of redemption that Jupiter Hammon had offered decades earlier. The change reflected no loss of faith in salvation but the anticipation of social revolutions in the lives of its pilgrims. Biblical fundamentalism remained in the language and thoughts of black New Yorkers. In the printed version of an 1809 Mutual Relief speech, the following poem was added:

> I long to lay this painful head,
> And aching heart, beneath the soil;
> To slumber in that dreamless bed,
> From all my toil.
>
> For misery stole me at my birth,
> And cast me naked on the wild,
> I perish, O my mother earth;
> Take home thy child.

Black men presented themselves as God's soldiers, and thereby made the abolition of slavery compatible with Christian redemption. As Peter Vogelsang prayed at the 1815 anniversary of the NYASMR: "O God! with pity look down upon our condition. How long, O dread majesty, shall we, a part of thy noblest work, remain a prey to oppression? How long shall prejudice continue us a way-mark for the finger of derision to point at? Shall thy immutable providence continue us hewers of wood and drawers of water?" Still blending radical religion with natural rights philosophy, Vogelsang concluded: "Hasten the time, O God! when slavery shall no more exist in these states; when every man in this republic, whether European, Indian, or African, shall be eligible to citizenship, and enjoy the immunities of liberty and the rights of man."[47]

Men and women in African associations preached and enforced moral conduct because they were not elite, because their life experiences had revealed the logic of that path, and because they had targeted their collective political will against slavery. The traditional logic casts them as obsequious supplicants before the white community and overbearing bullies in the black community. It achieves this rather intricate balance by making morality and aspiration white attributes. Black New Yorkers used voluntary associations to unleash evangelicalism's political mischief. "No man will question the importance of societies: whether we view them in a humane, social, or politic[al] light, their benefits are equally conspicuous—their necessities are founded in our very natures: no animal in creation requires so much care as man in his infancy, as if the economy of nature in this particular, was intended to teach man the social virtue. No man can say he has no need of his fellow man!" said Vogelsang.[48]

Black Christians did claim to hold "the keys of the kingdom," but the keys were minted from the metal of their own experiences in the fire of their own beliefs.

PART II

African Voluntary Associations and the Making of the Public Sphere

5

"The Inmates of My Sanctum Sanctorum"

African Voluntary Associations and the Public Sphere, 1808–1845

Nothing can afford to a philanthropic mind a more grateful and ex-
hilarating view than that of a race of men emerging from the numerous obstacles and oppressions which surround them, to a state
of competence and ease, and even to a participation in the most enlightened and rational enjoyments of civilized life—such a view is
afforded by the African Benevolent Societies of New York and
Brooklyn.   —Jacob Titus, 1818, quoted in *Afro-Americans in
New York Life and History*, July 1986

In September 1825, Epiphany Davis and Andrew Williams purchased land in a sparsely populated area of Manhattan, which became a part
of Central Park, from John and Elizabeth Whitehead. Davis—a feed dealer,
a trustee of Mother Zion Church, and a member of the New York African
Society for Mutual Relief—acquired twelve lots for $578. Williams—a boot-
black and a Mutual Relief member—paid $125 for three. The Whiteheads
sold Mother Zion six lots that same week. Over the next three years, three of
Zion's officers bought land there. "Mother A.M.E. Zion Church had a cemetery in the neighborhood of 86th Street and what is Central Park West," recalled Harry Williamson, the grandson of Albro Lyons, another NYASMR
member who lived in the area, "but whether or not any portion of the cemetery was included in the park is unknown to me." By 1832 the Whiteheads
had sold portions of their land to more than two dozen black families. The
settlement was Seneca Village, but white New Yorkers derisively called it
"Nigger Village" and they also ridiculed its poverty and rural style. Still, the

black households in the district were far more stable than their white counterparts. In 1855 half of all the black families in Seneca Village owned land, a rate 500 percent that for the city. Seneca's men met New York State's property qualification on Negro voters more often than black men in other sections of Manhattan. This might help to explain why Timothy Seaman and Charles Ray, both of the NYASMR, bought one and three lots, respectively, in Seneca but lived elsewhere. "The colored population of New-York is virtuous, orderly, and intelligent, when compared with the class of naturalized foreigners, who are, almost uniformly, disorderly, ignorant, and ready for riot," is how one editorial blasted the property qualification. Several African-society families, including the Garnets, Lyons, Millers, Seamans, Burchells, and Browns, acquired land in Seneca. The area also attracted institutions. Besides Zion, the African Union Church, All Angel's Church, and Colored School No. 3 found their way to the hamlet. In 1855 the municipality began consolidating the land that became Central Park. It paid Andrew Williams almost nineteen times his initial investment for his lots and home, probably less than their worth but still a handsome profit. Bishop Christopher Rush argued on behalf of the estate of his Mutual Relief brother Epiphany Davis in an unsuccessful attempt to improve his compensation. The building of the park destroyed a thriving African neighborhood and eliminated historic institutions such as the colored school and the Zion and Union churches.[1]

Weeksville, a settlement of free people of color in Brooklyn, had a similar origin and a better fate. In 1832 William Thomas of the NYASMR purchased thirty acres of land on the outskirts of Brooklyn's Bedford section. In 1835 Henry C. Thompson, president of the Brooklyn African Woolman Society, bought a neighboring parcel of land. He then transferred a portion of his holding to James Weeks, who divided it into plots and named the area. Weeksville became the largest free black settlement in Kings County. In 1847 Concord Baptist Church and Bethel Tabernacle (A.M.E.) were organized there. In 1849 the Reverend James Gloucester, an absentee landowner in Manhattan's Seneca Village, founded Siloam Presbyterian Church in Weeksville. That year the neighborhood housed about one hundred black families. White Brooklynites sarcastically labeled the enclave "Crow Hill"[2]; nonetheless, Weeksville provided Kings County's men and women of color with a district in which they could become landowners and build separate institutions. Weeksville survived into the twentieth century and was absorbed into the rapidly expanding districts of Bedford-Stuyvesant and Crown Heights.

It is not necessary to believe that African associations constructed neighborhoods to understand the role that some society members played in forming villages. African societies were a hybrid of religious benevolence and African American nationalism. Encouraged by the social focus of black Christianity, these societies steeped their initiates in a collective spiritual and political culture that tied every aspect of life to the destruction of slavery. Families never had to decide to build a village, they only had to act in such a way as to bring on the moment of moral reformation. The dominance of African society initiates in so many aspects of community life was likely an effect of the dominance of voluntary associations over the black public sphere: a social and intellectual space in which the ruling proslavery and racist politic was critiqued and the needs of the black community debated and addressed. In Philadelphia, Richard Allen and Absalom Jones of the Free African Society studied the pattern of black settlement in the city before choosing the site of the city's first black church. Churches, schools, and associations soon transformed the Cedar Ward district into black Philadelphia's institutional hub; and, according to Gary Nash, "black institutions became the envy of whites in racially mixed neighborhoods."[3]

The black communities of New York and Brooklyn wrapped themselves in a web of associations that together imposed principles—drawn largely from African evangelicalism—that they hoped to make universal. In moments of crisis, the major independent men's and women's societies engaged in secret and, at times, extralegal activities; otherwise, their functions were varied but ordinary. As in many precapitalist societies, antebellum black associations created a parallel and alternative social world based on, what Emilio Zamora terms, the "ethic of mutuality": a set of commonly held values, elaborated through voluntary associations, that laid the foundations for nationalist politics.[4]

Black New Yorkers displayed that ethic during the June 1808 meeting at which the artisans who originally planned the NYASMR decided to shun the trade-specific basis for admission. "There were signs of a tiny but healthy black artisan community in Jeffersonian New York," writes Sean Wilentz, "among the founding members of the New York African Society for Mutual Relief were six bootmakers; the society's first president was a house carpenter and its secretary a mechanic." Shane White calculates that, in 1800, 37.8 percent of the black men heads-of-household in Manhattan were artisans and a minority were in unskilled labor. (White warns that the sources underreport unskilled and service workers.) The black mechanics accepted open admission although they needed the protection of a labor association. Among the black craftsmen who opted for greater inclusion were carpenters William Hamilton, Mutual Relief's first president, and James Latham, a founder and officer. Both soon had their livelihoods threatened. In 1816 the white residents of Stone Street, concerned about property values, unsuccessfully attempted to have the "two coloured men, of sober, industrious habits" evicted from their carpentry shop. A sympathetic jury spared them.[5]

Black craftsmen did not avoid the individualistic, occupational basis of white working-class associations because of the rising exclusion of men of color from the skilled trades—such discrimination was an incentive to organize as laborers—rather, the founders of the African Society for Mutual Relief expressly rejected that model for political reasons. As Peter Vogelsang remembered the moment: "In the early part of the year 1808, a few mechanics of the people of colour in this city, taking into consideration the importance of providing for a sick day, and of devising means to administer assistance to those of their friends, whom the vicissitudes of time or the freaks of fortune might reduce to want, held several consultations for that purpose." As originally designed, the association initiated only craftsmen in order to avoid the fate of a benevolent association (probably the New York African Society) that was in financial ruin because it offered assistance to all distressed people of color whether or not they were members. "But after more mature deliberations, the gentlemen concluded, that to open the door for the admission of all moral characters of colour, would be to lay a good foundation for the improvement of morals among us," the secretary said.[6]

Mutual Relief became the most successful of Manhattan's African benevolent associations. Ninety-seven free black men, nearly a quarter of all the men who became members in its history, joined the NYASMR in its first year. While promising to meet monthly, pay dues, and assist members, their widows, and children when in need, these men made the society more than a self-help organization. The charisma and reputation of William Hamilton, John Teasman, and Peter Williams Jr. drew in many black men, while the possibility of raising the African community to a new level of cooperation attracted others.

As one dominant association fell, another rose at the center of black public life. The NYASMR carefully assumed that social role. In January 1809, the members appealed for incorporation to the legislature. "To strengthen our compact, to consolidate our interest, and to raise us to the dignity of a body politic," explained Secretary Peter Vogelsang. Incorporation was also an important symbolic victory, providing legal evidence of their humanity and citizenship. They put together all the necessary paper work and twice had New York City mayor DeWitt Clinton carry their petition to Albany. Clinton "employed his eloquence, till both houses went into a decision in your favor," Teasman reported to the members. On March 23, 1810, an act of the legislature incorporated the New York African Society for Mutual Relief.[7]

Three weeks later, when the stage brought the news, the members determined that it was worth celebrating. At the annual celebration of the NYASMR, the members and their guests sang James Latham's incorporation song. They also decided to parade, a popular form of entertainment and political action, but feared that a mob might form against them. A few white men expressed concern that "the authorities would be entirely powerless to protect you on the streets, and you would be torn in pieces by howling mobs." The founders responded, "We will go though death stare us in the face." More than a hundred black men from the New York African Society for Mutual Relief, carrying painted silk banners from their first anniversary, hoisting a sign "inscribed with the figure of a black man, and the words 'AM I NOT A MAN AND A BROTHER'"—the symbol and motto of the British Committee for the Abolition of the Slave Trade—accompanied by musicians and members of the black community, paraded through the main streets of Manhattan. The ode was sung, the charter read, and an oration delivered. "Secure in their manhood and will, they did parade, in large number, on the appointed day, easily thrusting aside by their own force the small impediments which blocked their way," wrote a later member.[8]

"Erected upon the firm basis of mutual good, this society in a short time attained a prosperity to which, no preceding institution of the kind, among us, had ever risen," said Vogelsang. The dues and initiation fee under the original constitution are unknown, but by the Civil War initiation cost fifty dollars and monthly dues were twenty-five cents. The original payment structure—probably an initiation fee of five or ten dollars that could be pro-rated and a quarter for monthly dues—created an impressive financial base. In 1815 the NYASMR had five hundred dollars in bank stock, "a respectable sum in cash," and a small hall. On August 18, 1820, the African Society purchased an $1,800 tenement on Orange (Baxter) Street in Manhattan in the Five Points area. The investment was made after considerable deliberation. The members believed that the area was about to be redeveloped through the expansion of the commercial district. The anticipated improvements did not occur, but the rapid growth of Manhattan's population inflated the property's value while rentals paid for its cost. In the rear of the apartment house the society erected a building, commonly called "African Society Hall" or "Society Hall," where it held its meetings and hosted the gatherings of other associations.[9]

With the increase of Manhattan's population, Five Points became the central locale of the European immigrant poor and the society one of many slumlords, while the black population moved north where open land could still be found. The Orange Street property met all of the African Society's hopes: it provided a steady stream of income to pay for sick and death benefits, it was physical evidence of the thrift of black Manhattanites, it was the gathering place of the black community, and a trap door in the floor of African Society Hall allowed them to secretly fulfill their role as a station on the Underground Railroad.

Black Gothamites' establishment of community organizations with multiple private and public functions set them apart from their white neighbors. The African societies' closest analogue in the white community arose in the "Burned-over District," the vast upstate territory west of the Hudson that was repeatedly swept by the religious fire of revivalism. The New York Manumission Society and the Quaker organizations never constituted a broad reform movement; rather, white religious radicalism came later and had a limited social agenda. By the 1830s, Burned-over radicalism brought a "benevolent empire," a web of societies, the "Great Eight," advocating such reforms as temperance, missions, Bible propagation, Sunday schools, Sabbath observance, and antislavery. However, according to Gilbert Hobbs Barnes, "British precedent was the highest authority" for New York's white evangelists. New York State's white Christian reformers imitated and deferred to English religious culture; and, if Bernard Semmel is correct, Britain's Methodist leadership used missions and societies to check the revolutionary potential of religious fanaticism by diverting its energies into movements for limited national reforms and foreign evangelizing.[10]

White associations also suffered a narrow definition of social work. Seeking to invite the Holy Spirit to save the degenerate, white "ultraism" counted individual souls in determining the success of religion. Burned-over thought stressed personal readiness for salvation. "The major weakness of the religious radicals was their exaggerated concern for the individual soul," argues Whitney R. Cross. By the 1830s revivals were bringing "masses of individuals" into the church and leading to thoughts about the coming of the millennium, but they did little to push white New Yorkers toward secular social change. This shortcoming was not limited to the new evangelical movements. When enough Christian families or persons find themselves gathered in a neighborhood, wrote the Puritan divine Cotton Mather in *Bonifacius* (1710), it is useful for them to form religious societies. These spiritual associations existed to practice and perfect Christianity, to protect young men from temptation and sin, and to suppress disorders. He confined "reform societies" to uprooting local vices that threatened salvation. Although Mather instructed Christians that "Excellent Zeal should be carried into our *Neighborhoods,*" his understanding of intervention did not go beyond the basic charities—the relief of widows, orphans, and paupers—and evangelizing.[11]

White evangelists were consumed with personal salvation and stumbled when translating beliefs into collective struggle. "The ultraists had highly individualized personal inspiration and convictions which poorly matched their zeal for concerted action," Cross remarks on the contradiction. They were largely "one-idea men" who were drawn to a sequence of social movements that offered "the single panacea for the ills of their age." Antislavery had a short lived appeal in the Burned-over District. It overthrew temperance as the thrust of social reform but died out as soon as the area had recorded its opposition to human bondage. At that point, with their souls saved, there was little more to be achieved. With the noticeable exception of the Wesleyan Methodists of the early 1840s, even strident abolitionists were unwilling to refuse fellowship with slaveholders and divide white churches. They remained antislavery but also conceded the political limitations of the movement. White Christians were creatures of an individualism that allowed one to be freed from responsibility for social sins by personal decree. As Barnes describes the problem: "Denunciation of the evil came first; reform of the evil was incidental to that primary obligation."[12]

In the 1830s, Burned-over radicalism invaded Gotham through the Chatham Street Chapel and the Broadway Tabernacle. Prominent Manhattan activists were among the rulers of the state's "benevolent empire." Arthur and Lewis Tappan invested their money and used their influence to bring Charles Finney, the foremost upstate revivalist, to Manhattan. Already publishing the *New York Evangelist,* a radical Finneyite tract, wealthy white Manhattanites were behind several attempts to train and attract clergy for the metropolis and bring a democratic and enthusiastic

Christianity to the city.[13] However, white benevolence in New York remained individualistic and single-issue oriented.

Irish benevolent associations offer another counterexample to African societies, for New York's beleaguered Irish community formed a number of voluntary associations. The Friendly Sons of St. Patrick (1784) was organized in Manhattan, as was the later Hibernian Universal Benevolent Society. New York also hosted societies that united Irish Catholics and Protestants, including the Association of the Friends of Ireland and the Shamrock Friendly Association. Brooklyn housed several Irish organizations. The Emerald Benevolent Association (1839) raised funds to support the local Roman Catholic Orphan Asylum. The Shamrock Benevolent Society (1841), the St. Patrick's Society, and the Emmet Benevolent Society (1847) offered members sick aid and a burial fund. In 1855 the Erin Fraternal Beneficial Association was constituted with the purpose of "lending mutual support to each other, as sojourners in a strange land."[14]

The prevalence of secret societies in Ireland has created speculation about their impact on United States urban politics. By 1815 the Orangemen gained a following among New York craftsmen. That anti-Catholic tradition, organized through a secret society, brought rioting in July 1824 when Irish Protestants in Manhattan attempted to celebrate the anniversary of William of Orange's conquest. In a collection of essays on Ireland's secret societies, T. Desmond Williams documents the presence of "organised groups which have pursued political, ideological or economic objectives by secret means and very often through violent action." The cabal was established through oaths that tied the agents to a political cause, not through contrived secrets and rituals. These societies repeatedly found themselves at odds with those associations that sought to sustain the status quo, and they were forced to secrecy as they were criminalized. Williams argues that the revolutionary potential of Irish societies led to a prohibition against policemen having such attachments.[15] Nonetheless, there is little evidence that New York's Irish benevolent associations engaged in subversive acts.

While Irish labor organizations eventually did call upon these traditions, local Irish benevolent societies did not, nor did they match the breadth of the African associations' social work. The Irish gangs that patrolled working-class districts provided the extralegal muscle to defend the interests of their communities. Irish benevolent societies were more akin to white Protestant voluntary associations.[16] For all their poverty and persecution, Irish New Yorkers differed from African Americans in the significant fact of their continued enjoyment of a legitimate political voice, while the legal vulnerability and political isolation of free black communities invited their societies to take on multiple, even secret, functions.

White working-class societies in New York City included trade organizations, benevolent associations, political assemblies, and fraternal orders. They were binary, combining a defined demographic with a single dominant purpose. Among the major ethnic associations were the Scotch St. Andrew's Society (1756), the German Society (1784), and the Anglo St. George's Society (1786). There were also general benevolent organizations like the Provident Society (1791), the Benevolent Society (ca. 1790), and the St. Stephen's Society (1793). The more significant white organizations protected craftsmen during the transformation from artisan to capitalist culture, which included organizing resistance to the erosion of the independent crafts. The General Society of Mechanics and Tradesmen (1785) united artisans of every rank. It evolved into a workers' fraternity that supported a school for the children of poor members and even made occasional forays into politics. Mutual aid and benevolent societies also served the individual interests of middling craftsmen; for instance, in 1794, printers established the Franklin Typographical Society, the city's first, permanent, philanthropic labor association. Unconventional clubs and groups of young working men blended liquor and leisure for sport, self-defense, or to menace the city. However, white workingmen's organizations primarily protected trades and wages; they reflected the decline of artisan life and the encroachment of bourgeois culture more than they established a white parallel to black associations.[17]

Black societies were conspicuously unlike white voluntary organizations. If the possibility of salvation generated among white Protestants an individualism that sought to display faith through personal perfection, then among black evangelists the method became social: the spiritual regeneration of the community in order to destroy bondage and bring on earthly and then heavenly redemption. African Christians imposed a collective style on their institutions and used evangelicalism's social culture to channel the community's energies toward political action.

Moreover, secrecy and opposition continued to characterize black organizations. The enslavement of Africans and the denial of the civil liberties of free black people forced African associations toward disloyalty. Moral reformation must be viewed as the ultimate objective of a broad-based social movement in order to understand the African societies' expanding and contracting functions. It is worth looking past the romanticism of society rhetoric, the seeming egalitarianism, the Christian metaphors, and the offer of racial reconciliation, to recall that the objective was radical social change. In his study of African American religion, Joseph R. Washington Jr. asserts that the Philadelphia African society existed "to keep black Methodists legal":

> When the little band marched out it formed the Free African Society. . . . The Free African Society was subversive. . . . In a word, power was sought from God not merely for the purpose of worshipping him but also for the purpose of internal unity to fight external oppression.[18]

The voluntary society fulfilled its constitutional objectives, but it also bound its members to greater social causes. "The chief purpose of any voluntary association consists in providing its members with mutual aid or protection, whether it is religious, cultural, social, recreational, physical, economic or political," argues Fei-Ling Davis in a history of Chinese secret societies. Those that combine these elements become "latently political (that is, prepared to seize political power)." Examining nineteenth-century secret societies, Davis explains that these organizations were little more than voluntary associations forced into opposition. Their major functions were benevolent. They defended initiates from attacks and threats, offered economic relief, settled disputes, protected members' money and property, hosted social functions, arranged funerals, and guarded the groups' investments (e.g., meeting halls). E. P. Thompson writes that nineteenth-century British "friendly societies" demanded discipline from workingmen. Raising funds, conducting meetings, and settling disputes were lessons in self-government that forged "a sub-culture out of which the less stable trade unions grew, and in which trade union officers were trained." "In the very secretiveness of the friendly society, and in its opaqueness under upper-class scrutiny," continues Thompson, existed the social space for subversion. Early European history provides another example. Roman officials feared the ease with which voluntary associations could forge subaltern cultures and engage in subversive acts. This preoccupation made them particularly suspicious of the bands of Christians who emerged during the second century.[19]

A parallel can also be found in the Diaspora. Cuba's colonial authorities were intolerant of the *cabildos de nación* because these African associations prevented people of color from being absolutely loyal to Spain. African mutual aid societies organized social events, kept African heritage current, unified local communities, and preserved "the memory of

Africa and of slavery." The government saw the suppression of the *cabildos* as the only way to stop the separatist threat "in which free blacks could rule themselves, isolated from the dominant culture."[20]

Black voluntarism had a unique sociology. In his examination of black Freemasonry, William Alan Muraskin criticizes scholars' tendency to combine black secret societies, mutual relief associations, and fraternities into a single set of institutions not grouped by function or class. He hypothesizes that "originall[y] the mutual aid societies were not primarily concerned with social activities, and the secret fraternal orders were not primarily concerned with mutual aid, each group tended, over time, to influence and take on some of the features of the other."[21] Muraskin assumes that black societies were striving to imitate white associations—that African societies had no peculiar cultural origin and no particular cultural design. He uses the idiosyncrasies of white institutional culture as a universal blueprint for institutional formation, and, thus, the distinctions of black institutional culture become failures to meet the white standard.

The limitations of the evidence and a general belief that all African organizations were fairly crude has limited interest in these societies' overlapping social roles and their distinctive sociology. Black people designed voluntary organizations to have multiple, and often secret, functions. The capacity to act secretively was a source of influence and power. Mutual relief associations preceded the fraternal organizations and, at their genesis, carried out social responsibilities. Antebellum black fraternities typically emerged from African societies and almost always assumed a similar range of activities. For instance, Manhattan's black Masons—although organized around the same contrived secrets and rituals as the white Craft—had a public career that mirrored that of the NYASMR. Among New York's African associations, burial and relief aid were organizing principles that fulfilled ethical obligations but did not limit social work. The major independent funeral and aid associations engaged in public charity, hosted lectures, built schools, supported churches, organized parades and political gatherings, and consciously determined and addressed the needs of the greater community. Internally, all societies were hierarchical, many had ranks, uniforms, and regalia, and their business was financial, spiritual, and political. The appointment of chaplains secured their religious atmosphere, and social work brought the temporary assignment of sergeants at arms, masters of ceremony, lecturers, ushers, and liaisons. Many societies achieved technical secrecy by incorporating oaths into their constitutions, keeping their membership rolls hidden, and imposing private initiations and ceremonies. They also seized the right to translate social ideas into social action and solve the plight of Africans in America.

Procedural similarities further complicate the task of separating African societies from secret and fraternal associations. Both "friendly" and "revolutionary" societies in precapitalist social movements shared certain characteristics. The universal elements were initiations, which bound individuals to the group; ceremonies, which served to unite the members and publicize their unity; practical rituals, like signs and passwords, which facilitated secrecy; and symbolism, especially banners and emblems, which connected ideology to structure and provided a recognizable mark of the group's existence.[22] African benevolent and secret societies met all these criteria. They constituted a quasi-secular world of obligations and attachments at the foundation of the black community.

Freemasonry offers the most illuminating example. On September 19, 1826, white Masons in Batavia and Canandaigua, New York, framed, abducted, and murdered William Morgan, once a Freemason himself, because he intended to publish the order's secrets. The resulting firestorm over the killing and the order's ability to protect the culprits brought the advent of the Antimasonic party and a decade of decline in the membership of the white secret society. The moral cloud over white Masonry extended beyond the Morgan affair. Much of the early history of the brotherhood transpired in taverns, and in England and the United States it was little more than a drinking and sporting club. The white American contribution to Freemasonry was extravagant, protracted pseudoreligious ritual. Many white evangelists in New York, including the Reverend Charles Grandison Finney, an initiate, feared that Freemasonry was an ancient and clandestine conspiracy against Christianity. The bastardization of biblical narrative within their rituals and the allure of a male world, separate from Protestant churches, made secret societies a danger to true religion. "The rise of fraternal orders at mid-century provides evidence of the emergence of a middle-class institution parallel to evangelical Protestantism," writes Mark C. Carnes of the tension, and the two "remain[ed] irreconcilably opposed to each other."[23]

In contrast, in antebellum New York City, Prince Hall Masonry—the common name of the black Freemasons—experienced no equivalent decline in status or membership; in fact, the number of black Masons and Masonic lodges in Manhattan and Brooklyn increased at the exact moment that the white order was in crisis. In Boston, the African Meeting House, the African Lodge, and the African Society were intimately connected; similarly, Prince Hall Masonry entered Manhattan through Mother Zion and the African Society for Mutual Relief. On February 16, 1812, the Prince Hall Grand Lodge of the Free and Accepted Masons in Massachusetts warranted Boyer Lodge No. 1 in the City of New York. (The name honored Jean Pierre Boyer, the Haitian-born, French-trained general who joined in the Haitian Revolution and, later, as president, united all of San Domingo into the Republic of Haiti.) Sandy Lattion, a member of Mother Zion and later a trustee of the African Asbury Church, served as the first worshipful master of Boyer. Eight anonymous black men joined Lattion in constituting the Manhattan lodge. James Varick and William Miller probably organized Boyer with Lattion, argues Bishop William J. Walls, "for they worked closely together in the church and other African organizations," such as the NYASMR and the African Bible Society of New York. The same year as the Morgan scandal, the Massachusetts Grand Lodge warranted two new Manhattan lodges, Celestial No. 2 and Hiram No. 4, and one Brooklyn lodge, Rising Sun No. 3. Over the next two decades, the four lodges grew in membership and influence, and, on March 14, 1845, they founded the Boyer Grand Lodge of New York State. The Grand Lodge was a Manhattan operation but quickly began chartering new lodges across the state and beyond (see table 5.1).[24]

Although black secret and benevolent societies had discrete memberships—limited by initiations and behavioral codes—they were generally viewed as community organizations. White people experienced and saw Freemasons as an elite tied through secret obligations and goals, while black New Yorkers knew Masons as a group who accepted and fulfilled social obligations that, in the public mind, overshadowed their esoteric relationships. Black Masons exploited the ethical focus of the Craft in order to define and attack slavery and racial inequality as immoral; for instance, Boyer regularly used its resources to organize and host political gatherings. Moreover, Prince Hall Masonry was not associated with the debaucherous drinking and sporting world of the early white lodges. From its beginnings, the black Craft's leadership was drawn from the African community's religious and moral stewards. Black people outside the Royal Art saw entrance into Freemasonry as a step in the larger community's moral reformation. In fact, Freemasonry was the single most important secular bond between the men who dominated political and

TABLE 5.1
The Growth of Prince Hall Masonry from Boyer

Lodge	Location	Warrant
Boyer No. 1	Manhattan	1812
Celestial No. 2	Manhattan	1826
Rising Sun No. 3	Brooklyn	1826
Hiram No. 4	Manhattan	1826
King Solomon No. 4	Manhattan	ca. 1850
Meridian No. 5	Manhattan	1850
Covenant No. 7	Manhattan	1850
Olive Branch No. 5	San Francisco, CA	1855
King Solomon No. 6	Jersey City, NJ	ca. 1856
Mount Olive No. 10	Manhattan	1858
Stone Square No. 6	Brooklyn	1859
Widow's Son No. 1	Brooklyn	1859
Evening Star No. 19	Oswego	1859
Jeptha No. 13	Albany	1860
Adelphic Union No. 14	Manhattan	1863
Hiram No. 21	Brooklyn	1863
Morning Star No. 19	Williamsburg[a]	1864
Mount Zion No. 13	Staten Island	1864
Wethington No. 8	San Francisco, CA	1865
Saint John's No. 16	Buffalo	1865
Mount Nebo No. 8	Elmira	1865

[a] In 1855 the City of Brooklyn annexed the City of Williamsburg.
NOTE: Lodges in italics were warranted by the Prince Hall Grand Lodge of Massachusetts. After 1845 the Boyer Grand Lodge of New York State warranted the state's lodges. In the 1850s, Boyer divided into two separate Grand Lodges—the National Compact and the United—over the issue of joining a national governing body for Prince Hall Masonry.
SOURCE: Harry A. Williamson, "Prince Hall Masonry in New York State," unpublished typescript, vol. V, 11, 74–89, passim. Harry A. Williamson Collection, Writings, Box 1 (1), Schomburg Collection, NYPL.

religious life in antebellum black New York. By subordinating their organization to the community's goals and committing it to collective action, Manhattan's Prince Hall Masons followed the NYASMR into a social space shaped by the persecution of black people.

The Boyer Masonic Lodge's dependent relationship to the NYASMR accounts for much of its success and acceptance. For decades, according to Masonic records, the Boyer Lodge and the Grand Lodge meeting rooms were in the African Society Hall at 42 Baxter Street, although they occasionally rented space from African School No. 2. It was not until May 7, 1860, that the Grand Lodge opened its own hall at Broome and Forsyth Streets. In addition, Masonic historian Harry Williamson found that as late as 1857 "the Grand Master reported the Grand Lodge was indebted to the 'Mutual Relief Soc. $150.00.'" The unnamed grand master was Manhattan craftsman Alexander Elston, enrolled into the NYASMR in 1823, initiated into the Boyer Lodge in 1827, and an officer and a future president of Mutual Relief.[25]

In the preceding century, Masonry had taken deeper root in the black community than the white. On June 5, 1730, the Duke of Norfolk appointed Daniel Cox, of the Grand Lodge of England, grand master of the colonies at New York, New Jersey, and Pennsylvania. Three years later, Henry Price was made grand master of New England. Racial segregation was an assumption of white American Masonry at its founding. African men were not initiated into the Craft until Irish and British soldiers occupied New England and the Mid-Atlantic during the Revolution. On March 6, 1775, Prince Hall, Thomas Sanderson, and Boston Smith came to Masonry through an Irish military lodge among the British soldiers garrisoned at Boston. The black men functioned as a lodge for almost a decade and even initiated new members, although the English Grand Lodge did not officially charter African Lodge, No. 459, until September 29, 1784. (In New York City, tavern-keeper Samuel Fraunces became a member of Holland Lodge, No. 8.) On June 24, 1791, the Boston group reorganized as the African Grand Lodge and later renamed itself in honor of its founder. The racial division of the American Craft continued. In the two decades before the Civil War, white Masons wrote detailed rituals for new degrees and declared British ritual "corrupt." Prince Hall Masonry underwent revisions but still identified with the English lodges and their truncated rituals, which allowed for social activity among Englishmen and political activity among black men. Well into the twentieth century, white Masons were contesting the legitimacy of Prince Hall Masonry.[26]

During the Revolution, black Americans encountered a Masonry stained with the antislavery sentiments of the British occupational forces. White Masonry, an American invention, was proslavery and thus segregated, offering a perverted message that allowed for the holding of people as property while simultaneously claiming universal fellowship. According to the Reverend Charles Finney, an officer of a New York Masonic lodge who dissociated, the white Grand Lodge of New York State codified racial exclusion in a series of acts that were copied by other states.[27] Thus, Prince Hall represented a separate branch of British Freemasonry in America, one marked by antislavery radicalism.

The Royal Art had another obvious attraction: although historically weak, Freemasonry's symbolically rich assertion of origins in the ancient profession of masonry and the resulting claim that the members of that occupation alone held special knowledge made the Masons the European organization that most resembled a West African secret society. That similarity came from the Masons' exploitation of a real social relationship. At best, the Craft had late-medieval derivation, but it alleged origins in the biblical account of the building of King Solomon's temple. By collapsing the secular and the spiritual, it moved even closer toward the African model. Similarly, the secret societies of Sierra Leone prepared many Africans for their initial encounter with and embrace of Freemasonry.[28] As the Royal Art spread any connections that existed between the trade and the society were lost and it came to be defined primarily by a contrivance, but the imagery remained potent for Africans' introduction to the Craft in eighteenth-century America. Freemasonry enjoyed unparalleled acceptance among black men throughout the Diaspora.

The close ties between African societies, churches, and fraternities protected and promoted black Freemasonry. The connection that Bishop Walls made between Manhattan's Boyer Lodge and the A.M.E. Zion Church is not at all tenuous. Because of their common political and social appeal, Prince Hall Masonry and African Methodism traveled hand in hand in black communities. Stephen C. Bullock argues that "Masonic values could even be used to challenge the injustices of the dominant culture, an ability seen in the experiences of Prince Hall and the 'African Lodge.'" Born in Bridgetown, Barbados, Prince Hall emigrated to the Boston colony as a teenager. Within a decade, he purchased property and qualified to vote. On the eve of the Revolution, he was drawn into Methodism and Masonry. Having lost close friends like Crispus Attucks at the Boston Massacre, Hall served with the colonials in the war. Later, while grand master of the African Lodge, he presided over the Boston African Society and the organization of the city's first black church. In 1815, Richard Allen and Absalom Jones established the Grand Lodge of Pennsylvania. Prince Hall Masonry and the black church also overlapped in New York. After the Civil War, black Freemasonry entered the South on the coattails of Methodism. The Reverend James Walker Hood, a future bishop of the A.M.E. Zion Church, established the Craft while ministering in North Carolina. In Georgia, Masonry was closely tied to the A.M.E. Church. (In the early twentieth century, Bishop Levi Jenkins Coppin established Prince Hall Masonry in Capetown, South Africa.) "Once established," writes Muraskin, "North or South, the two institutions continued to maintain their connecting links." While no connection was greater than that between Masonry and Methodism, clergy were also leaders of other fraternal associations. For instance, Bishop Abram Grant was a founder of the Heroines of Jericho, and Bishop Cornelius Thaddeus Shaffer served the Grand Lodge as an international delegate of the Good Templars.[29]

Manhattan's Philomathean Literary Society provides further evidence of the incorporation of secret ritual into antebellum African associations and it further exposes the gray area between secret and benevolent organizations. Ostensibly, the community of men and boys in the PLS appreciated literature, oratory, and music, but they also shared secrets. In 1842, the Philomatheans, already owning a meeting hall, consolidated and expanded their fraternal features and sought to become a lodge within a secret society, the Odd Fellows. The Grand Lodge of New York "treated [their request] with contempt" because the petitioners were men of color. Peter Ogden, a black sailor initiated into the Odd Fellows in England, brought their appeal to his Victoria Lodge, Liverpool, and on March 1, 1843, it chartered the Philomathean Lodge, No. 646, New York City, of the Grand United Order of Odd Fellows. (The following year the Philadelphia Library Company and Debating Society reorganized into an Odd Fellows lodge.) Ogden served as the Odd Fellows' United States agent, to the dismay of many white men seeking incorporation. From its first full year in Manhattan to 1849, when its headquarters moved to Philadelphia, the Fellowship attracted almost two thousand men. NYASMR members were disproportionately represented in the Odd Fellows' leadership: the Reverend John Peterson—"the born gentleman, the finished scholar, the renowned teacher of youth"—was a grand master and a director. Timothy Seaman was deputy grand master, James McCune Smith was grand secretary, William Fenwick, who was also initiated into the Boyer Masonic Lodge in 1827, was grand treasurer, and Thomas Hoffman and Edward V. Clark were directors. George T. Downing, the son of Mutual Relief's Thomas Downing, served a term as grand master. In 1844 the Hamilton Lodge, No. 710, New York City, was organized in honor of William Hamilton. (The Hamilton lodge held one of the oldest social events in black Manhattan, the Masquerade and Civic Ball, which began in 1869 as a haughty formal gathering and which by the late 1920s was transformed into an interracial Harlem drag contest popularly derided as the "Faggots' Ball.")[30]

The Philomatheans' conversion to Odd Fellowship was logical given that, in the words of Grand Master Benjamin Arnett, it was "a perfect organization for mutual aid and relief." Its rituals and mysteries fostered unity, its benefits brought a covenant of obligations, and the Judeo-Christian moralism at the core of the society's doctrines informed its political advocacy. Thus, as with Freemasonry, Odd Fellowship in the United States divided along racial lines as white men defended slavery from the rhetoric of fraternalism. In December 1806 the first local Odd Fellows lodge was organized at the Shakespeare House on Fair Street in Manhattan. Ten years later a second New York chapter was established, and in 1819 a lodge was begun in Baltimore. On October 23, 1820, the English lodge chartered the American society. Mark Carnes finds that within a decade, white Odd Fellows were transforming the association into a middle-class and temperate organization consumed with ritual. After 1845 they broke with England to protect the excessive ritual that was the source of their new success and renamed themselves the Independent Order of Odd Fellows. Carnes argues that these men sought the psychological comfort of an artificial male world in a rapidly changing society. The space that they created was as racialized as it was gendered. White American Odd Fellows objected to racially mixed fraternalism and black men becoming officers through England. They perceived the danger that the rhetoric of universal fellowship posed to human bondage. The decision to break with England allowed for independent, racially exclusive lodges. The black order kept ties with the British lodge. Black men saw the order's potential as an antislavery weapon and many of Manhattan's foremost black abolitionists were Odd Fellows. They instituted relief and burial programs for members, their widows, and orphaned children. In 1857 they established a women's auxiliary, the Household of Ruth, into which any woman who was an immediate relative of a fifth-degree Odd Fellow could be initiated. By 1882 the Grand United Order of Odd Fellows (America) had more than eight hundred lodges in the United States, Canada, and the Caribbean, and more than 32,000 members.[31]

African benevolent associations sired the major black secret societies and transferred their communitarian focus onto the fraternal organizations; in turn, black fraternities provided the ritual and rhetoric of secrecy that further cloaked the extralegal functions of voluntary organizations. The African society created a mode of community organization that transcended the institutional and cultural divisions of New York's and Brooklyn's black communities. The historical record is kind to only the major associations, those with the wealth, membership, and organizational purpose to sustain themselves and to document their work. However, the smaller and ephemeral associations—such as Frères Réunis—

known by single, third-person mentions and one-time newspaper an-
nouncements of their meeting or formation, are even more important.
Those organizations highlight a network that drove black institutions
and shaped daily life. Societies defined community leadership, they organized political action, and, as Mutual Relief's involvement in the Underground Railroad displayed, they possessed the ability to engage in extralegal and illegal acts when necessary.

The constitutions that descend from that of the NYASMR record only
the legal and public objectives of these associations; however, occasionally evidence appears of their extralegal functions. An 1843 letter from
Mutual Relief's William Powell, published in *The Liberator*, provides an
interesting glimpse at the significance of societies in black New York. A
carriage carrying black passengers raced into the city. The local Africans
were alarmed, suspecting that the unidentified travelers might be fugitives. "The denizens of Gotham (or at least the inmates of my *sanctum
sanctorum*) were . . . thrown into a sudden feverish excitement," recalled
Powell. Black people gathered. The car "was surrounded by the crowd,
who were anxious to liberate the interesting strangers, and take them
under their protection, 'peaceably if they can, forcibly if they must.'" The
throng was so large that it took the nervous driver several minutes to pry
the door. The interventionists grew restless. The door was finally opened.
Powell and his family stepped out, "and such a rejoicing you never witnessed."[32] The crisis ended.

There is another message in Powell's account. The qualifying phrase,
"or at least the inmates of my *sanctum sanctorum*," is cryptic. The sanctum sanctorum refers to the Masonic lodge, metaphorically Solomon's
temple with its inner-sanctuary, the Most Holy Place.[33] It is telling that, as
the white Craft lingered in crisis, Powell chose to highlight the unity of
the black metropolis with an image imported directly from the ritual of
Prince Hall Masonry. Powell used the secrets of Freemasonry to celebrate
the culture of the black public sphere.

6

In the Company of Black Men

Manhood and Obligation in the African Confraternity, 1808–1857

> I am still here fighting, fighting, fighting the needful battles . . . there is not quite the sociability here that there used to be, or perhaps we are growing older and do not go out so much to seek society—at least I do not. Some have gone to spirit lands, but they come back and commune with us. Some have scat[t]ered, but New York is still NY in many respects. Zuille, the Reasons, Hamilton, Garnett, Smith, Simmons, Peterson and many more whose names would awaken pleasant thoughts and cause your bosom to heave, are around.
> —George T. Downing to Rev. Alexander Crummell, April 12, 1860

In July 1827, Samuel Hardenburgh of the New York African Society for Mutual Relief, "a splendid-looking black man, in cocked hat and drawn sword, mounted on a milk-white steed," was grand marshal of a parade celebrating the statutory end of slavery in New York State. His deputies were also "on horseback, dashing up and down the line" of men and boys, "five or six abreast," who hoisted their society banners and wore their society colors. The African men's societies of New York City proceeded in order of rank, "splendidly dressed in scarfs of silk with gold-edgings, and with colored bands of music, and their banners appropriately lettered and painted." Eleven-year-old Henry Highland Garnet and fourteen-year-old James McCune Smith were among the phalanx. From the sidewalks, women and girls cheered on their male relatives. As the marchers reached City Hall, Hardenburgh saluted the mayor and then led the parade down Broadway toward the Battery. "It was a proud day for the Societies and their officers; it was a proud day, never to be forgotten by young lads, who, like Henry Garnet, first felt themselves impelled along that grand procession of liberty," recalled McCune Smith.[1]

"In an age when literacy was limited and mass communication media primitive, the ritual and oratory embedded in public gatherings contained deep political and cultural significance for Americans of both European and African descent," writes Elizabeth Rauh Bethel of a later festival in Boston. Manhattan's Wilberforce Philanthropic Association, founded on June 8, 1812, dominated African parading in New York and Brooklyn. Its pomp and pageantry at African ceremonies earned it a reputation similar to that of the militaristic African Greys of Providence, Rhode Island, and the African Society of Salem, Massachusetts. Societies sponsored such spectacle and decided the political, spiritual, and historical themes. Through such ceremonies, African Americans constructed a "collective identity." African societies used alternative holidays and substitute heroes to repair the national history by countering white people's historical constructions, which denied any African contributions to the queue of great moments that composed the national past.[2]

These public spectacles were also performances of black masculinity, a means of passing social roles and responsibilities across generations. Because white New Yorkers believed that black men's race compromised their right to exercise the privileges of manhood, they cast all expressions of black masculinity in distinctly political terms. However, the assumption that assertions of black masculinity were directed at white people is destructive because it neglects black men's commitment to patriarchy and dislocates the community functions of masculine discourse. Black men viewed their manhood as a manifest fact and their subordinate political and legal status as measures of a broader social immorality. The 1827 parade reflected a preexisting patriarchal authority. Notions of manliness were being forged but they were intended to usher young boys like Garnet and Smith into adulthood. The ideology of manhood—the constructed social meaning of being male, including its privileges and burdens—is an ongoing cultural process, argues Gail Bederman.[3] In antebellum New York City, African voluntary associations used oratory, performance, and spectacle to socialize boys into men.

Within African men's associations, members used the language of fraternalism—the brotherhood of men—to express social obligations. The force of fraternalism comes from its capacity to fit new social relationships and actions into a traditional culture. By asserting brotherhood, associations of men co-opted the language and symbols of their community—based in actual kinship—and established new relations, obligations, and privileges. Parades, initiations, oaths, and other rituals reinforced those fictive bonds.[4]

The confraternity allowed groups of black men to organize around their shared interests while respecting, at least metaphorically, the authority of blood relations.

In her study of antebellum Philadelphia, Susan G. Davis asserts that "when the image of a unified black community with moral and political claims on the rest of society was projected into the streets, whites felt their prerogatives threatened." White New Yorkers also reflexively viewed public expressions of black manhood as acts of political warfare. In historicizing their own racial and gender status, white working-class men so completely erased African Americans from history that any black person who stepped into the streets of New York City on a national holiday risked assault. The violent defense of this subjective national past was at its root a defense of white manhood. Before the end of the eighteenth century, white working-class men were using public celebrations to display and reenforce the antiaristocratic but racist message of the Revolution. White men rationalized their political and economic power through gendered and racialized notions and by ruthlessly imposing a white masculine standard on public space and propriety. As white working men assumed control over public life, early-eighteenth-century organizations like the New York Cordwainers Benefit Society established "uncompromised affirmation of their value to society and their place in the republic." For instance, the Society of Mechanics and Tradesmen in New York City, which united white men both as workers and through secret initiations and rituals, grew disgusted with the "aristocratical" nature of the political parties. The Mechanics responded with race- and gender-segregated workers' celebrations of George Washington's birthday and the Fourth of July.[5]

Voluntary societies assumed the task of providing surrogate cultural experiences for the black community. White mob violence limited apolitical parading among African Americans and brought an even greater reliance upon society-sponsored activities. On April 23, 1827, seven society members called "a large and respectable Meeting of the People of Colour, held in the Mutual Relief Hall." The community chose July 5 as its own holiday. It also decided against parading to protect people of color from the white toughs who roamed the city streets. The decree reflected the growing dissatisfaction of the activists with the willingness of some black folk to participate in public parades but not in political work. The societies then organized a community celebration. That same year, members of the New York Union, Clarkson, Wilberforce, and Brooklyn Woolman societies hosted a celebration of the seventeenth anniversary of the incorporation of the NYASMR. Mutual Relief's members held the positions of honor at Mother Zion Church, where the assembly took place. Men from all the societies wore their paraphernalia, flew their banners, and delivered orations.[6]

The voluntary societies' monopoly over public ceremony had obvious African parallels. West African secret societies often dominated social ritual and gender socialization. For example, Poro and Sande controlled the entry of boys and girls, respectively, into adulthood. The dramatic result was that they achieved universal participation by initiating all children during adolescence. Poro's role in socializing boys—which included its own schools and its right to decide the social meaning of puberty—guaranteed its perpetual power in West Africa. Similarly, the woman's Nyama society in Nigeria exercised broad authority over the family because it prepared women for marriage.[7]

This control over socialization can also be seen in the Diaspora. Cuban mutual aid societies shaped social life, worked to keep the memory of enslavement current, reminded black Cubans of their African heritage, and struggled to achieve group unity. The African brotherhoods of Brazil had parallel functions. Besides governing the rise of African Brazilian Christianity, the black brotherhoods of Rio provided mutual aid and burial assistance, acted as savings associations for enslaved Africans attempting to purchase their freedom, and, in some cases, even controlled entrance into crafts. "In many ways, brotherhoods were the most important socio-religious institutions of the early nineteenth century," argues Mary C. Karasch. They shaped the social world of Rio's Africans, and their religious responsibilities included organizing holidays and festivals to honor black saints.[8]

To establish that New York societies shared with many associations in West Africa and the Diaspora the right to socialize children and dominate community institutions, public spectacle, and the coming-of-age process is to make only a gross connection. Far deeper were the ethics of mutualism and collectivism that ordered social relations, a subculture of obligations and expectations that defined social life in black Manhattan. Those bonds transcended the associations and were described in the language of patriarchy.

The black public sphere had a masculine idiom, and it was sustained through the constant production of young intellectuals in community institutions. Young men were socialized in a discourse about masculinity and responsibility, community leaders were groomed in a sociopolitical culture of manhood. It approaches what E. Anthony Rotundo defines as "communal manhood," a notion of manliness as a set of obligations and expectations that arises in communities in which personal behavior has broad social consequences.[9]

Oppression exaggerates the social impact of personal behavior, and it can function to legitimize public authority over individual development. Manhood was not simply a role exercised to the community's benefit, it was a station created at the community's expense. African societies took responsibility for educating, training, and apprenticing black boys regardless of their backgrounds—functions that society members cherished and protected. Men completed the cycle when they fulfilled their social obligations by raising up boys and teaching them their ancestral and social duties.

For example, black Manhattanites were caring for fugitive, orphaned, and impoverished children long before the founding of the Association for the Benefit of Colored Orphans (1836), the committee of white women who governed the Colored Orphan Asylum. Pierre and Juliet Toussaint adopted their orphaned niece Euphemia and raised her as a daughter, and they regularly brought orphaned boys to live in their home. They housed and educated the boys until they were old enough to apprentice. (The Toussaints provided considerable support to the Roman Catholic Orphan Asylum although it refused to admit black children.) In 1839, the matrons of the Colored Orphan Asylum mentioned the depths of these informal networks while admitting ten-year-old Joseph Turner, a homeless boy, who was "sometimes sleeping in the streets, and at others being lodged and fed by poor coloured people." The COA's register also documents the type of hardship that the black community had been addressing. In 1837 Jacob Becket entered. His mother died four years earlier and slave catchers hunted down his father, a fugitive from Virginia, and returned him to bondage. The following year they received John Tomata, an eight-year-old enslaved boy from Havana, Cuba. Tomata's owner, likely a seaman, abandoned the severely injured child in New York City. Tomata died a few months later.[10]

Black women were the day-to-day operatives of social work, but men's voluntary associations governed the black community's response to such misfortune. Henry Highland Garnet was one of many fugitives to use African societies and less-formal community resources to plot their own social rise. It was through the Phoenix Literary Society (1833) that young

Garnet trained as a public speaker. An 1838 disagreement between the leaders of Phoenix and the Colored Orphan Asylum is revealing. Black New Yorkers heartily applauded the work of the COA, but they were noticeably absent from its list of financial supporters. African-society initiates like David Ruggles, Henry Scott, and Philip Bell made one-time, individual donations of three dollars, as did Rebecca Downing. Peter Williams Jr. was a regular donor, he invited the orphaned children to St. Philip's to collect special offerings, and he attended the funeral of at least one deceased child at the institution. But black organizations generally left it to the COA's administration to raise money in the white community. The Reverend Samuel Cornish, Simeon Jocelyn, and Thomas Van Rensselaer even challenged the asylum's leadership when the Manumission Society gave the COA money that William Turpin willed for the support of an educational facility for black people. The African men argued that the funds should go to Phoenix. The Asylum's governors and advisers decided to compromise, paying Phoenix four hundred dollars to drop all claims to the Turpin bequest.[11] The conflict did not reflect a lack of interest in the white-run asylum; rather, it was an indicator of black people's commitment to the values imbedded in their own associations.

Antebellum black institutions cultivated social men: individuals who rose through personal and community sacrifice and who accepted the resulting obligations. "Black culture in New York . . . was therefore in some ways very much a youth culture," observes Sterling Stuckey, "characteristically devoted, if the logic of the evidence and inference holds, to ancestral values." Societies initiated a dialogue between generations that passed cultural traditions, political forms, and leadership from fathers to sons. "Take the orphan by the hand," said Vice President John Teasman to the NYASMR. "Wipe away the tear; condole the afflicted; be worthy: they will rise and call you blessed; and you shall take an eminent seat in the circles of well organized and faithful societies; and there sit undisturbed, known by the name of the New York African Society for Mutual Relief."[12]

Teasman's career displays the process. How he became free is not clear, but he was born enslaved in New Jersey about 1754. He enjoyed a remarkable rise. At the time that New York State adopted a manumission law, Teasman was free, had a profession as a teacher and a principal, and was the highest-salaried black person in Manhattan. In January 1797, the prominent white trustees of the New York Manumission Society appointed Teasman as assistant teacher in the African school they had established a year earlier. Within a year Teasman and schoolmaster William

Pirsson were supplementing their salaries and exceeding their mandate by running an evening school for adults. In March 1799, Teasman succeeded Pirsson as principal.[13]

"The black principal immediately began training future leaders of the free black community," charges Robert J. Swan. He defended black New Yorkers against the New York Manumission Society's attempts to control the education and behavior of black Manhattanites. He helped guide the development of African church- and society-based schools. Over the Manumission Society's objections, Teasman organized the July 5, 1800, African parade in celebration of New York State's Gradual Manumission Act of 1799.[14]

Teasman was a founder of the NYASMR, serving as its first vice president and then succeeding William Hamilton in the presidency. In 1809, the Manumission Society fired Teasman for chairing the committee that organized the African celebration of the end of the slave trade to the United States. Mutual Relief put Teasman and his wife to work running two African schools that they sponsored. Black-run schools were numerous and competitive enough to allow black people to increase their autonomy in schools run by white New Yorkers. The Reverends Peter Williams Jr. and William Miller—both members of the NYASMR, and Miller a founder of the Wilberforce Philanthropic Association—were agents for African schools, traveling throughout the city to encourage black children's attendance.[15]

It was at such a school that young James McCune Smith began his intellectual journey. In 1824, when French general Lafayette visited New York, Smith was chosen to address him. "Here, sir, you behold hundreds of the poor children of Africa sharing with those of a lighter hue in the blessings of education; and while it will be our pleasure to remember the great deeds you have done for America, it will be our delight also to cherish the memory of General Lafayette as a friend to African emancipation, and as a member of this institution," the eleven-year-old commented.[16]

Four years later Isaiah G. DeGrasse, the son of Mutual Relief member George DeGrasse, wrote a letter to the American Convention for Promoting the Abolition of Slavery. The fifteen-year-old described himself as "a poor descendant" of an "injured people." He thanked the assembly for taking up the cause of African freedom and he blasted the inhumanity of bondage. He assured them of the progress of students at the New York African schools. "The different branches that are taught in this school, are reading, writing, arithmetic, geography, navigation, astronomy, and map drawing. Our schools which now contain 700 male and female scholars, continue to be conducted on the Lancasterian system, and the improvement of the scholars is such, as to be satisfactory to the trustees, and all visiters [*sic*] who come to the school." The young man concluded by sending them the thanks and blessings "of a descendant of Africa."[17]

Virtually all African societies offered educational programs. The Brooklyn African Woolman Benevolent Society promised to relieve its members' distress and to educate children of color. Its actual community functions were even broader. In 1815, Woolman's charter president, Peter Croger, opened his home to Brooklyn's first African school, holding day and evening classes for children and adults. In 1827 Woolman raised money to build an African school, church, and library after the local public school evicted the black class from its quarters in order to accommodate more white children. Henry Thompson, who followed Croger in the presidency, organized children's exhibitions and contests. The African Marine Fund assisted "poor African children, whose parents are unable to educate them," relieved distress in the greater black community, and provided benefits to members. The New York African Clarkson Association also made educational uplift a constitutional objective. The young men of the Garrison Literary and Benevolent Association pledged to encourage "the diffusion of knowledge, mental assistance, moral and intellectual improvement." In April 1834, "Plutarch" visited the boys and found "150 little ones, from the age of 5 to 14" writing and delivering orations, reciting, and composing. In the summer of 1848, Bishop Christopher Rush purchased a plot of land in Essex County, New York, on behalf of the A.M.E. Zion denomination, for the establishment of "Rush Academy," an institute for the religious training of young black men. Rush served as treasurer of the school and booster for its planned building.[18]

Black women's service societies were even more active in raising money, caring for the poor and orphaned, and addressing community needs. In 1833, at the beginning of his public career, David Ruggles lectured before the African Dorcas Association—formed in 1827 by a group of ministers—on the benefits of African women's organizations. Dorcas, like other women's associations, occasionally provided audiences for young black men emerging as public speakers and community leaders. Ruggles's dependence upon black women's societies continued. He was a founder and the guiding spirit of the New York Vigilance Committee, formed to assist fugitives and resist slave catchers in the metropolis. During its 1837 anniversary meeting, the Vigilance Committee called on the attendees to raise three thousand dollars to support its future work. In its first year, the black men who served as officers faced considerable expense in assisting 335 Africans. "The principal part of the subscriptions raised by the exertions of the general committee, has been obtained by the efforts of the Ladies, who collect from their friends one penny a week," confessed Chairman Theodore Wright and Secretary Ruggles in the *Annual Report.* Black women were the fundraising arm of black Manhattan's radical Vigilance Committee.[19]

Sojourner Truth came into the company of a black women's society during her two years in Gotham. She was attracted to them because at "that time, the 'moral reform' movement was awakening the attention of the benevolent in that city." The group looked to reach out to the lowliest of New York's women and even established independent prayer meetings. Truth eventually left the association because of her objections to these women's emotional displays while worshipping.[20]

In 1833 Maria Stewart moved from Boston to New York City, living there and in Williamsburg for the next two decades. A widow of the War of 1812, she became a powerful speaker in New England but never learned to write. Black women from New York tutored Stewart and she joined a local African women's literary society. Alexander Crummell, aware of the gender gap in educational opportunities, recalled that when he and his friends Henry Highland Garnet and Thomas Sidney returned to Manhattan from their travels to school, they were pleased to find Maria Stewart, "a young woman of my own people full of literary aspiration and ambitious authorship." "There were a few young women in New York who thought of these higher things, and it was a surprise to find another added to their number," he continued. Crummell sat in Stewart's audience on many occasions.[21]

Women sustained many of black Manhattan's institutions. Through the African Dorcas Association, women provided clothing and aid to poor children at the colored schools. Clothes were loaned in exchange for steady school attendance, and slackers were stripped of their allotment. In the 1830s, black women established the Female Mite Society to support the community's ministry. Black women and schoolchildren made and collected clothing and raised money for the Colored Orphan Asylum and the equally well-known Home for Aged Colored People. (The Quaker-supported Society for the Relief of Worthy Aged, Indigent Colored Persons in New York City was incorporated in 1845.) It assisted the elderly poor assigned by the commissioner of the alms house in New York, directly reducing black people's reliance upon public charity.[22]

Significantly, Sojourner Truth's brief tarriance and Maria Stewart's disappearance from public life underscore the patriarchal and man-centered culture of black Manhattan; in fact, African educational and cultural institutions' primary function was to socialize boys. Nineteenth-century secret societies succeeded, in part, because they created a social world apart from the woman-dominant culture of evangelical Christianity. Radical religion still influenced constructions of manhood. "There can be no doubt that the models of black manhood provided by the black church constitute one of its most important contributions, over the years, to the cause of black liberation," writes William H. Becker.[23] Black Christianity generated masculine examples, but the woman-dominant culture of the church was not the appropriate site for socializing boys. The fraternal experience was an important unifying force for black men's voluntarism. Manhattan's black men were not merely mimicking or submitting to the gender politics of the greater society. They were fully committed to progress through patriarchy.

The NYASMR's members dominated the public sphere by gathering communities of men to exercise the authority of men. On January 17, 1817, the Reverend William Miller of the NYASMR opened his house at 36 Mulberry Street—where he was already conducting a school—to the African Bible Society of New York, which became an auxiliary of the American Bible Society later that year. Miller served as president and was joined by several of his peers from New York's societies and fraternities. James Varick and Thomas Miller were vice presidents, George Collins was secretary, Lewis Carter was treasurer, and George DeGrasse, Sandy Lattion, Robert F. Williams, Andrew Smith, and William Lambert were managers. Within two years, the African Female Bible Society of New York appeared. The two shared the mission of spreading the Good Book in the black community.[24]

In 1829 the Philomathean Literary Society was formed and hosted weekly debates and recitations on a variety of subjects. In 1831 John De-Grasse, the younger son of George DeGrasse, received the association's annual essay prize and lectured on the Philomathean's work for intellectual advancement. "The address was very well written, and was pronounced with much eloquence and animation," remarked an observer. Philomathean's governors included young African society notables like

James McCune Smith, Philip Bell as chair, Thomas Jennings, and Henry Sipkins, all of whom looked to replicate the organization among the colored youth of other cities. That was accomplished in 1834, when William Jennings organized and served as prefect of the Boston Philomathean Society. By 1833 Bell and the board were offering a public lecture series out of Philomathean's Hall at No. 161 Duane Street.[25]

That year the Phoenix Society was founded to encourage black children's school attendance, nourish the intellectual pursuits of local adults, assist young black men pursuing education, establish moral societies, secure employment for the needy, and provide occupational training. It had Boston Crummell on its board, the Reverend Christopher Rush as its president, and real estate and clothing merchant Thomas Jennings and Peter Vogelsang as active members. Phoenix, notes Leonard Curry, "quickly establish[ed] a library, reading rooms, reading and discussion groups, and a course of lectures, but it also formed subordinate ward societies charged with performing some of the same functions in their smaller communities and with visiting all black families in their wards and urging upon them the benefits of education and intellectual development." Phoenix Hall, at Chapel Street (now West Broadway), challenged African Society Hall as the primary site of community gatherings and meetings. The Reverend Samuel Cornish was a Phoenix agent, soliciting memberships and encouraging support of the antislavery press. The cost of its programs were underwritten by a quarterly dues system on a pay-what-you-can-afford basis. To facilitate its work, Phoenix undertook a census of black Manhattan. The most ambitious endeavor was an attempt to raise ten thousand dollars to open a manual labor college.[26]

This goal was never achieved, but, as late as 1847, Alexander Crummell and James McCune Smith drove a resolution for a black men's college past the weighty opposition of Frederick Douglass, Henry Highland Garnet, and Thomas Van Rensselaer at the National Colored Convention in Troy, New York. "Their views were concurred in by a large party in the Convention, but more especially by the New York delegation," reported William C. Nell. Later, McCune Smith wrote Crummell on behalf of St. Philip's vestrymen to inform him that he was the unanimous choice for rector. He told his boyhood friend and political ally of St. Philip's financial and physical condition and quickly suggested some social work: "There is great need of a good grammar school for our youth in this city, in which Philadelphia and Pittsburgh have us at disadvantage." Smith was among the trustees of the New York Society for the Promotion of Education Among Colored Children, formed in 1847. He was joined by several NYASMR members, including editor Philip A. Bell, William P. Powell, George D. Jamison, Daniel Elston, the Reverend Charles B. Ray, Albro Lyons, jeweler Edward V. Clark, pickle and preserve merchant Henry Scott, Sampson White, who ministered in Washington, Brooklyn, and Manhattan, and the Reverend John Peterson. In 1854, McCune Smith continued to advocate a mechanical school for young black men that would deliver an education "as shall keep them from menial employments of every kind."[27]

The source of harmony within the African Society for Mutual Relief was not cultural but ideological; in fact, the key to its success was the ability to transcend ethnic and cultural divisions. If nationalism gave black New Yorkers a means of subordinating such distinctions in a discourse of collectivism and mutualism, manhood provided a guide for fulfilling the consequent obligations. Other African associations and institutions in New York proved that distinctions of wealth and culture could easily be observed and enforced within the constructs of intraracial gatherings. The social currents within Mutual Relief also tended toward disunity; however, the members shared a belief that African slavery meant a permanent inequality for black people everywhere. The African Society's harmony came from its members' ability to see its creation and success as antislavery gestures. There was a single common theme that overpowered whatever differentiated them: they were African men—enslaved, once enslaved, or sons of the enslaved.

There was a wide generation gap in Mutual Relief. When the organization was founded, John Teasman was in his fifties, William Hamilton in his thirties, Peter Williams Jr. in his twenties, and Henry Sipkins was a teenager. Hamilton said of the youngest men, "If we continue to produce specimens like these, we shall soon put our enemies to the blush, abashed and confounded they shall quit the field, and no longer urge their superiority of souls." As Teasman approached his sixtieth birthday, he too spoke of the brotherhood: "In the [meeting] house, and by the way, I am received, and met with all due respect and civility; not only by my co[n]temporaries; but also by my young friends, who treat me with much respect, gratitude, and attention."[28]

There were also dramatic educational distinctions. Boston Crummell, "the man who could not be enslaved," was the icon of the free black community's rise from bondage, illiteracy, and poverty. James McCune Smith was born free and became one of the best-educated men in New York

City. He was a well-known writer, served a brief stint as editor of the *Colored American*, had a successful pharmacy, "Apothecary's Hall," an equally lucrative medical practice, and earned a reputation so broad that local directories invariably instructed their readers that he was still a black man.[29] On the other hand, Mutual Relief included men who could neither read nor write and whose names are not found anywhere in the historical record except in the papers of the NYASMR.

Ethnicity was strikingly unimportant in society politics. Men born in the South, those born in Manhattan, Africans, and Caribbeans blended together at meetings. McCune Smith celebrated the inclusion and style of people born in Africa and the West Indies in the 1827 parade sponsored by the NYASMR: "Not a few with gay bandanna handkerchiefs, betraying their West Indian birth; neither was Africa itself unrepresented, hundreds who had survived the middle passage, and a youth in slavery joined in the joyful procession."[30]

Religious distinctions were grayed in the society in a way that they were not in the larger community of black Manhattan. Peter Williams Jr. was rector of St. Philip's Episcopal; Charles B. Ray ministered Bethesda (Congregational) Church for two decades; and Thomas Jennings was a founder and trustee of Abyssinian Baptist Church where Sampson White was pastor. James Varick, Christopher Rush, and William Miller were founders and bishops of the independent African Methodist Episcopal Zion church. (Never as large as the A.M.E. denomination, the "Freedom Church" was nonetheless a force in the national affairs of people of color. Sojourner Truth, Harriet Tubman, and Frederick Douglass, a licensed local preacher, were all affiliated with A.M.E. Zion.)[31] Presbyterians, Methodists, an occasional Catholic, the influential African Methodist Episcopal cohort, the A.M.E. Zion core, and those who claimed no organized version of God moved through the society with little friction.

Nor was there any discord between the growing number of thousandaires who sat beside cartmen and whitewashers at society meetings. Of the NYASMR's wealthier men, Martin R. Delany noted that Thomas Downing—Boyer member, philanthropist, and restaurateur—"has made 'three fortunes.'" He once extended a ten thousand dollar loan to the *New York Herald* to keep it afloat. Henry Scott was equally affluent. "There have doubtless been many a purser, who cashed and filed in his office the bill of Henry Scott, without ever dreaming of his being a colored man." Philip Bell inherited and improved the intelligence agency of William Hutson. "It is said to be not unusual, for the peasantry of Liverpool, to speak of Mr. Bell, as a benefactor of the emigrant domestics." Jeweler Edward V. Clark "has a respectable credit, even among the urbane denizens of Wall street." In 1870 the *New Era* described the NYASMR's men as "Master builders, tailors, shoemakers, machinists, and blacksmiths, printers, farmers, notary public and commissioner, seamen, longshoremen and common laborers."[32]

Masculinity and fraternalism were guides for individual behavior. They offered a language for individual identity and a mechanism that allowed individual aspiration to survive in a collectivist culture. "Fathers, I speak to you: have you done all that God and nature have placed in your power, to draw yourselves and offspring from the depth of disgrace in which our colour lies?" Peter Vogelsang asked the NYASMR. The division between private and public was grayed, for the individual man held the key to the group's resurrection. Vogelsang warned his audience to "awake from this lethargy, or never expect the privileges of a citizen." In an 1855 tribute to Frederick Douglass, Dr. James McCune Smith—who was trained under the founders of the earliest African organizations and was initiated into several African societies—betrayed how fully moral uplift was tied to notions of masculinity:

> When a man raises himself from the lowest condition in society to the highest, mankind pay him the tribute of their admiration; when he accomplishes this elevation by native energy, guided by prudence and wisdom, their admiration is increased; but when his course, onward and upward, excellent in itself, furthermore proves a possible, what had hitherto been regarded as an impossible, reform, then he becomes a burning and shining light, on which the aged may look with gladness, the young with hope, and the down-trodden, as a representative of what they may themselves become.[33]

Collectivist claims did not negate individualism. The methodical life produced individual and group rewards. The exchange was not that a man's accomplishments became community attainments, but that private achievements had public meaning. Black Manhattanites offered singular praise for singular accomplishments, as Smith delivered to Douglass and as Smith himself received from black Manhattan, then in affirming group competence that acclamation was augmented by reminders of the extraordinary social barriers that the individual faced.

When men accepted their obligations to a community that sacrificed to allow individual mobility, they confirmed the power of collectivism. It was in the fraternal culture of the voluntary association that this exchange occurred. William Hamilton's sons, William, Robert, and Thomas, were raised among pioneering intellectuals of the antebellum era like churchmen Christopher Rush and Charles Ray. Society initiates James McCune Smith, Philip Bell, Thomas Sidney, George Moore, Samuel Ringgold Ward, Peter Vogelsang, John Peterson, and George Downing were educated with Freemasons Alexander Crummell, the son of Boston Crummell; Patrick Reason, the master engraver; and Charles Reason, black New York's finest teacher, in African schools. African schools also trained such outstanding young men as emigrationist minister Henry Highland Garnet; Ira Aldridge, the Shakespearean actor and a Prince Hall Mason; and Isaiah DeGrasse, a leading minister who also taught many of the younger men. In 1831, as they outgrew the African schools, they were again united when Boston Crummell, Thomas Downing, and Peter Williams Jr. began Canal Street High School and employed a white teacher to instruct in Latin and Greek. These friendships lasted lifetimes. As late as 1860, Ira Aldridge was writing from Europe to his boyhood friend Dr. James McCune Smith of New York. Albro Lyons had an illuminating childhood experience. He was taught by the Reverend John Peterson (Garrison Association, NYASMR, Freemason, and Odd Fellow) in a Quaker School. Lyons went on to join Mutual Relief and his grandson, Henry ("Harry") Albro Williamson, became a grand officer and a leading historian of Prince Hall Masonry.[34]

The treacherous journey facing a black man who sought to climb the social ladder made community support imperative. When Charles Ray moved to the campus of Wesleyan College, white students protested to the administration and funded his return home. Thomas Jennings Jr. studied for years under a Boston dentist to establish himself in that profession. Bishop Onderdonk allowed Isaiah DeGrasse to attend classes at Manhattan's General Theological Seminary (Episcopal) but refused to permit him to live in the dormitory, apply for admission, or claim membership in the school. In an 1837 letter, Henry Highland Garnet gave Alexander Crummell a brief and prophetic account of DeGrasse's humiliation: "Mr. DeGrasse was stuck up in a corner to eat by himself in the Seminary, he has left, and takes private lessons." For a time, DeGrasse pastored Christ Episcopal Church in Providence, and he later established St. Matthew's Episcopal Church in Manhattan. John DeGrasse studied in the same African schools. In 1840, at age fifteen, he enrolled at Oneida Institute, and later at Clinton Seminary. He went to France and attended college for two years, returning to New York in 1845 to study medicine under Dr. Samuel Childs, supplementing that education by taking classes at Bowdoin College in Maine. Graduating in May 1849, DeGrasse again went to France and traveled throughout Europe working in hospitals. He returned to the United States in 1852 and established a practice in Boston. On August 24, 1854, John DeGrasse became the first black man admitted to the Massachusetts Medical Society. He also served as grand master of the Massachusetts Prince Hall Masons.[35]

James McCune Smith was for some time black Manhattan's foremost young scholar. "History, antiquity, bibliography, translation, criticism, political economy, statistics,—almost every department of knowledge,— receive emblazon from his able, ready, versatile, and unwearied pen," William Wells Brown wrote of his friend. Martin Delany estimated, "Dr. Smith is a man of no ordinary talents, and stands high as a scholar and a gentleman in the city, amidst the *literati* of a hundred seats of learning." In 1832, nineteen-year-old James Smith, a graduate of the African Free School who was rejected from Columbia University's medical school and the medical school at Geneva, New York, because of their racial proscriptions, left to study at the University of Glasgow, Scotland.[36]

In 1810 David Ruggles was born free in Norwich, Connecticut. He came to New York City at the age of seventeen and established a grocery. In 1833 he lectured to the Dorcas Society, and the following year he was serving on the Executive Committee of the Garrison Literary and Benevolent Association. Ruggles made his reputation in the Underground Railroad; secreting, according to one estimate, more than six hundred enslaved people to freedom. When he arrived in New York during his escape from enslavement in Maryland, Frederick Douglass was hurried to Ruggles. "He was a whole-souled man, fully imbued with a love of his afflicted and hunted people," wrote Douglass of his protector. Ruggles also arranged for the Reverend J. W. C. Pennington to preside at Douglass's marriage and then sent the couple to New Bedford, Massachusetts, where Douglass could gain employment and be out of danger. David Ruggles's early lectures encouraged the use of the press as an antislavery instrument. From 1833 to 1837, he worked as an agent for the *Emancipator* and apprenticed under Samuel Cornish, a Freemason and agent of the Phoenix Society. Ruggles then established his own paper, the public voice of the New York Vigilance Committee.[37]

Alexander Crummell was reared in black New York's institutional web. He entered Prince Hall Masonry and, later in his career, organized benevolent societies in Washington, D.C. His father was a leader of the NYASMR and his in-laws, the Elston family, were also prominent in

Mutual Relief and Masonry. Like other men of his generation, Crummell's scholarly pursuits were interrupted by the social obstacles of caste. His early education was under black and white instructors, and his spiritual guidance came from the Reverend Peter Williams Jr. He attended African School No. 2 with George Downing, James McCune Smith, and Isaiah and John DeGrasse. With Henry Highland Garnet, he enrolled in a school at Canaan, New Hampshire, established without race or gender limitations. The white townspeople were so opposed to the experiment in equality that Crummell and his friends feared for their lives. Crummell recalled that "the boys in our boarding house were molding bullets, expecting an attack upon our dwelling. About eleven o'clock at night the tramp of horses was heard approaching; and as one rapid rider passed the house he fired at it. Garnet quickly replied to it by a discharge from a double barrelled shotgun which blazed away through the window."[38]

In 1839 General Theological Seminary refused Crummell admission because of its color bar, citing Isaiah DeGrasse's application as precedent. Crummell received private tutoring under clergymen in Delaware. In 1842 Bishop Lee ordained Crummell. The new minister took an assignment in Providence, then, in 1846, journeyed to Philadelphia, where Bishop Onderdonk declared, "I cannot receive you into this Diocese unless you will promise, that you will never apply for a seat in my Convention, for yourself or for any church that you may raise in this city." Crummell rejected the conditions and left for England to raise money for the Church of the Messiah in New York. In 1851 he enrolled at Queens College, Cambridge University, graduating two years later. He ministered in Liberia for nineteen years, while remaining active in political issues in the United States and returning for brief visits to New York City. Maritcha Lyons, a child in Manhattan when Crummell was one of its leading figures, described him as a "man of princely bearing, of illustrious learning and matured experience." In 1872 Crummell settled in Washington, D.C., to pastor St. Luke's Episcopal Church.[39]

Samuel Ringgold Ward, a fugitive from bondage, also found refuge in the institutional world of black Manhattan. In the summer of 1837, Ward delivered a speech to the Phoenix Literary Society, in which he was a member, before an audience that included the white abolitionist Lewis Tappan. According to a contemporary, Ward was "'the ablest thinker on his legs' which Anglo-Africa has produced, whose powerful eloquence, brilliant repartee, and stubborn logic are as well known in England as in the United States." His parents escaped from bondage in Maryland, carrying the little boy to freedom. They first moved to New Jersey and lived among Quakers, and later settled in Manhattan. Their young son was educated in Manhattan's African schools and societies. In 1833 Thomas Jennings of the NYASMR put the young man to work as a clerk, and he later worked for David Ruggles.[40]

After deciding to pursue the ministry, he was sent to replace J. W. C. Pennington as teacher of the African school at New Town, Long Island. He followed his 1837 maiden speech with an address at the Broadway Tabernacle. The latter appearance led to the formation of a new African literary society with Ward as founder. He was married in 1838. A year later, Ward was licensed to preach and spent the next two years as an agent of the American and New York Anti-Slavery Societies. Traveling through Western New York lecturing against bondage, he was invited to dine with some leading men of Butler Township. After delivering a sermon, he was offered the pulpit of the Congregationalist Church in South Butler, New York. "The Church and congregation were all white persons save my own family," wrote Ward of the courage displayed "in calling and sustaining and honouring as their pastor a black man, in that day, in spite of the too general Negro-hate everywhere rife."[41]

Ward decided to take charge of the church, fully aware that his performance would either discredit or bolster caste and bondage but equally determined to reward the virtue of the parishioners: "They heard a preacher: they supposed and believed that he preached God's truth. That was what they wanted, and all they wanted. The mere accident of the *colour* of the preacher was to them a matter of small consideration." Ward served Butler for two years, leaving because of illness. He later ministered in Geneva, New York, worked for the Liberty party, and edited two newspapers in Syracuse. In October 1851 Samuel Ringgold Ward emigrated to Montreal, Canada, fleeing the United States because of its domination by slaveholders and the man-stealing that erupted after the passage of the Fugitive Slave Act.[42]

An equally incredible journey brought Henry Highland Garnet to the ministry of an African church in Troy, New York. He was one of the exceptional students in Manhattan's African schools, but his life had been far less fortunate than his peers' lives. The Trusty family escaped from New Market, Kent County, Maryland, in league with their relatives, Samuel Ringgold Ward's parents. They left with their owner's permission to attend a funeral but never returned. "Henry's father, mother, sister, and seven others, including himself, composed this company," McCune Smith wrote. "For several days they slept in the woods and swamps, traveling all night long." The duty of carrying the nine-year-old boy was shared by his father and uncles. Arriving in Delaware, they were aided by a Quaker, Thomas Garret. From there they split up, with the Wards going to New Jersey while the Trustys went to Pennsylvania and later to New York.[43]

In Manhattan the family received their new names. The father presided over the "baptism to Liberty" by informing his wife that she would no longer be called Henrietta but Elizabeth. His daughter was no longer Mary but Eliza. With his young son sitting atop his knee, he declared, "Your name is Henry." "My name is George Garnet."[44]

Henry Garnet went to sea at age thirteen to spend a year as a cabin boy rather than burden his family with his upkeep and education. He returned to Manhattan to find that his family had almost been captured by slave hunters. His mother was jailed for a while but released when she convinced authorities that she was falsely accused. The family's possessions were destroyed. Henry Garnet, now fourteen, was enraged. He bought a "large clasp-knife, openly carried it in his hand and sturdily marched up Broadway, waiting and hoping for the assault of the men-hunters." To relieve his family's plight, Garnet indentured himself to a Long Island Quaker for two years. After an injury to his leg, which was later amputated, he returned to his family in New York. He attended the Canal Street School, began lecturing at Phoenix and became a founder and officer of the Garrison Association. By the age of nineteen, he was studying at Oneida Institute. He was initiated into Freemasonry in Manhattan, and in the summer of 1837 he helped found the Colored Young Men, an organization of Manhattan youths determined to defend the civil rights of free black people. In 1840, three years before his ordination, Garnet was called to pastor Troy's new Liberty Street Presbyterian Church.[45]

William Hamilton, a founder and the first president of the NYASMR, was the primary architect of the institutions through which these young men passed. Hamilton was arguably the most important public figure in antebellum black Manhattan. In the first edition of the *Weekly Advocate*, the editors informed its readers: "Departed this Life, on Friday the 9th of December [1836], Mr. WILLIAM HAMILTON, Sen. in the 63rd year of his age. In recording the death of Mr. Hamilton, we are aware that we allude to no common man. He was one of sterling virtue and truth, and all his dealings thro' life were marked by a strict adherence to truth and justice." Governed by future NYASMR member Timothy Seaman, the Philomathean Literary Society marked the influence that Hamilton exercised over two generations of black Manhattanites. At a Philomathean meeting held shortly after Hamilton's death, Mutual Relief's John Peterson issued a resolution that was seconded by Philip Bell:

> Whereas it has pleased the Great Disposer of Events, in his all-wise Providence, to remove from this state of existence, Mr. WILLIAM HAMILTON, Sen. and whereas the deceased was a man of correct and upright deportment, a cultivated mind, of a sound and discriminating judgment, and also an active and efficient member of our Benevolent and Literary Societies, and of every other institution, whose object was the moral, and intellectual elevation of our people, therefore be it Resolved, That the Philomathean Society, of which the deceased was an Honorary Member, do deeply sympathize with the family and friends of the deceased, and with the community at large, in consequence of the loss which they have sustained in the death of this excellent man.
>
> Resolved, That as a token of respect for the virtues of the deceased, we will wear the usual badge of mourning for the space of 60 days at all meetings of the Society.
>
> Resolved, That the Scribe be instructed to address to the family a letter of condolence, accompanied with a copy of these Resolutions[.]
>
> Resolved, That the above Resolutions be published in the Weekly Advocate.
>
> TIMOTHY SEAMAN, Prefect.
WILLIAM BRADY, Scribe.[46]

Almost a year later, on September 27, 1837, Hamilton was still being saluted when a large audience assembled in the lecture room of the Broadway Tabernacle to welcome James McCune Smith, M.D., from his studies at the University of Glasgow. In five years Smith earned the bachelor's, master's, and doctor of medicine degrees. Mutual Relief's John J. Zuille, Dr. John Brown, and John Peterson (the latter two were also in the Garrison Association and were officers of the Boyer Masonic Lodge) served as vice presidents of the meeting. Daniel J. Elston (NYASMR) and Charles Reason (Freemason) were the secretaries. Ransom F. Wake (Freemason) presided, and declared that "we have assembled to celebrate a proud and signal triumph over this foul and hideous slavery-begotten monster, which the American people are cherishing in their bosoms." Wake detailed the honoree's early educational accomplishments and his academic blossoming in Europe after he left his mother and friends in the summer of 1832. Dr. James McCune Smith entered the room to thunderous applause. Smith took the podium and thanked his audience and hosts for their kindness. He was pleased to be "once more upon my native soil, once more in my native city, and amid those scenes which are endeared to me by the thousand happy recollections of boyhood and of youth." He extended thanks to the University of Glasgow and the people of Scotland "amongst whom I went a young and friendless exile, by whom I was received and treated as a brother and an equal." He then turned to the state of affairs in Manhattan, and, by necessity, to the death of William Hamilton Sr., the quintessential social man:

> There is a great man fallen in Israel—William Hamilton is no more! The kind father, the benevolent man, the able and profound reasoner, the sterling patriot, who had at heart the good of the whole country, and who obtained and richly merited the title of a patriarch among the people, has passed away from the earth. And whilst I would sympathize with you for his loss, I would also impress upon you the necessity of following the example which he set during life.[47]

Upon returning to New York, Smith established a medical practice and a pharmacy at 55 West Broadway in Manhattan but was refused membership in the New York Academy of Medicine. "The store had a backroom which became historical," recalled Smith's goddaughter. In the rear of the pharmacy was an impressive library where he hosted "discussions and debates on all the topics of the day," which were informal but well attended. In 1841 Dr. Smith joined the New York African Society for Mutual Relief. His shop operated as a training ground for black pharmacists and physicians, including doctors Peter W. Ray, Philip A. White, and George Philips. Ray attended Bowdoin College and the Vermont Medical College. He had a pharmacy in Williamsburg for fifty years and was a Brooklyn College of Pharmacy founder, a Prince Hall Mason, and the first black man admitted to the Kings County Medical Society. White, an initiate of the Garrison Association and Smith's brother in Odd Fellowship, ran a pharmacy in lower Manhattan and lived in Brooklyn. He later served on the Brooklyn Board of Education. McCune Smith was also physician to the New York Colored Orphan Asylum.[48]

The socialization offered by Manhattan's African societies deserves attention, for there were other bases upon which an appeal for equality could be made. Charleston also saw the rise of major benevolent societies among the men of color, but an examination offers a strikingly different account of their impact. In Charleston, class divisions figured prominently in shaping non-white communities. Foremost among the South

Carolina associations was the Brown Fellowship Society, established on November 1, 1790. The Brown Fellowship comprised wealthy men of mixed ancestry, most of whom were also masters. On the eve of the Civil War, the members owned thirty-six people, a sharp decline from earlier years. A fifty dollar initiation fee further curtailed intake. The Fellowship had its own cemetery on Pitt Street in Charleston, offered a rich package of benefits, and, at the close of the Civil War, its members established two local churches. The Humane Brotherhood, organized on June 19, 1843, was a poor cousin to the BFS. Fewer of its members were slave owners, the initiation cost was lower, the benefits more slight, and the average member was significantly less wealthy than his Fellowship counterpart. The Brotherhood owned a Pitt Street cemetery adjacent to that of the Brown Fellowship.[49]

In New York, black communities achieved relative unity by promoting social manhood. Manhood was an expression of collectivism, and it was regulated by a battery of voluntary associations. Men evolved in society, a term that referred to a spiritual community of personally interdependent and emotionally attached people. It implied a common fate and a singular purpose. It suggested something familial. The Reverend Samuel Ringgold Ward succinctly captured the connotations while describing his family's flight from slavery. Fearing the possibility of being sold apart, his mother convinced his father that they had to escape bondage. They bolted for freedom carrying their three-year-old son. "Upon this rescue," wrote Ward, "depended their continued enjoyment of each other's *society*."[50]

7

"A Single Voice"

African Societies, the Press, and the Public Sphere, 1827–1861

Have the sons of Africa no souls? feel they no ambitious desires? shall the chains of ignorance forever confine them? shall the insipid appellation of "clever negroes," or "good creature," any longer content them? Where can we find amongst ourselves the man of science, or a philosopher, or an able statesman, or a counsellor at law? Show me our fearless and brave, our noble and gallant ones. Where are our lecturers on natural history, and our critics in useful knowledge? There may be a few such men amongst us, but they are rare.

But give the man of color an equal opportunity with the white, from the cradle to manhood, and from manhood to the grave, and you would discover the dignified statesman, the man of science, and the philosopher.

But there is no such opportunity for the sons of Africa. . . . O ye sons of Africa, when will your voices be heard in our legislative halls, in defiance of your enemies, contending for equal rights and liberty?
—Maria W. Stewart, February 27, 1833 (quoted in
The Liberator, April 27, 1833)

"Added to poverty," Samuel Ringgold Ward wrote of New York, "in the case of a black lad in that city, is the ever-present, ever-crushing Negro-hate, which hedges up his path, discourages his efforts, damps his ardour, blasts his hopes, and embitters his spirit." "I am quite popular among the people," quipped Henry Highland Garnet, "and were I not so well acquainted with the comity of the world there would be some danger of [my] being ruffed up." The two cousins knew that black New Yorkers were not going to physically overwhelm their oppressors.

Ideas and words were the most potent weapons they had to combat racial injustice in the antebellum city. Confronting a tide of animosity and social censure, black Manhattanites brought their message to antislavery theaters across the nation and in Europe and the Caribbean. The history of black newspapers begins in Manhattan. Black New Yorkers' reliance upon the press to focus attention on the civil liberties of people of color distinguished them from other free black communities.[1] A handful of young editors were among that generation of black people who preached human rights to an international audience. Black Manhattan's earliest editors were men who trained as lecturers, writers, and leaders in the African voluntary associations of New York.

From July 7 to 12, 1834, white mobs roamed the streets of Manhattan looking to break up gatherings of black people. The trouble began on the evening of the Fourth of July, when a white horde interrupted black parishioners at the Chatham Street Chapel. Three days later, white toughs again attacked Chatham to disrupt a prayer meeting and lecture. This time Thomas Jennings floored the leader who took a quick retreat through a window, injuring himself further. The mob later returned with reinforcements. When the police arrived, they arrested the black men. "For the crime of being publicly assaulted by several white persons, I was locked up in the watchhouse throughout the night. Shortly after my imprisonment, four others were brought into the same cell by the officers of peace and justice, for the same crime," Ward wrote caustically. "My oath of allegiance to the antislavery cause was taken in that cell on the 7th of July, 1834."[2]

On the tenth, a gang robbed and burned the home of the white abolitionist Lewis Tappan. The following night a rabble invaded St. Philip's Church. The houses of black families on Mulberry Street were ravished along with the colored school. "About twenty poor African (native American) families, have had their all destroyed, and have neither bed, clothing, nor food remaining. Their houses are completely eviscerated, their furniture a wreck, and the ruined and disconsolate tenants of the devoted houses are reduced to the necessity of applying to the corporation for bread," read a New York periodical.[3]

On the twelfth, New York Episcopal bishop Benjamin T. Onderdonk punished the Reverend Peter Williams Jr. of St. Philip's for the violence. "In a move to preserve religious unity and eradicate any disruptive influences, New York Episcopal authorities attempted to silence antislavery agitation by Negro ministers," contends Leon Litwack. Assuring Williams of the "sincere sympathy which I feel for you and your people," the bishop nonetheless moved to strike the stain of antislavery radicalism from his houses of worship. By his own account, Williams was not the most radical figure in the American Anti-Slavery Society (AAS). The Reverends Theodore S. Wright and Samuel Cornish, Philip Bell, Thomas Van Rensselaer, and Bishop Christopher Rush were officers, and Dr. James McCune Smith was auditor. "It was my anxiety to promote the object of the Ph[o]enix Society, which is the improvement of the people of color in this city, in morals, literature, and the mechanic arts, that brought me to an acquaintance with the members of the Anti-Slavery Society," explained Williams, who was still unsure if St. Philip's would reopen. Williams claimed to be a conservative force in the AAS. Having already segregated his seminaries, Onderdonk forced the pastor of St. Philip's Church to abandon his public support of antislavery. "Let me advise you to resign, at once, your connexion, in every department, with the Anti-Slavery Society, and to make public your resignation," the prelate instructed. Williams obliged in a lengthy public letter in which he recounted the heroism of his father and his own work to improve black Manhattan in order to ensure that his departure from the AAS not be misread as an endorsement of colonization.[4] Williams walked a fine line in accepting the bishop's mandate while subtly questioning its logic and offering his brethren the humble apologies of a minister protecting his parish.

Like this exercise of church authority, many white people who claimed to champion the Negroes' cause were odious. In 1845, former New York City mayor James Harper took the presidency of the new African Education and Civilization Society, founded with a membership of elite men, including politicians and ministers, from across the nation. The AECS declared its goal to "educate Young Persons of Color as Teachers, to go to Africa, and devote their time to the Instruction of the Natives in the Arts and Sciences, and in disseminating the principles of Civil and Religious Liberty" to "ameliorate the condition of that long neglected and degraded people." The white African society published its contempt for people of color in its organizing document. "Africa, the great fountain-head of the Vice, Ignorance and Oppression which we deplore, remains unreclaimed, a vast tide of evil will perpetually roll its desolating influences over the millions of her unfortunate Sons," stated the preamble. To repay African Americans for their "unrequited [*sic*] labor," the AECS planned to build a seminary for the instruction of people of color who agreed "to make Africa their permanent home."[5] They thus solved two problems by evangelizing Africa while liberating themselves from the problem of free Negroes.

The press served racists equally well. In 1850 a white oysterman used a white newspaper to attack the African Society for Mutual Relief's Thomas Downing, an oyster dealer, owner of a popular Manhattan restaurant, and one of the wealthier black men in the city. John Smith wrote to complain about Downing and, unintentionally, confessed his own shortcomings. "There is a colored man by the name of Downing, who keeps an oyster cellar in Broad street, which is daily frequented by hundreds of merchants, both of this city and from the South," Smith snarled. "Downing has become wealthy from the patronage thus bestowed." There were other black men dealing in oysters. Smith accused Downing of being "a notorious abolitionist" and all the black dealers held "the same heinous and destructive sentiments." Smith soon revealed his intent: if the black oystermen were restricted, "I think I might get my stock off my hands, and soon afford to supply a fresh article on moderate terms, and, at the same time, receive a just reward for my devotion to the Constitution."[6]

New York City's white press took part in physically curtailing the free speech of black people, and these violent assaults spread to white abolitionists as their movement gained strength. City editors encouraged mobs by publishing the locations and schedules of meetings that attracted their disapproval. A telling example came in 1850 when the *New York Herald* lathered up its readers for the anniversary of the American Anti-Slavery Society. It charged abolitionists with inciting slave revolts and ran stories of savage Negroes raping white women. The black man became "wild, crude, a cannibal, stupid, and but one remove from the ourang outang, and but two from the little monkeys of the forests." He was "brutal, beastly, barbarous, ferocious, and possessing every vice without one virtue," the article continued. Careful instructions about the time and place of the meetings were given: "They commence tomorrow morning, at the Tabernacle; on Wednesday and Thursday they are to be continued at the New-York Society Library Rooms, No. 318 Broadway." The editor insisted that white men respond:

> Now is the time for New York to express an opinion in favor of the Union and the constitution. Let our whole population turn out, and declare their devotion to that instrument. Let the merchant, whose fortunes are interwoven with the South, leave his counting-room or his store, and go forth in support of his rights. Let the mechanic, the laborer, and every honest citizen who values the honor of the city and the safety of his race, leave his work for one or two days, and devote them to his country, to humanity, and the safety of his fellow man in another section.

The suggestion that the "manly" rebuttal might also be expressed "peaceably" was impotent.[7] The meetings were violently disrupted.

For these and other reasons, a generation of black Americans took the antislavery message beyond the United States in an attempt to find a sympathetic audience and to try slavery in the larger court of world opinion. From 1830 to the eve of the Civil War, argues R. J. M. Blackett, these Americans "developed a well-oiled and pretty efficient propaganda machine" aimed at turning European public opinion against American bondage. African Americans raised money in Europe to support various organizations from churches to the New York Committee of Vigilance. They destroyed the possibility of a union of American and English colonizationists, and they were central in convincing British churches to isolate and refuse fellowship with proslavery American churches. At various points in time, the struggle included New Yorkers like the Reverend J. W. C. Pennington, African society members William Powell, Peter Williams Jr., and Henry Highland Garnet, and Prince Hall's Alexander Crummell. However, it was the 1832 arrival of young James McCune Smith in Scotland that launched the growing international popularity of the narratives of enslaved Africans, a global debate on bondage, and the unprecedented rise of Frederick Douglass.[8]

In 1836 James McCune Smith was on the managerial committee of the newly formed Glasgow Emancipation Society. At their second annual meeting, Smith spoke forcefully against seven-year apprenticeships as an alternative to immediate emancipation. The Glasgow Society passed resolutions declaring slavery to be antithetical to the teachings of Jesus Christ, appointing American abolitionists George Thompson, William Lloyd Garrison, and Arthur Tappan honorary and corresponding members, and condemning prejudice against color.[9]

A decade after McCune Smith's return to the United States, Douglass stormed across Scotland. He damned as immoral the connection between the international Christian church and the slaveholders of the southern United States, pilloried the use of the law to bolster slavery, blasted the silence of the masses on the issue of human bondage, and delivered forceful firsthand accounts of the slave's lot in America and slavery's impact on the larger national psychology and morality. He also challenged the people of Scotland to separate themselves and their churches from the Slave Power and "send slavery reeling towards its grave as if struck by a bolt from heaven."[10]

From 1848 to 1851, the Reverend Alexander Crummell evangelized

Peter Williams (1815), one of the founders of the African Methodist Episcopal Zion Church in New York in the late eighteenth century, purchased his freedom from trustees of the John Street Methodist Episcopal Church, where he was a sexton for many years. Artist unknown. Courtesy of the Schomburg Center for Research in Black Culture, New York Public Library.

James Varick, first bishop of the African Methodist Episcopal Zion Church. No date, artist unknown. Courtesy of the Schomburg Center for Research in Black Culture, New York Public Library.

The Reverend William Miller. Courtesy of the Library Company of Philadelphia.

Reverend Christopher Rush, 1840. Courtesy of the Library of Congress.

Portrait of James McCune Smith. No date, artist unknown. Courtesy of the Schomburg Center for Research in Black Culture, New York Public Library.

Philip A. Bell, founder of the *Colored American,* the second black newspaper in the United States, in 1837. Artist unknown. Courtesy of the Schomburg Center for Research in Black Culture, New York Public Library.

Reverend Samuel Cornish, pastor of the first African Presbyterian Church in the city of New York. No date, painted by J. Paradise, engraved by F. Kearny. Courtesy of the Schomburg Center for Research in Black Culture, New York Public Library.

Drawing of George Thomas Downing. No date, artist unknown. Courtesy of the Schomburg Center for Research in Black Culture, New York Public Library.

Portrait of Samuel Ringgold Ward. No date, artist unknown. Courtesy of the Schomburg Center for Research in Black Culture, New York Public Library.

Reverend Henry Highland
Garnet. Courtesy of the
Library of Congress.

Portrait of Albro Lyons Sr., ca.
1880s. Photographer: Douglass, Brooklyn, L.I. Courtesy
of the Schomburg Center for
Research in Black Culture,
New York Public Library.

Portrait of Henry (Harry) Albro Williamson. No date, photographer unknown. Courtesy of the Schomburg Center for Research in Black Culture, New York Public Library.

Dedication service at the original site of Mother Zion Church, April 6, 1969. Courtesy of the Schomburg Center for Research in Black Culture, New York Public Library.

England to raise funds to build a permanent home for the Church of the Messiah P. E. in Manhattan. Originally named St. Matthew's, the church was founded by John Peterson under the pastorate of John DeGrasse. Crummell inherited the project after DeGrasse tired of racial animosity in the United States and left for the Caribbean. Bearing letters of introduction from American bishops and a Cambridge degree, Crummell was quite successful. He collected two thousand pounds for the effort. Part of his success came from his characterization of the problem: Messiah could not raise funds in the United States because there racial hatred and injustice retarded Christianity, and only through a moral revolution led by Africans could it recover. Crummell appealed to England through a restatement of the moral reform philosophy that he learned in black Manhattan. As one newspaper captured it:

> Notwithstanding some of the singularly excellent features of American Christianity, and some of the peculiar phases of American character, yet, unfortunately, the Christianity of his country lacked the great element of humanity. It needed a stronger presence of the idea of brotherhood. It was his firm conviction that this same African race, despised and scorned of men— they, and they alone, could furnish this needed element to the religion and civilization of that country. They both would remain unhealthy and incomplete, until the negro race were raised up and received as brethren.[11]

While Smith, Crummell, Douglass, and others lobbied Europe, black New Yorkers fashioned the local opposition press. Black Manhattan's antebellum newspapers were anticolonization, although they published debates on the subject; dedicated great space to the civil rights of free people of color; carried regular reports on conditions and events in Haiti; served as platforms for the antislavery message; and were the most consistent proponents of the moral reform ideology.

Manhattan was the birthplace of black journalism, and young men trained in local societies managed that rise. In 1827 John B. Russwurm, the first black person to graduate from an American college, and the Reverend Samuel B. Cornish, of the Phoenix Literary Society, founded *Freedom's Journal*, the nation's first black newspaper, in the home of NYASMR's Boston Crummell at 139 Leonard Street. Mutual Relief's Thomas Jennings was chair and Peter Williams Jr. was secretary of the group of stockholders who financed the venture. "Daily slandered, we think that there ought to be some channel of communication between us and the public; through which a single voice may be heard in defense of *five hundred thousand free people of colour*," declared the editors. Because of James Varick's interest in its success, *Freedom's Journal* was published for at least a year out of Mother Zion at 152 Church Street. The radical David Walker (Cornish's brother in Prince Hall Masonry) became agent for the *Journal* in Boston and even contributed articles to the paper.[12]

Two years later, Cornish began the *Rights of All*, an ephemeral anticolonization paper. The NYASMR's Philip A. Bell published the short-lived *Struggler*. In 1837 Bell established the *Weekly Advocate*, renamed the *Colored American*, for which John J. Zuille was printer. In his first issue, Bell pledged to advocate Christianity, anticolonization, temperance, universal suffrage, universal education, the rights of free people of color, and immediate emancipation. He included a special note to "Females of Colour" urging that they use their strengths for the good of the community. Fiscal trouble brought the paper under the control of a committee chaired by Thomas Jennings. Charles B. Ray replaced Bell, and Dr. John Brown of the NYASMR later edited the paper. Ray appointed Alexander Crummell agent for New York and the eastern states.[13]

The journalistic tradition broadened. From 1837 to 1842, Bell and Cornish edited the *Colored Man's Journal*. While working as an agent for the *Emancipator*, young David Ruggles, of the Garrison Literary and Benevolent Association, stridently promoted the press as a tool for mass education and communication. Between 1837 and 1841, he published the *Mirror of Liberty* for the New York Vigilance Committee, and then edited the *Genius of Freedom*. Mutual Relief's Dr. James McCune Smith united with the Reverend J. W. C. Pennington to publish a periodical from Hartford and New York. The Reverend Samuel Ringgold Ward, of the Phoenix Society, edited the *Impartial Citizen* from Boston. In 1852 Ward and Pennington joined with William H. Day to publish the *Alienated American* out of Cleveland, Ohio. While ministering and teaching in Troy, Henry Highland Garnet, Ruggles's brother in the Garrison Association, assisted the publisher of the *National Watchman* and then edited the *Clarion*. William Hamilton's son, Thomas, was co-editor of Troy's *People's Press*. On the eve of the Civil War, Thomas Hamilton was publishing the nation's first black magazine, the *Weekly Anglo-African*, with the goal "to present a clear and concise statement of the present condition, the past history, and the prospects of the colored population of the United States, free and enslaved." Early in 1861 George Lawrence Jr., son of a NYASMR member, assumed control of the *Anglo-African*, and Robert Hamilton edited the magazine during the Civil War. Thomas Hamilton edited the

People's Press and continued publishing and distributing books, as did printer and teacher John J. Zuille, whose business also served as publishing house for the local African societies.[14]

The advent of the black press, like that of the black church, profoundly questioned white people's moral authority to speak on issues of racial justice. It was not just a defensive reaction to the open hostility of Manhattan papers. Through a separate press, black men sought to critique their whole society. The very act of starting their own papers redefined the other New York City media as a white press, expressing the opinions of their white constituents, and publishing in the interests of white people. Four years after the founding of *Freedom's Journal*, white laboring-class New Yorkers responded to a similar political necessity when they voted to establish "a press that will advocate the principles of the mechanics & workingmen."[15] Black papers broke open the public dialogue on race and answered the numerous charges against the community.

That they saw themselves as an opposition press, not a race press, can be seen in the fact that, although black Manhattan already had its own local newspaper, it celebrated the establishment of *The Liberator*. In February 1831, a month after William Lloyd Garrison launched the antislavery tract, New York's African community met in the Boyer Lodge room to build support for the Boston journal. Peter Vogelsang and Thomas Jennings of the NYASMR served as chair and secretary of the meeting, respectively. Mutual Relief's Philip Bell was New York City's agent to *The Liberator* with the tasks of soliciting subscribers and distributing the paper. That summer, "the young men of color of the city of New-York" were plotting ways to increase readership of *The Liberator* and the *Genius of Universal Emancipation* among black New Yorkers. Garrison noted the key support of African Americans in sustaining the paper in its early years. Black subscribers outnumbered white and were more faithful in paying their bills. In 1832 Peter Williams, William Hamilton, Thomas Sipkins, and Thomas Jennings also helped Garrison publish his *Thoughts on African Colonization*.[16]

The opposition press brought an honesty to the public discussion of slavery that earlier African church sermons and lectures had captured. It focused public attention on the emotional and physical brutality of bondage. Not allowing slavery to be described as an economic system similar to others and fostering similar relations, black journalists defined and publicized the system by its inhumane features and its results. An 1827 article in *Freedom's Journal* captured the torture of enslaved Africa:

"He sees the mother of his children stripped naked before the gang of male negroes and flogged unmercifully; he sees his children sent to market to be sold at the best price they will fetch; he sees himself, not a man, but a *thing*."[17] While typically man-centered, the editorial was still a powerful critique of servitude.

It was through the black press that Dr. James McCune Smith offered essays and articles on abolition and the condition of enslaved and free black people. Smith chose the pseudonym "Communipaw"—or the "commune of Pauw," the vast land holdings of Michael Pauw, one of New Netherland's patroons. The pen name was not a simple geographical allusion for Smith. His fellow Manhattanites, black and white, understood the sarcasm of the selection. In 1808 Washington Irving published his popular *Diedrich Knickerbocker's A History of New York*, which was in circulation throughout Smith's childhood. Knickerbocker, the fictional author, uses Communipaw to satirize old Dutch New Netherland and its ways. Of particular importance is his description of "the Dutch negroes at Communipaw, who, like most other negroes, are famous for their risible powers." As the story unfolds, the reader encounters the Dutch as lazy, stubborn, and *niggardly* and the Africans ruling over the village. "These negroes, in fact, like the monks in the dark ages, engross all the knowledge of the place, and being infinitely more adventurous and more knowing than their masters, carry on all the foreign trade." The author reports that the enslaved transport the goods to market, predict the weather, display prowess on the fiddle, and control the animals with a lexicon of whistles. "And from their amazing skill at casting up accounts upon their fingers, they are regarded with as much veneration as were the disciples of Pythagoras of yore, when initiated into the sacred quaternary of numbers," he concluded.[18] Thus, Dr. Smith signed his more political and piercing public writings with a literary prod that few New Yorkers would have missed.

McCune Smith was also one of a few men who publicly discussed the violent eradication of slavery. In February 1841 he delivered a speech on Toussaint L'Overture to benefit the Colored Orphan Asylum. Borrowing on all of the ideological and stylistic developments of the early society founders, Smith presented a subject that continued to divide white and black New Yorkers. Viewing Haiti as the culmination of God's plan for African freedom, black New Yorkers celebrated the Revolution and its conductor. White New Yorkers viewed it as a horrific example of barbarity and an unacceptable precedent against property. Dismissing the con-

cerns of those who opposed the Revolution, Smith reminded his audience that the army of once-enslaved Africans whom L'Overture eventually brought against the French had been converted "into industrious laborers, by the simple expedient of *paying them for their labor.*" Haiti became proof that the African people were destined to liberty, and white
New Yorkers' insistence that the island was worse off became evidence of
their willingness to contort reality to defend bondage in their own nation. Thinking of slavery in the United States, Smith warned that "these
revolutions constitute an epoch worthy of the anxious study of every
American citizen."[19]

In the spring of 1851, McCune Smith compiled and published an ex-
haustive study of Manhattan's free people of color for the Committee on
the Social Condition of the Colored Race. He presented the findings at
Bethel Church following a convention of clergymen who had met to discuss the Fugitive Slave Act. The assembly continued over several days, and
the citizens of Brooklyn and Williamsburg were invited. The benefit of
urbanization, the report began, was in the density of the black population
and the resultant ease of communication and organizing. The city also allowed for a concentration of educational resources. Yet the disadvantages
of urban life were numerous; "City life is, after all, a kind of hot-house
forcing of human beings," the report continued. Mortality exaggerated
the number of widows and orphans in the local population. The deaths
of husbands and fathers stretched the resources of the community: "Our
benevolent societies have been obliged to cut off the widows and orphans, in order to help the sick." The city was also a cauldron of temptation. Vice houses offering cards, gambling, billiards, and liquor were a
particularly urban problem. And, while "women hastening through the
streets with their bonnets untied" does not seem to be the great moral
lapse that the report contended, half-dressed men standing on corners or
"gutter-tumbling" were worth addressing. In the city it was easier for
white workers to exclude men of color from the mechanical trades, while
black craftsmen had not the capital or plant to hire apprentices and jour-
neymen. Limiting black men to menial employment debased their manhood. The effects of capitalism were to "grind the face of the poor in the
cities, and render them more and more the slaves of lower wages and
higher rents." In early 1859, McCune Smith published detailed articles in
the *Anglo-African Magazine* on the growth of the German immigrant
population and its impact on African American labor and life.[20]

The scope of his work mirrored the expansive social agenda that the local societies had assumed, and the prescriptions were a bold application of the collectivist style. It called for the establishment of a "Colored Savings Institution" to allow the black community to purchase tenements and regulate rents through competition. After paying depositors 6 percent on their accounts, the surplus could provide business, home, and farm loans. The urgency of such an act was shown in the report's conclusion that the 2,500 black families of Manhattan paid a combined $25,000 rent above market price. Those families could save $20,000 on groceries and $10,000 on apparel. The report brought collectivism to business through "the establishment of a mutual bank, in which all the depositors should be, at the same time, stockholders, and which should have power to buy and sell real estate, to discount paper, to lend money on bond and mortgage, and to deal merchandise." The attendees passed resolutions for a savings and loan association and a protective labor union.[21] While the proposal was sweeping, it was also well thought out. Smith had immediate access to the NYASMR's successful experiences in real estate, the rental market, and mortgaging. Through its businessmen members, he had accurate information about clothing, fuel, and food suppliers, prices, and consumption in Manhattan.

Smith offered a telling account of the African struggle in the introduction to Frederick Douglass's autobiography, *My Bondage and My Freedom* (1855). "I cannot resist the belief," he wrote of Douglass, "that the boy who learned to read and write as he did, who taught his fellow slaves these precious acquirements as he did, who plotted their mutual escape as he did, would, when a man at bay, strike a blow which would make slavery reel and stagger." He provided a lengthy salute to Douglass's career, but perhaps his greatest compliment was that this was the book that he would hand to his own son. "It is an American book, for Americans, in the fullest sense of the idea," he concluded.[22]

He was joined by a number of talented writers. Bell and the other editors of the *Colored American* focused on the fight for universal manhood suffrage. Mocking the very phrase "free man of colour," Bell countered that "no man of colour, be his talents, be his respectability, be his worth, or be his wealth what they may, enjoys, in any sense, the rights of a freeman." In support of that comment, Ray examined the cowardice of the Constitutional Convention of 1822, which stripped the right to vote from free black men in New York State by imposing a $250 property qualification on them alone. What was clear was that the rights of some men had been enlarged at the expense of others.[23]

Thomas and Robert Hamilton had long careers as journalists and print-ers in the city, publishing local periodicals for the black community and major works in African American and antislavery history. They were regu-lars at the National Colored Conventions. They participated in the city's an-tislavery societies and were fierce advocates of the rights of free black peo-ple. In 1859 Thomas Hamilton brought all those interests together in the *Anglo-African*. Robert Hamilton and Henry Highland Garnet followed him as editors. William J. Wilson—the Brooklyn schoolteacher and the newspa-per correspondent "Ethiop"—wrote the editorials.[24]

Robert Hamilton used the *Anglo-African* to publicize the role that Af-rican Americans played in the struggle against slavery. "No matter what may be urged by his foes—foes to the country—the advance of the black man is as much indebted to his own positive progress as to anything else," read a Hamilton editorial. The editor paid tribute to black people's long contest for liberty by attaching the limited label "Anti-Pro-Slavery-Party" to the Republicans. William Powell sent letters of encouragement and support to his antislavery friends in New York and New England. To the abolitionists, he wrote: "In our humble opinion, after thirty years of anti-slavery experience, we have proved to the world that the cause of vital Christianity and humanity is indebted to that noble band of men and women for their unswerving devotion to the truths contained in that blessed book." Proslavery men had many weapons, but "we have God, the slave, and his flaming two-edged sword of truth—the Bible—on our side." George Downing was including an interesting rider in his letters: "Yours, for the freedom for which Attucks died."[25]

In 1858 Philip Bell, now fifty years old, migrated to San Francisco, where he founded and edited the *Pacific Appeal* and the *Elevator*. Although schol-ars of eastern cities reacted to Bell's departure with disinterest, writes one California historian, his activities on the West Coast solidified his posi-tion as "the most talented Negro journalist in the United States in the nine-teenth century." Bell remained active in the black churches and fraternities, assisted fugitive slaves, and used his role as publisher to provide assistance, especially information on jobs and housing, for black migrants to Califor-nia. When he died in 1889, Bell had engineered an unmatched journalistic career.[26]

Black New Yorkers enhanced a tradition of intellectual activism as they exploited the new international arenas and the weapon of the press.

8

When Black Men Spoke of Freedom

Voluntary Associations and Nationalist Culture, 1809–1865

> You act as though you were made for the special use of these devils. You act as though your daughters were born to pamper the lusts of your masters and overseers. And worse than all, you tamely submit, while your lords tear your wives from your embraces, and defile them before your eyes. In the name of God we ask, are you men? Where is the blood of your fathers? Has it all run out of your veins? Awake, awake; millions of voices are calling you! Your dead fathers speak to you from their graves. Heaven, as with a voice of thunder, calls on you to arise from the dust.
>
> Let your motto be RESISTANCE! RESISTANCE! RESISTANCE!
>
> —Rev. Henry Highland Garnet, *An Address to the Slaves of the United States of America* (1843)

By the 1780s, black New Yorkers had established a separate institutional culture grounded in spiritualism and mutualism. However, the first decade of the nineteenth century presented the black community with the possibility of assimilating into the larger society. The free black population was increasing, free people of color awaited some civil liberty, the slave trade had come to an official end, and African churches had denominational affiliations with white Christianity. There was a manifest logic to fighting for full inclusion. In 1808 a group of black men founded the New York African Society for Mutual Relief despite this evidence of "progress."

In *Slave Culture*, Sterling Stuckey marks William Hamilton's leadership in the organizing of the NYASMR as an important moment in black nationalist history. At a time when the status of black New Yorkers was "fluid," Hamilton challenged the black community to sustain indepen-

dent institutions. Examining Hamilton's 1809 address to the African Society, Stuckey asserts that "no black leader was more conscious of the
need for black institutions after the winning of freedom than Hamilton."
He was "a pioneer among Northern blacks in his discovery of sufficient
spiritual resonance in the values and heritage of his people for him to oppose absorption into the larger white world."[1] He saw the necessity of independent churches, voluntary societies, secret and fraternal associations, and schools. Beginning in the eighteenth century with his involvement in founding Manhattan's first black church and ending after his
historic address before the 1834 National Colored Convention, Hamilton
helped voice an intellectual current that preserved and promoted the gifts
of black culture.

Black nationalism, according to John Bracey Jr., August Meier, and Elliot Rudwick, has cultural, economic, political, and religious expressions,
but even these categories do not capture all of its manifestations. This
rather ungovernable ideology has resisted definition and bedeviled attempts to relate it to other political ideas like emigration. Taking advantage of the separatist possibilities of nationalist thought, Bracey writes
that emigration was "the purest expression of nationalist ideology." Howard Brotz also finds in antebellum emigration a rare occasion when the
boldness of political action approached that of nationalist rhetoric. Brotz
views nationalism as a product of a failed assimilationist campaign. In
the *Golden Age of Black Nationalism*, Wilson Jeremiah Moses complicates
the discussion. Nationalism and emigrationism were not as neatly tied as
scholars have suggested, notes Moses, recapturing the tensions of antebellum black politics. Nationalism was intimately connected to, overlapped with, and depended upon other political thrusts. Many black people freely appropriated nationalist rhetoric in pursuit of political objectives unrelated or even opposed to emigration. Stuckey's work frees the
study of nationalism from assimilationist assumptions by focusing on
how an ethnically diverse African population forged a common culture in
North America that gave rise to a fully elaborated concern for Africans
throughout the Diaspora.[2]

Assimilationist arguments give white people an agency in a discourse
in which they were only objects. Assimilation and emigration were strategies adopted by black people in reaction to white people's political behavior. Nationalism was not. It was never subordinate to or dependent upon
that black-white dialogue. It did not respond to the ebbs and tides of
white people's tolerance for racial progress. Nationalism was the ideological

superstructure of black politics and it operated fairly independent of such strategic concerns.

One of Stuckey's contributions is that his work situates nationalism as a part of African American culture. Africans forged a nationalist culture during the first decades of the New Netherland colony.[3] Nationalism was the political expression of collectivism, and it began with the assertion that Africans in the Diaspora constituted a historic community. It expressed *an overarching concern for the physical and political self-determination of people of African ancestry.* It neither dictated political strategies (e.g., emigration) nor precluded political goals (e.g., suffrage). It even accommodated contradictory notions. (For instance, black Christians held onto a belief in the interconnectedness of African peoples while simultaneously asserting the religious backwardness of Africa.) Nationalism was the most stable aspect of antebellum black political thought. It has been mistakenly described as a volatile and cyclical body of political ideas because of the tendency to define it as a reaction to white people's politics or as anti-white rhetoric.

The best measure of antebellum nationalism was not how fully one sought to integrate or escape white America but how committed one was to the self-determination of Africans in the Diaspora. The habit of casting black nationalism as a reply to white people has damaged our understanding of black political ideology. For instance, the dramatic act of emigrating was not necessarily a nationalist act. Leading Manhattanites and nationalists like the Reverend Samuel Ringgold Ward and William Powell[4] emigrated to Canada and England (not Haiti or Liberia). Their decisions were not predicated on nationalist logic but on personal and strategic concerns. Black Americans could emigrate without fully evaluating the impact of that act on African peoples, and black Americans could oppose removal because it threatened to weaken their fight to uplift the African race.

The men of the New York voluntary associations provide an interesting lens on this moment because of their dominance in the city's black communities. Citywide leadership emerged through voluntary associations, and community leaders could be grouped more easily by their societal connections than by their religious affiliations. In the culture of Manhattan, African Americans diverged in their tendency to satisfy their needs through collective action—a habit of gathering that cannot be explained as a mere by-product of white racialism.[5] The opening of the African Society, Philomathean (Odd Fellows), Phoenix, and Boyer Masonic halls allowed societies to organize and host local conventions with little church influence. The results included greater ecumenicalism and lay leadership. Moreover, because of their local success, the leaders of Manhattan's African voluntary associations became black New York's representatives at national assemblies.

Because of Hamilton's generation, voluntary associations were available to guide the black metropolis in the 1820s, a period when political institutions hardened against antislavery and white voters attacked the civil liberties of free black people. Political strategies such as emigration were hotly debated. Emigration was tactical, and it responded directly to white people's behavior; however, it also contained a critique of white people's capacity for social justice and moral transformation. For that reason, it fit comfortably into a nationalist framework.

The notion of "assimilation" has emerged in the historiography to describe those black people who rejected emigration. The assimilationist outlook was elaborated most clearly in the African-Christian promise of racial redemption and interracial reconciliation, the predictions of moral reform; however, even this offer was predicated upon a fundamental reconstitution of society and, more significantly, it came from religious separatists. Thus, nationalist rhetoric could defend either emigration or assimilation. On the eve of the Civil War, George Downing rejected emigration by blending black nationalism with the promise of social redemption: "Whilst I feel for Africa, whilst I would have Hayti great, prosperous, and strong, yet I do not any the less desire that *my country* shall be great, prosperous, and strong, and, withal, just. Nor am I without the hope that it will be so, and as I cherish that hope, I feel through it the greater obligation to remain in the country and help bring about the desired end."[6] Downing was a nationalist who rejected emigration and sought to make the United States a *just* nation in which he could submit to citizenship.

The political inventions of the antebellum decades were designed to protect black people's self-determination. In the decades before the Civil War, black New Yorkers denounced the work of the American Colonization Society with a ferocity that they occasionally admitted was greater than the threat of their removal. African nationalist rhetoric was an early casualty of this campaign. Africa went from being a national to an ancestral reference as black people asserted civil claims upon the United States. In February 1831, a meeting was held in Manhattan's Boyer Lodge Room to discuss the ACS. The attendees insisted "that we claim *this country, the place of our birth, and not Africa*; as our mother country; and all attempts to send us to Africa, we consider as gratuitous and uncalled for." Once Africa had been a universal element of black people's declarations, but responding to the Colonization Society meant shunning the use of Africa as a political symbol. That summer a meeting was held at Brooklyn's African Society Hall. The Woolman Society's Henry C. Thompson, George Woods, and the Reverends J. W. C. Pennington and George Hogarth delivered addresses and wrote the public statement. Borrowing New York's language, the Brooklynites accused the ACS of plotting "to remove us, the free people of color, from this, our beloved and native land, to the coast of Africa; a country unknown to us in every respect." Thompson prayed to see the day "when the sable sons of America will join with their fairer brethren, and re-echo liberty and equal rights in all parts of Columbia's soil."[7]

The rhetorical retreat from African signifiers was political; it did not mark the end of nationalism. Black New Yorkers continued to see themselves as a historic national group. The choice of language corresponded to a change of strategy, but it did not represent a reconceptualization of the community. Dr. James McCune Smith, reflecting upon the nationalist politics of his childhood, recalled the moment when black New Yorkers ceased describing themselves as Africans: "It was in after years, when they set up their protest against the American Colonization Society and its principles that the term 'African' fell into disuse and finally discredit." In the twentieth century, W. E. B. Du Bois made this connection, but his interpretation did not stress the political motivation; rather, he charged that black Americans adopted white people's contempt for Africa: "When the Cotton Kingdom of the 19th century built on black slavery led to a campaign in church and society to discount Africa, its culture and history, American Negroes shrank from any ties with Africa and accepted in part the color line."[8]

Scholarly interest in black people's reactions to white people must be balanced with a respect for the greater intentions of African American intellectualism. Nationalism was the broadest context of black politics, not a broken and clumsy dialogue with white people. Antebellum campaigns for equal citizenship in the body politic did not include the promise of cultural assimilation. Black Manhattanites believed political liberty was fully compatible with the group's integrity. In New York and Brooklyn, African signage received its death blow at meetings of black men held in African society halls. The process transpired in nationalist institutions.

The belief that Africans were entitled by natural and divine law to decide their own fates was at the root of nationalist sentiments. African symbolism declined—a step that preserved the collective claim to civil liberty—but black nationalism remained constant.

At the moment when black Manhattanites accelerated their campaign against the ACS, there was little chance of the removal of any significant portion of the black population. The Colonization Society had failed to win federal support for its objectives and it was struggling to remain active in the political scene. The fear was not of removal but of the political damage that colonization did. The crusade to relocate African Americans compromised their self-determination. In an 1839 address, McCune Smith called the ACS a band of "men whom we never solicited" and who "thrust their advice upon us." When black people did not heed the ACS's counsel, they were persecuted, continued Smith. "What is the Colonization Society?" he asked.

> We are told it consists of all the good and great men in our land. That it may have a few good men I will not deny, but that it has many great men in its ranks is, alas, too true. Senators, Chief Justices, Members of Legislatures, Divines, Physicians and Lawyers, M.C's, D D's, LL.D's, M.D's, Colonels, &c. &c., may be said to constitute this society. It is remarkable that its members are all of them titled men, or men grasping at titles.

Ten years later, Frederick Douglass was in Manhattan when society leaders Boston Crummell, George Lawrence, William Powell, and George Downing crafted a harsher statement of the same principle. Alexander Crummell had written to warn them that ACS agents were in Britain making false claims about African Americans' position on colonization. The New Yorkers assured Brits "that we will not remove to Africa except by the exercise of force." The very name of the ACS was insulting. To colonize oneself was voluntary, but to colonize others was an act of supremacy.[9] The ACS's work presupposed white people's right to intrude into the lives of enslaved and free black people. It empowered white people to decide the fates of free people of color. The fact that many moderate and progressive white men were committed to this goal did even more violence to black people's claim to the most basic civil liberty.

Black people displayed their opposition to the ACS in a refusal to volunteer for removal and an intolerance for political deviants. Over its half-century career, the ACS, by its own account, removed fewer than three hundred people, not even six each year, from all of New York State. In

1829 John B. Russwurm, co-founder of *Freedom's Journal*, announced his support for colonization and was burned in effigy. Russwurm was later cast as little more than a race traitor when he accepted a position with the Maryland Colonization Society. He remained faithful to his convictions. Later that year the newsman emigrated to Liberia, where he eventually became superintendent of schools and founded and edited the *Liberia Herald*. "I long to see young men, who are now wasting the best of their days in the United States, flocking to this land as the last asylum to the unfortunate—I long for the time when you, my dear friend, shall land on the shores of Africa, a messenger of that Gospel which proclaims liberty to the captive, and light to those who sat in great darkness!" explained Russwurm. In 1835 he became governor of the Cape Palmas settlement. Manhattan's young men were equally stern with Charles C. Andrews, a founder of the New York Manumission Society. As the teacher at African School No. 2, Andrews's colonizationist beliefs angered many of Manhattan's leading black men, including Hamilton, Sipkins, and Downing of the New York African Society for Mutual Relief. Those who had been Andrews's students split with those who had not. The "old heads" in the community eventually triumphed and Andrews was spared, but he still faced potent opposition. Later, Andrews's career was settled when he beat young George Downing for referring to a woman of color as a "lady." Thomas Downing reacted harshly and the "incident furnished the spark to the powder that was already in the city, of discontent with white teachers, and the result was—[black men instructors] John Peterson and Ransom F. Wake," wrote a contemporary.[10]

The 1831 meeting issued an "Address to the Citizens of New-York," in which it laid out black Manhattan's critique of colonization: the men of the ACS were powerful and influential, and many were motivated by humanitarian concerns, confessed the authors. "But we do protest strongly against the means which that Society uses to effect its purposes." If black people's sin was their degradation, it was a greater Christian sin for the ACS to twist such misery into an accusation. Second, the ACS spoke of and for a black population whom they did not know. They claimed Africa as the home of men, women, and children born in the United States. They offered assurances that "the poor ignorant slave" will be miraculously "transformed into a 'missionary,' to instruct in the principles of Christianity, and the arts of civilized life" through deportation. Moreover, the ACS encouraged the exclusion of free colored people from trades, schools, churches, and politics in order to create the inferiority upon which their argument for removal rested. They used a social inequity that they themselves erected as proof of black people's natural inferiority. "A difference of color is not a difference of species," the committee reminded New York:

> The time must come when the Declaration of Independence will be felt in the heart, as well as uttered from the mouth, and when the rights of all shall be properly acknowledged and appreciated. God hasten that time. This is our home, and this is our country. Beneath its sod lie the bones of our fathers: for it, some of them fought, bled, and died. Here we were born, and here we will die.[11]

At the root of what many scholars have described as the political innovations of antebellum black Manhattan—a distinct style in the National Colored Conventions, a growing militancy, and a palpable mistrust of white people—was a covetousness of the right to self-determination. The themes were captured in an 1830 address at St. Philip's Church during which Peter Williams Jr. accused the American Colonization Society of scheming to rid the nation of free black people and of defaming free people of color in order to create the necessity of their removal.[12] However, voluntary associations soon seized the front line of the struggle.

The National Colored Conventions were far less nationalistic in tone than the Manhattan assemblies. Their interracial audiences and the influence of Richard Allen and the Philadelphia delegates forced a certain moderation. Still, nationalists and nationalism were not altogether absent. The Manhattan representatives to the first Annual National Convention of the People of Color—the Reverend William Miller, Henry Sipkins, William Hamilton, and Thomas L. Jennings, all of the NYASMR—were experienced anticolonization advocates. The proceedings ran for five days, beginning June 6, 1831. Jennings and Sipkins served on the influential Report Committee, which wrote the final communication, calling on free people of color in the United States to support Canadian settlement, hold annual conventions, work for moral reform, raise a convention fund, support education, practice economy and temperance, and condemn the American Colonization Society. Provisional committees were formed in the major cities to organize and carry out these objectives. New York's committee comprised Mutual Relief members Peter Williams Jr., Boston Crummell, Philip Bell, Thomas Downing, and Peter Vogelsang. Adam Ray, a founder of the NYASMR, served on the Newark, New Jersey, committee.[13]

On June 4, 1832, when the second National Colored Convention opened in Philadelphia, the New York City delegates—Bell, Hamilton, Sipkins, and Jennings—were again from the NYASMR. The attendees elected Sipkins president and Bell secretary. Hamilton sat on the Report Committee, which offered support for Canadian settlement and an even stronger repudiation of the ACS. Hamilton helped construct a brief resolution encouraging delegates "to discountenance, by all just means in their power, any emigration to Liberia or Hayti, believing them only calculated to distract and divide the whole colored family." That stance was transposed to the public statement, which described the concerns of the delegates as "the effects of Slavery on the bond and Colonization on the free."[14]

The New Yorkers' imprint on the third Annual Convention in 1833 was bolder. Hamilton and Jennings again led the New York City contingent. Mutual Relief brother Henry Sipkins was the delegate from Catskill and Hudson, New York. William Brown, later to found the African Tompkins Association, and Henry Thompson of the African Woolman Society represented Brooklyn. The Manhattan men pushed the delegates to endorse the establishment of local literary and benevolent societies patterned on those in Gotham:

> Moved by William Hamilton, seconded by Thomas L. Jinnings, that this Convention earnestly recommends the formation of Phoenix Societies in every State, after the form, and on the principles of the Phoenix Societies of the City of New-York, and that the constitution of the said Societies be attached to the printed minutes of this Convention.[15]

The fourth National Convention was held in New York City and took a distinctly different tone. Hamilton, Sipkins, Hardenburg, and Vogelsang of the NYASMR were representing New York. Mutual Relief's Thomas Thompson was in the Brooklyn delegation, along with Abraham Brown and Henry Brown of the later BATA and Henry Thompson of the BAWBS. The founder of the African Society for Mutual Relief strayed far from his earlier pronouncements. Bracey, Meier, and Rudwick cite William Hamilton's opening address to the 1834 assembly as an important exception to the "assimilationist" focus of the National Conventions. Although African symbolism receded from black people's rhetoric, Hamilton stressed black unity and charged that white New Yorkers were retaliating against free black people for their consistent antislavery posture.[16]

Hamilton divided the nation into three distinct groups: the white man, the enslaved, and the free colored man. He then warned his audience that "under present circumstances it is highly necessary [that] the free people of color should combine, and closely attend to their own interest." He saw an army of enemies who targeted free black people. First among them was the American Colonization Society. Earlier that year, the Manhattan branch of the ACS outfitted a ship, the *Jupiter,* to carry out their relocation plan, and local white women organized the Female Society for the Support of Schools in Africa. Hamilton called colonization a proslavery step, intended to rid the nation of free colored people, remove its most potent antislavery voice, erase the evidence of black people's fitness for liberty, and reestablish the unchallenged relations of master and slave. He decried the ACS as "the great Dragon of the land," which cloaked itself "in the garb of angels of light" but sought only to "sacrifice the free people of color" to the interest of servitude. He scored the Colonization Society for blaming free black people for racial amalgamation, for accusing them of exciting revolts, for intimidating legislatures to deny their rights, for pressuring Congress to relocate them, and for preventing the establishment of educational institutions for their benefit.[17] The principle of self-determination held these themes together. The violation of this basic human right united enslaved and free black people, and the ACS was the trespasser.

Hamilton's impassioned inquiry into the state of free black people was accompanied by a more violent attack on slavery than any that he had made before. Earlier, Hamilton had lamented slavery in moral tones that took advantage of the common religious culture of black and white New Yorkers. Now he demanded that free black men do the "work of moral improvement" to bring about the moment when "slavery, that Satanic Monster, that beast whose mark has been so long stamped on the forehead of the nations, shall be chained and cast down into blackness and darkness forever." Hamilton offered his clearest statement of the moral reform ideology:

> Aside from the future day of judgment and retribution, there is always a day of retribution at hand. That society is most miserable that is most immoral—that most happy that is most virtuous. Let me therefore recommend earnestly that you press upon our people the necessity and advantage of a moral reformation. It may not produce an excess of riches, but it will produce a higher state of happiness, and render our circumstances easier.[18]

Sipkins served as president, and the views of the Manhattan men dominated. They formed committees to explore the decline of their civil rights, scrutinize skilled crafts that were closed to black labor, survey the racial pro-scriptions at manual labor schools, devise ways to increase support for black and abolitionist periodicals, investigate the work of the Colonization Soci-ety, and search state legislatures for laws harmful to black people and de-velop opposition strategies. There were also committees to draft a constitu-tion and to write an address to the free people of color.[19]

There were impressive accomplishments. The report of the committee on the Colonization Society brought a resolution sharply condemning the ACS's "principles which aim at the root of our liberty." The delegates agreed to counter the ACS through local organizations and to continue inspecting its work in the United States and Liberia. The attendees urged free black people to patronize businesses and conveyances that offered equal treat-ment. After some debate they decided to discourage public parades and processions because they were time consuming, expensive, and left people of color vulnerable to violent assaults. They called on all "auxiliary soci-eties" to commit to the "patronage and circulation" of abolitionist papers. They promoted a project to build a high school in Hartford, Connecticut, for black youths. They even wrote their boldest declaration. Calling the lowly condition of the colored people of the United States unparalleled in the "history of nations," they bemoaned a fall from ancestors who "for their excellence of attainment in the arts, literature and science, stood before the world unrivalled." The public statement attacked "*American slavery* and *American prejudice*" as the culprits. It went on to address and detail their concerns in prosecutorial style. Blending the language of moral reform with the forcefulness of the New Yorkers, it read:

> We rejoice that we are thrown into a revolution where the contest is not for landed territory, but for freedom; the weapons not carnal, but spiritual; where struggle is not for blood, but for right; and where the bow is the power of God, and the arrow the instrument of divine justice; while the victims are the devices of *reason*, and the prejudice of the human heart. It is in this glorious struggle for civil and religious liberty, for the establish-ment of peace on earth and good will to men, that we are morally bound by all the relative ties we owe to the author of our being to enter the arena, and boldly contend for victory.

It concluded by proclaiming "moral warfare" against injustice.[20]

The National Conventions exposed the New York style. A power strug-gle between Manhattan and Philadelphia marred the movement from its beginning. The schism was not just a product of the many egos in the two cities, it mirrored real ideological differences between the communities. Bishop Allen and the power of the African Methodist Episcopal Church secured the first conventions for Philadelphia, but soon the force of black Manhattan's businessmen and editors was felt. The 1834 events betrayed the ideological gap. The New York delegation was "skeptical of some phases of the theoretical humanitarianism of the Boston and Philadelphia groups, and . . . placed its confidence in the power of the press to arouse public action, and in specific local efforts to get results," argues Howard Holman Bell in his history of the conventions. The Philadelphians recaptured the national conventions through the American Moral Reform Society, sparking a boycott from the New York group. After 1835, black Manhattan's leadership—drawn from Mutual Relief and its subordinates—left the national organization and concentrated on statewide conventions, which became the first to demand equal suffrage, lobby the legislature, and court the Liberty party. That departure also responded to the conspicuous presence of white missionaries, colonizationists, and solicitors at the conventions. The New York State gatherings excluded white people and thus became "the first of the Negro conventions on record to declare its independence of white meddling."[21]

Nationalism echoed in the culture of black Gotham. The Manhattanites were committed to convening as a method of creating community consensus for political actions and declarations, airing their political differences, and bringing young men into the antislavery struggle; however, they exhibited little faith in the idea that the convention was itself a political act. Moreover, their growing unease with white people's involvement worked against any more active participation. Although African references had receded from their language, the unity of African peoples remained their goal. The rhetorical shift was motivated by neither assimilation nor separatism. It occurred in defense of self-determination.

In fact, as African symbolism declined, black New Yorkers were displaying greater unity. On November 20, 1835, David Ruggles joined with Thomas Van Rensselaer, the Reverends Samuel Cornish and Theodore Wright, and other local black men to form the New York Committee of Vigilance, which instituted the principles of self-defense, self-reliance, and self-determination in Gotham. On July 23, 1836, George Jones, a free black man, was arrested at work and brought without counsel before a justice. The bounty hunters swore that he was a runaway slave, and Richard Riker, Recorder of New York City, upheld their claim. Within a few hours of his arrest, reported Ruggles, he was "bound in chains, dragged through the streets, like a beast to the shambles!" The Underground Railroad leader argued that extremism was justified because the law did not protect black people from kidnappers.

> We must no longer depend on the interposition of Manumission or Anti-Slavery Societies, in the hope of peaceable and just protection; where such outrages are committed, peace and justice cannot dwell. While we are subject to be thus inhumanly practised upon, no man is safe; we must look to our own safety and protection from kidnappers; remembering that 'self-defence is the first law of nature.'

Ruggles called a gathering of black men to address the crisis. After being freed, George Jones presented the committee with a small cash donation and two trunks of clothing to aid fugitives.[22]

Like defending black people from slave catchers, assisting fugitives from bondage was an act justified largely in nationalist terms. In Brooklyn, the Reverend Charles B. Ray, Allen Stewart, William Still, and Albro Lyons were all conductors on the Underground Railroad, combining at times with Brooklyn minister Henry Ward Beecher, the brother of Harriet Beecher Stowe, to protect fugitives. In Manhattan, society men like David Ruggles, George T. Downing, the Reverend J. W. C. Pennington, Charles Reason, Henry Highland Garnet, and Dr. James McCune Smith were active in the Railroad. Mutual Relief's John J. Zuille was posthumously credited with assisting 120 fugitives. Ray served as secretary of the New York State Vigilance Committee. In addition, Philip Bell and Thomas Van Rensselaer were delegates of the United Anti-Slavery Society of New York City, and Samuel Cornish and Theodore Wright were leaders of the Evangelical Union Anti-Slavery Society.[23]

Manhattan set the pace for Brooklyn and Williamsburg. By the 1840s John Zuille was acting as Manhattan's representative to the suburbs. Williamsburg followed Brooklyn in adopting a political stance parallel to the New Yorkers. Believing that the black people of his village had been left out of the great political discussions, Willis Hodges organized a caucus at the town's black church. "At this meeting Armstrong Archer and myself were elected delegates to represent the Williamsburg people of color in the [1840] Albany convention," recalled Hodges. In 1832 Armstrong Archer became a member of Abyssinian Baptist and in 1848 he joined the African Society for Mutual Relief. Hodges continued to represent Williamsburg at regional and national conventions, he founded the Williamsburg Union Temperance Benevolent Society, and he published the *Ram's Horn* with Thomas Van Rensselaer and Frederick Douglass as editors.[24]

The 1843 National Colored Convention in Buffalo, New York, confirmed the vitality of nationalism. A lecture from Henry Highland Garnet, now a pastor in Troy, consumed the proceedings. Garnet's youth—he was only twenty-seven—must have struck the black men seated before him. Equally daunting was the fact that Garnet's antislavery credentials were spotless. He had already attracted considerable attention as a minister and an abolitionist in New York State, and he did not waste the chance to extend his radical reputation. On the second day, Garnet delivered *An Address to the Slaves of the United States of America*, which Stuckey describes as "a contribution to nationalist theory" that "could hardly have been more African in spirit." It was the most extreme exposition to appear in the United States since David Walker's *Appeal to the Coloured Citizens* (1829). Walker's influence was obvious. Later, in introductory remarks to the *Appeal*, Garnet described Walker's contribution with envy:

> This little book produced more commotion among slaveholders than any volume of its size that was ever issued from an American press. They saw that it was a bold attack upon their idolatry, and that too by a black man who once lived among them. It was merely a smooth stone which this David took up, yet it terrified a host of Goliaths. When the fame of this book reached the South, the poor, cowardly, pusillanimous tyrants, grew pale behind their cotton bags, and armed themselves to the teeth. They set watches to look after their happy and contented slaves.[25]

Garnet used his position as chair of the Business Committee to speak a truth rooted in the experiences of his own life, a truth directed to black people enslaved in the South. He spoke so honestly that day that the attendees ultimately refused the *Address*. Certainly, free black men and women across the nation had privately uttered similar words, but to publish them required a different kind of courage. Garnet divided the dissenters into two groups: those who thought the statement a revolutionary appeal for violence, and those who feared for their lives should it wear their signatures. He faced the weighty opposition of the Reverends Charles Ray and James Gloucester of New York City, and Frederick Douglass, representing Boston. Ray and Gloucester's disapproval is interesting. Ray's editorials never shied away from extreme positions and, fifteen years later, Gloucester and his wife Elizabeth were sending money to support John Brown's campaign against slavery. But the moment did not seem right to them. The Reverend Theodore Wright supported Garnet.[26]

The delegates surely recalled the events of David Walker's murder, and to that extent Garnet's *Address* was all too familiar. The young Troy minister did not limit himself to reformulating or restating Walker's thoughts. As Stuckey notes, Garnet used the concept of a black Diaspora to position himself to demand the violent liberation of Africans.[27]

Looking past the free black communities, he turned to the enslaved themselves and particularly to bondsmen. The lecture began with a brief but sharp critique of the National Colored Conventions. Their discussions and debates were too eulogistic, and the tendency "to weep over your unhappy condition" too great. It was time to act. To prove this, Garnet offered two reversals reminiscent of the public speeches of William Hamilton and Peter Vogelsang. The first insisted that if Christians found themselves under the rule of heathens and, thus, the reign of a false God, it would be their religious duty to resist. It was equally true that anyone enslaved by Christians must throw off that oppression since servitude is an un-Christian condition. The second asserted that if white men were slaves and black men were masters, the nation would be embroiled in endless turmoil. Africans, then, had no justification for being "a patient people."[28]

Defining nationalism in distinctly masculine terms, the *Address* summoned the courage of black men, who, as "children of Africa," were tied regardless of their condition. The history of African degradation in the Americas required a response. The minister summarized "all the dark catalogue of this nation's sins." He assured his audience that the oppressors had caused their own downfall. White Christians' evil brought them to "ruin." "They have cursed you—they have cursed themselves—they have cursed the earth which they have trod," Garnet prophesied.[29]

The once dominant hope for peaceful social resolution was gone. New York's leadership claimed a more active role in the great struggle against bondage. Their strategy shifted from persuasion to intervention. The Vigilance Committee, the antislavery speeches in Europe, and the Underground Railroad typified their abolitionism. Even extralegal resistance to slavery was justified; moreover, it was a direct result of the moral failure of white Christians. Garnet could therefore call slave owners "devils," for he no longer feared alienating white people generally. The speech betrayed the philosophical distance between the nation's foremost black intellectuals. Ray convinced the delegates to send the *Address* to a special committee so that the language could be negotiated. It was voted on two days after it was heard. "Douglass rose and made some forcible remarks against its adoption," read the proceedings. It was rejected by a single ballot, and there remained enough discomfort to force another hearing.[30]

The most radical element was the thinly veiled call for revolt. If it was a sin for Christians to enslave their fellow men, then it was "SINFUL IN THE EXTREME FOR YOU TO MAKE VOLUNTARY SUBMISSION." No person could allow another man's evil to keep him or her from heaven. A wholly different salvation journey emerged in which freedom and redemption became synonymous. "THEREFORE, IT IS YOUR SOLEMN AND IMPERATIVE DUTY TO USE EVERY MEANS, BOTH MORAL, INTELLECTUAL, AND PHYSICAL, THAT PROMISES SUCCESS," Garnet chided.[31]

The Troy pastor went further. He asked each man to place his name on that great list of historical revolutionaries. His words could be nothing but a call to arms: "You had far better all die—*die immediately*, than live slaves, and entail your wretchedness upon your posterity." He lamented that "there is not much hope of Redemption without the shedding of blood." Join Denmark Vesey, he appealed, for, while the rebel did not succeed, "History, faithful to her high trust, will transcribe his name on the same monument with Moses, Hampden, Tell, Bruce, and Wallace, Touissaint L'Overteur, Lafayette and Washington." Garnet pointed with pride to Nat Turner and the Africans of the *Amistad*. He repeatedly reminded the unfree that they were three million strong.[32]

The minister questioned the behavior of bondsmen. He instructed them to tell their masters in every way possible the truth of human justice and Christian righteousness. It was time to make a final stand against bondage, time to defend their women and their souls.

> Fellow-men! patient sufferers! behold your dearest rights crushed to the earth! See your sons murdered, and your wives, mothers, and sisters doomed to prostitution! In the name of the merciful God! and by all that life is worth, let it no longer be a debateable question, whether it is better to choose LIBERTY or DEATH!

Therefore Garnet's rejection of violence, offered at the end of the *Address* and slight in force, was quite unconvincing. "We do not advise you to attempt a revolution with the sword, because it would be INEXPEDIENT," he said. He quickly followed that caveat with another reminder that the bondspeople numbered three million and that it was better for them to die free than live bound.[33]

An Address to the Slaves is a complicated historical document. Speaking formerly unspoken thoughts and concerns to an absentee audience, the bondspeople of the South, was not its sole purpose; in fact, it might fairly be viewed as a device. The pastor was fully aware that his primary audience, regardless of the essay's title, comprised free black people in the North and white Christians. Garnet sought to radicalize the politics of the former while underscoring the crisis of slavery for the latter. His immediate political concern was the free black men in his audience. The essay's shock value varied widely given the ideological differences among the attendees. However, those listening to Garnet could not have missed the fact that if the pastor had sternly censured bondsmen for inconsistent resistance to slavery, then, by necessity, he had extended a far ruder assessment of free black *manhood*. These realities helped the delegates refuse the essay altogether. The opposition had grown by the final day of the meeting, and even Wright sided against its adoption.[34]

Of course, the controversy did not end at Buffalo. Shortly after, Garnet sent a letter to Maria Chapman, of the Boston Female Antislavery Society, in response to her criticisms of the *Address* and its author. "My crime is, that I have dared to think, and act, contrary to your opinion," the minister responded in a tone that captured black New Yorkers' frustration with white abolitionists.

> . . . the address to the slaves you seem to doom to the most fiery trials. And yet, madam, you have not seen that address—you have merely *heard* of it; nevertheless, you criticised it very severely. You speak, at length, of myself, the author of the paper. You say that I 'have received bad counsel.' You are not the only person who has told your humble servant that his humble productions have been produced by the '*counsel*' of some anglo-saxon. I have expected no more from ignorant slaveholders and their apologists, but I really looked for better things from Mrs. Maria W. Chapman, an antislavery poetess, and editor *pro tem.* of the Boston Liberator. I can think on the subject of human rights without the 'counsel,' either from the men of the West, or the women of the East. . . . In a few days I hope to publish the address, then you can judge how much treason there is in it. In the mean time, be assured that there is one black American who dares to speak boldly on the subject of universal liberty.[35]

As Chapman did, it is easy to misread the radical message of Garnet's *Address*. The speech competes with Walker's *Appeal* as the quintessential expression of nineteenth-century African American nationalism because it is a fearless defense of African liberty. The nationalist roots of both documents are not contained in their rejection of white people or their perceived anti-white rhetoric. That focus confuses mechanics (or tactics) with political intent. Walker and Garnet were lending their voices to the struggle for the self-determination of African peoples. The relationship between black and white people was, at best, secondary.

In 1848 John Brown paid to publish Garnet's *Address to the Slaves*. Brown was attracted to the increasingly militant posture of the New York City men. From 1852 to 1855, Garnet worked as a Presbyterian missionary in Jamaica, returning in 1856, following the death of Theodore Wright, to minister Manhattan's Shiloh Presbyterian Church. During Garnet's absence, according to W. E. B. Du Bois, Brown placed himself "in the confidence of McCune Smith and the able Negro group of New York who had developed a not unnatural distrust of whites." Besides Smith, the cadre likely included Bell, Ray, and Zuille, the most seditious of Manhattan's black men. "It is difficult to say how much Garnet and militants like him influenced Brown," asserts Stephen B. Oates, but the radical minister clearly affected Brown's political writings. Brown kept close ties to the New York men until his assassination after his failed raid on Harper's Ferry, Virginia.[36]

In New York City, nationalism was the framework of antebellum black politics. Black men in Manhattan and Brooklyn responded to the 1850 Fugitive Slave Act with the Committee of Thirteen. "Each member of which was pledged to keep the letter but to violate the spirit of [that] unholy enactment," wrote Maritcha Lyons, the goddaughter of James McCune Smith. The group determined to resist the law and aid runaways. Members of the New York African Society for Mutual Relief were its backbone. John J. Zuille was chair. Philip Bell was one of two secretaries, and James McCune Smith and Thomas Downing sat as members. George Downing, grand master of the Odd Fellows, was a member, as were the Reverend John Raymond of Zion Baptist Church and William Hamilton's son Robert. The Thirteen also spent considerable time organizing black Manhattan's resistance to the Colonization Society. In 1852 they called a special meeting in Manhattan to respond to the work of the ACS and to reject their "hypocritical philanthropy."[37]

The reign of the Fugitive Slave Act made Mutual Relief's William Powell—the proprietor of Manhattan's Colored Seamen's Home—one of the city's leading abolitionists. In late September 1850, bounty hunters seized James Hamlet (or James Hamilton Williams), and Powell revealed his talents as an organizer and a spokesman. "The slave . . . was given up by the bloodhounds of the north to the bloodhounds of the south," lamented Harriet Jacobs, a fugitive herself. With an entourage of black seamen, Powell marched upon City Hall to find out if Mayor Woodhull was willing to protect free persons of color in Manhattan. Days later the mayor instructed New York authorities not to assist in the capturing of runaways. On the First of October, Powell reported the exchange during a mass meeting at Mother Zion. Robert Hamilton and Charles Ray also spoke. Albro Lyons served as vice president. Powell declared that had his friend Robert Hamilton been seized, "we would not allow him to be taken out of the city." He then asked, "Shall we resist oppression? Shall we defend our Liberties? Shall we be *Freemen* or *Slaves*?" Imploring his audience, he continued:

> Shall the blood-thirsty slaveholder be permitted by his unrighteous law to come into our domiciles, or workshops, or the places where we labor, and carry off our wives and children, our fathers and mothers, and ourselves, without a struggle—without resisting, even if need be, unto death? . . . You are told to peaceably submit to the laws; will you do so? You are told to kiss the manacles that bind you; will you do so?

The cry "No!" overtook the room. Harriet Jacobs contrasted the worlds of New Yorkers: "While the [white] fashionables were listening to the thrilling voice of Jenny Lind in Metropolitan Hall, the thrilling voices of poor hunted colored people went up, in an agony of supplication, to the Lord, from Zion's church."[38]

African society members and fellow travelers attended and helped organize meetings in Brooklyn and Williamsburg. Within two days, eight hundred dollars had been raised to purchase Hamlet's freedom. On October 5, 1850, the antislavery factions of New York and Brooklyn held a rally in a Manhattan park. Powell shook Hamlet's hand as a freeman, and hundreds of free black people escorted Hamlet back to his home in Williamsburg. A few days later Robert Hamilton delivered the address at the Williamsburg celebration of Hamlet's return. There Hamlet took the stage and gave a wrenching account of his captivity.[39]

A pacifist who remained loyal to William Lloyd Garrison, Powell was arguably one of the most "assimilationist" of Manhattan's black leaders. In 1851 he moved himself and his family to England in search of a better future for his children. His Mutual Relief brother Albro Lyons took over his Colored Seamen's Home during his absence. Upon arriving in London, he wrote Garrison to assure him of his safe arrival. He announced his plan to immediately pick up his antislavery work in a visit to Scotland, and he sent firsthand accounts of American abolitionists in London and Liverpool.[40] Interestingly, Powell emigrated to a predominantly white nation. His emigration judged white Americans' capacity for transformation, but it kept a basic faith in the possibility of an integrated and equal society.

Powell's departure anticipated the rise of a potent emigrationist movement, organized around Emigration Conventions that met in 1854, 1856, and 1858. That final year, Henry Highland Garnet, Robert Hamilton, and the Reverend Sampson White helped organize the interracial African Civilization Society, an emigrationist and missionary organization. An impressive collection of black minds, including Dr. Martin R. Delaney and the Reverend J. W. C. Pennington were members and officers. Garnet served as president.[41]

Thus, in the spring of 1860, Henry Highland Garnet divided from his friends over his involvement in the Civilization Society. Garnet was already the local agent for emigration to Haiti. Philomathean's George T. Downing and the members of the NYASMR led the attack. At the first gathering, the debate between Downing and Garnet became so heated that the lights in the hall had to be extinguished in order to bring the meeting to a close. A second and much larger convocation was held at Zion the following night. Downing and Garnet were again the main combatants, but the speakers also included the Reverends Charles Ray and J. W. C. Pennington. Provocative handbills were distributed:

COLORED MEN, READ!

It is said we should be slaves! It is said we should go to Africa! A new society has been formed to send us there! It is collecting money for this purpose. Shall this be? Come out! Will you be shipped off? A public meeting to oppose the same is to be held on Thursday evening, the 12th of April, at Zion Church, Church street. It will be addressed by many speakers. Let nothing prevent you, come out, crowd old Zion! Admittance free.[42]

A strident dialogue followed. To great laughter, William Tyson, in the chair, said he "hoped the colored men would have more respect for themselves than to copy after the rowdy meetings of white men." The early evening was spent establishing that the Civilization Society could not claim the support of black New Yorkers. Downing proposed a series of sharp resolutions against the new organization that climaxed with a statement that "we believe the African Civilization Society to be no other than an auxiliary of the negro-hating American Colonization Society," which was broadly applauded. "I was in search a few days ago for matter[s] with which to battle (you know that I am fond of fighting the 'African Civilization Society[)]," Downing joked to his boyhood friend Alexander Crummell. He seriously feared that the emigrationist society might pull attention from immediate political struggles. "I was in John Zuille[']s printing office yesterday talking about exertions in behalf of the elective franchise; it is to be submitted to the people this fall. It might be obtained—yes it would be, with proper exertions," he concluded. Prince Hall officer Ransom Wake chose harsher words to move the meeting to action. He called his audience slaves and, while pointing at Garnet, told them to "obey your master." "Canes and fists became very unsteady by this time," wrote a reporter. The meeting was eventually called to an end with all of its business being tabled.[43]

Dr. Smith delivered a final knock on colonization by slapping his childhood rival in the press. In an open letter targeting Garnet's African Civilization Society, Smith charged that "your schemes of emigration have neither the charm of novelty nor the prestige of success." He accused the Civilization Society of doing the American Colonization Society's bidding. Smith, no mild flatterer of Haiti when it fit his purposes, issued an unwarranted attack on the nation to further discredit the "African Civilization scheme." "Your duty to our people is to tell them to aim higher. In advising them to go to Hayti, you direct them to sink lower," barked Smith. Language barriers and the vast cultural divide awaiting Protestants in a Catholic nation would alone foil the attempt; yet, Garnet, from the safe distance of the United States, encouraged the endeavor. "Shake yourself free from these migrating phantasms, and join us with your might and main," the doctor snapped.

> As the beloved pastor of a large and intelligent people in the centre of a metropolis which appreciates your talents and acknowledges your genius, you have ample room and verge enough for the marked abilities with which it has pleased God to endow you, without wasting your vigor in the vain attempt to people an island within the tropics.[44]

In fact, the issue of colonization was largely settled within the community of black Manhattan. Few free black people opted to emigrate; most free black people opposed colonization and were suspicious of emigrationists.

The disagreement between McCune Smith and Garnet was as much personal as ideological. "Allow me to express the hope, that you will continue to improve, until you shall cease to grieve your friends by no longer prostituting your extensive learning and brilliant talents, to purposes which you ought to consider beneath you," ripped Garnet in reaction to Smith's letter. Garnet denied Smith's charges that the African Civilization Society was a tool of the American Colonization Society and pointed out the errors of Smith's argument. He called Smith's insinuations "sly, wicked, and cunning."

> Sir, you effect to be much interested for my welfare, and say that you value my humble labors in this country, and especially in this city—you say that I have considerable influence in a large influential and central congregation—all of which you delight in, and desire to be continued, and then you labor like a giant filled with new wine to blacken my name, and to ruin me in the estimation of my church and my friends, by trying to prove me to be in complicity with slavery and the slave trade.

Garnet challenged Smith to explain what greater work he had done to advance the cause of freedom. He then issued his most scathing attack while capturing the eternal pull of emigration:

> You anti-emigrationists seem to desire to see the hundreds of colored men and women who have good trades to stay here and be the drudges and menials of white men, who will not employ or work with them. Go to our hotels and private mansions of the rich, and on board of our steamboats, and you will find many skillful carpenters, masons, engineers, wheelwrights, and blacksmiths, millers, as well as female mechanics, who are wasting their talents for a mere pittance. You will see many of them borne down with discouragement, and they will tell you that the reason they do not work is because they have been told over and over again when they have applied for work—"We dou't [*sic*] employ niggers."

Garnet accused Smith of behaving the same way toward black labor and passing by the black merchants of New York in favor of white ones. Even on the site of the stately Sixth Avenue mansion that Dr. Smith was having constructed, not a single sable face was at work.[45]

The popular definition of nationalism makes it difficult to explain Garnet's politics. His strategic decisions to talk tough to white folk and to support emigration did not mark the boundaries of his nationalist views. Garnet's career shows that he was always a nationalist. His teenage years working with the "sons of Africa" in the Garrison Literary Association entertained the integrationist possibilities of nationalism, his 1843 *Address* captured its revolutionary potential, and his missionary work in the West

Indies and presidency of the African Civilization Society exploited its potent separatist option.

On Sunday, February 12, 1865, the Reverend Henry Highland Garnet delivered a sermon before the United States Congress. Garnet moved to Washington from New York a year earlier to minister to colored troops and to pastor the Fifteenth Street Presbyterian Church. He was invited to the House by congressional chaplain William Channing. The hall was packed. The presence of a black choir and an integrated audience was alone remarkable in that setting, noted an attendee, "and it was a sight stranger still to see this colored divine stand up in the dignity of his high office as a priest of the Most High in that Speaker's desk." A friend later wrote that Garnet was "the most radical of the Republicans. A citizen and an agitator; a soldier and a peace-maker. How strangely and wonderfully is his history mingled with the history of our land."[46]

Garnet came forward and read scripture with the voice of "one who wrestled with an angel." He preached of the biblical figures who taught false doctrines, who used their learning and power to serve themselves and not God, and who knew the moral good but were not inclined to embrace it. The point was unmistakable. Everyone in that hall knew that there were modern-day Pharisees who "hated and wronged a portion of their fellowmen, and waged continual war against the government of God." These new despots, continued Garnet, "are faithful to their prototypes of ancient times." They spent their energy and talent shoring up an evil and defending a falsehood. They were drawn from everywhere, and they led their contemporaries down the path of destruction. They exercised such power that they transferred the lie to the church and the state. Some of them, such as New York City mayor Fernando Wood, stood in that very hall and declared that black people were suited by heaven and nature for no higher pursuit than servitude. "I was born among the cherished institutions of slavery," Garnet informed his audience. "My earliest recollections of parents, friends, and the home of my childhood are clouded with its wrongs." He knew the whip and the chain of bondage; he was perfectly prepared to show them "this demon, which the people have worshipped as a God." Its most loathsome feature was that it preyed on human beings, not things, not animals, not ideas. All the rhetoric of the world could not erase that evil. That peculiar property is a man, "God made him such, and his brother cannot unmake him." The whole sin began with "the ruthless traders in the souls and bodies of men [who] fastened upon Christianity a crime and stain at the sight of which it shudders and shrieks."[47]

He pointed to Africa, having suffered centuries of persecution, but still loved by its descendants. In contrast, measure your reward for the national investment in bondage, Garnet urged. Slavery has torn apart your political institutions, drawn vice, greed, and murder upon you, led to godlessness and blasphemy, and "caused the bloodiest civil war recorded in the book of time." He listed the great men from antiquity to the present who opposed servitude. He turned to the future. The status of black Southerners and the limits of reform were the central questions of the moment. Garnet answered both at once because they were inseparable. Agitation would end at the hour of moral reformation:

> When all unjust and heavy burdens shall be removed from every man in the land. When all invidious and proscriptive distinctions shall be blotted out from our laws, whether they be constitutional, statute, or municipal laws. When emancipation shall be followed by enfranchisement, and all men holding allegiance to the government shall enjoy every right of American citizenship. When our brave and gallant soldiers shall have justice done unto them. When the men who endure the suffering and perils of the battle-field in the defence of their country, and in order to keep our rulers in their places, shall enjoy the well-earned privilege of voting for them. When in the army and navy, and in every legitimate and honorable occupation, promotion shall smile upon merit without the slightest regard to the complexion of a man's face. When there shall be no more class-legislation, and no more trouble concerning the black man and his rights, than there is in regard to other American citizens. When, in every respect, he shall be equal before the law, and shall be left to make his own way in the social walks of life. . . . When caste and prejudice in Christian churches shall be utterly destroyed, and shall be regarded as totally unworthy of Christians, and at variance with the principles of the gospel. When the blessings of the Christian religion, and of sound religious education, shall be freely offered to all, then, and not till then, shall the effectual labors of God's people and God's instruments cease.[48]

The nation had thrown off the disgrace of bondage by accident, but it needed to face the challenge of democracy by intent. Enfranchisement was a necessary step in social reorganization. Garnet still clung to the basic nationalist principle of the self-determination of black people and rejected uncritical assimilation. Americans had paid a heavy price, but the collective sin was greater and the atonement incomplete. "Eternal justice holds heavy mortgages against us," continued Garnet, "and prosperity and peace can be purchased only by blood, and with tears of repentance." That day, Brooklyn schoolmaster William J. Wilson was in the hall. An experienced reporter and writer, even he had difficulty describing the impact that Garnet had on the people crowded there. Overwhelmed by the sight, he wrote:

> Men who went to the house to hear a colored man, came away having heard a MAN in the highest and fullest sense. Many who went there with feelings of curiosity, came away wrapped in astonishment. Not only a man, but a great representative man had spoken, and they were amazed.[49]

Slavery's eulogy was delivered to Congress by a one-legged African, claimed as a fugitive slave, whose brilliance carried him to the ministry through the African societies of New York City. The white people gathered in the hall learned that the highest national virtues received their most eloquent plea when black men spoke of freedom.

PART III

The Transformation of African American Voluntarism

9

"The Gaudy Carnival"

The African Declension in the NYASMR, 1863–1945

And even on such a theme I know I must prepare myself for the re-buff from many—"Why talk to *us* of fatherland? What have *we* to do with Africa? *We* are not Africans; we are Americans. You ask no peculiar interest on the part of Germans, Englishmen, the Scotch, the Irish, the Dutch, in the land of their fathers, why then do you ask it of us?"

Alas for us, as a race! so deeply harmed have we been by oppression that we have lost the force of strong, native principles, and prime natural affections. Because exaggerated contempt has been poured upon us, we too become apt pupils in the school of scorn and con-tumely. Because repudiation of the black man has been for centuries the wont of civilized nations, black men themselves get shame at their origin and shrink from the terms which indicate it.

—Alexander Crummell, *The Future of Africa*, 1862

On July 16, 1863, Peter Vogelsang—a member the New York African Society for Mutual Relief and the son of one of its founders—was wounded during a fierce battle at James Island, South Carolina, where he was serving with the Massachusetts Fifty-Fourth Infantry. At that mo-ment, thousands of New York's Irish and German workers were in the middle of a week of antidraft and antiwar rioting during which they murdered dozens of black people and chased hundreds of others from Manhattan as their homes and institutions were destroyed. Three months earlier, on April 17, Vogelsang left his family and a job as a clerk in Brook-lyn to join the army. "I ought to have written you long ago that your man Vogelsang was accepted, and is a Sergeant in one of the new companies.

He is very efficient," Colonel Robert Gould Shaw, commander of the Fifty-Fourth, wrote to his father, who had recommended the recruit. He was the oldest man in the regiment, almost forty-eight at the time he joined, and by the war's end he had risen to regimental quartermaster and to the rank of first lieutenant. Vogelsang organized the first Prince Hall Masonic military lodge.[1]

The motivations that brought Vogelsang, a free black man, to risk his life to wage war against bondage were gathered from his experiences in New York, and they were shared by others. In 1861, with the outbreak of the Civil War, William Powell returned to the United States. From New Bedford, Massachusetts, he immediately began pushing for abolition. He turned his pen against the rebels:

> [I]t is a war—a shameful, outrageous war, to perpetuate the damnable institution of concubinage, cradle-robbing, and women-whipping—a war to obliterate from the statute-books of every nominally free State, all laws granting our people the least protection and political rights—a war to reestablish the accursed African slave-trade![2]

That summer, Alexander Crummell returned from Africa to a reception at the Bridge Street A.W.M.E. Church in Brooklyn. With the leading ministers and society men of New York and Brooklyn in attendance, Crummell declared that "wherever the black man is, he is my brother, preeminently so. Our race is indomitable; no other race could have undergone the oppression we have suffered and survived. But we have not only survived, but progressed; we have taken hold of the pillars of the country, and shaken them to their foundation."[3]

Powell soon followed Crummell back to New York City. "I must confess that, heretofore, I have held in utter contempt the United States flag, because it gave us no protection," he wrote of the new optimism that the war brought. He saw a chance for the uplift of the race. His son William was commissioned as a surgeon in the army. Powell himself took a naval commission. He reestablished his Sailor's Home at No. 2 Dover Street—Mutual Relief brother Albro Lyons ran a Sailor's Home on Vandewater Street and opened a seamen's outfitting shop on Roosevelt Street—and began labor organizing among black sailors. He again emerged as a vocal opponent of slavery and a forceful advocate of abolition as a military strategy.[4]

Early in January 1863, Powell and several other black men organized a celebration of the Emancipation Proclamation at Cooper Union. The

Reverend Henry Highland Garnet delivered the address on behalf of the Committee of the Sons of Freedom. "The old monster dies very hard," Garnet warned. The black men of New York City had already volunteered their military services to the governor. The Reverend John Peterson of the NYASMR also spoke that evening.[5]

Yet, as free black people became more excited about the inevitability of slavery's demise, white New Yorkers became increasingly agitated about the costs of a war that now seemed to benefit not the nation but the Negro. Beginning July 13, 1863, Irish and German workers rioted in Manhattan for days. The violence spread to Brooklyn and the other suburbs. Black people were cursed, chased, slapped, stabbed, kicked, punched, blinded, bitten, scratched, lynched, mutilated, roasted, clubbed, dismembered, stoned, and gouged. Dozens were killed and hundreds were injured. Henry Highland Garnet barely escaped with his life. The Colored Orphan Asylum and other African institutions were torched. "At 1 o'clock, yesterday, the garrison of the Seventh avenue arsenal witnessed a sad and novel sight. Winding slowly along 34th street into Seventh avenue, headed by a strong police force, came the little colored orphans, whose asylum had been burned down on Monday night," noted a local paper. A train of more than two hundred people, including a band of black men and women carrying all their possessions, was escorted to the East River and then to Riker's Island that night by officers and soldiers wielding rifles with bayonets. "I saw a poor negro hanging by the neck on a tree. He was entirely naked, and a slow fire burning under him! His feet were partially roasted; his body scorched in several places, and lifeless! A crowd of low people,—men, women, and children,—were looking on; rude boys were poking the poor corpse with sticks; while others of the crowd were making derision with their victim," reported Noyes Wheeler.[6]

William Powell distinguished himself as an abolitionist and business-man; therefore, on July 18 the pacifist's Seamen's Home was sacked. "A lawless, infuriated New York mob" attacked the house that afternoon and it was "invaded by a mob of half-grown boys," Powell wrote to Garrison.

> As a man of peace, I have religiously, and upon principles eternal as the heavens, never armed myself with deadly weapons of defence, and thus have been at the mercy of the blood-thirsty Vandals. It was the wisdom of one insignificant man that once saved a besieged city. I thank God, who has given me the victory—to rely wholly upon His all-protecting arm. It was better that all my property should be destroyed, as it has been, and my family stripped of everything except the clothing in which they escaped

with their lives, than that one drop of blood should be shed in defence of their lives. Let us thank God that He still reigns, and that He will yet make the wrath of man to praise him. From 2, P.M., till 8, P.M. myself and family were prisoners in my own house to king mob, from which there was no way to escape but over the roofs of adjoining houses. About 4, P.M., I sent a note to Superintendent Kennedy for protection, but received none, from the fact that he had been seriously injured by the mob in another part of the city. Well, the mob commenced throwing stones at the lower windows until they had succeeded in making an opening. I was determined not to leave until driven from the premises. My family, including my invalid daughter, (who is entirely helpless,) took refuge on the roof of the next house. I remained until the mob broke in, and then narrowly escaped the same way. This was about 8 1/2, P.M. We remained on the roof for an hour; still I hoped relief would come. The neighbors, anticipating the mob would fire my house, were removing their effects on the roof—all was excitement. But as the object of the mob was plunder, they were too busily engaged in carrying off all my effects to apply the torch. Add to this, it began to rain as if the very heavens were shedding tears over the dreadful calamity. "Hung be the heavens with black!"

How to escape from the roof of a five-story building with four females—and one a cripple—besides eight men, without a ladder, or any assistance from outside, was beyond my *not* excited imagination. But the God that succored Hagar in her flight came to my relief in the person of a little deformed, despised Israelite—who, Samaritan-like, took my poor helpless daughter under his protection in his house; there I presume she now is, until friends send her to me. He also supplied me with a long rope. I then took a survey of the premises, and fortunately found a way to escape; and though pitchy dark, I took *sounding* with the rope, to see if it would touch the next roof, after which I took a clove-hitch around the clothes-line which was fastened to the wall by pulleys, and which led from one roof to the other over a space of about one hundred feet. In this manner I managed to lower my family down to the next roof, and from one roof to another, until I landed them in a neighbor's yard. We were secreted in our friend's cellar till 11, P.M., when we were taken in charge by the police, and locked up in the Station-house for safety.

Powell and his family remained there for a day with more than seventy other men, women, and children suffering broken bones, other injuries, and bruises. The following evening the police escorted them to the New Haven ferry. Powell's family survived the Draft Riots of 1863; his property did not. Rioters stole or destroyed three thousand dollars worth of his possessions that day.[7]

A mob also swarmed upon the home of the NYASMR's Albro Lyons—Powell's former partner—intent on destroying any vestiges of his hard work. In the first assault they broke windows, tore down the shutters, and kicked in the front door. Lyons and his wife Mary got their children to safety and returned home. Their daughter later recalled:

As the evening drew on, a resolute man and a courageous woman quietly seated themselves in the exposed hall, determined to protect their property, to *sell their lives as dearly as maybe* should the need arise. Lights having been extinguished, a lonely vigil of hours passed in mingled darkness, indignation, uncertainty, and dread. Just after midnight, a yell announced that a second mob was gathering to attempt [an] assault. As one of the foremost of the rioters attempted [to] ascend the front steps, father advanced into the doorway and *fired point blank into the crowd*. Not knowing what might be concealed in the darkened interior, the fickle mob more disorganized than reckless, retreated out of sight hastily and no further demonstration was made that night.[8]

Officer Kelly from the local precinct visited the Lyons that evening and, overwhelmed by the damage and unable to afford them protection, "sobbed like a child." The next day a third rabble took the house.

This sent father over the back fence to the Oak Street [police] station, while mother took refuge on the premises of a neighbor. This was a friendly German who in the morning had loosened boards of intervening fences in anticipation of an emergency. This charitable man, some weeks after, was waylaid and severely beaten by "parties unknown."[9]

When the police cleared the house it was in ruins and the rioters had even attempted to burn it to the ground. That night the police escorted Mary Lyons and the children to Brooklyn on the Williamsburg ferry. Other fugitives from the riots hid in Manhattan hotels. Many refugees escaped to Weeksville, Brooklyn, where the black men were armed to protect evacuees. Albro Lyons stayed in Manhattan to salvage what remained of his property and to prevent looting. Mary Lyons took the children on a long and lonely trek across Long Island over the Sound and through New England to Salem, Massachusetts. She and her husband lost more than fifteen hundred dollars in property.[10]

A group of outraged white businessmen assisted the victims of the riots, and Garnet, Ray, and Peterson constructed black Manhattan's response to the Committee of Merchants for the Relief of Colored People. "When in pursuit of our peaceful and humble occupations we had fallen among thieves, who stripped us of our raiment and had wounded us, leaving many of us half dead, you had compassion on us. . . . You hastened to express your sympathy for those whose fathers, husbands, sons, and brothers had been tortured and murdered. You also comforted the aching hearts of our widowed sisters and soothed the sorrows of orphan children," the black men wrote in praise.[11]

The Draft Riots redrew the map of black New York, bringing a minor exodus of black Manhattanites to the surrounding areas, particularly Brooklyn. The African Society for Mutual Relief, which had always been a New York organization with a few hearty members from outside the city, was transformed into a Brooklyn association with a Manhattan address. Many of the key older members moved to Brooklyn, and, although the majority of the new initiates were New Yorkers, the officers came from a group of young and dynamic Brooklyn residents. For instance, Edward V. C. Eato and John W. Dias, whose families moved from Manhattan to Brooklyn in the postwar years, served in the presidency for most of the association's last six decades.[12]

The Civil War was also a turning point in the social history of African American institutions. After the war, New York's traditional African societies retreated from the public sphere and never again controlled the black community's political and social life. African societies struggled to sustain themselves in the absence of a unifying political goal, in the face of the shifting site of black national politics, under the pressures of an expanding capitalist culture, and in competition with the national appeal of general men's fraternities. The conclusion of the Civil War marked the end of the African society as a dominant institution in black New York's public sphere. The greatest challenge came from within these associations. For instance, the NYASMR suffered most from an internal—and ideological—crisis that divided those who sought to deal with discrimination and other external pressures by making the association a business partnership for the benefit of its members and those who held on to its history of public obligation supported by private financial ties.[13] Mutual Relief abandoned the public sphere as its members split over its collectivist tradition and confronted a growing contempt for African heritage.

The moral and political purpose of the antebellum era was gone. At a similar moment in Cuba the division between Africans and mulattos scarred many of the benevolent organizations that evolved from the earlier *cabildos*.[14] In New York, members of the African Society for Mutual Relief lost any sense of a global struggle and determined to fight for justice for themselves alone. They united around the narrowest of principles: protecting the material interests of a few dozen men.

In short, the NYASMR followed groups like the Society of the Sons of New York into a self-created, exclusive space that sociologist E. Franklin Frazier dubs "the gaudy carnival": a fantasy of black high society. On March 14, 1865, the benevolent Lincoln Literary and Musical Association was organized as an elite social club. In the 1880s the "better" men of color in Manhattan established the Society of the Sons of New York. A Daughters organization soon followed; however, both associations likely responded to the growing presence of black foreigners and Southerners in Gotham. In his zeal to dismantle the fiction of a black elite, Frazier dismissed a complex sociopolitical culture with the accusation of vulgar racial mimicry. The problem of black aspirants to the bourgeoisie was not their race, and if they were guilty of excess, then they were apt students of American middle-class culture. Responding directly to Frazier's work, Kevin K. Gaines warns that the postbellum black elite never sought to be white, rather they brought a boast of their own civility against the political and economic barriers of race. Their fault was their reluctance to challenge many of the racist notions in popular thought, which at times meant incorporating aspects of the broader racial mythology into their uplift program. There were two troublesome aspects of this phenomenon. The economic problem, with which Frazier was most concerned, was that this "high society" lacked the means to sustain its status.[15] The social problem, more relevant here, was its ideological and social isolation from the greater black community. For example, the most striking development in the NYASMR's postbellum history was its incapacity in the public sphere.

The postwar African Society never fit its preferred image as an Old New York elite men's association, and it did not actually have to for the claim to have effect. There were a few foreign-born men in the association, a couple of members were illiterate, and many were Southerners. They looked to break through the barrier of racial injustice by using gradations of color, separations of class, and distinctions of past as pretenses for exemption to caste. For those who were neither from elite backgrounds nor high society, it was even more important that the NYASMR be both. The shift was strategic. It did not negate their sense of unity with all people of African descent. It subordinated it.

Nationalist rhetoric served no purpose in the absence of real political commitments and real political action. Africa and Haiti quietly disappeared from their language and thoughts. The continent and the island that were once offered as the primary evidence of black people's universal right to liberty became uncomfortable symbols of the link between color and poverty. The members ceased thinking of themselves as a single group of men joined in a single cause, just as they stopped seeing their society as an instrument of the larger black community. That was clear from the conflicts they had, and it was also clear in the pattern of their growth. Native-born New Yorkers were always a dominant group, and, after the war, black men from Virginia and the Carolinas were the fastest-growing block. However, Robert A. Gordon (initiated in 1874), a porter living in Manhattan who emigrated from St. Thomas, was the last man to identify himself as foreign-born and still be admitted to the African Society. In 1887 R. S. Tobler, a Bermudan, applied and was swiftly rejected. Three years later, John A. Robinson, from St. Vincent, was turned down in spite of the fact that President Edward Eato vouched for him. More surprisingly, in April 1908 the status-conscious members rejected Robert C. Fraser, M.D., who was born in British Guyana.[16] By themselves, a handful of refusals do not establish the African Society's stance on ethnicity, but they fit rather neatly into a broader pattern.

The members proved unable to reconcile their growing individualism with the society's collectivist traditions. Some men even became publicly uncomfortable with the remnants of the association's nationalist past. In December 1888, William Russell Johnson, a Brooklyn clerk and a board member, moved to delete the word "African" from the name of the NYASMR—a motion that spoke to his hope to see the association avoid discrimination when conducting its public business and his desire to see it focus on matters private and not political. For the moment, the name's historical importance overwhelmed the perceived benefits of a change. The motion was not carried,[17] but the feelings that produced it remained.

In February 1910, William Russell Johnson asked for a special meeting at which he again proposed an amendment changing the name to "The Society for Mutual Relief of the City of New York." (In 1876 the African Methodist Episcopal Church voted down a proposal to change its name to American Methodist Episcopal; however, in 1954 the CME denomination replaced the term "Colored," renaming itself the Christian Methodist Episcopal Church.) Considerable discussion followed the second attempt to rename the NYASMR. The members elected to table the question and have a committee report on its advisability. A committee was selected: Charles Smith, an accountant who served as treasurer and a trustee of the society; former vice president William W. Brown, a Manhattan clerk; long-time member James Linwood; trustee Henry Cunningham, a member for thirty-five years and the father of the society's doctor; and secretary James S. Williams.[18]

This time the resolution received serious consideration. The report, presented at the next regular meeting and captured in the shorthand of the secretary, displayed both the goals of the name change and the self-examination it sparked. The committee's comments began rather blandly. They carefully detailed all the legal steps necessary for a name change. They informed the members that the cost would be $150 to $175. They warned that the new name was too close to that of the Mutual Relief Association of New York (chartered in 1879). Then they turned to the question of color, the central issue, and answered it with brutal honesty: the "momentary advantage gained based on the elimination of any racial prominence in the title, would soon thereafter disappear when the real and true status of the composition of the Society is known, comprehended, or discovered by white-Americans." They analyzed the word "African." If starting all over again, "your Committee freely admits that it would be more than doubtful that *such* [a] name would be chosen." However, "in the absence of some concrete, forceful or material reason why an honorable name handed down to us in unbroken suc[c]ession for over a hundred years by fearless, able and ag[g]ressive men of their day should be now changed, your Committee is forced to look upon such [a] change as unadvisable."[19]

The name was but a symptom of a greater internal problem. As Mutual Relief retreated from the public sphere, its members were pressed to find an organizational purpose. Stripped of their political objectives, African Society meetings were frustrating experiences, comprising excruciatingly dull statements of account and business ritual. The postwar members chose as their primary occupation that which the founders saw as a necessary inconvenience of their design. The early members were driven by their social work and found little need to manufacture internal ceremony. In the absence of social responsibilities, Mutual Relief was a bare benevolent society with a singularly corporate purpose.

Moreover, that raison d'être —death—was also a source of woe. By the end of the Civil War, the NYASMR had lost such icons as Dr. James McCune Smith and Thomas Jennings, the charter generation had passed, and there was but a handful of men who could bind the society to the visions of its founders and its dynamic early decades. When the radical editor and prominent minister Charles B. Ray died in September 1886, the members rushed his death benefit and remaining sick aid to his widow. A few months later the death of Peter Vogelsang Jr. again shook the brotherhood.[20]

Unable or unwilling to sustain a public role, the members attempted to manufacture ceremony and fraternalism around this burial function. In 1918 James Walker Rutledge's death was remembered with a page left blank in the *Minutes*. In 1923 Chaplain Robert Swan died. The members recorded his life by standing for a moment of silence during a regular meeting. When the Reverend Solomon W. Hutchings passed, the entire board of the NYASMR traveled to Burlington, New Jersey, to attend to his family. Hutchings had been a bishop of the Union American Methodist Episcopal Church. The Hutchingses later wrote the society to thank them for their "pilgrimage": "Though your mission was a sad one to us, still it makes the members of the family happy and proud to know of the great respect and high esteem that you held for one who has so suddenly passed from Life to Death."[21]

To stop its decline, the African Society had to become something more than a burial association. However, the members repeatedly rejected the tradition of public engagement and instead sought to copy the success of the men's fraternities by adopting a similar internal culture. Ironically, the black men's fraternities that had grown out of the earlier African societies became the model for Mutual Relief's resurrection. Under the presidency of Edward Eato, Masonic grand master, many fraternal features were imported into the African Society. However ill-fitted, this pomp did bring camaraderie to the group. The ode was sung to begin and end meetings. Attendance in regalia at funerals was stressed. The officers continued to distribute membership pins, the substitute for the badges and sashes of the antebellum era, and they regularly reminded members to wear them for social and official events. In fact, NYASMR pins were being purchased as late as 1938.[22] Regular dinners and celebrations were introduced, and awards for long-term members and officers completing lengthy terms reinforced the new fraternalism.

Stealing a sense of purpose from the national fraternities allowed the members to avoid political engagement, and it reinforced their image as a black bourgeois association—an organization of elite men joined naturally by their substance rather than artificially by their politics. They crafted an institutional history that was compatible with the reality they were constructing. That process occurred over decades. Free men of color like Thomas Downing were heralded, while enslaved men like John

Maranda were forgotten. From somewhere came the allegation that William Hamilton was the bastard son of Alexander Hamilton, and in the NYASMR rumor became reality.[23] Free-born Peter Williams Jr. gained prestige while George DeGrasse, the citizen-slave, went without mention. It was an unfortunate revision. It apologized for the actual origins of the association while it accentuated that which was least important; moreover, it eliminated any ideological reason for addressing the black community's needs.

By the spring of 1891, John J. Zuille had become so frustrated with Mutual Relief's declining significance that he secretly started researching and writing a history of the association. He had long been concerned about the passing of the antebellum generation and the growing self-interest of the younger men. At a regular meeting in April 1887, he offered an impromptu lecture on the history and purpose of the NYASMR, breaking with the strict business ritual. Speaking for a group of members who believed that the association had lost its moral purpose, he instructed the newer initiates that the society was greater than themselves. In May 1891 he read a historical essay. The members enthusiastically received the work and enlisted him to write a full history. "No one among our ranks of living members could more fitly fill the position of historian than Mr. John J. Zuille," remarked President Eato. By January 1893 the history was complete, and Mutual Relief paid to publish and print a hundred cloth-cover editions and two hundred paperback copies. The society donated *The Historical Sketch of the New York African Society for Mutual Relief* to several libraries and sold the remainder at twenty-five cents per copy. In the spring of 1894 John J. Zuille died.[24]

His history did not have the intended impact. The African Society continued to collect, preserve, and distribute its history, but largely for self-aggrandizement. Through the final decade of the nineteenth century, Zuille's *Historical Sketch* was kept in print, and special attention was paid to caring for the society's records. Shortly after the turn of the century, a Historical Committee was active and historians were irregularly elected. Although Zuille had intended to remind the members of their obligations, most members came to use the NYASMR's history as proof of their elite claims. At the annual collation in November 1928, bibliophile and historian Arthur Schomburg, who was tied to many of the African Society's members through Prince Hall Masonry, was invited to lecture on the NYASMR's history before a gathering that included the Reverends Hutchins Bishop, George Frazier Miller, and William McKinney, and Brooklyn Republican leader George Wibecan. Afterwards, the African Society went into a formal negotiation with Schomburg to write a second organizational history.[25] That project was never contracted; nonetheless, Schomburg collected information and published an article on the association.

Mutual Relief did regain a certain prominence, but it was wholly social. Its public image changed in two stages. First, a membership tax allowed the NYASMR to overcome constitutional prohibitions on donating money and to begin to shake off its image as a wealthy but distant association. Second, the officers began to exploit their connections to other black institutions in Manhattan and Brooklyn and their historical position among black men's organizations. Correspondence with black churches, societies, and political organizations allowed them to reenter public discourse while surgically avoiding politics.[26]

"Our fathers built upon a foundation wiser than they knew," said Eato in his annual address of 1905, "for in the Inaugural Address of the President in the year 1810, he expressed a hope that future generations might carry on their work. I am of the opinion that the most sanguine one did not anticipate that this Society would survive the trying ordeals of almost a century, broadening its operations for the material benefit of its members and their families." Eato's brother in Masonry, Samuel Scottron, writing for the *Colored American* magazine, agreed: "It is safe to say that membership in the New York African Society for Mutual Relief, carries with it a greater sense of special worth or ability, financially, to the member than can be said to be true of any other society among Afro-American New Yorkers. . . . In that respect it can't be matched in the United States among colored men."[27]

In the *Story of the Negro Race*, Booker T. Washington noted that the New York African Society for Mutual Relief had reached its centennial; however, the only recent accomplishment that he could point to was its wealth. In style and substance, the African Society became little more than a well-to-do, local men's fraternity. In the spring of 1907, the African Society was preparing for a grand social function to mark its one hundredth anniversary. A Centennial Committee planned the festivities. The guest list included Samuel Scottron, the Honorable Charles Anderson, the Reverends Hutchins C. Bishop and George Frazier Miller, and Bishop Alexander Walters. They began with a service at St. Philip's Protestant Episcopal Church on Sunday evening, June 7, 1907. The following Wednesday, June 10, carriages and automobiles emptied their occupants at the [Carnegie] hall, and the care and expense entailed by the absolutely charming gowns which bedecked the ladies was a matter of remark. The banquet hall was a bower of flowers and the sweet strains of the orchestra, hidden by large palms, gave the place almost an Oriental charm. The men wore conventional evening dress and when Toastmaster Charles H. Lansing called upon the Rev. William T. Dixon to bless the assemblage, the picture was one seldom witnessed.

Dixon pastored Brooklyn's Concord Baptist Church. The Carnegie Hall banquet also included D. Macon Webster's lecture on the NYASMR and a six-piece orchestra secured for the night.[28]

Eato saved Mutual Relief by encouraging its fraternal culture. When past-president William H. Anthony was elevated from treasurer to vice president, Eato congratulated him on his long and faithful service to the NYASMR. At the annual collation of that year, Anthony received a testimonial and was awarded "a beautiful gold badge suitably inscribed with the name of the society [and the] date of presentation." In 1910, when Eato resigned the presidency, the members gave him an engraved silver loving cup at the annual collation. Eato was so overcome that he could only respond, "I thank you." Two years later James Walker Rutledge received a gold coin for his service as chairman of the board from 1885 to 1910. In 1918 gossip about the age of the society's elder member, Mensor P. Saunders, brought a celebration of his birthday. (Saunders was also grand secretary of New York State Prince Hall Masonry.) "The New York African Society for Mutual Relief digressed long enough in its steady and venerable career of 110 years' existence to abandon its regular place of meeting in the World Building for Murray's Restaurant, 70 Pine street, Monday, to do honor to one of its oldest members, Mensor P. Saunders," reported the *New York Age*. During his party, Saunders "confessed to eighty years existence without regard to the years he had really lived." Dr. Walter N. Beekman, dentist to Manhattan's black celebrities, and Alonzo Skrine, Saunders's brother in Masonry, served as masters of ceremony. Saunders received a gold ring with the NYASMR seal. "I cannot speak too highly of the regard I have for the men of the Society, whose friendship I have had the pleasure to enjoy to no little extent since 1880," the honoree later wrote. Five years later, when Saunders died, the usual floral wreath was sent to the family, and members of the NYASMR acted as pallbearers at his funeral at Bridge Street A.W.M.E. Church. In 1936 Charles T. Smith was being honored for more than a quarter century of service as treasurer.[29]

In a sad irony, Mutual Relief had become a quaint and ineffective association—a fairly extravagant social club—at a time when black New Yorkers faced numerous problems and other, less wealthy, organizations were addressing those needs. At noon, Saturday, July 28, 1917, a coalition of benevolent societies displayed the type of leadership that antebellum African associations had exercised and for which postbellum black communities craved. Ten thousand black men, women, and children marched from Fifty-Sixth Street along Fifth Avenue to Twenty-Third Street at Madison Square Garden. The procession protested racial violence in Waco, East St. Louis, and Memphis, and, more broadly, lynching. The participants carried banners and placards but did not utter a sound. A drum beat was the only noise. The Silent Parade Against Lynching launched a new phase of political struggle in New York. "For once the American Negro, [British] West Indian Negro and Haitian worked in unison as black men," the *Age* triumphantly declared. The Bermuda Benevolent Association, the American West Indian Ladies Aid Society, the Danish West Indian Benevolent Society, the Montserrat Benevolent Association, the St. Vincent Cricket Club, and the Caribbean American Publishing Company joined with African American societies to fund and organize the protest.[30] The NYASMR was noticeably absent.

John E. Nail was the treasurer of the committee that coordinated the Silent Parade through St. Philip's. They plastered Manhattan with flyers announcing their public meetings. In the aftermath, the committee sent a letter to President Woodrow Wilson on behalf of "the colored people of Greater New York" and representing "the sentiment of the people of Negro descent throughout the land." They reminded Wilson that lynch mobs had slaughtered 2,867 black men and women over three decades, but the authorities had not produced a single murder conviction. A distinguished committee—including Fred Moore of the *Age*, James Weldon Johnson of the NAACP, Dr. W. E. B. Du Bois of the *Crisis*, millionaire industrialist Madame C. J. Walker, the Reverends Adam Clayton Powell of Abyssinian Baptist and George Frazier Miller of St. Augustine's, and John Nail—drafted the public statement and brought it to the White House. They were cordially refused an audience with the president.[31]

Nail, who joined the NYASMR five years after the parade, captured the African Society's evolution into an apolitical organization. His fame was also inherited. His father was John B. Nail, the owner of a fancy men's parlor in Manhattan and a wealthy Brooklynite who dabbled in Tammany Hall politics in the late nineteenth century. The younger Nail joined with Henry C. Parker to establish Nail and Parker, a leading Harlem real estate company. In 1909 Nail and Parker organized the sale of St. Philip's Church on West 25th Street (in a largely black neighborhood commonly called the Tenderloin) for the Reverend Hutchins C. Bishop. Upon moving to Harlem, the church sold its lower Manhattan building for $140,000, and in 1911 it sold its nearby cemetery for $450,000. St. Philip's purchased ten apartment buildings along 135th Street for $640,000 and a new house of worship in Harlem. Nail and Parker continued to handle St. Philip's business, and they were the agents when the "colored YMCA" moved to Harlem. The African Society cherished Nail's membership because he was proof of their claim to elite status among black organizations. Ironically, Nail used the African Society to boast about his membership in a prominent men's association and to glean a few opportunities to meet and mingle with current or future business partners. Earlier, Nail had lobbied to handle the society's real estate business, and his firm was among those that made offers to buy its properties. At no point was Nail a truly active member. He was president of the Negro Board of Trade in Harlem, vice president of the Republican Business Men's Club of New York City with its largely white membership, a member of the Mayor's Housing Committee, the first black man on the city's Real Estate Board, and a consultant to President Herbert Hoover's national commission on urban housing. In contrast, his attendance at NYASMR meetings lapsed, he forgot to pay his dues for almost a year, and ten years after he was initiated he was quietly removed from the rolls. More significantly, Nail's most public involvement in politics took place before he was ever a member of the NYASMR. That was, after all, no longer what the African Society did.[32]

It was not until the Great Depression that the members broke with their long pattern of isolation and again took a clear stance on a political issue facing the nation. In 1933 they voted to condemn the trial, conviction, and sentencing of nine black youths charged with the rape of two white women in Scottsboro, Alabama, a sequence of injustices that brought international criticism. (A year earlier, New York State's Prince Hall Masons appealed to Governor Franklin Delano Roosevelt for the commutation of the sentence of Ruth Brown, a black woman on death row. Grand Master Edward T. Sherwood Jr. wrote on behalf of the Craft, calling on the governor to reexamine the evidence against the condemned for justice's sake.) In April 1933, John Dias, on behalf of the African Society, instructed President Franklin Delano Roosevelt that the oldest incorporated organization of black Americans unequivocally rejected the decision in Scottsboro and called on him to intervene:

> The New York African Society for Mutual Relief, Inc., organized in 1808, chartered by the Legislature of the State of New York in 1810, and re-incorporated in 1901—at its regular meeting on Monday, April 10, 1933, the Pulitzer Building, New York, New York, deferred its regular course of business, to register an indignant and emphatic protest at this apparent and glaring miscarriage of justice, resulting from a pitiless bigotry and an unsatiable prejudice. The verdict flaunts the broad boast of American fair play, and shocks the keen sense of justice of all unbiased persons.

> This Society deeply regrets that such a sad condition should still obtain in this year of 1933, and it expresses the sincere hope that your kind offices as President of these United States may be enlisted, to find some means of relieving the victim in his dire straits, and vindicate what appears to be a travesty of law and justice, and to the end that the other impending victims in this case may be spared a similar fate.[33]

In but a few lines Dias had blended his knowledge of the organization's historic achievements with his conviction that the African Society was still relevant to the struggle against injustice. Members of the NYASMR participated in rallies and protests of the Scottsboro affair, but, more importantly, Scottsboro briefly brought a sense of purpose to the organization that had been absent since the Civil War.

Nonetheless, the African Society for Mutual Relief's involvement in the Scottsboro protests was an aberration, not a change of philosophy. The society's transition from a primarily political to a primarily financial association made it nearly impossible to sustain any political work. Its lack of faith in collective action also erased options that might have sustained the NYASMR as a benevolent organization.

That fact can best be seen in comparison. In the late 1930s, John Dias, president of the NYASMR, was the neighbor of William Ince, a founder, incorporator, director, and the third president of Brooklyn's Paragon Progressive Community Association (PPCA); in fact, most of Mutual Relief's officers lived in Bedford-Stuyvesant alongside Paragon's founders and directors. The two associations were on radically different trajectories. Begun on July 18, 1939, with a little money collected at its first meeting, PPCA thrived by bringing cooperative economics to black Brooklyn, while a few years later the NYASMR folded despite its impressive financial holdings. Nine black Brooklynites, most of Barbadian ancestry, founded Paragon. Rufus Murray, a leading Scottish Rite Mason, guided the efforts of Dr. St. Clair Critchlow, Ferrara Levi Lord, William Ince, Fitzroy Stephens, Rupert Jemmott, Clarence Medford, Lloyd Wilson, and Redmond Peyton. The PPCA followed Marcus Garvey's call for black collectivism and economic nationalism. Its headquarters were in a Fulton Street basement. It later moved to its own site. Paragon operated as a traditional benevolent society—offering sick aid and social events—with a less traditional business arm.[34]

The Paragon Progressive Federal Credit Union was chartered on January 29, 1941, and opened on February 24, 1941. It extended credit for "educational, medical, hospital and dental expenses; payment of various taxes, interest on mortgages and insurance premiums; purchase of fuel, clothing for the family, furniture, household appliances, automobiles, radios and a variety of other useful things necessary for their comfort and convenience." At their first meeting in 1939, the founders collected only $2.25, and within forty years Paragon had issued millions in loans and held $4.7 million in total assets.[35]

In contrast, by 1945 the NYASMR was not much of a society. The old tradition of association in intrigue was buried in the nineteenth century. In 1945, with its membership dwindling and unable to attract new initiates, the New York African Society for Mutual Relief folded.[36]

On Easter Sunday 1969, the Reverend George W. McMurray, pastor of Mother Zion, gathered with his choir, parishioners, bishop, and several politicians, including Manhattan borough president Percy Sutton, to unveil a copper and brass plaque at Church and Leonard streets, the site of New York's first black church. The day before, New York City mayor John Lindsay had posed with Zion's ministers and trustees at Gracie Mansion where a representation of the plaque was displayed for the media. The Negro History Association of New York City organized the ceremony and completed the historical research. That same year, writes Bishop William Walls, the surviving members of the NYASMR came together for a ceremony during which a plaque was placed on their old Baxter Street property.[37] Mutual Relief's observance went unnoticed.

The African declension was mostly ideological.

10

"Shall It Be a Woman?"

The Transformation of Black Men's Voluntarism, 1865–1960

> Methinks I heard a spiritual interrogation—
> 'Who shall go forward, and take off the reproach
> that is cast upon the people of color?
> Shall it be a woman?'
> And my heart made this reply—
> 'If it is thy will, be it even so, Lord Jesus!'
> —Maria W. Stewart, in *The Liberator*,
> November 12, 1832

That African Americans' material aspirations determined the culture of antebellum black organizations is a theme in the historiography; a corollary of this assertion is that black associations imitated the cultural patterns of white Americans. William Alan Muraskin asserts that Prince Hall Masonry was founded during the Revolution as a middle-class device. Organizations were a means of enforcing class boundaries in a community with few real material distinctions. Through associations, black people not only aspired upward, but mimicked their white betters. Besides giving ownership of national creeds to white Americans, Muraskin defines black people's ideals as antagonistic to and destructive of American norms. E. Franklin Frazier's work also accepts that black associations attempted to mirror the white bourgeoisie. "The mutual aid societies and the secret fraternal organizations first appeared among the free Negroes," writes Frazier. "Both types of organizations grew up in response to the needs of the Negro and reflected the influence of white patterns."[1]

Like Muraskin, Frazier offers the not-so-novel fact that free black people organized the first relief societies as proof that a self-conscious and self-interested middle class was seeking to divorce itself from the greater black community and attach itself to middling white Americans. It was exclusion from white associations, adds Gunnar Myrdal, that led to the formation of black societies. In his history of United States lodges, Charles Ferguson concurs and extends the perception of imitative and obsequious African American fraternalism in a chapter that wore the mean title, "Blackface: The Lodges of the American Negro." Concluding that white people were responsible for establishing the societal tradition among black Americans, Ferguson writes that "high-minded whites began early to dress the Negro in symbolic robes and breeches." In short, his position was not far from that of the Philadelphia woman who, on October 5, 1847, looked out of her window to see a procession of the local and New York lodges of the Grand United Order of Odd Fellows and declared, "La! it's the Nigger Masons."[2]

This historiography is encumbered by ill-founded assumptions. The most obvious error results from an inattention to the West African influences on early black American societies and concludes that African American institutions with white parallels must be Euro-American inspired. It also exploits the poverty of sources on the early African societies, a scarcity aggravated by their rapid postbellum collapse, to make their recent history definitive. The first result is an ahistorical conclusion that the early African societies were immature versions of postbellum black associations; in fact, societal life was far more vibrant among black men before the Civil War. The second error holds that black societies lived to nurture a middle-class tradition but fails to define the basis of that tradition. The middle class was not a fixed, or even stable, social group across that lengthy period. The problem is compounded because this position also mistakes the moralism of early African American discourse for a class affectation rather than a political strategy. Moral discourse was the cornerstone of an attack on slavery that, while carrying material consequences, was the hallmark of a church-based social movement. The overall effect is that the scholarship grants white actors title to the most universal social tenets and creates black associations as poor mimics of white social phenomena.

The ability of white Americans to isolate black people from middle-class status need not be complemented by the pretense that white people are the sole authors and carriers of the general social values. What these historians have missed is that white men's lodges and fraternities were themselves in flux, changing rapidly in the decades before and after the

Civil War from loosely structured drinking clubs into ritual-driven associations of temperate, middle-class men. Mark C. Carnes argues that the growth of incessant and lavish ceremony in these organizations was intended to give young men a moral and psychological guide to manhood in Victorian America. The explanation for "why [white] men joined organizations whose chief, and in some cases only, ostensible purpose was the performance of elaborate successions of initiatory rituals" was to be found in the transformation of male socialization in the preceding decades.[3] Black men's associations occupied a different cultural place and satisfied distinct social functions, a divergence that has not been explained by the scholarly assumption of cross-cultural aping.

The fact is that the ascendance of capitalism enveloped men's associations, black and white, in bourgeois culture. Individualism, thrift, and industry occur logically among and are generally understood by all the members of an acquisitive society. The antebellum demand for the emancipation of the enslaved constituted a revolutionary objective that put African societies in a hostile relationship to the established social order and the laws that protected it; after the Civil War, few African American associations extended an alternative vision of the social system, rather they worked to rid the industrial nation of its barbaric racial baggage. Postbellum associations called for full inclusion by wrapping themselves in the system's basic principles. It is true that African American societies became particularly middle class in their focus and philosophy in the aftermath of the war, but it is an act of pure self-flattery to read racial mimicry into that behavior and language when both were simply adjustments to the reigning social system.

Looking at the Western Native Township, South Africa, Hilda Kupler and Selma Kaplan found a similar transition in a wide variety of burial societies and savings associations premised "largely in the money values of the Western world." More than 65 percent of the sample population belonged to a burial society, and interviewees were almost four times as likely to save for and secure their futures through informal local associations than through the services of professional insurance dealers. "Stokfel" and "Mahodisana," the most common of these organizations, alone claimed a fifth of the respondents. Mixing mutual aid and personal thrift, they encouraged and facilitated property ownership. The attraction of such societies was probably their informality, which personalized the financial arrangement and allowed for flexibility and forgiveness. Their success reflected Africans' ability to apply culturally comfortable mechanisms to new social objectives. In the late 1920s A.M.E. bishop George Benjamin Young helped found the South African Burial Society, which became one of the largest businesses owned by the Bantu. Similarly, independent and church-based benevolent and burial societies adapted to the changing social conditions of the urban and rural United States. Toward the end of the century, historian, novelist, and abolitionist William Wells Brown wrote critically of the Southern phenomenon:

> To get religion, join a benevolent society that will pay them "sick dues" when they are ill, and to bury them when they die, appears to be the beginning, the aim, and the end of the desires of the colored people of the South. In Petersburg I was informed that there were thirty-two different secret societies in that city, and I met persons who held membership in four at the same time.[4]

After the Civil War, African societies declined. Their demise was not a product of capitalist culture but a reflection of changes in African American culture. For instance, while Brown continued to tie religion and relief, God was an immediate casualty of African associations' postwar transformation. Religious men still joined such organizations and maintained organizational connections to black churches, but these men no longer saw themselves as soldiers in a moral revolution that would bring on a social or spiritual redemption. Social work receded from their agendas. The African societies stopped being the agents of religious enthusiasm. Moreover, the disappearance of overarching political goals undermined their communitarian and nationalistic basis and allowed class and ethnic interests to more fully define the divisions between and within societies. The black associations that most easily incorporated individualistic values fared best.

The local and charitable focus of the African benevolent societies was a disadvantage in a competition with national associations organized around material concerns. Most instructive is the career of the International Order of Twelve of the Knights and Daughters of Tabor. In 1846 twelve black men met in St. Louis to plan the Knights of Liberty, a secret society with revolutionary aims. The original goal was to spread across the nation and eventually liberate the enslaved. The Knights soon abandoned that plan and became active in the Underground Railroad. The Reverend Moses Dickson, its founder, enlisted in the Union Army during the war, as did a number of its members. In 1871 Dickson formed the kindred Knights and Daughters of Tabor, spreading its tabernacles and temples nationally. No longer a society of black men combined in intrigue, the postwar Knights and Daughters tried to "break every chain of injustice" by mixing religion, education, accumulation, and temperance into a recipe for bourgeois success.[5]

The Coachmen's Union League Society, Inc. (CULS), adapted the African society form to a labor organization. The Coachmen's League was founded in 1864 and possibly influenced by the death of driver Abraham Franklin, who was pulled from his coach, tortured, and murdered—his body then savagely mutilated and displayed—by an Irish mob during the 1863 Draft Riots. The society's founders were Manhattan coachmen "fired with ambition and hopes, looking toward a new day of justice, freedom and achievement." The language of their constitution was taken from that of the NYASMR:

> We, the subscribers, reflecting daily upon the various vicissitudes of life to which mankind is continually exposed and stimulated by the desire of improving our condition do conclude that the most efficient method of securing ourselves from the extreme exigencies of life to which we are liable to be reduced is by uniting ourselves in a body for the purpose of raising a fund for the relief of our members.[6]

By 1925 the Coachmen had twelve hundred members and assets totaling more than $85,000. They held monthly lectures, ran an employment bureau, donated money to local and national civil rights and uplift organizations, and even attempted to confederate the black benevolent and fraternal societies of New York by purchasing a hall for their collective use. The latter plan failed, but alone the CULS bought a large, handsome building at No. 252 West 138th Street in Harlem. The Coachmen's Home included quarters for other associations, lodge rooms, recreational areas, and an eatery.[7]

In 1869 twelve black caterers, including George Green of the NYASMR, brought the mutual relief model into the Corporation of Caterers with the goals of protecting and promoting their business interests and regulating the quality of catering in New York City. In 1872 the organization began a mutual aid program and was renamed the United Public Waiters Mutual Beneficial Association. Admitting small businessmen and waiters, the United Public Waiters' membership exceeded one hundred, about a fifth of all the black waiters in the city. This benevolent labor association survived until 1905.[8]

The entrance of black men into the Knights of Pythias displayed an equally militant insistence upon political and material equality. In 1870 the Supreme Lodge rejected the application of several men of color. A year later John Parker, a white Pythian residing in Louisiana, advocated the acceptance of black men into the fraternity, an act which brought his expulsion and the nine-year revocation of the Louisiana Grand Lodge's charter. In reaction, men of light complexion in Mississippi applied for admission without mentioning that they were of African ancestry and were initiated. One of them, Dr. Thomas W. Stringer, immediately established the "Colored Knights of Pythias." On March 26, 1880, Lightfoot Lodge No. 1 was founded in Vicksburg, Mississippi. Two other lodges were formed along with a Grand Lodge and a Supreme Council. A month later, the "Constitution and By-Laws of the Supreme Lodge Knights of Pythias of North and South America, Europe, Asia and Africa Inclusive" were adopted. The black Pythians offered sick aid, burial assistance, widow and orphan relief, and intellectual and spiritual uplift. Politics were not to infect the fraternity, instead "obedience to law, loyalty to government, are its cardinal principles."[9]

In 1873 the Grand Fountain of the United Order of True Reformers was organized. White Reformers in Huntsville, Alabama, encouraged the formation of black fountains and promised complete autonomy. Under the administration of the Reverend William Washington Browne, once enslaved in Georgia, twenty-seven fountains were opened with about two thousand members. In 1881 Browne assumed control of the Richmond, Virginia, fountain by invitation of its members. The new grand worthy master of Virginia instituted a "mutual benefit" plan. Browne guided the True Reformers in creating a realty division, a bank, and an old age home. Working through the state's black churches, Browne looked to blend religion, reform, and relief "to break down crime, licentiousness, poverty and wretchedness." While the organization had its origins among white men in Alabama, the black Reformers insisted that "the United Order of True Reformers, as a Mutual Benefit Association, was founded by William Washington Browne, at a meeting of the True Reformers at the Orphan Asylum, at Richmond, Va., January 11, 1881." The Reformers established themselves in Brooklyn, apparently through Bridge Street Church, and, after the turn of the century, they opened a True Reformers Hall in Manhattan.[10]

The Invincible Sons and Daughters of Commerce wore their bourgeois objectives even more proudly. Brooklyn's Augustus M. Hodges helped found the organization, on the 1896 anniversary of Abraham Lincoln's birthday, as a secret society with "signs, grips, degrees, passwords, etc." The ISDC practiced economic nationalism, with the members sworn to purchase from black shopkeepers and use the organization's money to fund and support new businesses. The Sons and Daughters saw their economic focus as distinct in the history of black associations: "THE I.S.D.C. IS NOT A DEATH BENEFIT SOCIETY, BUT ONE TO BENEFIT YOU WHILE YOU LIVE. . . . We differ from the old societies."[11]

No society matched the rise of the black Elks. The Elks began as the "Jolly Corks," a band of white actors who came together in 1867 as a social club named for a drinking game. On February 16, 1868, after the funeral of a companion, they reorganized as the Benevolent and Protective Order of Elks. In 1890 the Elks constitutionally prohibited the initiation of non-white men. Black Elkdom began in 1896, the brainchild of Arthur J. Riggs, who organized Cincinnati's Knights of Pythias and served as Pythian Grand Chancellor of Ohio. That year, Riggs, a Pullman porter, secured a copy of the Elks' ritual on his train during the Grand Lodge meeting in Cincinnati. He then edited the ritual, brought it to a printer, and had it copyrighted. On November 17, 1898, Riggs called together the first black Elks Lodge at the Masonic Temple in Cincinnati. The white Elks, angered that their secrets were in the possession of black men, stormed in to dismiss the illegal gathering. The black men

> demanded that the Exalted white Ruler show us his copyright for his ritual. He said we were here first, and you Negroes have no right to use the B. P. O. E. Ritual. I said, look at this, and I produced my copyright signed by Uncle Sam and said, if I hear another word about a Negro Elk Lodge I will put the entire white Lodge in Jail for infringing on my copyright.

Riggs was later threatened with lynching and eventually fled Cincinnati, but black Elkdom flourished across the nation.[12]

In 1919 Cyril Briggs, an immigrant from St. Kitts, organized the socialist African Blood Brotherhood in New York, an organization with social functions that approached those of the antebellum African societies. The ABB was a "Negro secret organization," spread through small militaristic units and dedicated to "the liberation of Africa and the redemption of the Negro race." The Brotherhood offered a blend of nationalism and socialism that encouraged people of African descent to overcome their ethnic and cultural divisions, practice cooperative economics, prepare for self-defense, advance in the trades, improve their individual and group morality, control the education of black children and promote the history of African peoples, form literary groups, and push into the effort for race advancement at the grassroots level.[13] The Blood Brotherhood's platform was oddly reminiscent of the campaigns that emerged from African voluntary associations in antebellum New York.

National, political, and economic associations were stiff competition for African societies, and black entrepreneurs in banking and indemnity posed an equally daunting challenge. "For these benefits Negroes have turned to the more secure benefits of Negro insurance companies, which represent the greatest achievements of Negro business enterprise," writes Frazier of the challenge that African American businessmen presented. Gunnar Myrdal adds that "the most direct origin of the insurance company, of course is the benevolent society, of which there are a great number among the Negroes."[14]

National organizations controlled enough capital to respond. As early as 1906 the black Knights of Pythias had a Virginia bank with almost $100,000 in deposits. In 1911 the Masons partnered with the Odd Fellows and the Knights of Pythias to form a bank. In 1930 the Masons took complete control of the institution, which had $600,000 in total deposits. In the years that followed, local and statewide lodges created banks, credit unions, and loan associations that provided hundreds of thousands of dollars to fund organizational, individual, and community projects.[15]

Similarly, the Freemasons' entry into insurance occurred on a far grander scale than the African societies could achieve. The New York African Society for Mutual Relief influenced the 1888 founding of the Hiram Masonic Relief Association of the State of New York. Although established under a most worshipful grand master from Albany and chartered as a statewide organization, Masonic Relief was originally to be controlled by the Freemasons of New York City. The objective of the association was "to assist and render aid to the widows and orphans of worthy Master Masons." By 1894 Freemasons from Brooklyn and Manhattan accounted for more than 60 percent (124 of 204) of HMRA's members. "The work of the Hiram Masonic Relief Association, with its objects, demands our united and earnest support individually and also as a body representing this jurisdiction," wrote the Most Worshipful Grand Master Edward V. C. Eato in 1901. Eato, president of the NYASMR, was one of HMRA's strongest advocates.[16]

Local labor and ethnic associations had advantages over African societies in attracting members, particularly migrants and immigrants, in the changing city. The Southern League was the largest of the new benevolent associations, but it eventually suffered a financial collapse. In the 1890s the Society of the Sons of North Carolina appeared. By 1925 the North

Carolinians had more than four hundred members and a three-story meeting house in Brooklyn. In 1899 Brooklyn's Sons of Virginia was formed, and soon a Daughters association was organized. Eight years later, over a hundred men had joined the Virginia club, with two thousand dollars in assets. From the turn of the century to 1920, Manhattan saw the founding of the Sons and Daughters of Florida, the South Carolina Club, and the United Sons and Daughters of Georgia, the wealthiest state association. In 1897 San Juan Hill businessmen Clarence W. Robinson and George L. Joell organized the Bermuda Benevolent Association. During the next thirty years, Irma Watkins-Owens writes, several black West Indian organizations emerged: the Montserrat Progressive Society, the American West Indian Ladies Aid Society, the Grenada Mutual Association, the Sons and Daughters of Barbados, the Trinidad Benevolent Association (whose founder also began the political Caribbean Union), the women's West Indian Federation, the Virgin Island Industrial Association, and the St. Lucia United Association. State and "homeland" organizations offered mutual relief in the form of informal and formal savings and loans associations, sick aid, and burial insurance, and engaged in focused local, national, and international political and social action. Caribbean fraternal orders also appeared. The first was Manhattan's El Sol de Cuba No. 38, a Prince Hall lodge warranted on June 1, 1881. By the 1920s the Logia Hijos del Caribe, No. 75, Prince Hall, was active in New York. Black West Indians were heavily involved in New York State Masonry and had reached its highest ranks. Louis Alexander Jeppe, who was born in St. Thomas in 1869 and emigrated to the United States in 1888, served four terms as the worshipful master of a Brooklyn lodge, was the state lodge's first grand historian, and was later appointed grand orator.[17] Jeppe was also a leader of Brooklyn's West Indian Forum, a cultural association.

Before the Civil War, black organizations like the Masons and Odd Fellows were distinctly political; after the war, their international network and their culture of rituals eased the transition to apolitical organizing. Muraskin's argument that black Masonry had historically opposed any institutional involvement in politics more accurately describes its postbellum history. The ability to enter and exit politics without losing organizational purpose allowed the Elks and the Masons to experience extraordinary growth in New York and across the nation. By 1946 black Elkdom included half a million members, and by 1960 the black Craft had four hundred thousand.[18]

Limited to local recruiting, no longer enjoying mass cultural appeal, and offering only a citywide network, the New York African Society for Mutual Relief faltered. West Indian benevolent associations showed that the community and cultural basis of activism had not disappeared. Mutual Relief's major problem was its members' discomfort with localism. They looked to the national organizations with envy and grew peculiarly resentful of their responsibilities to the immediate community and of the fact that the organization was not suited to greater endeavors. On April 23, 1907, the Reverend R. A. Royster founded the Men's Aid Society, No. 1, of Sheepshead Bay, Brooklyn. "The object of the society is caring for the sick and burying the dead," reported the *Age*. It had eight charter members and a structure similar to the NYASMR's. By its first anniversary, the organization's membership had grown to fifty and it had assets of two hundred dollars. In short, the Men's Aid Society was a minor, local relief association, exactly what the NYASMR would have been if not for its antebellum investments. "The African Society for Mutual Relief is the oldest of its character in existence; it has always maintained its exclusive character as to the type of men to be admitted into membership which is restricted. However, over the years, that exclusiveness has been maintained but the 'exclusiveness' is not of its original character," prodded Harry Williamson, a leading Freemason and Odd Fellow from Brooklyn.[19]

Offering black men tens of thousands of members, lower costs, more secure benefits, and countless opportunities for advancement, the Masons, Odd Fellows, Elks, and Pythians redefined the pattern of black men's voluntarism. The power of the African association was ideological; and, in the absence of a universally accepted political cause, general men's fraternities proved more viable at recruiting in increasingly diverse and divergent black communities. Moreover, the appearance of intercollegiate fraternities among men of color—beginning with the Boulé or Sigma Pi Phi (1904), Alpha Phi Alpha (1906), Kappa Alpha Psi (1911), Omega Psi Phi (1911), and Phi Beta Sigma (1914)—sharpened the class distinctions among men's societies. Black sororities, especially Alpha Kappa Alpha (1908) and Delta Sigma Theta (1913),[20] had the same effect among women.

Predictably, the most significant presidency in the NYASMR's postbellum history came under a man who simultaneously led Prince Hall Masonry in New York. On October 17, 1905, grand master Edward V. C. Eato installed the officers and bestowed the credentials on the initiates of Brooklyn's Carthaginian Lodge, a name honoring "the land of our forefathers, Carthage." Black people from across Kings County, Manhattan, and the surrounding area came to Sumner Hall on Fulton Street to participate. Samuel

Scottron, a former grand secretary of the fraternity, reported that "three hundred ladies and gentlemen assembled, and all were fully impressed with the solemnity of the occasion as well as gratified with the lighter parts following, when ensued music, dancing and refreshments." Brooklyn's newest Masonic lodge included at least two members of the African Society for Mutual Relief.[21]

William Oscar Payne, with exaggerated tones, instructed a Brooklyn audience that "Masonry is the handmaid of religion and that toleration, truth, and justice are the most important tenets. The Jew, the Mohommedan, the Catholic, the Protestant, each professing his peculiar religion may retain their faith and yet be Masons. Masonry is the universal morality which is suitable to living man and to every creed."[22] Through Freemasonry, black men continued to find society without the burdens of the old African associations; for, Masonic culture adapted comfortably to apolitical pursuits.

A year after the Masonic initiation, the "colored Elks" held their national convention in Brooklyn. Again the proceedings were the source of excitement. Brooklyn Lodge No. 32 was the "mother lodge" of New York State and had four hundred members. The local Elks were established by James A. Roston, who had been promoted from private to lieutenant for his valor in the Philippines during the Spanish-American War. Roston's lecture captivated the audience and the convention was touted as the fraternity's most successful. By 1928 the Brooklyn Elks alone had eighteen hundred members. Elkdom also kept close relations with the black church; for instance, the minister of Brooklyn's Fleet Street A.M.E. Zion Church, Dr. W. C. Brown, was grand chaplain of the Elks. (The Reverend Brown was also a grand officer of the Knights of Pythias of New York State.)[23]

In the contest between men's associations, the African societies' appeal eroded with the loss of their social functions. For example, the African societies' control over black education in New York and Brooklyn slowly ended in the nineteenth century as the African schools were absorbed into the public system. Local black leaders joined the Board of Education, but black organizations no longer provided and governed schools for the community. The process can be traced rather neatly in Brooklyn, where the Woolman Society once supervised the education of black children. Just before the Civil War, the African schools were brought under municipal control. Black Brooklynites were given a seat on the Board of Education but lost community control. In 1882 Dr. Philip A. White, who studied under the NYASMR's James McCune Smith, became the first African

American appointed to serve on the Brooklyn Board of Education. In 1891 attorney and Democratic politician Thomas McCants Stewart began a term of service. From 1894 to 1898, Samuel Scottron sat on the Brooklyn Board.[24] In but a few decades the task of educating black children moved from community to municipal hands.

Similarly, the Fifteenth Amendment dramatically and immediately shifted the stage of black national politics in the United States to the South. New York State's black men received an unrestricted right to vote and soon became a presence in the regular Democratic and Republican organizations. Professional black politicians transformed the nature of leadership in the New York community and, in doing so, reshaped the political space within which black societies operated. John B. Nail—the father of Harlem realtor John E. Nail, a member of the NYASMR—emerged as the postbellum black underboss of Tammany Hall, Manhattan's Democratic machine. Nail came to New York from Baltimore during the war and began working in the local gambling clubs. By the 1880s he owned his own elegant parlor on Twenty-Eighth Street in the Tenderloin, and Tammany was courting him. Nail, like the politicians who followed, sought the support of black ministries and societies. On January 12, 1905, J. H. Anderson, Isaiah K. Berry, and William K. Scott organized the Monitor League, a political club in the San Juan Hill section of Manhattan that blended moral stewardship and benevolent outreach. The club offered a library, lecture series, and neighborhood improvement campaigns. Its leadership, actual and honorary, included the leading black businessmen and black Republican politicians of New York and Brooklyn. Twentieth-century leaders—including congressman Adam Clayton Powell Jr., the pastor of Abyssinian Baptist Church and a Mason; Manhattan borough president Percy Sutton, a Mason and a member of Kappa Alpha Psi; and New York Supreme Court justice Oliver Williams, a Mason—solidified their political power by drawing on community institutions. Carter G. Woodson offered an acerbic account of the new politics of black churches and fraternities:

> In one of our large cities, in which an election was recently held, the outstanding Negro preachers were bought up for a small sum. While one of our noted national figures at the head of a secret society was paid $250 for going into this local campaign and a Negro national politician known to fame for selling out in National Republican Conventions was paid the same amount, then local Negro preachers were paid only $25 each, and a politically dull Presbyterian minister was paid only $7.[25]

TABLE 10.1

Fraternal Ties of A.M.E. Bishops Consecrated 1900–1960

No.*	Bishop	Mason	O.F.	K.P.	Elk	Other	Boulé	ΑΦΑ	ΚΑΨ	ΩΨΦ	ΦΒΣ
29	Cornelius Shaffer					1					
30	Levi Coppin	•									
31	Edward Lampton	•									
46	William Fountain						•		•		
49	John Gregg	•		•	•		•	•			
51	Sherman Greene	•	•	•	•					•	
55	David Sims	•		•				•			
56	Henry Tookes	•									
59	Decatur Nichols									•	
61	Frank Reid	•		•	•			•			
62	Alexander Allen	•		•		2		•			
64	John Clayborn	•				3, 4			•		
67	Joseph Gomez	•						•			
69	William Wilkes	•									•
70	Carey Gibbs	•		•		4					
71	Howard Primm	•							•		
72	Frederick Jordan	•			•			•			
73	Eugene Hatcher	•			•						•
74	Francis Gow	•							•		
75	Ernest Hickman	•									
76	Samuel Higgins	•		•	•	5	•				•
77	William Ball	•									•
79	John Bright	•									
80	George Collins	•	•	•	•	3, 4					

* Order of consecration.

NOTES: 1, Good Templar; 2, Frontiers of America (Cleveland); 3, Eastern Star; 4, American Woodmen; 5, Shriner.

SOURCE: Bishop R. R. Wright, Jr., *The Bishops of the African Methodist Episcopal Church* (Nashville, TN: A.M.E. Sunday School Union, 1963), passim.

In the early nineteenth century, African men's societies defined leadership in black communities; a century later national fraternities and societies provided institutional constituencies for black leaders. The bishops of the African Methodist Episcopal Church offer an interesting case study (see table 10.1). By the twentieth century, their fraternal connections were multiplying despite the declining influence and presence of African societies. After 1950 nearly all newly consecrated A.M.E. bishops had fraternal relations. Masonry put its grip on the Methodist leadership, the Elks and Knights of Pythias established traditions, while the college fraternities made real inroads, but African societies had been swept from the competition.[26]

New York's A.M.E. Zion church continued its fellowship with the national fraternities. In the nineteenth century, the Boyer Masonic Lodge started launching its yearly round of meetings with a Divine Service at local black churches. In time, other lodges and societies began attending. In 1915 A.M.E.Z. bishop James W. Hood delivered the annual lecture at Mother Zion. Hood was past grand master of Prince Hall Masonry in North Carolina. James Brown, Mother Zion's pastor, was a member of Boyer, and his church was the usual site of the annual religious convocation, although occasionally the event was moved to other major black churches such as Abyssinian Baptist with its well-known pastor, Adam Clayton Powell Sr.[27]

In addition to forging closer ties to national organizations, black churches were more willing than African societies to meet local community needs. The Reverend Alexander Crummell—who later served as the first president of the American Negro Academy and was honored by the formation of a Crummell Historical Club in Washington—carried the spirit of the earliest African associations to D.C.'s black churches. Crummell complained that the great "Beneficial Societies"—like those of his childhood in New York City—"which spread from town to town, from city to city, from state to state, and which serve to save individuals and families, in times of sore distress, from deep and utter want," no longer reached the most vulnerable people. Challenging black ministers to engage in the charitable and service functions that the community desperately needed, the St. Luke's pastor noted that

> the colored people have over 70 churches and church organizations, and yet we have the saddening fact that these churches have failed, with hardly an exception, to care for their own poor[,] their widows, their diseased members and their orphans. We build large churches; we are constantly dividing and sub-dividing our church organizations, and uprearing new and costly church edifices. Thousands and tens of thousands of dollars are constantly spent upon new church buildings; and poor people, in lanes and alleys, are almost exhausted, in meeting the demands for churches and chapels, which are almost annually erected for splits and divisions: but never a dollar do we hear of as expended for an orphanage or a hospital built by a colored church for the needy and the destitute.[28]

Crummell knew that church-based organizing benefited from an already united and captive audience. Conversely, African societies depended upon their political appeal to draw like-minds from the general population.

New York's black churches attempted to revive voluntary associations. After his speech before Congress, the Reverend Henry Highland Garnet returned to Shiloh Presbyterian in Manhattan. He became extraordinarily popular and "attracted many ambitious young men" by reestablishing the literary and debate societies of his youth. By the turn of the century, Brooklyn's growing Bethany Baptist Church had an active and effective women's relief society. Similarly, the Brooklyn Literary Union was founded in the basement of a church. The membership grew so large that it was twice relocated. The BLU encouraged the appreciation of literature and music. There were dues but no one was disallowed because of poverty. Attorney Thomas McCants Stewart and editor T. Thomas Fortune ably headed the association.[29]

In fact, Crummell's challenge to the black church was ultimately met; but, it was answered through the ascendance of black women's associations. Women's voluntary associations embraced localism at a time when traditional African men's societies were shunning such social and political responsibilities. The expansion of church-based social work dramatically altered gender roles in African American communities. Black women, organized to address the needs of black communities, expanded their traditional service and support functions within the church and achieved greater self-governance and self-determination. In a study of turn-of-the-century Chicago, Anne Meis Knupfer found that the range of black women's club activity included "kindergarten and mothering . . . suffrage, antilynching laws, literary contests, political debates, embroidery, sewing, municipal reform, philosophy, youth activities, child welfare, care for the elderly, drama, study, safe lodging for working women, health care, orphanages, home life, and rotating economic credit." New York's black women had a version of each of these. "Our churches are chiefly composed of pious, consecrated, self-sacrificing women, and there is not a Christian Association or Benevolent Society existing which does not depend chiefly upon female influence for stability and support," said the Reverend J. Francis Robinson of Halifax in 1899. In their history of African American Christianity, C. Eric Lincoln and Lawrence Mamiya agree, adding that the survival of the black church is a product of the efforts of women.[30]

Women dominated the mission work—domestic and foreign spiritual and social outreach—of the major black religious denominations. The church was especially vulnerable to black women's sequential movements for self-determination, gender equality, and national organization. Black Baptist missionaries appeared in the eighteenth century, and in 1840 the American Baptist Missionary Convention was established and did relatively little foreign outreach. In 1865 three regional bodies united to establish the Consolidated American Baptist Convention. On August 25,

1886, the National Baptist Convention was founded with the Woman's Auxiliary as its major foreign missionary arm. "While women may not have served as much pioneership on the foreign field as men, they have had more heart and leisure for consideration of the study of missions and have gone farther along in missionary thinking, giving, and sacrificing than the rest of the church. Our Foreign Mission Board believes that women more largely support and sustain these causes than the other church groups," write two historians. In the 1890s black women's campaign against sexism within the Baptist church brought demands for a national women's auxiliary, which, in 1900, gave birth to the Baptist Women's Missionary League. Methodist missions also survived on the efforts of black women. In 1876 the A.M.E. Zion denomination granted women voting rights and in 1894 it extended clerical rights across the gender line. In 1916 the Reverend Florence Spearing Randolph, a leader in the women's club movement, a missionary, and a suffragette, became president of the denomination's Woman's Home and Foreign Missionary Society.[31]

In New York City, the transition to church-based and woman-dominant voluntarism played out in the life of Maritcha Remond Lyons. The daughter of Albro Lyons (a member of the New York African Society for Mutual Relief, the city's foremost black benevolent society), she grew up in the shadows of the leading black men of Manhattan and Brooklyn. She was educated under Charles Reason and the NYASMR's Dr. James McCune Smith, her godfather and the best man at her parents' wedding (which was conducted by the Reverend Peter Williams Jr.). The young girl had the opportunity "to listen to Prof. Reason, George T. Downing, [Dr.] Philip A. White and Dr. [Alexander] Crummell in an intimate exchange of thought and opinion." Maritcha Lyons became an impressive orator in her own right. In 1864, while a teenager, she began her speaking career in Providence, Rhode Island, where her family had relocated after being assaulted during the New York Draft Riots. There, she spoke before the state legislature to gain admission to the public schools. The case was brought by her mother with the assistance of George T. Downing. "I, but sixteen years old, made my maiden speech and, in a trembling voice plead for the opening of the door of opportunity," remembered Lyons.[32]

For almost fifty years, from October 1869 to May 1918, Maritcha Remond Lyons worked as a teacher and, later, as an assistant principal in Brooklyn. She also organized and participated in local political and intellectual events. In 1901 the Constitution League invited her to speak at

Carnegie Hall in response to the recent anti-black riots in Manhattan. She lectured on suffrage in Rhode Island, Connecticut, Maine, and New York. In 1922, "I helped a little in the Anti-Lynching Crusade inaugurated by that distinguished race woman, the late Mary E. Talbert. My efforts were confined to Long Island," wrote an aging Lyons.[33]

Her antilynching work began decades earlier. In 1892 Maritcha Lyons debated "the afterwards famous lecturer against 'lynching', the noted 'Iola', Ida B. Wells (Barnett)." Hosted by the Brooklyn Literary Union, the debate resulted in the formation of the Women's Loyal Union of New York and Brooklyn, which engaged in civil rights and labor struggles, and charitable work. Social worker and editor Victoria Earle Matthews served as president. According to Deborah Gray White, "the New York–based Union formed sister clubs in Charleston, Memphis, and Philadelphia." Lyons and Wells began "a valued friendship." As Lyons wrote:

> For her grit, her determination, and patriotism, she ranks high as one of the foremost of our race leaders. I coached her in the art of extempore speaking, and I had the extreme satisfaction of listening to her when without notes she held an audience spell-bound for two hours.

In 1895 Victoria Earle Matthews and T. Thomas Fortune, editor of the *New York Age*, spoke at the Boston conference at which the National Federation of Afro-American Women was formed. Local and state societies established a decade earlier by black church women were the foundation for the rise of national women's organizations, both denominational and independent, at the end of the century. Women's groups from Brooklyn's Concord Baptist Church and New York's Bethel Church were in attendance at the 1895 convention. In 1896 the National League of Colored Women was officially constituted—although its nucleus was established in 1892—at a Washington convention. The two organizations merged to form the National Association of Colored Women, with Mary Terrell as president and Victoria Matthews as national organizer. Two years later, Matthews and Fortune were among the distinguished group that founded the National Afro-American Council as a voice against lynching and civil rights violations.[34]

In 1897 Matthews and Lyons founded Manhattan's White Rose Association, an industrial and aid mission for black women migrants from the South. White Rose agents met trains and boats arriving in New York City to offer advice and assistance to black women. Another Brooklyn woman, Rebecca J. Carter, who trained in social service through Concord Baptist

Church, was principal of the White Rose Mission in Clarksville, Tennessee, which was organized through the Women's Baptist Home Mission Society. In its first fifteen years, New York's White Rose assisted five thousand black women. By 1915 its workers provided lodging for black working women, meals, classes, a library, and lectures, and it had extended its services to black boys.[35]

Another officer of the NACW, Sarah Garnet, the second wife and widow of Henry Highland Garnet, founded the Equal Suffrage League of Brooklyn with her sister, Dr. Susan Smith McKinney Steward. The ESL kept close relations with the churches and the NACW. (In 1870 Susan Smith was valedictorian of the New York Medical College for Women. She kept offices in Brooklyn and Manhattan, and finished her career as the physician of Wilberforce College.) In 1892 Smith joined Victoria Matthews in forming the Women's Loyal Union, which engaged in civil rights, labor, and charitable work. In 1906 Steward became secretary of the NACW. At the Suffrage League's third convention, Verina Morton Jones, M.D., announced the opening of the Lincoln Settlement House, the first such institution run by and for black people in Brooklyn. The Equal Suffrage League also included Brooklyn's Addie Waits Hunton, an antilynching crusader and, later, an NAACP member. Hunton served with the Red Cross during the First World War. In 1925 Hunton was president of the Empire Federation of Women's Clubs.[36]

Earlier, in 1908, Hunton had been reelected national organizer for the NACW during its convention in Brooklyn. The sessions ran from August 24 to 28 and allowed for an interesting glimpse at the broad organizational networks of local black women. The Dorcas Missionary Society—descended from one of the city's oldest black women's associations—invited the National Association to Brooklyn, and a number of women's societies prepared for two hundred delegates from more than thirty states. Brooklyn's Alice Wiley, president of the Northeastern Federation of Women's Clubs, supervised the arrangements. Business meetings were conducted at Concord Baptist Church, which also provided the delegates with meals and a post office. The closing ceremonies were held at Bridge Street Church. During the week, the delegates were given tours of famed black institutions such as the Howard Colored Orphan Asylum. A semi-convention was held in the auditorium of the White Rose Home. Some association leaders discussed the results of their local organizing work before a packed audience. "It was thought that some account of the work which Negro women all over this land are engaged in doing, from the lips of the workers themselves, would bring inspiration and cheer into the lives of other women," noted the *Age*. Sarah Garnet then hosted the Equal Suffrage League and the NACW officers and executive board during a luncheon and discussion at the West Indian Forum.[37]

Addie Hunton was also a key figure in the establishment of New York's "colored YWCA." Black women, trained in black colleges and supported by black denominations, exploited the YWCA system to bring organized social work to their communities despite the institution's segregated structure. Attracted to the evangelical activism of the Y, New York's black women deflected the maternalism of the national organization and established an institution with broad social outreach and uplift programs. Judith Weisenfeld argues that New York's black women "negated simple distinctions between secular and religious work," and the Y offers an example of how they expanded the definition of Christian philanthropy by pursuing their goals on the local and national levels. In 1916 Eva Bowles, secretary of Manhattan's black Y, was appointed national secretary to work among black people in cities. Bowles and other black women were Jim Crowed in local offices while working for the National YWCA. "Obviously, YWCA officials were able to ignore the Christian creed of the 'Y' when it would require them to treat black women as equals," writes a historian of the organization.[38]

Churches were the primary arena of black women's activism. By the turn of the century, St. Mark's Methodist Episcopal Church in Manhattan was operating as a social service center. It had a unisex Mutual Aid Society, which paid sick and death benefits and was dominated by church members but open to all. In 1905 Maude K. Griffin reported that St. Mark's was subsidizing permanent social work missions in Harlem, Brooklyn, and the Bronx. The church ran a day nursery and donated liberally to orphan asylums and schools in the South. On St. Mark's drawing board were a home for aged colored people and the Epworth League. Planned primarily to assist black women migrants, the latter was to be "a place where self-respecting girls compelled to earn their own livelihood, may find shelter with home influences and comforts, yet at reasonable cost." Epworth was also to offer employment assistance and youth services.[39]

A 1915 study of educational facilities for black children in Manhattan made specific mention of the social work at St. Cyprian Episcopal Church. The women at St. Cyprian, most of Caribbean ancestry, ran social service programs, an employment agency for women domestics, and businesses from the parish house. The study went on to cite the "members of various church societies, the groups of girls connected with the Y. W. C. A. and some high school boys and girls" and suggested that college scholarships be given to those who sought to become professional social workers.[40]

Black women did much of the social service work that marked Adam Clayton Powell Sr.'s ministry at Abyssinian Baptist Church. The church ran a home for aged people—anyone who was a member of Abyssinian for five years was eligible regardless of their financial circumstances— with a number of women on staff. Among the varied local outreach programs, the women's Highway and Hedges Society fulfilled the church's pledge to provide for impoverished children in its neighborhood.[41]

In an examination of turn-of-the-century black Baptists, Evelyn Brooks Higginbotham notes that "women were crucial to broadening the public arm of the church and making it the most powerful institution of racial self-help in the African American community."[42] Higginbotham's assertion recognizes the fact that the black church did not always yield that kind of power. By transforming the church into the primary site of local action, women transformed the public sphere.

In the aftermath of the Civil War, the African voluntary societies of New York City folded, just as national fraternal associations and cultural and ethnic organizations rose. "There are several benevolent societies, and also several workingmen and women's protective unions, organized for mutual relief and protection. The oldest and most prominent is the 'New York African Society for Mutual Relief,'" reported a black Manhattanite to Washington's *New Era* in 1870.[43] However, the other societies were publicly silent and soon ceased their social work.

At the turn of the century, W. E. B. Du Bois confidently declared the church to be black Americans' only remaining institutional connection to the African past.[44] If the West African institutional influence in African American culture lived, then it survived in the company of black women.

Notes

NOTES TO THE INTRODUCTION

1. Paule Marshall, *Brown Girl, Brownstones* (1959; New York: Feminist Press, 1981), 11, 196, 207, 219–22, passim.

2. Robert L. Harris Jr., "Early Black Benevolent Societies, 1780–1830," *Massachusetts Review* (Fall 1979), 607.

3. Darlene Clark Hine and Earnestine Jenkins, eds., *A Question of Manhood: A Reader in U.S. Black Men's History and Masculinity* (Bloomington: Indiana University Press, 1999), 2.

4. Deborah Gray White, *Too Heavy a Load: Black Women in Defense of Themselves, 1894–1994* (New York: Norton, 1999), passim. Also, Tullia Brown Hamilton, "The National Association of Colored Women, 1896–1920" (Ph.D. dissertation, Emory University, 1978); Evelyn Brooks Higginbotham, *Righteous Discontent: The Women's Movement in the Black Baptist Church, 1880–1920* (Cambridge, MA: Harvard University Press, 1993); Judith Weisenfeld, *African American Women and Christian Activism: New York's Black YWCA, 1905–1945* (Cambridge, MA: Harvard University Press, 1997); Julia Sudbury, *"Other Kinds of Dreams": Black Women's Organizations and the Politics of Transformation* (London: Routledge, 1998); Cynthia Neverdon-Morton, *Afro-American Women of the South and the Advancement of the Race, 1895–1925* (Knoxville: University of Tennessee Press, 1989).

5. Robert L. Harris, Jr., "Early Black Benevolent Societies, 1780–1830," *Massachusetts Review* (Fall 1979), 603. A number of scholars have examined the black voluntary tradition and noted that black people were more likely to form and join voluntary associations. See, for instance, Nicholas Babchuck and Ralph V. Thompson, "The Voluntary Associations of Negroes," *American Sociological Review* (October 1962), 647–55; Howard W. Odum, *Social and Mental Traits of the Negro* (New York: Columbia University Press, 1910), 99, passim. The literature has generally cast white voluntary associations as definitive; black organizations are examined only in comparison and relation to white associations. See, for instance, Murray Hausknecht, *The Joiners: A Sociological Description of Voluntary Association Membership in the United States* (New York: Bedminster, 1962), 75–76, passim.

6. Melville J. Herskovits, *The Myth of the Negro Past* (1941; Boston: Beacon, 1990), 7, 160–66.

7. Thomas C. Holt, "Slavery and Freedom in the Atlantic World: Reflections on the Diasporan Framework," in Darlene Clark Hine and Jacqueline McLeod, eds., *Crossing Boundaries: Comparative History of Black People in Diaspora* (Bloomington: Indiana University Press, 1999), 35–37.

8. Robert Gregg, *Sparks from the Anvil of Oppression: Philadelphia's African Methodists and Southern Migrants, 1890–1940* (Philadelphia: Temple University Press, 1993), 1.

9. William D. Piersen, *Black Yankees: The Development of an Afro-American Subculture in Eighteenth-Century New England* (Amherst: University of Massachusetts Press, 1988), 59, passim.

NOTES TO CHAPTER 1

1. Melville J. Herskovits, *The Myth of the Negro Past* (1941; Boston: Beacon, 1990), 7, passim; E. Franklin Frazier, *The Negro in the United States* (New York: Macmillan, 1949), 3–11; Gary B. Nash, *Race, Class, and Politics: Essays on Colonial and Revolutionary Society* (Urbana: University of Illinois Press, 1986), 26.

2. Frazier, *Negro in the United States*, 12–13.

3. Herskovits, *Myth of the Negro Past*, 145; W. E. Burghardt Du Bois, ed., "The Negro Church: Report of a Social Study Made Under the Direction of Atlanta University together with the Proceedings of the Eighth Conference for the Study of the Negro Problems, Held at Atlanta University, May 26th, 1903," 2–4, in vol. 2 of W. E. B. Du Bois, ed., *Atlanta University Publications* (New York: Octagon, 1968); Carter G. Woodson, *The Negro in Our History* (1922; Washington, DC: Associated Publishers, 1941), 22–50; Joseph R. Washington Jr., *Black Sects and Cults* (Garden City, NY: Doubleday, 1972), 21–30; Sylviane A. Diouf, *Servants of Allah: African Muslims Enslaved in the Americas* (New York: New York University Press, 1998), 2, 49–93, 113–16.

4. Forrest G. Wood, *The Arrogance of Faith: Christianity and Race in America from the Colonial Era to the Twentieth Century* (New York: Knopf, 1990), 8–9. Although not convinced of the depth of African influences on African American culture, Eugene Genovese still recognizes the need for careful examination. That the African influence on black American culture cannot be quantified, Genovese responds to those who dismissed the links, in no way challenges the fact of its existence: "If that thrust had European counterparts, so be it. If those counterparts reinforced or encouraged certain features of black religion, well and good. Black America's tie with an African tradition nonetheless remained and helped shape a culture entirely its own." Eugene D. Genovese, *Roll, Jordan, Roll: The World the Slaves Made* (1972; New York: Vintage, 1976), 210.

5. Sidney W. Mintz and Richard Price, *The Birth of African-American Culture: An Anthropological Perspective* (1976; Boston: Beacon, 1992), 7–19, 62, 70.

6. Basil Davidson, *The African Genius: An Introduction to African Cultural and*

Social History (Boston: Little, Brown, 1969), 91–92; Herskovits, *Myth of the Negro Past*, 158–66; Carter G. Woodson, *The African Background Outlined, or Handbook for the Study of the Negro* (1936; New York: Negro Universities Press, 1968), 169–70; John Thornton, *Africa and Africans in the Making of the Atlantic World, 1400–1800* (1992; Cambridge, UK: Cambridge University Press, 1998), 218–19; Michael A. Gomez, *Exchanging Our Country Marks: The Transformation of African Identities in the Colonial and Antebellum South* (Chapel Hill: University of North Carolina Press, 1998), 100. William D. Piersen suggests that the use of so-cial satire in West African secret societies through oral communication and per-formed song has provocative parallels in black American culture: William D. Piersen, *Black Legacy: America's Hidden Heritage* (Amherst: University of Massa-chusetts Press, 1993), 54–57. For an in-depth look at the structure of an African secret society, see K. L. Little, "The Poro Society as an Arbiter of Culture," *African Studies*, Vol. 7, No. 1 (March 1948), 1–15.

7. Mintz and Price, *Birth of African-American Culture*, 14, 61–71.

8. For instance, Charles William Heckethorn documents the appearance of veiled associations in early history from Europe to the Middle East, and from Asia to Central and South America. Nesta H. Webster describes these mystic unions as an irresistible force that sparked and bolstered subversion. That belief introduced anti-Semitic tirades about grand, if not global, plots. Bernard Fay places the Revolutionary triumph of the United States on the shoulders of a Freemasonry that alone laid "the foundation for national unity" and kept George Washington's army united on the field. Charles William Heckethorn, *The Secret Societies of All Ages and Countries: A Comprehensive Account of Upwards of One Hundred and Sixty Secret Organisations—Religious, Political, and Social—from the Most Remote Ages Down to the Present Time*, 2 vols. (New York: New Amster-dam Book Company, 1897); J. M. Roberts, *The Mythology of Secret Societies* (New York: Charles Scribner's Sons, 1972), 6, 10–11; Nesta H. Webster, *Secret Societies and Subversive Movements*, 2nd ed. (London: Boswell, 1924), passim. Bernard Fay, *Revolution and Freemasonry, 1680–1800* (Boston: Little, Brown, 1935), 229, 245–47.

9. Margaret Washington Creel, *"A Peculiar People": Slave Religion and Com-munity-Culture among the Gullah* (New York: New York University Press, 1988), 48; Patrick R. McNaughton, *The Mande Blacksmiths: Knowledge, Power, and Art in West Africa* (Bloomington: Indiana University Press, 1988), 3; Kenneth Little, "The Political Function of the Poro" (Part I), *Africa*, Vol. 35, No. 4 (October 1965), 350–51; Alvin Magid, "Political Traditionalism in Nigeria: A Case-Study of Secret Societies and Dance Groups in Local Government," *Africa*, Vol. 42, No. 4 (October 1972), 289–304; Mwelwa C. Musambachime, "The Ubutwa Society in Eastern Shaba and Northeast Zambia to 1920," *International Journal of African Historical Studies*, Vol. 27, No. 1 (1994), 89–99; also Dugald Campbell, *In the Heart of Bantuland: A Record of Twenty-nine Years' Pioneering in Central Africa*

among the Bantu Peoples, with a Description of Their Habits, Customs, Secret Societies and Languages (1922; New York: Negro Universities Press, 1969), 96–117. Secret societies in the Congo used the spread of Christianity to oppose European colonialism. See Jean Comhaire, "Sociétès Secrètes et Mouvements Prophétiques au Congo Belge," *Africa,* Vol. 25, No. 1 (January 1955), 54–58.

10. Creel, *"A Peculiar People,"* 2, 60, passim.

11. "Act of the Director and Council of New Netherland Emancipating Certain Negro Slaves therein Mentioned" (passed 25 February 1644), in E. B. O'-Callaghan, compiler, *Laws and Ordinances of New Netherland, 1638–1674* (Albany, NY: Weed, Parsons, 1868), 36–37; Holland Society of New York, *New York Historical Manuscripts: Dutch* (Baltimore: Genealogical Publishing, 1980), GG (land papers): 36, 54–56; Graham Russell Hodges, *Root and Branch: African Americans in New York and East Jersey, 1613–1863* (Chapel Hill: University of North Carolina Press, 1999), 14, 17–18.

12. Joyce D. Goodfriend, *Before the Melting Pot: Society and Culture in Colonial New York City, 1664–1730* (Princeton, NJ: Princeton University Press, 1992), 10; Shane White, *Somewhat More Independent: The End of Slavery in New York City, 1770–1810* (Athens: University of Georgia Press, 1991), 3, 26; George Edmund Haynes, *The Negro at Work in New York City: A Study in Economic Progress* (1912; New York: AMS Press, 1968), 45–47; *Return of the Whole Number of Persons within the Several Districts of the United States, According to* "An Act Providing for the Enumeration of the Inhabitants of the United States," Passed March the First, One Thousand Seven Hundred and Ninety-One (Philadelphia: Childs and Swaine, 1791), 36; Edwin Olson, "The Slave Code in Colonial New York," *Journal of Negro History,* Vol. 29, No. 2 (April 1944), 147–48; Douglas Greenberg, *Crime and Law Enforcement in the Colony of New York, 1691–1776* (1974; Ithaca, NY: Cornell University Press, 1976), 44.

13. "Ordinance of the Director and Council of New Netherland Against Fugitives from Service . . ." (passed 9 August 1640), "Ordinance of the Director and Council of New Netherland Against Harboring Fugitive Servants" (passed 13 April 1642), in O'Callaghan, compiler, *Laws and Ordinances of New Netherland,* 24, 32; Holland Society of New York, New York Historical Manuscripts: Dutch (Baltimore: Genealogical Publishing, 1980), 5 (council minutes): 129.

14. "A Bill Concerning Masters[,] servants[,] Slaves[,] Labourers and Apprentices" (passed 24 October 1684), "An Act for Regulating Slaves" (passed 27 November 1702), in *The Colonial Laws of New York from the Year 1664 to the Revolution, Including the Charters to the Duke of York, the Commissions and Instructions to Colonial Governors, the Duke's Laws, the Laws of the Dongan and Leisler Assemblies, the Charters of Albany and New York and the Acts of the Colonial Legislatures from 1691 to 1775 Inclusive* (Albany, NY: State Printer, 1894), 1: 157–59, 519–21; John Cadman Hurd, *The Law of Freedom and Bondage in the United States,* 2 vols. (1858; New York: Negro Universities Press, 1968), 1: 280; Ira K.

Morris, *Morris's Memorial History of Staten Island, New York*, 2 vols. (West New Brighton, Staten Island, NY: Privately printed, 1900), 2: 49. The slave code in Montserrat was similar. See Howard A. Fergus, "The Early Laws of Montserrat (1668–1680): The Legal Schema of a Slave Society," *Caribbean Quarterly*, Vol. 24, Nos. 1–2 (March–June 1978), 34–43.

15. Roger Bastide, *The African Religions of Brazil: Toward a Sociology of the Interpenetration of Civilizations* (1960 [translation by Helen Sebba]; Baltimore: Johns Hopkins University Press, 1978), 83–90; R. K. Kent, "Palmares: An African State in Brazil," *Journal of African History*, Vol. 6, No. 2 (1965), 162, 170, 175; Orlando Patterson, *The Sociology of Slavery: An Analysis of the Origins, Development and Structure of Negro Slave Society in Jamaica* (London: Macgibbon and Kee, 1967), 198–202; Thornton, *Africa and Africans in the Making of the Atlantic World*, 281, 292–300.

16. Letter reprinted in Gabriel Furman, *Antiquities of Long Island* (1874; Port Washington, NY: Ira J. Friedman, 1968), 221–22. Emphasis mine.

17. James Riker Jr., *The Annals of Newtown, in Queens County, New-York: Containing Its History from Its Earliest Settlement, Together with Many Interesting Facts Concerning the Adjacent Towns; Also, A Particular Account of Numerous Long Island Families Now Spread over This and Various Other States of the Union* (New York: D. Fanshaw, 1852), 142–43; *Boston News-Letter*, February 2–February 9, 1708, February 16–February 23, 1708; Richard Shannon Moss, *Slavery on Long Island: A Study of Local Institutional and Early African-American Communal Life* (New York: Garland, 1993), 112–13; "An Act for Preventing the Conspiracy of Slaves" (passed October 30, 1708), in *Colonial Laws of New York*, 1: 631. A somewhat similar pattern was found in New England; see Robert K. Fitts, *Inventing New England's Slave Paradise: Master/Slave Relations in Eighteenth-Century Narragansett, Rhode Island* (New York: Garland, 1998), 115–17.

18. Letter from Rev. John Sharpe to the secretary of the Society for the Propagation of the Gospel in Foreign Parts, 23 June 1712, reprinted by Chaplain Roswell Randall Hoes, USN, in *The New York Genealogical and Biographical Record* (October 1890), 162–63; *Boston News-Letter*, 7 April–14 April 1712, 14 April–21 April 1712; letter from Governor Hunter to the Lords of Trade, 23 June 1712, and letter from Governor Hunter to Secretary Popple, 10 September 1713, in E. B. O'Callaghan, ed., *Documents Relative to the Colonial History of the State of New-York; Procured in Holland, England and France by John Romeyn Brodhead, Esq., Agent . . .* (Albany, NY: Weed, Parsons, 1855), 5: 339–43, 371; Kenneth Scott, "The Slave Insurrection in New York in 1712," *New-York Historical Society Quarterly* (January 1961), 43–74; Edward Robb Ellis, *The Epic of New York City* (New York: Coward-McCann, 1966), 112–13; Herbert Aptheker, *American Negro Slave Revolts* (1943; New York: International Publishers, 1987), 172–73; Thomas J. Davis, *A Rumor of Revolt: The "Great Negro Plot" in Colonial New York* (New York: Free Press, 1985), 54–55.

19. *Boston News-Letter*, 14 April–21 April 1712, 21 April–28 April 1712; Governor Hunter to the Lords of Trade, 23 June 1712, and Governor Hunter to Secretary Popple, 10 September 1713, in O'Callaghan, ed., *Documents Relative to the Colonial History*, 5: 339–43, 371; Scott, "Slave Insurrection in New York in 1712," 43–74; Ellis, *Epic of New York*, 112–13; Davis, *Rumor of Revolt*, 54–55.

20. Rev. John Sharpe to the secretary of the Society for the Propagation of the Gospel in Foreign Parts, 23 June 1712; *Boston News-Letter*, 14 April–21 April 1712.

21. Michael Mullin, *Africa in America: Slave Acculturation and Resistance in the American South and the British Caribbean, 1736–1831* (Urbana: University of Illinois Press, 1992), 67–68. On the social and ideological functions of blood oaths and blood brotherhood in Africa, see Geoffrey Parrinder, *West African Religion: A Study of the Beliefs and Practices of Akan, Ewe, Yoruba, Ibo, and Kindred Peoples* (1949; New York: Barnes and Noble, 1969), 135–36; E. E. Evans-Pritchard, "Zande Blood-Brotherhood," *Africa*, Vol. 6, No. 4 (October 1933), 369–401; J. H. M. Beattie, "The Blood Pact in Bunyoro," *African Studies*, Vol. 17, No. 4 (1958), 198–203; T. O. Beidelman, "The Blood Covenant and the Concept of Blood in Ukaguru," *Africa*, Vol. 33, No. 4 (October 1963), 321–42; Thomas J. Herlehy, "Ties That Bind: Palm Wine and Blood-Brotherhood at the Kenya Coast during the 19th Century," *International Journal of African Historical Studies*, Vol. 17, No. 2 (1984), 285–308.

22. The Directors of the West India Company to Peter Stuyvesant, 7 April 1648, in Hugh Hastings, ed., *Ecclesiastical Records of the State of New York*, 8 vols. (Albany: James B. Lyon, 1901–5), 1: 228–29; "Number of Negroes Imported from 1701–1726," in E. B. O'Callaghan, M.D., *The Documentary History of the State of New-York; Arranged under the Direction of the Hon. Christopher Morgan, Secretary of State*, 4 vols. (Albany, NY: Weed, Parsons, 1849), 1: 707; William Renwick Riddell, "The Slave in Early New York," *Journal of Negro History*, Vol. 13, No. 1 (January 1928), 70; Hodges, *Root and Branch*, 38.

23. Mullin, *Africa in America*, 13–14, 62–63; Barbara Kopytoff, "The Development of Jamaican Maroon Ethnicity," *Caribbean Quarterly*, Vol. 22, Nos. 2–3 (June–September 1976), 33–37, is particularly insightful on Coromantee cultural identity; Frederick P. Bowser, *The African Slave in Colonial Peru, 1524–1650* (Stanford, CA: Stanford University Press, 1974), 187–88; Karen Ordahl Kupperman, *Providence Island, 1630–1641: The Other Puritan Colony* (New York: Cambridge University Press, 1993), 170–71; Kent, "Palmares," 165–68; Bastide, *African Religions of Brazil*, 90–96, 103; Melville J. and Frances S. Herskovits, *Rebel Destiny* (1934; Freeport, NY: Books for Libraries Press, 1971), vii; Philip Wright, "War and Peace with the Maroons, 1730–1739," *Caribbean Quarterly*, Vol. 16, No. 1 (March 1970), 13–14; R. C. Dallas, *The History of the Maroons*, 2 vols. (1803; London: Frank Cass, 1968), 1: 68–69, passim; Bernard Marshall, "Slave Resistance and White Reaction in the British Windward Islands, 1763–1833," *Caribbean*

Quarterly, Vol. 28, No. 3 (September 1982), 36–40; Carey Robinson, *The Fighting Maroons of Jamaica* (Jamaica: William Collins and Sangster, 1969), 16–17; Mavis C. Campbell, *The Maroons of Jamaica, 1655–1796: A History of Resistance, Collaboration and Betrayal* (Granby, MA: Bergin and Garvey, 1988), 5, 44–50, passim; C. L. R. James, *The Black Jacobins: Toussaint L'Ouverture and the San Domingo Revolution* (1938; 2nd rev. ed., New York: Vintage, 1963), 20; Diouf, *Servants of Allah*, 20, 79–80, 145–63; Herbert Aptheker, "Maroons within the Present Limits of the United States," *Journal of Negro History*, Vol. 24, No. 2 (April 1939), 167–84; Leslie Howard Owens, *This Species of Property: Slave Life and Culture in the Old South* (New York: Oxford University Press, 1976), 87–88.

24. Captain F. W. Butt-Thompson, *West African Secret Societies: Their Organisations, Officials, and Teaching* (1929; Westport, CT: Negro Universities Press, 1970), 15–18, 21–30, 218–42; George E. Brooks, *Landlords and Strangers: Ecology, Society, and Trade in Western Africa, 1000–1630* (Boulder, CO: Westview Press, 1993), 45, 73–77; McNaughton, *Mande Blacksmiths*, passim; William P. Murphy and Caroline H. Bledsoe, "Kinship and Territory in the History of a Kpelle Chiefdom (Liberia)," in Igor Kopytoff, ed., *The African Frontier: The Reproduction of Traditional African Societies* (Bloomington: Indiana University Press, 1987), 123–42; Kenneth Little, "The Political Function of the Poro" (Part II), *Africa*, Vol. 36, No. 1 (January 1966), 66–70. Also see Parrinder, *West African Religion*, 128–35. On the modern history of West African secret societies, see M. D. W. Jeffreys, "The Nyama Society of the Ibibio Women," *African Studies*, Vol. 15, No. 1 (1956), 15–28; M. C. Jedrej, "Medicine, Fetish and Secret Society in a West African Culture," *Africa*, Vol. 46, No. 3 (1976), 247–57; Ruth B. Phillips, "Masking in Mende and Sande Society Initiation Rituals," *Africa*, Vol. 48, No. 3 (1978), 265–76; Emea O. Arua, "Yam Ceremonies and the Values of Ohafia Culture," *Africa*, Vol. 51, No. 2 (1981), 694–705. For examinations of this cultural form in other places, see Hilda Kuper and Selma Kaplan, "Voluntary Associations in an Urban Township," *African Studies*, Vol. 3, No. 4 (December 1944), 178–86; and A. G. Schutte, "Thapelo Ya Sephiri: A Study of Secret Prayer Groups in Soweto," *African Studies*, Vol. 31, No. 4 (1972), 245–60.

25. *Journal of the Legislative Council of the Colony of New-York. Began the 9th Day of April, 1691; and Ended the 27 of September, 1743* (Albany, NY: Weed, Parsons, 1861), 333; Hurd, *Law of Freedom and Bondage*, 1: 281–82; "An Act for Preventing[,] Suppressing and Punishing the Conspiracy and Insurrection of Negroes and Other Slaves" (passed December 10, 1712), in *Colonial Laws of New York*, 1: 761–67.

26. "A Law for Regulating Negro and Indian Slaves in the Night Time" (passed 10 March 1713), "A Law Restraining Slaves Negro[es] and Indians from Gaming with Moneys or for Moneys" (passed 20 February 1722), in *Minutes of the Common Council of the City of New York, 1675–1776*, 8 vols. (New York: Dodd, Mead, 1905), 3: 30–31, 277–78.

27. "An Act for the More Effectual Preventing and Punishing the Conspiracy and Insurrection of Negro and Other Slaves; for the Better Regulating Them and for Repealing the Acts Herein Mentioned Relating Thereto" (passed October 29, 1730), in *Colonial Laws of New York*, 2: 679–88.

28. Davis, *A Rumor of Revolt*, 250–63; Rev. J. R. Bayley, *A Brief Sketch of the Early History of the Catholic Church on the Island of New York* (New York: Catholic Publication Society, 1870), 45.

29. Daniel Horsmanden, *The New-York Conspiracy, or a History of the Negro Plot, with the Journal of the Proceedings Against the Conspirators at New-York in the Years 1741–2* (1810; New York: Negro Universities Press, 1969), 102, 135, 386–92.

30. Ibid., 242–43, 252–53; Sterling Stuckey, *Slave Culture: Nationalist Theory and the Foundations of Black America* (New York: Oxford University Press, 1987), 11. On ring ceremonies in African-Brazilian culture, see Bastide, *African Religions of Brazil*, 138, passim.

31. Horsmanden, *New-York Conspiracy*, 65, 98, 104–5, 130, 253; William D. Piersen, *Black Yankees: The Development of an Afro-American Subculture in Eighteenth-Century New England* (Amherst: University of Massachusetts Press, 1988), 79; Parrinder, *West African Religion*, 29–34, 115–27. On Hughson's role as fence, see Davis, *A Rumor of Revolt*, 3–5.

32. Horsmanden, *New-York Conspiracy*, 12, 39, 60–63, 74, 105. On the origins of Masonry in New York, see Harry A. Williamson, "A History of Freemasonry among the American Negroes" (unpublished manuscript, 1929), 8, Schomburg Collection, NYPL; and *Gould's History of Freemasonry throughout the World*, 6 vols., revised by Dudley Wright (New York: Scribner's Sons, 1936), 6: 40–65. On the purchase of the weapons, see Thomas J. Davis, "The New York Slave Conspiracy of 1741 as Black Protest," *Journal of Negro History*, Vol. 56, No. 1 (January 1971), 28.

33. Piersen, *Black Yankees*, 82–83; Olaudah Equiano, *The Interesting Narrative of the Life of Olaudah Equiano, Written by Himself* (1791; Robert J. Allison, ed., Boston: Bedford, 1995), 42–43, 185; Sylvia R. Frey and Betty Wood, *Come Shouting to Zion: African American Protestantism in the American South and the British Caribbean to 1830* (Chapel Hill: University of North Carolina Press, 1998), 56–58; McNaughton, *Mande Blacksmiths*, 3–12. Another interesting example is available in the recent history of Central Africa. During the Rhodesian conflict (1965–1979), which resulted in an independent Zimbabwe, spirit mediums used ancestral and religious beliefs to unify the masses and empower the guerrilla soldiers. The overthrow of colonial rule resulted from the application of traditional ideas and practices to new political objectives. See David Lan, *Guns and Rain: Guerrillas and Spirit Mediums in Zimbabwe* (Berkeley: University of California Press, 1985), passim.

34. E. J. Hobsbawm, *Primitive Rebels: Studies in Archaic Forms of Social Movement in the 19th and 20th Centuries* (New York: Norton, 1959), 13–23; Hodges,

Root and Branch, 100–102; Butt-Thompson, *West African Secret Societies*, 20, 281–84; Jean Chesneaux, *Secret Societies in China: In the Nineteenth and Twentieth Centuries*, translated by Gillian Nettle (Ann Arbor: University of Michigan Press, 1971), 60–63.

35. Ray A. Kea, "'I am Here to Plunder on the General Road': Bandits and Banditry in the Pre-Nineteenth-Century Gold Coast," in Donald Crummey, ed., *Banditry, Rebellion and Social Protest in Africa* (Portsmouth, NH: Heinemann, 1986), 109–32; Eric Hobsbawm, *Bandits* (New York: Delacorte, 1969), 22, 50.

36. *The Sociology of Georg Simmel*, translated, edited, and with an introduction by Kurt H. Wolff (New York: Free Press, 1950), 330–60; Roberts, *Mythology of Secret Societies*, 9; also see Wilson Carey McWilliams, *The Idea of Fraternity in America* (Berkeley: University of California Press, 1973), 58–60.

37. Thornton, *Africa and Africans in the Making of the Atlantic World*, 220, 300–303.

38. New York State Library, *Calendar of Council Minutes, 1668–1783*, 398, 435; A. J. Williams-Myers, "The African Presence in the Hudson River Valley: The Defining of Relationships between the Masters and the Slaves," *Afro-Americans in New York Life and History*, Vol. 12, No. 1 (January 1988), 93–95.

39. Quobna Ottobah Cugoano, a native of Africa, *Thoughts and Sentiments on the Evil and Wicked Traffic of the Slavery and Commerce of the Human Species, Humbly Submitted to the Inhabitants of Great-Britain*, edited by Vincent Carretta (1787; New York: Penguin, 1999), 15; Frey and Wood, *Come Shouting to Zion*, 37–38.

40. James, *Black Jacobins*, 55–56, 86–87; Diouf, *Servants of Allah*, 150–53; Creel, *"A Peculiar People,"* 154–55.

41. K. O. Laurence, "The Tobago Slave Conspiracy of 1801," *Caribbean Quarterly*, Vol. 28, No. 3 (September 1982), 1–9.

42. Mary C. Karasch, *Slave Life in Rio de Janeiro, 1808–1850* (Princeton, NJ: Princeton University Press, 1987), 298–99; João José Reis, *Slave Rebellion in Brazil: The Muslim Uprising of 1835 in Bahia*, translated by Arthur Brakel (1986; translation, Baltimore: Johns Hopkins University Press, 1993), 41–69; Diouf, *Servants of Allah*, 79, 153–63; Bastide, *African Religions of Brazil*, 95.

43. See Joseph T. Wilson, *The Black Phalanx: A History of the Negro Soldiers of the United States in the Wars of 1775–1812, 1861–'65* (1890; New York: Arno, 1968), 47; Edward Countryman, *A People in Revolution: The American Revolution and Political Society in New York, 1760–1790* (Baltimore: Johns Hopkins University Press, 1981), 288; Benjamin Quarles, *The Negro in the American Revolution* (Chapel Hill: University of North Carolina Press, 1961), 8, 56, 70, 98, 171–72; Thomas Jones, *History of New York during the Revolutionary War, and of the Leading Events in the Other Colonies at that Period*, 2 vols., edited by Edward Floyd de Lancey (New York: For the New-York Historical Society, 1879), 1: 334, 2: 76, 256–57.

44. Graham Russell Hodges, "Black Revolt in New York City and the Neutral Zone: 1775–83," in Paul A. Gilje and William Pencak, eds., *New York in the Age of the Constitution, 1775–1800* (Rutherford, NJ: Fairleigh Dickinson University Press and Associated University Presses, 1992), 20–40.

45. William C. Suttles Jr., "African Religious Survivals as Factors in American Slave Revolts," *Journal of Negro History*, Vol. 56, No. 2 (April 1971), 99, passim.

46. Du Bois, ed., "Negro Church," 5; Nicholas C. Cooper-Lewter and Henry H. Mitchell, *Soul Theology: The Heart of American Black Culture* (San Francisco: Harper and Row, 1986), 8–12; Piersen, *Black Yankees*, 74–86; Patterson, *Sociology of Slavery*, 182–88; Frey and Wood, *Come Shouting to Zion*, 39; Donald H. Matthews, *Honoring the Ancestors: An African Cultural Interpretation of Black Religion and Literature* (New York: Oxford University Press, 1998), 5.

47. Winthrop D. Jordan, *White over Black: American Attitudes toward the Negro, 1550–1812* (1968; New York: Norton, 1977), 180–87; Peter Kolchin, *American Slavery, 1619–1877* (New York: Hill and Wang, 1993), 143, 148–49.

48. Gomez, *Exchanging Our Country Marks*, 268; Washington Jr., *Black Sects and Cults*, 24; Carter G. Woodson, "Comments on Negro Education," *New York Age*, 29 August 1931.

49. Frey and Wood, *Come Shouting to Zion*, 14, 33–34; Diouf, *Servants of Allah*, 52–53.

50. Piersen, *Black Yankees*, 77; Patterson, *Sociology of Slavery*, 195–98; Karasch, *Slave Life in Rio de Janeiro*, 84–86; A. J. R. Russell-Wood, "Black and Mulatto Brotherhoods in Colonial Brazil: A Study in Collective Behavior," *Hispanic American Historical Review* (November 1974), 579–81.

51. Hodges, *Root and Branch*, 15; Debbie Officer, "Last Rites," *African Voices* (March 1994); Kirk A. Johnson, "The History in 'Dem Bones,'" *Heart and Soul* (February–March 1996); Anne Cronin, "The Struggle for Freedom and a Proper Burial," *New York Times*, 28 February 1993; Mechal Sobel, *The World They Made Together: Black and White Values in Eighteenth-Century Virginia* (Princeton, NJ: Princeton University Press, 1987), 218–21; Creel, *"A Peculiar People,"* 55; Genovese, *Roll, Jordan, Roll*, 197–201. By the end of the eighteenth century, the value of Manhattan's Negro Burial Ground increased so dramatically that there were multiple claims before the Common Council. The controversy began in the summer of 1790 while the cemetery was still in use. In February 1796 a subcommittee decided that the "claimants have no right to intrude upon or take possession of the Land leased to the memorialists." The city negotiated an exchange. Title to the Negro Burial Ground was delivered to the city, the land was prepared for the imposition of the regular street grid, and the Africans received a new Augustus Street lot suitable as a burial ground and additional property. The attempts of the Africans, including the trustees of Mother Zion, to find suitable burial lands were in part due to an outbreak of yellow fever that struck the city at the end of the summer of 1798, killing over fourteen hundred New Yorkers, including forty-one

Africans. The final land transfer with the city was made in 1800. See minutes of 23 June 1790, 24 September 1790, 13 November 1790, 30 April 1792, 29 February 1796, 27 June 1796, 25 July 1796, 12 May 1800, in *Minutes of the Common Council of the City of New York, 1784–1831*, 18 vols. (New York: Published by the City of New York, 1917), 1: 554, 598, 610, 709–10, 2: 221, 252–53, 264, 626; James Hardie, A.M., *An Account of the Malignant Fever, Lately Prevalent in the City of New-York* (New York: Hurtin and McFarlane, 1799), 142–45.

52. Wood, *Arrogance of Faith*, 8–9. "As part of the white attempt to control black religion, the slaveholders' regime tried to supervise slave funerals and feared their providing the occasion for insurrectionary plots," writes Eugene Genovese of this same phenomenon in the antebellum South. See *Roll, Jordan, Roll*, 194.

53. Hodges, *Root and Branch*, 54; Mrs. [Charlotte Rebecca] Bleecker Bangs, *Reminiscences of Old New Utrecht and Gowanus* (Brooklyn, 1912), 30.

54. Richard W. Pointer, *Protestant Pluralism and the New York Experience: A Study of Eighteenth-Century Religious Diversity* (Bloomington: Indiana University Press, 1988), 1–5, 11–14, 33, 38; "Report of Committee on the Remonstrance," 27 January 1650, and "Secret Instructions Sent by James II to Governor Dongan, of New York," 29 May 1686, in Hastings, ed., *Ecclesiastical Records of the State of New York*, 1: 266, 2: 915–16; Rev. David S. Sutphen, *Historical Discourse, Delivered on the 18th of October, 1877, at the Celebration of the Two Hundredth Anniversary of the Dutch Reformed Church of New Utrecht, L.I., and an Historical Address, by Hon. Teunis G. Bergen* (Brooklyn: Privately published, 1877), 47; "Marriage Fees; Deaths; Members and Other Miscellaneous Matter Culled from the Records of the Reformed Protestant Dutch Church of the Town of Flatbush, Kings Co., New York," translated by Frank L. Van Cleef (typescript, Brooklyn, 1915), 61. Thomas de Moor was a member of the Reformed Church. Maria Bastiaensz and Wyntie de Vries share surnames with Africans but are not designated as such. "List of the Members of the Dutch Reformed Church in New York in 1686, Arranged According to the Streets of the City," in Henricus Selyns, *Records of Domine Henricus Selyns of New York 1686–7, with Notes and Remarks by Garret Abeel Written a Century Later 1791–2* (New York: Holland Society of New York, 1916), 11–14. New York State Library, *Calendar of Council Minutes, 1668–1783* (Albany: State University of New York, March 1902), 58, 60.

55. Du Bois, ed., "Negro Church," 12–13; Goodfriend, *Before the Melting Pot*, 126–32; Hodges, *Root and Branch*, 119–28.

NOTES TO CHAPTER 2

1. Gary B. Nash, *Race, Class, and Politics: Essays on American Colonial and Revolutionary Society* (Urbana: University of Illinois Press, 1986), 309.

2. Cotton Mather, "Rules for the Society of Negroes, 1693," in Thomas James

Holmes, *Cotton Mather: A Bibliography of His Works*, 3 vols. (Cambridge, MA: Harvard University Press, 1940), 3: 936–37; Rev. James M. Simms, *The First Colored Baptist Church in North America, Constituted at Savannah, Georgia, January 20, A.D. 1788, with Biographical Sketches of the Pastors* (1888; New York: Negro Universities Press, 1969), 14–20; William D. Piersen, *Black Yankees: The Development of an Afro-American Subculture in Eighteenth-Century New England* (Amherst: University of Massachusetts Press, 1988), 59–60; Rev. W[illia]m. Douglass, *Annals of the First African Church, in the United States of America, Now Styled the African Episcopal Church of St. Thomas, Philadelphia* (Philadelphia: King and Baird, 1862), 13, 30–31. "The Free African Society was not a religious organization, but a means for the expression of freedom and protest," writes Joseph R. Washington Jr.; however, it did become "the major vehicle for deciding where and how Negroes should worship." Joseph R. Washington Jr., *Black Religion: The Negro and Christianity in the United States* (Boston: Beacon, 1964), 188.

3. John Daniels, *In Freedom's Birthplace* (1914; New York: Arno, 1969), 21; Daniel A. Payne, *History of the African Methodist Episcopal Church*, edited by Rev. C. S. Smith (1891; New York: Arno, 1969), 3; Christopher Phillips, *Freedom's Port: The African American Community of Baltimore, 1790–1860* (Urbana: University of Illinois Press, 1997), 133–35; Henry Reed Stiles, *A History of the City of Brooklyn. Including the Old Town and Village of Brooklyn, the Town of Bushwick, and the Village and City of Williamsburgh*, 3 vols. (Brooklyn: Privately printed, 1867–70), 3: 707; HABS, "African Baptist Society Church, North Side of York Street at the Corner of Pleasant Street, Nantucket, Nantucket County, Massachusetts" (Washington, DC: HABS, Office of Archeology and Historic Preservation, National Park Service, ca. 1971), 1–2, in the records of the Historic American Buildings Survey, Library of Congress; Margaret Washington Creel, *"A Peculiar People": Slave Religion and Community-Culture among the Gullah* (New York: New York University Press, 1988), 2, 181–82.

4. Arthur A. Schomburg, "Jupiter Hammon before the New York African Society," *New York Amsterdam News*, 22 January 1930; William J. Walls, *The African Methodist Episcopal Zion Church: Reality of the Black Church* (Charlotte, NC: A.M.E. Zion Publishing House, 1974), 26–27, 128. The NYAS was still functioning in the 1790s. See Sidney I. Pomerantz, *New York: An American City, 1783–1803* (New York: Columbia University Press, 1938), 469.

5. Simms, *First Colored Baptist Church*, 15; C. C. Adams and Marshall A. Talley, *Negro Baptists and Foreign Missions* (Philadelphia: National Baptist Convention, 1944), 12–13; Mary C. Karasch, *Slave Life in Rio de Janeiro, 1808–1850* (Princeton, NJ: Princeton University Press, 1987), 82–86; A. J. R. Russell-Wood, "Black and Mulatto Brotherhoods in Colonial Brazil: A Study in Collective Behavior," *Hispanic American Historical Review* (November 1974), 567–602; Manoel S. Cardozo, "The Lay Brotherhoods of Colonial Bahia," *Catholic Historical Review* (April 1947), 12–30.

6. Michael A. Gomez, *Exchanging Our Country Marks: The Transformation of African Identities in the Colonial and Antebellum South* (Chapel Hill: University of North Carolina Press, 1998), 268, E. Franklin Frazier, *The Negro in the United States* (New York: Macmillan, 1949), 15–16; Melville J. Herskovits, *The Myth of the Negro Past* (1941; Boston: Beacon, 1990), 208–13; W. E. B. Du Bois, ed., "The Negro Church: Report of a Social Study Made under the Direction of Atlanta University together with the Proceedings of the Eighth Conference for the Study of the Negro Problems, Held at Atlanta University, May 26th, 1903," 5, in Vol. 2 of W. E. B. Du Bois, ed., *Atlanta University Publications* (New York: Octagon, 1968); Eugene D. Genovese, *Roll, Jordan, Roll: The World the Slaves Made* (1972; New York: Vintage, 1976), 162, 210, 212; Walls, *African Methodist Episcopal Zion Church*, 15–22.

7. Forrest G. Wood, *The Arrogance of Faith: Christianity and Race in America from the Colonial Era to the Twentieth Century* (New York: Knopf, 1990), 139.

8. Percy Livingstone Parker, ed., *The Heart of John Wesley's Journal* (New York: Fleming H. Revell, 1903), 2–3, 8; Sylvia R. Frey and Betty Wood, *Come Shouting to Zion: African American Protestantism in the American South and British Caribbean to 1830* (Chapel Hill: University of North Carolina Press, 1998), 87–91.

9. Joyce D. Goodfriend, *Before the Melting Pot: Society and Culture in Colonial New York City, 1664–1730* (Princeton, NJ: Princeton University Press, 1992), 124–32; Albert J. Raboteau, *A Fire in the Bones: Reflections on African-American Religious History* (Boston: Beacon, 1995), 24, 154.

10. William Warren Sweet, *Methodism in American History* (New York: Abingdon, 1933), 41–46; on charity and the British Methodists, see Abel Stevens, *The History of the Religious Movement of the Eighteenth Century, Called Methodism, Considered in Its Different Denominational Forms, and Its Relations to British and American Protestantism*, 3 vols. (New York: Carlton and Porter, 1858–61), 2: 472–74; Orlando Patterson, *The Sociology of Slavery: An Analysis of the Origins, Development and Structure of Negro Slave Society in Jamaica* (London: Macgibbon and Kee, 1967), 207–15; Nash, *Race, Class, and Politics*, 331–33.

11. Richard W. Pointer, *Protestant Pluralism and the New York Experience: A Study of Eighteenth-Century Religious Diversity* (Bloomington: Indiana University Press, 1988), 42–46.

12. Garret Abeel, "Historical Notes about the City of New York, from 1609 to 1792," in Henricus Selyns, *Records of Domine Henricus Selyns of New York 1686–7, with Notes and Remarks by Garret Abeel Written a Century Later 1791–2* (New York: Holland Society of New York, 1916), 36–39; Joseph R. Washington Jr., *Black Sects and Cults* (Garden City, NY: Doubleday, 1972), 41–42.

13. L. C. Rudolph, *Francis Asbury* (Nashville, TN: Abingdon Press, 1966), 176–83; Frey and Wood, *Come Shouting to Zion*, 91–93; Adams and Talley, *Negro Baptists and Foreign Missions*, 13–15. On white Methodists' tortured journey with

slavery, see Donald G. Mathews, *Slavery and Methodism: A Chapter in American Morality, 1780–1845* (Princeton, NJ: Princeton University Press, 1965); *The African Repository and Colonial Journal*, May 1832, 127.

14. This interpretation is supported by Williams's prominent role in the African separation from the John Street Church. Sweet, *Methodism in American History*, 55–59; Peter Williams Jr. letter in the *African Repository and Colonial Journal*, Vol. 10 (August 1834), 186–88; Dr. Francis Bourne Upham, Pastor, *The Story of the Old John Street Methodist Episcopal Church 1766–1932* (New York: Privately printed, 1932); Rev. J. B. Wakeley, *Lost Chapters Recovered from the Early History of American Methodism* (New York: Printed for the Author, 1858), 438–44, 460–62, 463–65, 467–69. On the financial condition of John Street, see Pointer, *Protestant Pluralism and the New York Experience*, 105. Nicholas Bayard, the witness to Williams's manumission document, was one of Manhattan's leading masters. He advertised regularly in local papers for his runaways, including enslaved Africans and William Patterson (a.k.a. John O'Konnor), a 22-year-old Irish servant; James, a 40-year-old Indian man; and James Costlelicth, an indenture from Bristol; *New-York Evening Post*, 15 June 1747, 8 May 1749, 5 November 1750.

15. Washington Jr., *Black Sects and Cults*, 33; Letter from "W[illia]m. Hamilton a black man to his excellency John Jay Esqr Governor of the State of New York, 8 March 1796," No. 501, Box 5, John Jay Papers, Butler Library, Columbia University, New York City.

16. Stevens, *History of Methodism*, 1: 351; Sweet, *Methodism in American History*, 53–58; John Wesley, "To 'Our Brethren in America,'" in Albert C. Outler, ed., *John Wesley* (New York: Oxford University Press, 1964), 82–84; Letter from John Wesley to the Rev. Francis Asbury, 20 September 1788, in Herbert Welch, ed., *Selections from the Writings of the Rev. John Wesley, M.A.* (New York: Abingdon, 1918), 394–95; Pointer, *Protestant Pluralism and the New York Experience*, 108–9, 127–28. Also see Samuel A. Seaman, A.M., *Annals of New York Methodism: Being a History of the Methodist Episcopal Church in the City of New York from A.D. 1766 to A.D. 1890* (New York: Hunt and Eaton, 1892), passim.

17. Woman dominance in black Christianity can also be found in the Diaspora. In the eighteenth century, a "small coterie of British men and black evangelical women became the center of Methodism in Antigua and the cradle of conversion in the archipelago," Sylvia R. Frey and Betty Wood write. Women, white and black, shaped the social experience of revivalistic religion, and black women were the means through which African mysticism entered evangelical culture. Frey and Wood, *Come Shouting to Zion*, 105–9. The fraternalism of the Africans comes through the coldness of the record: when Thomas Miller married Elizabeth Hose on 2 August 1794 his classmate Peter Williams served as the witness. John Street Church, "Record Book 1B," 42–43, 62, and "Record Book 1A," 31–32, Methodist Episcopal Church Records, Manuscripts Division, New York Public Library.

18. James T. Campbell, *Songs of Zion: The African Methodist Episcopal Church in the United States and South Africa* (New York: Oxford University Press, 1995), 13; George Claude Baker Jr., *An Introduction to the History of Early New England Methodism, 1789–1839* (1941; New York: AMS, 1969), 49–50; Sweet, *Methodism in American History*, 237; *New York Age*, 26 September 1931; Walls, *African Methodist Episcopal Zion Church*, 40–41, 43–48; Christopher Rush (with George Collins), *A Short Account of the Rise and Progress of the African Methodist Episcopal Church in America* (New York: Published by the author, 1843), 9–10; C. Eric Lincoln and Lawrence H. Mamiya, *The Black Church in the African American Experience* (Durham, NC: Duke University Press, 1990), 56–57.

19. Frey and Wood, *Come Shouting to Zion*, 108–11; Rhys Isaac, "Evangelical Revolt: The Nature of the Baptists' Challenge to the Traditional Order in Virginia, 1765 to 1775," *William and Mary Quarterly*, Vol. 31, No. 3 (July 1974), 361.

20. The trustees, elected on September 8, 1800, were Francis Jacobs, George Collins, Thomas Sipkins, George E. Moore, George White, David Bias, Peter Williams, Thomas Cook, and William Brown. Rush, *Short Account of the Rise and Progress of the African Methodist Episcopal Church*, 9–15, 25–29; Carter G. Woodson, *The History of the Negro Church* (1921; Washington, DC: Associated Publishers, 1945), 67–68; Edward D. Smith, *Climbing Jacob's Ladder: The Rise of Black Churches in Eastern American Cities, 1740–1877* (Washington, DC: Smithsonian Institution Press, 1988), 39–40; Anne Cronin, "The Struggle for Freedom and a Proper Burial," *New York Times*, 28 February 1993; Lincoln and Mamiya, *Black Church in the African American Experience*, 56–57. On New York City's history of segregated Christianity and the attempts to stop Africans from burying their dead at night, see Goodfriend, *Before the Melting Pot*, 91, 122, 125–26.

21. Wood, *Arrogance of Faith*, 245; "To the Bishops and Preachers of the Philadelphia and New-York Conferences, assembled," in Rush, *Short Account of the Rise and Progress of the African Methodist Episcopal Church*, 61.

22. Rush, *Short Account of the Rise and Progress of the African Methodist Episcopal Church*, 16–23.

23. In 1763 Manhattan's first Baptist church was organized. In 1832 Africans organized the Zion Baptist Church on Spring Street under the direction of the Reverend John T. Raymond. A. Clayton Powell Sr., *Against the Tide: An Autobiography* (New York: Richard R. Smith, 1938), 161–62; Abyssinian Baptist Church, *The Articles of Faith, Church Discipline, and By-Laws of the Abyssinian Baptist Church in the City of New York, April 3, 1833* (New York: J. Post, 1833), 11–14; George H. Hansell, *Reminiscences of Baptist Churches and Baptist Leaders in New York City and Vicinity, from 1835–1898* (Philadelphia: American Baptist Publication Society, 1899), 24–26.

24. Minutes for 30 March 1807, 26 September 1808, 10 October 1808, 18 April 1814, in *Minutes of the Common Council of the City of New York, 1784–1831*, 18 vols. (New York: Published by the City of New York, 1917), 4: 389, 5: 272, 278,

7: 729. On the scope of this harassment, see Paul A. Gilje, *The Road to Mobocracy: Popular Disorder in New York City, 1763–1834* (Chapel Hill: University of North Carolina Press, 1987), 154–56.

25. Walls, *African Methodist Episcopal Zion Church*, 68.

26. Rush, *Short Account of the Rise and Progress of the African Methodist Episcopal Church*, 29–31.

27. Rev. Edwin Warriner, *Old Sands Street Methodist Episcopal Church, of Brooklyn, N.Y., An Illustrated Centennial Record, Historical and Biographical* (New York: Phillips and Hunt, 1885), 13; Stiles, *History of Brooklyn*, 3: 700–707; Clarence Taylor, *The Black Churches of Brooklyn* (New York: Columbia University Press, 1994), 8–14; Craig Steven Wilder, "A Covenant with Color: Race and the History of Brooklyn, New York" (Ph.D. dissertation, Columbia University, 1994), 37, 40.

28. Rush, *Short Account of the Rise and Progress of the African Methodist Episcopal Church*, 34–52, 58–59; Hood, *One Hundred Years of the African Methodist Episcopal Zion Church*, 8–9.

29. Rush, *Short Account of the Rise and Progress of the African Methodist Episcopal Church*, 34–52, 58–59; Bishop J[ames]. W[alker]. Hood, D.D., LL.D., *One Hundred Years of the African Methodist Episcopal Zion Church; or, the Centennial of African Methodism* (New York: A.M.E. Zion Book Concern, 1895), 8–9; Pointer, *Protestant Pluralism and the New York Experience*, 11–28. In 1848 the word "Zion" was officially added to the name of the denomination; Lincoln and Mamiya, *The Black Church*, 57–58.

30. Rush, *Short Account of the Rise and Progress of the African Methodist Episcopal Church*, 53–64, 75–76, 96–97; on the spread of Zion churches in Brooklyn and Williamsburgh, see Taylor, *Black Churches of Brooklyn*, 8–11; on Rossville AMEZ, see the publications of the Sandy Ground Historical Society.

31. Washington Jr., *Black Religion*, 197; *Substance of the Debate in the House of Commons, on the 15th May, 1823, on a Motion for the Mitigation and Gradual Abolition of Slavery throughout the British Dominions* (1823; New York: Negro Universities Press, 1969), 164, 178–80.

32. Schomburg, "Jupiter Hammon"; Arnett G. Lindsay, "The Economic Condition of the Negroes of New York Prior to 1861," *Journal of Negro History*, Vol. 6, No. 2 (April 1921), 191; Walls, *African Methodist Episcopal Zion Church*, 90.

33. Nash, *Race, Class, and Politics*, 328–47; J. H. Powell, *Bring Out Your Dead: The Great Plague of Yellow Fever in Philadelphia in 1793* (1949; New York: Time Reading Program, 1965), 102–3; Schomburg, "Jupiter Hammon"; Douglass, *Annals of the First African Church*, 15–31; Bishop Richard Allen, *The Life, Experience and Gospel Labors of the Rt. Rev. Richard Allen* (Privately printed, 1833), 14; Philip S. Foner, *History of Black Americans: From Africa to the Emergence of the Cotton Kingdom* (Westport, CT: Greenwood, 1975), 556–59; Julie Winch, *Philadelphia's Black Elite: Activism, Accommodation, and the Struggle for Autonomy, 1787–1848*

(Philadelphia: Temple University Press, 1988), 7; *Laws of the African Society; Instituted at Boston, Anno Domini, 1796* (Boston: Printed for the Society, 1802), 4–6, collection of the New-York Historical Society; Robert J. Cottrol, *The Afro-Yankees: Providence's Black Community in the Antebellum Era* (Westport, CT: Greenwood, 1982), 45–47; Robert L. Harris Jr., "Early Black Benevolent Societies, 1780–1830," *Massachusetts Review* (Fall 1979), 609–11; Philip S. Foner, *History of Black Americans: From the Emergence of the Cotton Kingdom to the Eve of the Compromise of 1850* (Westport, CT: Greenwood Press, 1983), 239. On the Boston African Society, also see William C. Nell, *The Colored Patriots of the American Revolution* (New York: Arno, 1968), 96–97; and Herbert Aptheker, ed., *A Documentary History of the Negro People in the United States* (1951; New York: Citadel, 1969), 38–39; "Statistical Inquiry into the Condition of the People of Colour, of the City and Districts of Philadelphia" (Philadelphia: Kite and Walton, 1849), 22–23, in the Daniel A. P. Murray Collection, Library of Congress. By 1826, the African Improvement Society of New Haven, Connecticut, was formed. African benevolent societies were also established in Albany, Troy, and Syracuse. Short-lived societies appeared throughout northern and western New York State.

NOTES TO CHAPTER 3

1. C. L. R. James, *The Black Jacobins: Toussaint L'Ouverture and the San Domingo Revolution* (1938; 2nd rev. ed., New York: Vintage, 1963), 151–58, 289–92.

2. The New England Puritans actually used the conversion experience as proof of election. Industry was an important marker of godliness. For instance, it influenced the "Half-Way Covenant," the Puritans' attempt to solve the problems of the declining population of saved people, the relationship of unregenerate souls to the church, and the baptizing of children. See Edmund S. Morgan, *Visible Saints: The History of a Puritan Idea* (1963; Ithaca, NY: Cornell University Press, 1965), passim.

3. Looking at Rockdale, Pennsylvania, Anthony F. C. Wallace comes to a conclusion comparable to Thompson's. Christian reformers "depoliticized" working-class culture by usurping its most salient issues. Religion did not plot against labor, but, by making work a spiritual duty, it certainly weakened the moral authority of the workers' critique of capitalism. In an insightful reexamination, Bernard Semmel argues that Britain's early "Methodist Revolution" was the parallel of the Jacksonian Era in the United States. Semmel charges that both balanced industrialization's disruptive effect on society by augmenting the power of the individual, through universal grace in England and white manhood suffrage in the United States. Evangelicalism's strength was not that it allowed individuals to emote but that its leadership could negotiate a nonviolent track by blending conservative economic politics with liberal social values. Thus, Methodism stood in the way of "a violent English counterpart to the French Revolution," and its

influence on other denominations made "increasingly possible the relatively orderly social transformation to a modern, individualistic society during the eighteenth and nineteenth centuries."

Paul E. Johnson notes that dutiful labor was a tenet of revivalistic faith in antebellum Rochester, New York. The transformation to bourgeois society, Johnson
stresses, "bore the stamp of evangelical Protestantism." With far more nuance
than the earlier studies, Johnson's analysis focused on entrepreneurs who were
able to determine the common Protestant's ethic by defining and rewarding
"moral" behavior. The substance of the religion was vulnerable to the "social experience" of the congregation as there was a subtle but regular interplay between
the interests of class and the obligations of faith. Christopher Hill, *The World
Turned Upside Down: Radical Ideas during the English Revolution* (1972; London:
Penguin, 1991), 324; Max Weber, *The Protestant Ethic and the Spirit of Capitalism*
(1930; New York: Routledge, 1992), 63, 79–81, 95; E. P. Thompson, *The Making of
the English Working Class* (1963; New York: Vintage, 1966), 365–72; Anthony F. C.
Wallace, *Rockdale: The Growth of an American Village in the Early Industrial Revolution* (1972; New York: Norton, 1980), 383–84; Bernard Semmel, *The Methodist
Revolution* (New York: Basic Books, 1973), 6–9, 170–72, 192–97; Paul E. Johnson,
*A Shopkeeper's Millennium: Society and Revivals in Rochester, New York, 1815–
1837* (New York: Hill and Wang, 1978), 6–8, 121–35.

4. Hill, *World Turned Upside Down*, 324. Colonial New England provides an
example of the importance of this division. In 1639 Robert Keayne, a Boston
merchant, was accused, tried, censured, and fined for overcharging his cus-
tomers. The ethic shaped the debate about Keayne's behavior more than it determined his actions. He eventually repaired his relationship to the church. Keayne
continued to live in shame, not only for the moral and social crime of dishonesty,
but also because of a public suspicion that he was guilty of the spiritual infrac-
tion of tampering with the evidence of divine election. Bernard Bailyn, ed., *The
Apologia of Robert Keayne: The Self-Portrait of a Puritan Merchant* (New York:
Harper Torchbooks, 1965), passim.

5. Semmel, *Methodist Revolution*, 94–95; John R. Tyson, ed., *Charles Wesley:
A Reader* (New York: Oxford University Press, 1989), 77; David Brion Davis,
The Problem of Slavery in Western Culture (Ithaca, NY: Cornell University Press,
1966), 438, passim; Eric Foner, *Tom Paine and Revolutionary America* (New York:
Oxford University Press, 1976), 111; Lewis V. Baldwin, *"Invisible" Strands in Afri-
can Methodism: A History of the African Union Methodist Protestant and Union
Methodist Episcopal Churches, 1805–1980* (Metuchen, NJ: Scarecrow Press, 1983),
12–14.

6. John Wesley, A.M., *Thoughts upon Slavery*, 25, 33–35, 56, passim (London:
1774), in *A Collection of Religious Tracts* (Philadelphia: Joseph Crukshank, 1773).

7. Ibid., 15, 17, 39–40, 47, passim.

8. John Woolman, *The Journal of John Woolman* (Boston: Houghton Mifflin,

1871), 103, passim; Thomas Paine, "African Slavery in America," 8 March 1775, in Moncure Daniel Conway, ed., *The Writings of Thomas Paine*, 4 vols. (New York: Putnam's Sons, 1894), 1: 1–9; Foner, *Tom Paine*, 73.

9. Sylvia R. Frey and Betty Wood, *Come Shouting to Zion: African American Protestantism in the American South and British Caribbean to 1830* (Chapel Hill: University of North Carolina Press, 1998), 91; Letter from John Wesley "to a friend," 26 February 1791, in Herbert Welch, ed., *Selections from the Writings of the Rev. John Wesley, M.A.* (New York: Abingdon, 1918), 399.

10. Gilbert Hobbs Barnes, *The Antislavery Impulse, 1830–1844* (New York: D. Appleton-Century, 1933), 18; New York Manumission Society, "Rules for the Government of the Said Society," 25 January 1785, and "Report[s] of the Standing Committee," 9 November 1786, May 1787, Vol. 5, Records of the New York Manumission Society, collection of the New-York Historical Society. New York's white Christian elite was equally patronizing in its social work among Jews. For instance, when Peter Augustus Jay resigned as a director and treasurer of the American Society for Meliorating the Condition of the Jews, he prayed for the "spiritual welfare" of the Jews, whose "present infidelity is among the strongest evidences of the Religion they reject" and whose conversion promised to bring earthly joy. See letter from Peter Augustus Jay to the President of the American Society for Meliorating the Condition of the Jews, 10 November 1822, Jay Family Papers, collection of the New-York Historical Society. Thomas Clarkson, *An Essay on the Slavery and Commerce of the Human Species, Particularly the African; Translated from a Latin Dissertation, which was Honoured with the First Prize in the University of Cambridge for the Year 1785*, 2nd ed. (rev. and enlarged). In 1784 King's College (founded 1754) was renamed Columbia College.

11. C. Eric Lincoln and Lawrence H. Mamiya, *The Black Church in the African American Experience* (Durham, NC: Duke University Press, 1990), 56; Letter from "W[illia]m. Hamilton a black man to his excellency John Jay Esqr Governor of the State of New York, 8 March 1796," No. 501, Box 5, John Jay Papers, Manuscripts Division, Butler Library, Columbia University, New York City. Hamilton may also have been influenced by Quobna Ottobah Cugoano's 1787 essay, which shared similar themes of slavery as anti-Christian, slaveholders as thieves, and divine goodness protecting the enslaved. Quobna Ottobah Cugoano, a native of Africa, *Thoughts and Sentiments on the Evil and Wicked Traffic of the Slavery and Commerce of the Human Species, Humbly Submitted to the Inhabitants of Great-Britain*, edited by Vincent Carretta (1787; New York: Penguin, 1999), 24, 34–35, 60, 66–67.

12. Hugh I'Anson Fausset, *William Cowper* (New York: Harcourt, Brace, 1928), 73–91; John Newton and Richard Cecil, *The Life of the Reverend John Newton, Rector of St. Mary Woolnoth, London. Written by Himself in A.D. 1763, and Continued to His Death in 1807, by Rev. Richard Cecil, Minister of St. John's Chapel, London* (New York: American Tract Society, 185?), 151–56; Norman

Nicholson, *William Cowper* (London: Longmans, 1960), passim; Henry Thomas Griffith, ed., *Cowper*, 2 vols. (Oxford: Clarendon, 1874–75), 2: 189–91. Cowper was likely familiar with the enslaved African American author Phillis Wheatley's protest poetry, which had already been published in the United States and England. Wheatley was also an evangelical Christian. On Wheatley's work, see John C. Shields, "Phillis Wheatley's Struggle for Freedom in Her Poetry and Prose," in Shields, ed., *The Collected Works of Phillis Wheatley* (New York: Oxford University Press, 1988), 229–70.

13. See Rev. T. S. Grimshawe, A.M., F.S.A., M.R.S.L., ed., *The Works of William Cowper: His Life, Letters, and Poems* (New York: Robert Carter and Brothers, 1851), 618–19. James Robert Boyd, ed., *The Task, Table Talk, and Other Poems of William Cowper, with Critical Observations of Various Authors on His Genius and Character, and Notes, Critical and Illustrative* (New York: A. S. Barnes and Co., 1853); Martin Priestman, *Cowper's Task: Structure and Influence* (Cambridge, UK: Cambridge University Press, 1983), 71, 208n; Thomas Clarkson, M.A., *The History of the Rise, Progress, and Accomplishment of the Abolition of the African Slave-trade, by the British Parliament* (Philadelphia: James P. Parke, 1808), 152–53.

14. Bishop Richard Allen, *The Life, Experience and Gospel Labors of the Rt. Rev. Richard Allen* (Privately printed, 1833), 6–8; James T. Campbell, *Songs of Zion: The African Methodist Episcopal Church in the United States and South Africa* (New York: Oxford University Press, 1995), 6; Rev. Edwin Warriner, *Old Sands Street Methodist Episcopal Church, of Brooklyn, N.Y., An Illustrated Centennial Record, Historical and Biographical* (New York: Phillips and Hunt, 1885), 69–70.

15. Letter from "J.N." to "Dear Sir," 2 June 1792, in Rev. John Newton, *Letters and Conversational Remarks, by the late Reverend John Newton, Rector of St. Mary Woolnoth, Lombard Street, London,* edited by John Campbell (New York: S. Whiting, 1811), 5–6; Newton and Cecil, *Life of the Reverend John Newton,* 124–25, 216; John Newton, *The Journal of a Slave Trader, 1750–1754, with Newton's Thoughts upon the African Slave Trade,* edited by Bernard Martin and Mark Spurrell (London: Epworth, 1962), passim; Rev. T[homas]. Clarkson, M.A., *An Essay on the Impolicy of the African Slave Trade, in Two Parts* (1788; Freeport, NY: Books for Libraries Press, 1971), 30–67; James Field Stanfield, Late a Mariner in the African Slave Trade, *Observations on a Guinea Voyage. In a Series of Letters Addressed to the Rev. Thomas Clarkson* (London: James Phillips, 1788), 1.

16. Warriner, *Old Sands Street Methodist Episcopal Church,* 69–73.

17. Arthur A. Schomburg, "Jupiter Hammon before the New York African Society," *New York Amsterdam News,* 22 January 1930; Leo H. Hirsch, Jr., "The Negro and New York, 1783 to 1865," *Journal of Negro History,* Vol. 16, No. 4 (October 1931), 384–85.

18. Eugene D. Genovese, *Roll, Jordan, Roll: The World the Slaves Made* (1972; New York: Vintage, 1976), 162; Karl Marx, "Contribution to the Critique of

Hegel's Philosophy of Law," in *Karl Marx and Frederick Engels: Collected Works* (New York: International Publishers, 1975), 3: 175–87.

19. Phillis Wheatley, *Poems on Various Subjects, Religious and Moral* (1773), 18, in Shields, ed., *Collected Works of Phillis Wheatley*; Jupiter Hammon, "An Address to Miss Phillis Wheatly, Ethiopian Poetess, in Boston, who came from Africa at eight years of age, and soon became acquainted with the gospel of Jesus Christ," in "Six Broadsides Relating to Phillis Wheatley (Phillis Peters)," Schomburg Collection, NYPL; Helen M. MacLam, "Black Puritan on the Northern Frontier: The Vermont Ministry of Lemuel Haynes," in David W. Wills and Richard Newman, eds., *Black Apostles at Home and Abroad: Afro-Americans and the Christian Mission form the Revolution to Reconstruction* (Boston: G. K. Hall, 1982), 3–7.

20. Donald H. Matthews, *Honoring the Ancestors: An African Cultural Interpretation of Black Religion and Literature* (New York: Oxford University Press, 1998), 23.

21. Mechal Sobel, *The World They Made Together: Black and White Values in Eighteenth-Century Virginia* (Princeton, NJ: Princeton University Press, 1987), 221–25; also see Matthews, *Honoring the Ancestors*, 29.

22. Jupiter Hammon, "An Address to the Negroes of the State of New-York," in Carter G. Woodson, ed., *The Mind of the Negro as Reflected in Letters Written during the Crisis 1800–1860* (Washington, DC: Association for the Study of Negro Life and History, 1926), xii.

23. Ibid., vii–viii.

24. Ibid., viii–xii.

25. Ibid., xii–xiii.

26. Thompson, *Making of the English Working Class*, 365.

27. Hammon, "Address to the Negroes," viii–xii.

28. H. Richard Niebuhr, *The Kingdom of God in America* (Hamden, CT: Shoe String Press, 1956), 12.

29. Elizabeth Rauh Bethel, *The Roots of African-American Identity: Memory and History in Antebellum Free Communities* (New York: St. Martin's, 1997), 59; Lewis Perry, *Radical Abolitionism: Anarchy and the Government of God in Antislavery Thought* (Ithaca, NY: Cornell University Press, 1973), 18–54.

30. Hammon, "Address to the Negroes," xv.; See Sondra A. O'Neale, *Jupiter Hammon and the Biblical Beginnings of African-American Literature* (Metuchen, NJ: American Theological Library Association and Scarecrow Press, 1993), 205.

31. Hammon, "Address to the Negroes," xv.

32. Thomas J. Davis, *A Rumor of Revolt: The "Great Negro Plot" in Colonial New York* (New York: Free Press, 1985), ix, 54–55; Richard Shannon Moss, *Slavery on Long Island: A Study of Local Institutional and Early African-American Communal Life* (New York: Garland, 1993), 113–14.

33. "For the group, the small, well-defined community of believers became

the spiritual, social, material, and, above all, symbolic center of the slave community, the fountainhead of their unity and survival, of their cultural and ultimately ethnic identity, in a very real sense, of their freedom," Sylvia Frey writes of the impact of black Christianity in the Revolutionary era. "Unlike Anglo-Americans, for whom the concept of freedom implied autonomy, for African-Americans, as for their African forebears, freedom meant social bonds, attachment to a group." See Sylvia R. Frey, *Water from the Rock: Black Resistance in a Revolutionary Age* (Princeton, NJ: Princeton University Press, 1991), 284.

34. William Alexander, compiler, *Memoir of Captain Paul Cuffee, A Man of Colour: To which is Subjoined "The Epistle of the Society of Sierra Leone, in Africa, & c."* (London: W. Alexander, 1811), 25–27.

35. "To the People of Color," in Allen, *Life, Experience and Gospel Labors*, 51–52.

36. Hammon, "Address to the Negroes," xv.

37. George H. Williams, "The Religious Background of the Idea of a Loyal Opposition: A Protestant Contribution to the Theory and Practice of Ecumenical Dialogue," in D. B. Robertson, ed., *Voluntary Associations: A Study of Groups in Free Societies: Essays in Honor of James Luther Adams* (Richmond, VA: John Knox Press, 1966), 55–89; Edmund S. Morgan, *The Puritan Dilemma: The Story of John Winthrop* (Boston: Little, Brown, 1958), 203; Edmund S. Morgan, ed., *The Diary of Michael Wigglesworth, 1653–1657* (New York: Harper Torchbooks, 1946), 38; Perry Miller, *The New England Mind: The Seventeenth Century* (1939; Cambridge, MA: Harvard University Press, 1982), 398–505.

NOTES TO CHAPTER 4

1. John H. Bracey, Jr., August Meier, and Elliott Rudwick, *Black Nationalism in America* (Indianapolis, IN: Bobbs-Merrill, 1970), xxvi.

2. W. E. B. Du Bois, *The Autobiography of W.E.B. Du Bois: A Soliloquy on Viewing My Life from the Last Decade of Its First Century* (New York: International Publishers, 1968), 344; letter from Peter Williams Jr. to Paul Cuffe, 26 June 1816, in Rosaline Cobb Wiggins, ed., *Captain Paul Cuffe's Logs and Letters, 1808–1817: A Black Quaker's "Voice from within the Veil"* (Washington, DC: Howard University Press, 1996), 418.

3. Ellen Tarry, *The Other Toussaint: A Modern Biography of Pierre Toussaint, a Post-Revolutionary Black* (Boston: Daughters of St. Paul, 1981), 287; Shane White, *Somewhat More Independent: The End of Slavery in New York City, 1770–1810* (Athens: University of Georgia Press, 1991), 143, 155, 161; Society for the Prevention of Pauperism, "A Record Book with the Names of Heads of Families on Church, Franklin, Broadway, Leonard, and White Streets" (1820), Records of the Society for the Prevention of Pauperism, collection of the New-York Historical Society.

4. African nationalism is also displayed in black New Yorkers' tendency to

speak of Africa as a single entity—a nation, a country, and a homeland—rather than an assortment of states. Italics mine. Letter from "W[illia]m. Hamilton a black man to his excellency John Jay Esqr Governor of the State of New York, 8 March 1796," No. 501, Box 5, John Jay Papers, Butler Library, Columbia University, New York City; William Hamilton, *Address to the New York African Society, for Mutual Relief, Delivered in the Universalist Church, January 2, 1809* (New York: Privately printed, 1809); James McCune Smith, M.D., "Introduction" to Rev. Henry Highland Garnet, *A Memorial Discourse; by Rev. Henry Highland Garnet, Delivered in the Hall of the House of Representatives, Washington City, D.C. On Sabbath, February 12, 1865* (Philadelphia: Joseph M. Wilson, 1865), 24.

5. John L. Rury, "Philanthropy, Self Help, and Social Control: The New York Manumission Society and Free Blacks, 1785–1810," *Phylon: The Atlanta University Review of Race and Culture*, Vol. 46, No. 3 (1985), 238; Daniel Perlman, "Organizations of the Free Negro in New York City, 1800–1860," *Journal of Negro History*, Vol. 56 (1971), 181–97; William Alan Muraskin, "Black Masons: The Role of Fraternal Orders in the Creation of a Middle-Class Black Community" (Ph.D. dissertation, University of California, Berkeley, 1970), 6–8, 48–49, 63–64, 183.

6. "The Minutes and Proceedings of the First Annual Meeting of the American Moral Reform Society, Held at Philadelphia, in the Presbyterian Church in Seventh Street, below Shippen, from the 14th to the 19th of August, 1837" (Philadelphia: Merrihew and Gunn, 1837), 2–3, 28, passim, in the Daniel A. P. Murray Collection, Library of Congress.

7. Letter from Peter Williams Jr. to Capt. Paul Cuffe, 13 May 1815, and letter from Abraham Thompson, president, and Peter Williams Jr., secretary (of the New York African Institution) to the Friendly Society at Sierra Leone, 20 November 1815, in Wiggins, ed., *Captain Paul Cuffe's Logs and Letters, 1808–1817*, 60–61, 357, 396; Joseph Mason Andrew Cox, *Great Black Men of Masonry, 1723–1982* (Bronx, NY: Blue Diamond Press, 1982), 6, 50–52; Peter Williams Jr., *Discourse Delivered on the Death of Capt. Paul Cuffe, Before the New-York African Institution, in the African Methodist Episcopal Zion Church, October 21, 1817* (New York: African Institution, 1817), 4, 8–10, 15–16; on Cuffe's relations with black New Yorkers, see James Oliver Horton, *Free People of Color: Inside the African American Community* (Washington, DC: Smithsonian Institution, 1993), 113.

8. Peter Paul Simons, "Lecture Delivered before the African Clarkson Association, New York, New York," 23 April 1839, reprinted in C. Peter Ripley et al., eds., *The Black Abolitionist Papers*, 5 vols. (Chapel Hill: University of North Carolina Press, 1991), 3: 288–92.

9. Frances E. W. Harper, "Enlightened Motherhood: An Address before the Brooklyn Literary Society," 15 November 1892, Daniel A. P. Murray Collection, Library of Congress.

10. Ann Ducille, "Blues Notes on Black Sexuality: Sex and the Texts of Jessie Fauset and Nella Larson," *Journal of the History of Sexuality*, Vol. 3, No. 3 (1993), 423.

11. Emilio Zamora, *The World of the Mexican Worker in Texas* (College Station: Texas A & M University Press, 1993), 86–88, 99–103. Examining nineteenth-century England, E. P. Thompson notes that working-class consciousness was forged through the institutional culture of the friendly societies, political discourse, and "moral rhetoric." E. P. Thompson, *The Making of the English Working Class* (1963; New York: Vintage, 1966), 424. Moreover, New York City did not produce a black aristocracy with the wealth and privilege of the group that emerged in Philadelphia. See Julie Winch, *Philadelphia's Black Elite: Activism, Accommodation, and the Struggle for Autonomy, 1787–1848* (Philadelphia: Temple University Press, 1988), passim.

12. Simons, "Lecture Delivered before the African Clarkson Association," 291–92; Kevin K. Gaines, *Uplifting the Race: Black Leadership, Politics, and Culture in the Twentieth Century* (Chapel Hill: University of North Carolina Press, 1996), xiv–xv, 31–32. There are other examples of black New Yorkers clearly separating ideological and class positions. For instance, they usually dismissed white colonizationists as proslavery while they never seriously accused black emigrationists of such a motivation. The Reverend Henry Highland Garnet was eventually insulted in black Manhattan because he favored emigration, but he was never exiled. In the context of the group, emigration was a strategy, a political device, that in no way marked its advocates as alienated from or opposed to the greater community interest, and only black people who allowed themselves to become the agents of white colonizationists received the ultimate censure of exile. An acquaintance captured this aspect of Garnet's life: "Our friendship towards him and his towards us was no servile admiration on either side, but a full appreciation by each, of what each thought worthy in the other. He and I knew each other well; we differed in political sentiment—we differed in religious belief, but we were each a self-respecting friend; and neither demanded the subordination of any fraction of [illegible] in our mutual intercourse." Hon. Jas. Matthews, "Oration, on the Life and Character of Hon. Henry Highland Garnet, Delivered at Albany, NY, April 17, 1882," in Misc. Manuscripts, John E. Bruce Collection, Schomburg Collection, NYPL.

13. Rebecca J. Scott, *Slave Emancipation in Cuba: The Transition to Free Labor, 1860–1899* (Princeton, NJ: Princeton University Press, 1985), 66, 163–64, passim; Sylviane A. Diouf, *Servants of Allah: African Muslims Enslaved in the Americas* (New York: New York University Press, 1998), 105; A. J. R. Russell-Wood, "Black and Mulatto Brotherhoods in Colonial Brazil: A Study in Collective Behavior," *Hispanic American Historical Review* (November 1974), 594–95. On the concept of social medicine, see William P. Murphy, "Secret Knowledge as Property and Power in Kpelle Society: Elders versus Youth," *Africa*, Vol. 50, No. 2 (1980), 197–200.

14. A Member [Peter Vogelsang], *An Address Delivered before the New-York African Society for Mutual Relief, in the African Zion Church, 23d March 1815,*

Being the Fifth Anniversary of Their Incorporation (New York: Printed for the Society, 1815), 3–4, collection of the New-York Historical Society.

15. *The Constitution of the New York African Society for Mutual Relief*, Passed June 6th, 1808. Amended February 8th, 1869 (New York: Bunce and Co., 1869).

16. A number of men waited for years after their emancipation to join Mutual Relief. Saving money for the initiation fee and the dues was a consideration in this delay, but the death benefit also became a more potent draw toward the end of men's lives. Jacob Francis (1833), Peter Nichols (1837), Henry Williams (1839), John Brown (1844), and William Jackson (1845) all waited two or three decades after their manumissions to join the NYASMR. There is considerable room for error in compiling this type of a list because many of the names are common, and public records are often casual with the names of enslaved and free black people. The ages of the black men who are listed as manumitted from 1800 to 1820 and joining the NYASMR from 1830 to 1845 have been used to insure that they are compatible with this claim. Harry B. Yoshpe, "Record of Slave Manumissions in New York during the Colonial and Early National Periods," *Journal of Negro History*, Vol. 26, No. 1 (January 1941), 78–103; the index of manumission records, Vol. 3, Francis Cook's manumission is available in Vol. 1, Records of the New York Manumission Society, New-York Historical Society.

17. Yoshpe, "Record of Slave Manumissions in New York," 100. On February 12, 1813, Emma Miller manumitted "my male slave named James Varick, hereby willing & declaring that the sd. James Varick shall & may at all time & times hereafter, exercise, hold & enjoy all & singular the liberties, rights, privileges and immunities of a free man, as fully to all intents & purposes as if he had been born free." The manumission document is in Vol. 3, Records of the New York Manumission Society. Bishop J[ames]. W[alker]. Hood, D.D., LL.D., *One Hundred Years of the African Methodist Episcopal Zion Church; or, the Centennial of African Methodism* (New York: A.M.E. Zion Book Concern, 1895), 162, 530; William J. Walls, *The African Methodist Episcopal Zion Church: Reality of the Black Church* (Charlotte, NC: A.M.E. Zion Publishing House, 1974), 84–95. Varick's birthday is unclear; some sources date it as early as 1750. I have used the date offered in Bishop R. R. Wright, Jr., *The Bishops of the African Methodist Episcopal Church* (Nashville, TN: A.M.E. Sunday School Union, 1963), 385.

18. Rush's preachers' society was "for the benefit of destitute superannuated preachers, their widows and orphans." Membership was limited to pastors with at least five years in the connection, and the authors agreed to a modest initiation fee of one dollar and annual dues of one dollar. Interestingly, the money was turned over to the A.M.E. Zion Book Concern in the form of a loan. The Book Concern thus received its startup money while the members were assured of a reasonable rate of return. The general agent of the Concern governed the distribution of interest to each conference according to its needs and its membership. When the Concern was able to retire the loan, the fund was to be invested in real

estate with the general agent continuing to distribute profits to the conferences. The society's other business was placed in the hands of a committee of ministers selected from each conference. Edward D. Smith, *Climbing Jacob's Ladder: The Rise of Black Churches in Eastern American Cities, 1740–1877* (Washington, DC: Smithsonian Institution Press, 1988), 67; Christopher Rush (with George Collins), *A Short Account of the Rise and Progress of the African Methodist Episcopal Church in America* (New York: Published by the author, 1843), 119; letter from John Alsop, Walter Livingston, and William Duer for the Committee Appointed by the Corporation for the Relief of Clergymen, Widows, and Children in Communion with the Church of England, to Examine into the Accounts of Jacob LeRoy Esqr., Late Treasurer of the Said Corporation, dated 23 September 1785, in Box 5, Rutherfurd Papers, collection of the New-York Historical Society; Abel Stevens, *The History of the Religious Movement of the Eighteenth Century, Called Methodism, Considered in Its Different Denominational Forms, and Its Relations to British and American Protestantism*, 3 vols. (New York: Carlton and Porter, 1858–61), 2: 465–66; Hood, *One Hundred Years of the African Methodist Episcopal Zion Church*, 168, 528–30; [Historical Records Survey, WPA], *Inventory of the Church Archives of New York City: The Methodist Church* (New York: Historical Records Survey, 1940), 35.

19. Also appears as Moranda and Marander. I have used the most consistent spelling from the records of the New York African Society for Mutual Relief. His identity has been confirmed through city directories and censuses.

20. Yoshpe, "Record of Slave Manumissions in New York," 81, 84, 85.

21. Peter Williams Jr. was a guiding spirit and probably a founder of the New York African Society for Mutual Relief, although his name does not appear on the petition for incorporation, the later act, or the histories of the society compiled after the fire of 1867. There are early publications that confirm that Williams was a member and served as chaplain and vice president of the society for at least a year. John Street Church, "Record Book 1A," 4, Methodist Episcopal Church Records, Manuscripts Division, New York Public Library; Rev. J. B. Wakeley, *Lost Chapters Recovered from the Early History of American Methodism* (New York: Printed for the Author, 1858), 446–61.

22. Wilson Jeremiah Moses, *Alexander Crummell: A Study of Civilization and Discontent* (Amherst: University of Massachusetts Press, 1992), 11–12; Rev. William J. Simmons, D.D., *Men of Mark: Eminent, Progressive and Rising* (1887; New York: Arno, 1968), 530–35.

23. *Laws of the State of New York, Passed at the Thirty-Fifth Session of the Legislature* (Albany, 1812), 189–90; Yoshpe, "Record of Slave Manumissions in New York," 84, 89, 92, 95, 101; Perlman, "Organizations of the Free Negro in New York City," 185; Philip S. Foner, *History of Black Americans*, 2 vols. (Westport, CT: Greenwood, 1975, 1983), 1: 241; *Laws of the State of New York, Passed at the Sixty-Eighth Session of the Legislature* (Albany, 1845), 242–43.

24. Letter from "W[illia]m. Hamilton a black man to his excellency John Jay Esqr Governor of the State of New York, 8 March 1796."

25. Theodore Hershberg, "Free Blacks in Antebellum Philadelphia: A Study of Ex-Slaves, Freeborn, and Socioeconomic Decline," *Journal of Social History* (Winter 1971–72), 192–200; also see Robert L. Harris, Jr., "Early Black Benevolent Societies, 1780–1830," *Massachusetts Review* (Fall 1979), 614–15.

26. The Brooklyn African Woolman Association patterned its constitution on that of the NYASMR:

> The reflection of the various vicissitudes to which mankind are continually exposed, has been productive of various means to alleviate their distresses—provision is made for almost every species of wretchedness—the afflicted, the widow and orphan generally, have a source to look to for relief, and we, the subscribers, do conclude, that the most efficient method of securing ourselves from the extreme exigencies to which we are liable to be reduced, is, by uniting ourselves in a body for the purpose of raising a fund for the relief of its members; consequently, we have associated ourselves, under the name and stile of the *Brooklyn African Woolman Benevolent Society*, with the pleasing hope of ameliorating the occasional distresses of each other by our mutual endeavors.

On January 28, 1831, it was incorporated under New York State law. *Constitution of the Brooklyn African Woolman Benevolent Society*, Adopted March 16, 1810 (Brooklyn, NY: E. Worthington, 1820), collection of the New-York Historical Society; *Laws of the State of New York, Passed at the Fifty-Fourth Session of the Legislature* (Albany, 1831), 12–13; *Constitution of the African Marine Fund, for the Relief of the Distressed Orphans, and Poor Members of This Fund* (New York: John C. Totten, 1810), passim, collection of the New-York Historical Society; "Constitution of the Garrison Literary and Benevolent Association, New-York," *The Liberator*, 19 April 1834; *Constitution and By-Laws of the Abyssinian Benevolent Daughters of Esther Association of the City of New York.* Adopted April 19th, 1839 (New York: Zuille and Leondard, 1853), collection of the Society for the Preservation of Weeksville and Bedford-Stuyvesant History; James B. Browning, "The Beginnings of Insurance Enterprise among Negroes," *Journal of Negro History* (October 1937), 421–22.

27. Letter, written in French, from Michel Castor, A. Lambert, B. Duplessy, D. G. Cerci, and Jean L. Chabert to Monsieur [Pierre Toussaint], 19 November 1839, Pierre Toussaint Papers, Manuscripts Division, NYPL; Ellen Tarry, *The Other Toussaint: A Modern Biography of Pierre Toussaint, a Post-Revolutionary Black* (Boston: Daughters of St. Paul, 1981), 334.

28. Foner, *History of Black Americans*, 2: 250; *The Liberator*, 6 August 1831; Willis Augustus Hodges, *Free Man of Color: The Autobiography of Willis Augustus Hodges*, edited with an introduction by Willard B. Gatewood Jr. (Knoxville:

University of Tennessee Press, 1982), 49, 53. The title, *The Ram's Horn*, is biblical; see Joshua 6:1–21. In 1832 the Reverend John Lewis, a black clergyman, founded the Providence Temperance Society, and one of the leaders of the Temperance movement in Rochester, New York, was Austin Steward, a black grocer. See Robert J. Cottrol, *The Afro-Yankees: Providence's Black Community in the Antebellum Era* (Westport, CT: Greenwood, 1982), 62; Paul E. Johnson, *A Shopkeeper's Millennium: Society and Revivals in Rochester, New York, 1815–1837* (New York: Hill and Wang, 1978), 117–18.

29. Howard H. Turner, *Turner's History of the Independent Order of Good Samaritans and Daughters of Samaria, Together with a Concise History of the Ancient Samarians as Spoken of in the Bible* (Washington, DC: R. A. Waters, 1881), 25–26, 64–65.

30. [Vogelsang], *An Address Delivered before the New-York African Society for Mutual Relief*, 11–13.

31. Minutes for 14 and 28 December 1807, in *Minutes of the Common Council of the City of New York, 1784–1831*, 18 vols. (New York: Published by the City of New York, 1917), 4: 663, 682.

32. Peter Williams Jr., *An Oration on the Abolition of the Slave Trade; Delivered in the African Church in the City of New York, January 1, 1808* (New York: Samuel Wood, 1808), 11–12, passim, Schomburg Collection, NYPL; Walls, *African Methodist Episcopal Zion Church*, 144.

33. Williams Jr., *Oration on the Abolition of the Slave Trade*, 12–13.

34. Ibid., 13–19.

35. Ibid., 13–20.

36. Ibid., 24–26.

37. Henry Sipkins, a descendant of Africa, *An Oration on the Abolition of the Slave Trade, Delivered in the African Church in the City of New-York, January 2, 1809*, Schomburg Collection, NYPL.

38. Ibid.

39. Ibid.; on the Quaker impact on New York, see Arthur J. Worrall, *Quakers in the Colonial Northeast* (Hanover, NH: University Press of New England, 1980).

40. [Vogelsang], *An Address Delivered before the New-York African Society for Mutual Relief*, 14–15.

41. The Union Society probably took its name from Manhattan's African Union Methodist Church. There is a less convincing explanation for the Union Society's name. About 1807 Abraham Thompson and June Scott, black Manhattan's elder preachers, joined a white former Quaker named John Edwards in erecting a small church and two preachers' residences at No. 101 Green Street. The ephemeral and Quaker-ish Union Society was born. Edwards sought a place to occasionally preach, and Thompson and Scott, according to contemporaries, were drawn to the free accommodations. Zion's trustees discovered the plan. Thompson denounced it and returned to Zion; Scott attached himself to another

church. The Union church folded. On Bishop Francis Asbury and Methodist an-
tislavery, see Albert J. Raboteau, *Slave Religion: The "Invisible Institution" in the
Antebellum South* (1978; New York: Oxford University Press, 1980), 143–45. On
John Woolman and Quaker antislavery, see Jean R. Soderlund, *Quakers and Slav-
ery: A Divided Spirit* (Princeton, NJ: Princeton University Press, 1985). On the
Union Society, see Rush, *Short Account of the Rise and Progress of the African
Methodist Episcopal Church*, 28–29; Carter G. Woodson, *The History of the Negro
Church* (1921; Washington, DC: Associated Publishers, 1945), 67–68. On William
Wilberforce, Thomas Clarkson, and the British Quakers, see Elizabeth Rauh
Bethel, *The Roots of African-American Identity: Memory and History in Antebel-
lum Free Black Communities* (New York: St. Martin's, 1997), 145–47; David Brion
Davis, *The Problem of Slavery in the Age of Revolution, 1770–1823* (Ithaca, NY:
Cornell University Press, 1975), passim. Also see Thomas Clarkson's *An Essay on
the Slavery and Commerce of the Human Species, Particularly the African; Translated from a Latin Dissertation, which was Honoured with the First Prize in the
University of Cambridge for the Year 1785*, 2nd ed. (rev. and enlarged); *An Essay on
the Impolicy of the African Slave Trade, in Two Parts* (London: J. Phillips, 1788);
*The History of the Rise, Progress, and Accomplishment of the Abolition of the Afri-
can Slave-trade, by the British Parliament*, 2 vols. (Philadelphia: James P. Parke,
1808). On the Quaker women's Clarkson Association, see Society for the Prevention of Pauperism, *Fourth Annual Report of the Managers of the Society for the
Prevention of Pauperism, in the City of New-York. Read and Accepted, January,
1821* (New York: E. Conrad, 1821), 14, Records of the (New York) Society for the
Prevention of Pauperism, collection of the New-York Historical Society. On Clinton and Tompkins in the Craft, see *Gould's History of Freemasonry throughout the
World*, 6 vols., revised by Dudley Wright (New York: Scribner's Sons, 1936), 6:
48–53.

The Manhattan African societies inspired other African organizations over a
wide area. As late as 1848 the Reverend Henry Highland Garnet, a founding
member of the Garrison Association, was lecturing before the Female Benevolent
Society of Troy, New York, where he was pastor of a Presbyterian church. Julia
Williams, who married Garnet in 1840, belonged to that society. Sterling Stuckey,
Slave Culture: Nationalist Theory and the Foundations of Black America (New
York: Oxford University Press, 1987), 166; Smith, "Introduction" to Garnet,
Memorial Discourse, 32.

42. Larry Gara, *The Liberty Line: The Legend of the Underground Railroad*
(Lexington: University of Kentucky Press, 1961), 79; David Brion Davis, *The
Problem of Slavery in Western Culture* (Ithaca, NY: Cornell University Press,
1966), 299–326; Sipkins, *An Oration on the Abolition of the Slave Trade*. This limitation in Quaker antislavery thought was present from the beginning. George
Fox's 1657 and 1679 epistles on slavery implored Friends to evangelize their enslaved Africans and Indians, and not to find themselves standing in the way of

conversions to Christ. George Fox, *A Collection of Many Select and Christian Epistles, Letters and Testimonies, Written on Sundry Occasions, by That Ancient, Eminent, Faithful Friend, and Minister of Christ Jesus*, 2 vols. (Philadelphia: Marcus T. Gould, 1831), 1: 144–45, 2: 160–62.

43. Hamilton, *Address to the New York African Society, for Mutual Relief.*

44. Ibid.

45. Ibid.; [Vogelsang], *An Address Delivered before the New-York African Society for Mutual Relief*, 14.

46. Hamilton, *An Address to the New York African Society for Mutual Relief.*

47. Sipkins, *An Oration on the Abolition of the Slave Trade*; [Vogelsang], *An Address Delivered before the New-York African Society for Mutual Relief*, 16.

48. Ibid., 4.

NOTES TO CHAPTER 5

1. Roy Rosenzweig and Elizabeth Blackmar, *The Park and the People: A History of Central Park* (1992; New York: Henry Holt, 1994), 65–89; Harry A. Williamson, "Folks in Old New York and Brooklyn" (Bronx, NY: Unpublished manuscript, July 1953), 11, Schomburg Collection, NYPL; *The Liberator*, 27 April 1834.

2. Harold X. Connolly, *A Ghetto Grows in Brooklyn* (New York: New York University Press, 1977), 9–12; Craig Steven Wilder, "A Covenant with Color: Race and the History of Brooklyn, New York" (Ph.D. dissertation, Columbia University, 1994), 41–42; on Gloucester in Seneca Village, see Rosenzweig and Blackmar, *Park and the People*, 73. White people in Flushing, Queens, also labeled a local African neighborhood "Crow Hill." See Henry D. Waller, *History of the Town of Flushing, Long Island, New York* (Flushing, NY: J. H. Ridenour, 1899), 177.

3. Gary B. Nash, *Race, Class, and Politics: Essays on American Colonial and Revolutionary Society* (Urbana: University of Illinois Press, 1986), 307–9, 311.

4. The fact that opposition groups must provide social alternatives has been captured succinctly by Jean Chesneaux, who notes that the anti-Confucian societies that operated in China for centuries found themselves in the paradoxical situation of having to substitute elaborate conventions and codes for those they opposed. Jean Chesneaux, *Secret Societies in China: In the Nineteenth and Twentieth Centuries*, translated by Gillian Nettle (Ann Arbor: University of Michigan Press, 1971), 7–9. Emilio Zamora, *The World of the Mexican Worker in Texas* (College Station: Texas A & M University Press, 1993), 86–90.

5. Sean Wilentz, *Chants Democratic: New York City and the Rise of the American Working Class, 1788–1850* (New York: Oxford University Press, 1984), 48n; Shane White, *Somewhat More Independent: The End of Slavery in New York City, 1770–1810* (Athens: University of Georgia Press, 1991), 158; the report of the jury's decision is reprinted in Howard B. Rock, ed., *The New York City Artisan, 1789–1825: A Documentary History* (Albany: State University of New York Press, 1989), 172–73.

6. A Member [Peter Vogelsang], *An Address Delivered before the New-York African Society for Mutual Relief, in the African Zion Church, 23d March 1815, Being the Fifth Anniversary of Their Incorporation* (New York: Printed for the Society, 1815), 3–4, collection of the New-York Historical Society.

7. Ibid., 6, 8–11; John Teasman, *An Address Delivered in the African Episcopal Church, on the 25th March, 1811. Before the New York African Society, for Mutual Relief; Being the First Anniversary of Its Incorporation* (New York: J. Low, 1811), 7.

8. "Thomas L. Jennings," *Anglo-African Magazine*, Vol. 1, No. 4 (April 1859); John J. Zuille, *Historical Sketch of the New York African Society for Mutual Relief* (New York: Privately printed, 1893), 6–7, 24. Five years earlier, George DeGrasse sought to be a citizen while still enslaved. On July 5, 1804, he was naturalized in the United States; more striking was that he managed to do this before he was free. He had been in the country for over five years and in the city for more than one when he applied:

City of New York, ss.

    Be it remembered, that George DeGrasse, of the city of New York, servant, who hath resided within the limits and jurisdiction of the United States for the term of five years, and within this State of New York for the term of one year at least, appeared in the Court of Common Pleas, called the Mayor's Court, and which is a common law court of record held in and for the city and county of New York in the State of New York, on Thursday, the fifth day of July, in the year one thousand eight hundred and four, and having made proof to the satisfaction of said Court that he is a person of good moral character, attached to the principles of the Constitution of the United States, and well disposed to the good order and happiness of the same, and having in the said Court taken the oath prescribed by law to support the Constitution of the United States, and did in open Court absolutely and entirely renounce and abjure all allegiance and fidelity to every foreign prince, potentate, state or sovereignty, and particularly to the King of the United Kingdom of Great Britain and Ireland, of whom he was then a subject, the said George DeGrasse was thereupon, pursuant to the laws of the United States in such case made and provided, admitted by the said Court to be, and his is accordingly to be, considered a citizen of the United States.

    Given under the seal of the said Court, the day and year above written.
        Per curiam,

T. WOODMAN, *Clerk.*

In 1815 DeGrasse joined the NYASMR. William C. Nell, *The Colored Patriots of the American Revolution* (New York: Arno, 1968), 316. W. E. Burghardt Du Bois, ed., *Economic Co-operation among Negro Americans* (Atlanta: Atlanta University Press, 1907), 96; James McCune Smith, M.D., "Introduction" to Rev. Henry Highland

Garnet, *A Memorial Discourse; by Rev. Henry Highland Garnet, Delivered in the Hall of the House of Representatives, Washington City, D.C. on Sabbath, February 12, 1865* (Philadelphia: Joseph M. Wilson, 1865), 20–21; Thomas Clarkson, M.A., *The History of the Rise, Progress, and Accomplishment of the Abolition of the African Slave-Trade, by the British Parliament*, 2 vols. (Philadelphia: James P. Parke, 1808), 1: 153. The charter was renewed every fifteen years until 1855 when it was allowed to expire. In 1869 the society was incorporated under the general laws of New York State.

9. My estimation of the dues and initiation fee is based upon those of contemporary organizations. [Vogelsang], *An Address Delivered before the New-York African Society for Mutual Relief*, 5, 8; Zuille, *Historical Sketch of the NYASMR*, 16; Samuel R. Scottron, "New York African Society for Mutual Relief Ninety-Seventh Anniversary," *Colored American Magazine* (December 1905), 688.

10. Gilbert Hobbs Barnes, *The Antislavery Impulse, 1830–1844* (New York: Appleton-Century, 1933), 17–19, 20–25; Richard W. Pointer, *Protestant Pluralism and the New York Experience: A Study of Eighteenth-Century Religious Diversity* (Bloomington: Indiana University Press, 1988), 132–33; Bernard Semmel, *The Methodist Revolution* (New York: Basic Books, 1973), 17–18, 167–69. Similarly, in his study of Rockdale, Pennsylvania, Anthony F. C. Wallace notes that businessmen funded white societies and missions and directed them toward a decidedly moderate and class-conscious reform program. Anthony F. C. Wallace, *Rockdale: The Growth of an American Village in the Early Industrial Revolution* (1972; New York: Norton, 1980), 296, 332–37.

11. Robert L. Harris, Jr., "Early Black Benevolent Societies, 1780–1830," *Massachusetts Review* (Fall 1979), 613–14; Whitney R. Cross, *The Burned-over District: The Social and Intellectual History of Enthusiastic Religion in Western New York, 1800–1850* (Ithaca, NY: Cornell University Press, 1950), 198–201, 271; Cotton Mather, *Bonifacius: An Essay Upon the Good, That is to Be Devised and Designed by Those Who Desire to Answer the Great End of Life, and to Do Good While They Live* (Boston: B. Green, 1710), 73–88, 167–74.

12. Cross, *Burned-over District*, 263–67, 275; William Warren Sweet, *Methodism in American History* (New York: Abingdon, 1933), 241–53; Barnes, *Antislavery Impulse*, 25.

13. Cross, *The Burned-over District*, 165–69; Barnes, *Antislavery Impulse*, 17–24; Keith J. Hardman, "Charles G. Finney, the Benevolent Empire, and the Free Church Movement in New York City," *New York History* (October 1986), 411–35.

14. Paul A. Gilje, *The Road to Mobocracy: Popular Disorder in New York City, 1763–1834* (Chapel Hill: University of North Carolina Press, 1987), 133–34; Leo Hershkowitz, "The Irish and the Emerging City: Settlement to 1844," in Ronald H. Bayor and Timothy J. Meagher, eds., *The New York Irish* (Baltimore: Johns Hopkins University Press, 1996), 13; Edwin G. Burrows and Mike Wallace, *Gotham: A History of New York City to 1898* (New York: Oxford University Press, 1999), 542–43; Henry R. Stiles, *A History of the City of Brooklyn, Including the Old*

Town and Village of Brooklyn, the Town of Bushwick, and the Village and City of Williamsburgh, 3 vols. (Brooklyn: Privately printed, 1870), 3: 856.

15. Wilentz, *Chants Democratic*, 85; T. Desmond Williams, ed., *Secret Societies in Ireland* (New York: Barnes and Noble, 1973), 1–7.

16. Noel Ignatiev, *How the Irish Became White* (New York: Routledge, 1995), 92–121; Nash, *Race, Class, and Politics*, 311. On gang culture in the city, see Richard B. Stott, *Workers in the Metropolis: Class, Ethnicity, and Youth in Antebellum New York City* (Ithaca, NY: Cornell University Press, 1990), 230–31.

17. Wilentz, *Chants Democratic*, 38–46, 55–60; Sidney I. Pomerantz, *New York: An American City, 1783–1803* (New York: Columbia University Press, 1938), 469; Rock, ed., *New York City Artisan*, 21–30, 199–213. For a more general history of New York benevolent associations, see M. J. Heale, "Patterns of Benevolence: Associated Philanthropy in the Cities of New York, 1830–1860," *New York History* (January 1976), 53–79.

18. Joseph R. Washington Jr., *Black Sects and Cults* (Garden City, NY: Doubleday, 1972), 51.

19. Fei-Ling Davis, *Primitive Revolutionaries of China: A Study of Secret Societies in the Late Nineteenth Century* (1971; Honolulu: University Press of Hawaii, 1977), 72–78; E. P. Thompson, *The Making of the English Working Class* (1963; New York: Vintage, 1966), 418–22; Robert L. Wilken, *The Christians as the Romans Saw Them* (New Haven, CT: Yale University Press, 1984), 8–47.

20. Rebecca J. Scott, *Slave Emancipation in Cuba: The Transition to Free Labor, 1860–1899* (Princeton, NJ: Princeton University Press, 1985), 265–67.

21. William Alan Muraskin, "Black Masons: The Role of Fraternal Orders in the Creation of a Middle-Class Black Community" (Ph.D. dissertation, University of California, Berkeley, 1970), 2–3. Later published as William A. Muraskin, *Middle-Class Blacks in a White Society: Prince Hall Freemasonry in America* (Berkeley: University of California Press, 1975).

22. E. J. Hobsbawm, *Primitive Rebels: Studies in Archaic Forms of Social Movements in the 19th and 20th Centuries* (1959; New York: Norton, 1965), 150–53.

23. A minister and seceding Mason from the period offered a lengthy treatment of the Morgan murder. See Lebbeus Armstrong, *William Morgan Abducted and Murdered by Masons, in Conformity with Masonic Obligations; and Masonic Measures, to Conceal That Outrage Against the Laws; a Practical Comment on the Sin of Cain. Illustrated and Proved in a Sermon, Delivered in Edinburgh, Saratoga County, Sept. 12, 1831* (New York: L. D. Dewey, 1831). Wallace, *Rockdale*, 342–47; Rev. C. G. Finney, *The Character, Claims, and Practical Workings of Freemasonry* (Cincinnati: Western Tract and Book Society, 1869), passim; Cross, *The Burned-over District*, 114–23; Mark C. Carnes, *Secret Ritual and Manhood in Victorian America* (New Haven, CT: Yale University Press, 1989), 23–27, 31–32, 72–79; Paul E. Johnson, *A Shopkeeper's Millennium: Society and Revivals in Rochester, New York, 1815–1837* (New York: Hill and Wang, 1978), 66–69.

252 | Notes to Chapter 5

24. Harry A. Williamson, "A History of Freemasonry among the American Negroes" (New York: Unpublished manuscript, 1929), 19–30, Schomburg Collection, NYPL; H. P. Davis, *Black Democracy: The Story of Haiti* (New York: Dial, 1928), 114–15; Rayford Logan, *Haiti and the Dominican Republic* (New York: Oxford University Press, 1968), 32–33; William J. Walls, *The African Methodist Episcopal Zion Church: Reality of the Black Church* (Charlotte, NC: A.M.E. Zion Publishing House, 1974), 90.

25. Harry A. Williamson, "Prince Hall Masonry in New York State," unpublished typescript, Vol. 1: 7–10, Vol. 2, Part 2: 119, 129, passim, Harry A. Williamson Collection, Writings, Schomburg Collection, NYPL.

26. *Gould's History of Freemasonry throughout the World*, 6 vols., revised by Dudley Wright (New York: Scribner's Sons, 1936), 6: 40–65; Williamson, "History of Freemasonry," 3–8; Harold Van Buren Voorhis, *Negro Masonry in the United States* (New York: Henry Emmerson, 1949), 10–22; Joseph Mason Andrew Cox, *Great Black Men of Masonry, 1723–1982* (Bronx, NY: Blue Diamond Press, 1982), 6, 50–52, 84–85, 123; Julie Winch, *Philadelphia's Black Elite: Activism, Accommodation, and the Struggle for Autonomy, 1787–1848* (Philadelphia: Temple University Press, 1988), 7–9; Carnes, *Secret Ritual and Manhood*, 25, 28–29; Bertram L. Baker, "Masonic Notes," *New York Age*, 16 July 1932.

27. Finney, *Character, Claims, and Practical Workings of Freemasonry*, v–viii, 186–90.

28. The name "Royal Art" is a biblical reference to the Golden Rule, which Saint James described as the Royal Law. It was intended to capture the culture of fraternalism in Masonry. Samuel Seabury, *A Discourse Delivered in St. James' Church, in New-London, On Tuesday the 23d of December, 1794: Before an Assembly of Free and Accepted Masons, Convened for the Purpose of Installing a Lodge in That City* (New London, CT: Brother Samuel Green, 1795), 14–15. Michael A. Gomez, *Exchanging Our Country Marks: The Transformation of African Identities in the Colonial and Antebellum South* (Chapel Hill: University of North Carolina Press, 1998), 101. On the origins of Freemasonry, see David Stevenson, *The Origins of Freemasonry: Scotland's Century, 1590–1710* (Cambridge, UK: Cambridge University Press, 1988), 1–9, passim. For the biblical description of Solomon's temple, see 1 Kings 5–8; 1 Chronicles 22; 2 Chronicles 2–5. A completely speculative connection can be made between Mother Zion and Masonry from this account. While Zion appears several times in scripture, it is prominent in the temple narrative. After the building of the temple, Solomon gathered the holy men and leaders of the tribes to bring the ark of the covenant of the Lord and other sacred artifacts from Zion, the city of David, and place them in the temple's Most Holy Place.

29. Steven C. Bullock, *Revolutionary Brotherhood: Freemasonry and the Transformation of the American Social Order, 1730–1840* (Chapel Hill: University of North Carolina Press, 1996), 158; George W. Crawford, *Prince Hall and His Fol-*

lowers: Being a Monograph on the Legitimacy of Negro Masonry (New York: The Crisis, 1914), 13–19; Winch, *Philadelphia's Black Elite*, 7–8; Elizabeth Rauh Bethel, *The Roots of African-American Identity: Memory and History in Antebellum Free Black Communities* (New York: St. Martin's, 1997), 64–67; Muraskin, "Black Masons," 83–89; Bishop R. R. Wright, Jr., *The Bishops of the African Methodist Episcopal Church* (Nashville, TN: A.M.E. Sunday School Union, 1963), 146–50, 191–92, 301.

30. In October 1847, the New York Odd Fellows participated in a grand parade in Philadelphia. *The Ram's Horn*, 5 November 1847, includes a description of the festivities and a history of the Odd Fellows; Charles B. Wilson, *The Official Manual and History of the Grand United Order of Odd Fellows in America. Authorized by the Third B.M.C., and Approved and Published by the Sub-Committee of Management* (Philadelphia: George F. Lasher, 1894), 11–19, 65–67; Williamson, "Prince Hall Masonry in New York State," Vol. 2, Part 2, 129; George Chauncey, *Gay New York: Gender, Urban Culture, and the Making of the Gay Male World, 1890–1940* (New York: Basic Books, 1994), 257–63. For a short account of the rise of black fraternities and the racial conflict for control of these associations, see Noel P. Gist, *Secret Societies: A Cultural Study of Fraternalism in the United States* (Columbia: University of Missouri Press, 1940), 64.

31. Rev. Benjamin W. Arnett, P.G.M., *Biennial Oration before the Second B.M.C. of the Grand United Order of Odd Fellows* (Dayton, OH: Christian Publishing House, 1884), 10–23; Carnes, *Secret Ritual and Manhood*, 25–29, passim.

32. *The Liberator*, 8 September 1843.

33. On the sanctum sanctorum in Masonic ritual, see Finney, *Character, Claims, and Practical Workings of Freemasonry*, 138–42. On the use of biblical temple imagery in Masonry, see Eugen Lennhoff, *The Freemasons: The History, Nature, Development and Secret of the Royal Art*, translated by Einar Frame (New York: Oxford University Press, 1934), 15; Stevenson, *Origins of Freemasonry*, 1–9; Joseph Fort Newton, *The Builders: A Story and Study of Freemasonry* (New York: Macoy Publishing and Masonic Supply, 1930), 74–79.

NOTES TO CHAPTER 6

1. James McCune Smith, M.D., "Introduction" to Rev. Henry Highland Garnet, *A Memorial Discourse; by Rev. Henry Highland Garnet, Delivered in the Hall of the House of Representatives, Washington City, D.C. on Sabbath, February 12, 1865* (Philadelphia: Joseph M. Wilson, 1865), 24–25.

2. Elizabeth Rauh Bethel, *The Roots of African-American Identity: Memory and History in Free Antebellum Communities* (New York: St. Martin's, 1997), 3–7; *Laws of the State of New York, Passed at the Thirty-Fifth Session of the Legislature* (Albany, NY: 1812), 189–90; Daniel Perlman, "Organizations of the Free Negro in New York City, 1800–1860," *Journal of Negro History*, Vol. 56 (1971), 185; Philip S.

Foner, *History of Black Americans*, 2 vols. (Westport, CT: Greenwood, 1975, 1983), 1: 241; Robert J. Cottrol, *The Afro-Yankees: Providence's Black Community in the Antebellum Era* (Westport, CT: Greenwood, 1982), 63.

3. James Oliver Horton and Lois E. Horton, "Violence, Protest, and Identity: Black Manhood in Antebellum America," in Darlene Clark Hine and Earnestine Jenkins, eds., *A Question of Manhood: A Reader in U.S. Black Men's History and Masculinity* (Bloomington: Indiana University Press, 1999), 393–95; Gail Bederman, *Manliness and Civilization: A Cultural History of Gender and Race in the United States, 1880–1917* (Chicago: University of Chicago Press, 1995), 7.

4. Mary Ann Clawson, *Constructing Brotherhood: Class, Gender, and Fraternalism* (Princeton, NJ: Princeton University Press, 1989), 11, 21–25, 42–45; Wilson Carey McWilliams, *The Idea of Fraternity in America* (Berkeley: University of California Press, 1973), 9–29.

5. Susan G. Davis, *Parades and Power: Street Theatre in Nineteenth-Century Philadelphia* (Philadelphia: Temple University Press, 1986), 46–47; David R. Roediger, *The Wages of Whiteness: Race and the Making of the American Working Class* (New York: Verso, 1991), 100–111, passim; Howard B. Rock, ed., *The New York City Artisan, 1789–1825: A Documentary History* (Albany: State University of New York Press, 1989), 3–25; Society of Mechanics and Workingmen of New York City, *Minutes of Meetings of the General Executive Committee*, 5 February 1830, 18 May 1831, 27 June 1831, collection of the New-York Historical Society.

6. The resolution read:

> Resolved, That the object of our celebrating the Fourth Day of July, being to express our gratitude for the benefits conferred on us by the honorable Legislature of the state of New York, we will do no act that may have the least tendency to disorder; we shall therefore abstain from all processions in the public streets on that day.
>
> Resolved, Therefore, that the Committee of Arrangements do now, on this twenty sixth day of June, enter their PROTEST, in behalf of the aforesaid Meeting; the Mutual Relief Society; the Asbury and Presbyterian Churches; against any public Procession whatever in the streets on the fifth of July.
>
> JOHN MARANDA, *Chairman*
> THOMAS L. JENNINGS, *Sec'ry*
> JOHN ROBERTSON,   }
> HENRY SCOTT,   }
> Wm. MILLER,   } *Comm. of Arrangements*
> MOSES BLUE [Blew],}
> GEO. HOWARD.   }

Interestingly, the NYASMR was mentioned before the churches. *Freedom's Journal*, 30 March 1827, 29 June 1827; Edwin G. Burrows and Mike Wallace, *Gotham:*

A History of New York City to 1898 (New York: Oxford University Press, 1999), 546–47.

7. M. C. Jedrej, "Medicine, Fetish and Secret Society in a West African Culture," *Africa*, Vol. 46, No. 3 (1976), 250–51; K. L. Little, "The Poro Society as an Arbiter of Culture," *African Studies*, Vol. 7, No. 1 (March 1948), 5–10; Kenneth Little, "The Political Function of the Poro," *Africa*, Vol. 35, No. 4 (October 1965), 356–60; M. D. W. Jeffreys, "The Nyama Society of the Ibibio Women," *African Studies*, Vol. 15, No. 1 (1956), 15–28. On the link between African and African American socialization patterns, see Margaret Washington Creel, *"A Peculiar People": Slave Religion and Community-Culture among the Gullah* (New York: New York University Press, 1988), 288–91.

8. Rebecca J. Scott, *Slave Emancipation in Cuba: The Transition to Free Labor, 1860–1899* (Princeton, NJ: Princeton University Press, 1985), 265–67; A. J. R. Russell-Wood, "Black and Mulatto Brotherhoods in Colonial Brazil: A Study in Collective Behavior," *Hispanic American Historical Review* (November 1974), 588–99; Mary C. Karasch, *Slave Life in Rio de Janeiro, 1808–1850* (Princeton, NJ: Princeton University Press, 1987), 82–86.

9. E. Anthony Rotundo, *American Manhood: Transformations in Masculinity from the Revolution to the Modern Era* (New York: Basic Books, 1993), 2, 10–18.

10. M. N. L. Couve de Murville, Archbishop of Birmingham, England, *Slave from Haiti: A Saint for New York? A Life of Pierre Toussaint* (London: Catholic Truth Society, 1995), 15–16; Colored Orphan Asylum, *Admissions, 1837–1866,* 12, 48, 56–57, Records of the Association for the Benefit of Colored Orphans, collection of the New-York Historical Society. The constitution of the Association for the Benefit of Colored Orphans is included in the Minutes of the Board Meetings, entry for 9 December 1836, Records of the Association for the Benefit of Colored Orphans. It was likely derived from the "By-Laws and Regulations of the Society for the Relief of Poor Widows with Small Children. To Which is Added a List of the Subscribers and of Donations Made to the Society, from November 1811 to November 1813," Records of the Society for the Relief of Poor Widows with Small Children, collection of the New-York Historical Society.

11. Joel Schor, *Henry Highland Garnet: A Voice of Black Radicalism in the Nineteenth Century* (Westport, CT: Greenwood, 1977), 19; Leonard P. Curry, *The Free Black in Urban America 1800–1850: The Shadow of the Dream* (Chicago: University of Chicago Press, 1981), 185, 205; Colored Orphan Asylum, *Minutes of the Board Meetings, November 26, 1836–December 18, 1840,* on the funeral see the entry for 12 January 1838, on the conflict see the entries for 13 July 1838 and 14 September 1838, on the contributions see the entries for 9 February 1838, 12 October 1838, 12 April 1839, 14 February 1840, and the Treasurer's Reports, passim, Records of the Association for the Benefit of Colored Orphans, collection of the New-York Historical Society.

12. E. P. Thompson, *The Making of the English Working Class* (1963; New

York: Vintage, 1966), 421–24; Sterling Stuckey, *Slave Culture: Nationalist Theory and the Foundations of Black America* (New York: Oxford University Press, 1987), 142; John Teasman, *An Address Delivered in the African Episcopal Church, On the 25th March, 1811. Before the New York African Society, for Mutual Relief; Being the First Anniversary of Its Incorporation* (New York: J. Low, 1811), 12.

13. Robert J. Swan, "John Teasman: African-American Educator and the Emergence of Community in Early Black New York City, 1787–1815," *Journal of the Early Republic* (Fall 1992), 334–37; Arthur J. Alexander, "Federal Officeholder in New York State as Slaveholders, 1789–1805," *Journal of Negro History*, Vol. 28, No. 3 (July 1943), 326–49; on the creation of the Manumission Society's school, see "Report of the Standing Committee," 11 May 1786, and "Negro School Fund with John Murray Jun'r.," Vol. 5, Records of the New York Manumission Society, collection of the New-York Historical Society.

14. From the turn of the century to the War of 1812, Teasman was active in New York State Republican politics. In 1804 he was one of twenty prominent black men invited to dine with Republican gubernatorial candidate Aaron Burr. He campaigned for New York City Republicans, and, at the start of the War of 1812, he was chair of the Colored Republican General Committee. Swan, "John Teasman," 338–44, 349–53.

15. *New York Age*, 13 July 1905; Paul A. Gilje and Howard B. Rock, eds., *Keepers of the Revolution: New Yorkers at Work in the Early Republic* (Ithaca, NY: Cornell University Press, 1992), 238–39; Swan, "John Teasman," 351; Foner, *History of Black Americans*, 2: 238.

16. George G. Williams, *History of the Negro Race in America, from 1619 to 1880*, 2 Vols. (New York: G. P. Putnam's Sons, 1883), 2: 167–68.

17. "Minutes of the Adjourned Session of the Twentieth Biennial American Convention for Promoting the Abolition of Slavery, and Improving the Condition of the African Race, Held at Baltimore, Nov. 1828," in *The American Convention for Promoting the Abolition of Slavery and Improving the Condition of the African Race: Minutes, Constitution, Addresses, Memorials, Resolutions, Reports, Committees and Anti-Slavery Tracts*, 3 vols. (New York: Bergman Publishers, 1969), 1: 67–68.

18. Bishop J[ames]. W[alker]. Hood, D.D., LL.D., *One Hundred Years of the African Methodist Episcopal Zion Church; or The Centennial of African Methodism* (New York: A.M.E. Zion Book Concern, 1895), 528; Craig Steven Wilder, "The Rise and Influence of the New York African Society for Mutual Relief, 1808–1865," *Afro Americans in New York Life and History* (July 1998), passim; Craig Steven Wilder, "A Covenant with Color: Race and the History of Brooklyn, New York" (Ph.D. dissertation, Columbia University, 1994), 35–36; Rhoda Golden Freeman, *The Free Negro in New York City in the Era before the Civil War* (New York: Garland, 1994), 65; Sandra Shoiock Roff, "The Brooklyn African Woolman Benevolent Society Rediscovered," *Afro-Americans in New York Life*

and History, Vol. 10, No. 2 (July 1986), 55–57; *The Liberator*, 21 April 1832, 19 April 1834; *Constitution of the Brooklyn African Woolman Benevolent Society*, Adopted March 16, 1810 (Brooklyn, NY: E. Worthington, 1820), collection of the New-York Historical Society; *Constitution of the African Marine Fund, for the Relief of the Distressed Orphans, and Poor Members of This Fund* (New York: John C. Totten, 1810), passim, collection of the New-York Historical Society; *Laws of the State of New York, Passed at the Fifty-Second Session of the Legislature* (Albany, 1829), 380–81.

19. Dorothy B. Porter, "David Ruggles, an Apostle of Human Rights," *Journal of Negro History*, Vol. 28, No. 1 (January 1943), 28; *The First Annual Report of the New York Committee of Vigilance, for the Year 1837* (New York, 1837), in Herbert Aptheker, ed., *A Documentary History of the Negro People in the United States* (1951; New York: Citadel, 1969), 161–63.

20. Sojourner Truth, *Narrative of Sojourner Truth; A Bondwoman of Olden Time, with a History of Her Labors and Correspondence Drawn from Her "Book of Life"* (1850; New York: Oxford University Press, 1991), 86–87. The New-York Historical Society staff found an order of admission to a Dorcas Society in an 1841 *American Masonic Register*, which shows the ease with which secret ritual could be imported into women's service societies. In this ritual, an official "clad in solemn fantastic canonicals" delivered an oath, tracing the origins of such associations to Antiquity, to a kneeling candidate. A crumb taken from a fancy platter was brought to the mouth of the initiate and then suddenly pulled away to dramatize the importance of sacrifice. See "Order of Admission to the Dorcas Society," Misc. Manuscripts, Dorcas Society, collection of the New-York Historical Society. The records of a Civil War–era Dorcas Society are available. These women did both charitable work for the church and outreach to the greater community. The latter included sewing uniforms and undergarments for Union soldiers. See St. Mark's Church, Ladies Benevolent (Dorcas) Society, *Minute Book, 1861–1864*, passim, collection of the New-York Historical Society.

21. Letter reprinted in Marilyn Richardson, ed., *Maria W. Stewart: America's First Black Woman Political Writer* (Bloomington: Indiana University Press, 1987), 93–95.

22. In 1860 some of the more prominent black women of New York and Brooklyn held a fair to benefit the Colored Orphan Asylum. Dorothy Sterling, ed., *We Are Your Sisters: Black Women in the Nineteenth Century* (New York: Norton, 1984), 110, 118; George E. Walker, *The Afro-American in New York City, 1827–1860* (New York: Garland, 1993), 64–72; *The Liberator*, 29 June 1833, 13 March 1863; Foner, *History of Black Americans*, 2: 238, 240–43.

23. Mark C. Carnes, *Secret Ritual and Manhood in Victorian America* (New Haven, CT: Yale University Press, 1989), 70–89; William H. Becker, "The Black Church: Manhood and Mission," in Hine and Jenkins, eds., *A Question of Manhood*, 322–23, passim.

24. William J. Walls, *The African Methodist Episcopal Zion Church: Reality of a Black Church* (Charlotte, NC: A.M.E. Zion Publishing House, 1974), 90–91; *Third Report of the American Bible Society, Presented May 13, 1819, with an Appendix, Containing Extracts of Correspondence* (New York: Printed for the Society, 1819), 30, 35.

25. *The Liberator*, 10 December 1831, 5 January 1833; Walker, *Afro-American in New York*, 74–78.

26. *The Liberator*, 19 June 1833; Walker, *Afro-American in New York*, 74–78; Schor, *Henry Highland Garnet*, 19; Curry, *The Free Black in Urban America*, 185, 205; Charles H. Wesley, "The Negroes of New York in the Emancipation Movement," *Journal of Negro History*, Vol. 24, No. 1 (January 1939), 83.

27. *The Liberator*, 6 October 1847, 14 April 1854; Wilson Jeremiah Moses, *Alexander Crummell: A Study of Civilization and Discontent* (Amherst: University of Massachusetts Press, 1992), 14; James McCune Smith to Alexander Crummell, undated, in Letters, Alexander Crummell Papers; Freeman, *Free Negro in New York City*, 253–54.

28. William Hamilton, *An Address to the New York African Society, for Mutual Relief, Delivered in the Universalist Church, January 2, 1809* (New York: Privately printed, 1809); Teasman, *An Address Delivered in the African Episcopal Church*, 8.

29. Moses, *Alexander Crummell*, 11–12; Rev. William J. Simmons, D.D., *Men of Mark: Eminent, Progressive and Rising* (1887; New York: Arno, 1968), 530–35; Foner, *History of Black Americans*, 2: 235–36. A contemporary visited Smith's pharmacy while in New York. See William C. Nell, *The Colored Patriots of the American Revolution* (New York: Arno, 1968), 156–57.

30. Smith, "Introduction" to Garnet, *Memorial Discourse*, 24.

31. Carter G. Woodson, *The History of the Negro Church* (1921; Washington, DC: Associated Publishers, 1945), 73, 89–90, 106, 152; "Thomas L. Jennings," *Anglo-African Magazine*, Vol. 1, No. 4 (April 1859); C. Eric Lincoln and Lawrence H. Mamiya, *The Black Church in the African American Experience* (Durham, NC: Duke University Press, 1990), 57–58.

32. Martin R. Delany, *The Condition, Elevation, Emigration and Destiny of the Colored People of the United States* (1852; Baltimore: Black Classic Press, 1993), 102–7; Aptheker, ed., *Documentary History of the Negro People in the United States*, 1: 623; on the loan to the *Herald*, see the clippings in the Thomas and George Downing photo file, Schomburg Collection, NYPL.

33. A Member [Peter Vogelsang], *An Address Delivered before the New-York African Society for Mutual Relief, in the African Zion Church, 23d March 1815, Being the Fifth Anniversary of Their Incorporation* (New York: Printed for the Society, 1815), 15, collection of the New-York Historical Society; Dr. James M'Cune Smith, "Introduction," in Frederick Douglass, *My Bondage and My Freedom* (1855; New York: Dover, 1969), xvii.

34. Simmons, *Men of Mark*, 1003–4; Smith, "Introduction" to Garnet, *Memorial Discourse*, 22–23; Stuckey, *Slave Culture*, 145–48; James Oliver Horton, *Free*

People of Color: Inside the African American Community (Washington, DC: Smithsonian Institution Press, 1993), 57–59; Joseph Mason Andrew Cox, *Great Black Men of Masonry, 1723–1982* (Bronx, NY: Blue Diamond Press, 1982), 4, 161–62, 187; Michel S. Laguerre, *American Odyssey: Haitians in New York City* (Ithaca, NY: Cornell University Press, 1984), 167; Herbert Marshall and Mildred Stock, *Ira Aldridge: The Negro Tragedian* (1958; Washington, DC: Howard University Press, 1993), 219; Harry A. Williamson, "Folks in Old New York and Brooklyn" (Bronx, NY: Unpublished manuscript, July 1953), 6, 16, Schomburg Collection, NYPL; *New York Age*, 3 August 1905; Moses, *Alexander Crummell*, 16.

35. Leon F. Litwack, *North of Slavery: The Negro in the Free States, 1790–1860* (Chicago: University of Chicago Press, 1961), 117, 201–2; Curry, *Free Black in Urban America*, 189; *The Liberator*, 11 February 1842; Henry H. Garnet to Alexander Crummell, 13 May 1837, in Letters, Alexander Crummell Papers; Williams, *History of the Negro Race in America*, 2: 133–34; Nell, *Colored Patriots of the American Revolution*, 317–18.

36. William Wells Brown, *The Black Man, His Antecedents, His Genius, and His Achievements* (New York: Thomas Hamilton, 1863), 205–6; Delany, *Condition, Elevation, Emigration and Destiny*, 110; Williams, *History of the Negro Race in America*, 2: 167–68; Curry, *Free Black in Urban America*, 92; David W. Blight, "In Search of Learning, Liberty, and Self Definition: James McCune Smith and the Ordeal of the Antebellum Black Intellectual," *Afro-Americans in New York Life and History* (July 1985), 7–9.

37. C. Peter Ripley et al., eds., *The Black Abolitionist Papers*, 5 vols. (Chapel Hill: University of North Carolina Press, 1991), 3: 175–76n; Douglass, *My Bondage and My Freedom*, 340–41; Porter, "David Ruggles," 23–50; Cox, *Great Black Men of Masonry*, 48–49; *The Liberator*, 6 August 1836; *Colored American*, 11 March 1837.

38. Cox, *Great Black Men of Masonry*, 72; Alexander Crummell, *Destiny and Race: Selected Writings, 1840–1898*, edited by Wilson Jeremiah Moses (Amherst: University of Massachusetts Press, 1992), 3–4, 56; Litwack, *North of Slavery*, 118; quoted in Simmons, *Men of Mark*, 530–35.

39. Ibid., Alexander Crummell, "1844–1894: The Shades and the Lights of a Fifty Years' Ministry. Jubilate. A Sermon by Alex. Crummell, Rector. And a Presentation Address by Mrs. A. J. Cooper. St. Luke's Church, Washington, D.C., December 9th, 1894" (Washington, DC: R. L. Pendleton, 1894), 6–16, in the Daniel A. P. Murray Collection, Library of Congress; Maritcha Remond Lyons, "Memories of Yesterdays, All of Which I Saw and Part of Which I Was: An Autobiography" (unpublished manuscript, ca. 1924), 53, in Williams [Lyons] Family Papers, Schomburg Collection, NYPL.

40. Smith, "Introduction" to Garnet, *Memorial Discourse*, 23; Samuel Ringgold Ward, *Autobiography of a Fugitive Negro: His Anti-Slavery Labours in the United States, Canada, and England* (London: John Snow, 1855), 30–34, 49–50, 79–83, 128–33.

41. Ibid.
42. Ibid.
43. Schor, *Henry Highland Garnet*, 6–28; Smith, "Introduction" to Garnet, *Memorial Discourse*, 17–25.
44. Ibid.
45. Ibid.; Schor, *Henry Highland Garnet*, 6–28; Cox, *Great Black Men of Masonry*, 87.
46. *Weekly Advocate*, 7 January 1837.
47. After Smith's speech, the following resolutions passed unanimously:

> *Resolved*—That we hail with lively joy, the safe return of our friend and fellow-citizen Dr. James McCune Smith, A.M., to his native land, and feel that the abundant testimonials of moral works joined to professional abilities with which he comes furnished from abroad, justly claim for him a pre-eminence in the minds of his friends and community who have this night assembled to give him their united and hearty welcome.
>
> *Resolved*—That we have full and implicit confidence in the professional ability and skill, as well as the unexceptionable moral character of our highly esteemed friend, and do therefore most earnestly recommend him to the patronage of the American public.
>
> *Resolved*—That in behalf of the colored citizens of New York, do tender our sincere and most grateful thanks to the noble-hearted, the philanthropic of Glasgow, for the deep and lively interest manifested by them for us, the disfranchised and oppressed of America, in their kind and courteous treatment toward our cherished fellow-citizen Dr. Smith, during his five years residence within the walls of their ancient University.

Colored American, 28 October 1837.
48. Brown, *The Black Man*, 205–6; Lyons, "Memories of Yesterdays," 77; Harold X. Connolly, *A Ghetto Grows in Brooklyn* (New York: New York University Press, 1977), 23; Williams, *History of the Negro Race in America*, 2: 167–68; Curry, *Free Black in Urban America*, 92; Cox, *Great Black Men of Masonry*, 160; Blight, "In Search of Learning, Liberty, and Self Definition," 10.
49. In 1818 an African society in Charleston purchased a plot of land for the construction of an A.M.E. Church. Robert L. Harris, Jr., "Charleston's Free Afro-American Elite: The Brown Fellowship Society and the Humane Brotherhood," *South Carolina Historical Magazine*, Vol. 82, No. 4 (October 1981), 289–310. The Brown Fellowship sponsored the education of Daniel Alexander Payne, who became the sixth bishop of the A.M.E. Church. See Bishop R. R. Wright, Jr., *The Bishops of the African Methodist Episcopal Church* (Nashville, TN: A.M.E. Sunday School Union, 1963), 266–67.
50. Ward, *Autobiography of a Fugitive Negro*, 20–23.

NOTES TO CHAPTER 7

1. Samuel Ringgold Ward, *Autobiography of a Fugitive Negro: His Anti-Slavery Labours in the United States, Canada, and England* (London: John Snow, 1855), 28; Henry Highland Garnet to Alexander Crummell, 13 May 1837, in Letters, Alexander Crummell Papers, Schomburg Collection, NYPL; Howard Holman Bell, "A Survey of the Negro Convention Movement, 1830–1861" (Ph.D. dissertation, Northwestern University, 1953), 43.

2. Ward, *Autobiography of a Fugitive Negro*, 46–49.

3. Leon F. Litwack, *North of Slavery: The Negro in the Free States, 1790–1860* (Chicago: University of Chicago Press, 1961), 202–3; *American Anti-Slavery Reporter*, Vol. 1, No. 7 (July 1834), 111–12; "On the Condition of the Free People of Color in the United States," *Anti-Slavery Examiner*, No. 13 (New York, 1839), 22.

4. Litwack, *North of Slavery*, 202–3; Charles H. Wesley, "The Negroes of New York in the Emancipation Movement," *Journal of Negro History*, Vol. 24, No. 1 (January 1939), 77–78; Letters in the *African Repository and Colonial Journal*, Vol. 10 (August 1834), 185–88; Leo H. Hirsch Jr., "The Negro and New York, 1783 to 1865," *Journal of Negro History*, Vol. 16, No. 4 (October 1931), 456.

5. *Report of the Formation of the African Education and Civilization Society, Containing the Preamble and Resolutions Passed at Their First Meetings, the Constitution and Officers of the Society, Together with a Statement of the Objects of the Society by the Executive Committee* (New York: Privately printed, 1845), 2–8, collection of the New-York Historical Society.

6. *The Liberator*, 20 December 1850. Later, Downing expressed his frustrations with the growing intolerance of the nation. In the aftermath of the Dred Scott decision, when Downing found himself being sued in court over a debt, he refused to be sworn in on the grounds that the Supreme Court had said that black men enjoyed no rights as citizens. The judge pondered the claim and decided that Downing would be a citizen and a human being for the purposes of the case. See Freeman, *The Free Negro in New York City*, 76.

7. *New York Herald*, 6 May 1850.

8. R. J. M. Blackett, *Building an Antislavery Wall: Black Americans in the Atlantic Abolitionist Movement, 1830–1860* (1983; Ithaca, NY: Cornell University Press, 1989), 13, 77–78, 81–82, 129, 196, passim. On the Vigilance Committee, see William J. Walls, *The African Methodist Episcopal Zion Church: Reality of the Black Church* (Charlotte, NC: A.M.E. Zion Publishing House, 1974), 157. Peter Williams Jr.'s return from London was covered in *The Colored American*, 11 March 1837.

9. *The Liberator*, 6 August 1836.

10. Blackett, *Building an Antislavery Wall*, passim; Frederick Douglass, "Address at Abbey Church, Arbroath, Scotland, February 13, 1846," in Philip S.

Foner, ed., *The Life and Writings of Frederick Douglass*, 5 vols. (New York: International Publishers, 1975), 5: 22–27.

11. "Condition of the Black and Coloured Population of the United States," "To the British Churchmen and the British Public," and "African Episcopal Church, New York," articles and pamphlets, in Letters, Alexander Crummell Papers.

12. Carter Godwin Woodson, *The Negro Professional Man and the Community, with Special Emphasis on the Physician and the Lawyer* (1934; New York: Negro Universities Press, 1969), 17; Lerone Bennett Jr., "Founders of the Black Press," *Ebony* (February 1987); Wilson Jeremiah Moses, *Alexander Crummell: A Study of Civilization and Discontent* (Amherst: University of Massachusetts Press, 1992), 13; Joseph Mason Andrew Cox, *Great Black Men of Masonry, 1723–1982* (Bronx, NY: Blue Diamond Press, 1982), 48–49, 190–91; *Freedom's Journal*, 16 March 1827; Walls, *African Methodist Episcopal Zion Church*, 92; *David Walker's Appeal, in Four Articles; Together with a Preamble, to the Coloured Citizens of the World, but in Particular, and Very Expressly, to Those of the United States of America*, edited with an introduction by Charles M. Wiltse (1829; New York: Hill and Wang, 1965), 56n.

13. Woodson, *Negro Professional Man*, 17; W[illiam] Wells Brown, M.D., *The Rising Son; or, The Antecedents and Advancement of the Colored Race* (Boston: A. G. Brown, 1874), 473; Wesley, "Negroes of New York in the Emancipation Movement," 70–71, passim; *Weekly Advocate*, 7 January 1837; Charles Ray to Alexander Crummell, 28 October 1839, in Letters, Alexander Crummell Papers; *Weekly Anglo-African*, 12 January 1861, 16 March 1861; Rhoda Golden Freeman, *The Free Negro in New York City in the Era before the Civil War* (New York: Garland, 1994), 130–36.

14. Ibid.; C. Peter Ripley et al., eds., *The Black Abolitionist Papers*, 5 vols. (Chapel Hill: University of North Carolina Press, 1991), 3: 175–76n; Martin R. Delany, *The Condition, Elevation, Emigration and Destiny of the Colored People of the United States* (1852; Baltimore: Black Classic Press, 1993), 127–28; Dorothy B. Porter, "David Ruggles, an Apostle of Human Rights," *Journal of Negro History*, Vol. 28, No. 1 (January 1943), 30–31; Wesley, "Negroes of New York in the Emancipation Movement," 90, 94–95; Martin E. Dann, ed., *The Black Press, 1827–1890: The Quest for National Identity* (New York: Putnam's Sons, 1971), 20; Arnett G. Lindsay, "The Economic Condition of the Negroes of New York Prior to 1861," *Journal of Negro History*, Vol. 6, No. 2 (April 1921), 199. Also see Donald Franklin Joyce, *Gatekeepers of Black Culture: Black-Owned Book Publishing in the United States, 1817–1981* (Westport, CT: Greenwood, 1983).

15. Society of Mechanics and Workingmen of New York City, *Minutes of Meetings of the General Executive Committee*, 5 May 1831, collection of the New-York Historical Society.

16. In 1833 Thomas Jennings, Peter Vogelsang, and Henry Sipkins led a local meeting to discuss William Lloyd Garrison's planned antislavery tour in Britain.

While only black men could truly speak for black people, it was decided that Garrison—familiar enough with the sentiments of the nation's leading men of color and having shown a similar politic in his *Thoughts on African Colonization* (1832)—warranted their support. The conference resolved to "highly approve" of Garrison's mission and to take up a collection to defer some of the cost. *The Liberator*, 12 March 1831, 20 August 1831, 11 May 1833; Wesley, "Negroes of New York in the Emancipation Movement," 76; "Thomas L. Jennings," *Anglo-African Magazine*, Vol. 1, No. 4 (April 1859); William Lloyd Garrison, *Thoughts on African Colonization* (1832; New York: Arno, 1968).

17. *Freedom's Journal*, 6 April 1827.

18. J. J. Clute, *Annals of Staten Island: From Its Discovery to the Present Time* (New York: Chas. Vogt, 1877), 16; Washington Irving, *Diedrich Knickerbocker's A History of New-York* (1808; 1854; Tarrytown, NY: Sleepy Hollow Press, 1981), 90–91.

19. John Russwurm, Charles Reason, Peter Paul Simons, David Ruggles, and Henry Highland Garnet also discussed violence as a solution to slavery. James Oliver Horton and Lois E. Horton, "Violence, Protest, and Identity: Black Manhood in Antebellum America," in Darlene Clark Hine and Earnestine Jenkins, eds., *A Question of Manhood: A Reader in U.S. Black Men's History and Masculinity* (Bloomington: Indiana University Press, 1999), 385–90; James McCune Smith, M.A., M.D., "Toussaint L'Ouverture and the Haytian Revolutions," in Alice Moore Dunbar, ed., *Masterpieces of Negro Eloquence: The Best Speeches Delivered by the Negro from the Days of Slavery to the Present Time* (New York: Bookery Publishing Company, 1914), 19–32. Dr. Smith was a public critic of William Lloyd Garrison and, like many of Manhattan's black men, early parted company with the editor. He accused Garrison and white antislavery advocates of ignoring the plight of free black people and failing to treat black men as equals. Speaking of Douglass's relationship to Wendell Phillips and Garrison, Smith wrote, "These gentlemen, although proud of Frederick Douglass, failed to fathom, and bring out to the light of day, the highest qualities of his mind: they did not delve into the mind of a colored man for capacities which the pride of race led them to believe to be restricted to their own Saxon blood." Obviously, the charges put him in the good company of Douglass but beyond the approval of a few colleagues, including William P. Powell of the NYASMR. Powell was not an unquestioning supporter of Garrisonian thought, he simply did not suspect Garrison's motives. As early as 1839, Powell publicly expressed his allegiance to the editor. David W. Blight, "In Search of Learning, Liberty, and Self Definition: James McCune Smith and the Ordeal of the Antebellum Black Intellectual," *Afro-Americans in New York Life and History* (July 1985), 15; Dr. James M'Cune Smith, "Introduction," in Frederick Douglass, *My Bondage and My Freedom* (1855; New York: Dover, 1969), xxii; *The Liberator*, 19 July 1839, 7 February 1845.

20. Ibid., 4 April 1851, 11 April 1851; James McCune Smith, "The German Invasion," *Anglo-African Magazine*, Vol. 1, Nos. 2 and 3 (February–March 1859).

21. *The Liberator*, 19 July 1839, 7 February 1845.

22. Smith, "Introduction" to Douglass, *My Bondage and My Freedom*, xvii–xxxi.

23. *Weekly Advocate*, 14 January 1837; *Colored American* 4 March 1837.

24. Philip S. Foner, ed., *The Life and Writings of Frederick Douglass*, 5 vols. (New York: International Publishers, 1975), 5: 381; Craig Steven Wilder, "A Covenant with Color: Race and the History of Brooklyn, New York" (Ph.D. dissertation, Columbia University, 1994), 62–63; Woodson, *The Negro Professional Man*, 17; Freeman, *The Free Negro in New York City*, 134–36.

25. *Weekly Anglo-African*, 5 January 1860; *The Liberator*, 18 February 1859, 16 March 1860.

26. Douglas Henry Daniels, *Pioneer Urbanites: A Social and Cultural History of Black San Francisco* (Berkeley: University of California Press, 1990), 54, 72, 114–15.

NOTES TO CHAPTER 8

1. Sterling Stuckey, *Slave Culture: Nationalist Theory and the Foundations of Black America* (New York: Oxford University Press, 1987), 201–2; William Hamilton, *Address to the New York African Society, for Mutual Relief, Delivered in the Universalist Church, January 2, 1809* (New York: Privately printed, 1809).

2. John H. Bracey, Jr., August Meier, and Elliot Rudwick, ed., *Black Nationalism in America* (Indianapolis, IN: Bobbs-Merrill, 1970), xxvi–xxx, 77; Howard Brotz, ed., *Negro Social and Political Thought, 1850–1920* (New York: Basic Books, 1966), 2–12; Wilson Jeremiah Moses, *The Golden Age of Black Nationalism, 1850–1925* (New York: Oxford University Press, 1978), 32–33, 45; Harold Cruse, *The Crisis of the Negro Intellectual* (New York: Morrow, 1967), 4; Stuckey, *Slave Culture*, passim.

3. Graham Russell Hodges, *Root and Branch: African Americans in New York and East Jersey, 1613–1863* (Chapel Hill: University of North Carolina Press, 1999), 88, passim.

4. On Ward in Canada and England, see Samuel Ringgold Ward, *Autobiography of a Fugitive Negro: His Anti-Slavery Labours in the United States, Canada, and England* (London: John Snow, 1855), passim. William Powell was a central figure in shaping the NYASMR that emerged in the 1850s. Powell was born in New York State about 1807. He was the son of an enslaved African who was freed under New York's manumission law. Educated while serving on board a whaler, he later settled in Massachusetts, where he opened a sailors' home. He was a supporter of Garrison, a signer of the constitution of the American Anti-Slavery Society, and an early member of the New England Anti-Slavery Society. In 1839 Powell began the Colored Seamen's Home at 70 John Street in lower Manhattan to provide safe accommodations for the itinerant black men who passed through New York on

commercial ships. He continued to exercise influence over the Massachusetts and New England Anti-Slavery Societies while active in the black community of Manhattan. In 1840 he joined the New York African Society for Mutual Relief. That same year he became a founder of the Manhattan Anti-Slavery Society. In 1842 he served on the Committee of Arrangements for the anniversary celebration and annual meeting of the American Anti-Slavery Society, which was held at Broadway Tabernacle in Manhattan. Abolitionist and author Lydia Maria Child was recording secretary. See Philip S. Foner, *History of Black Americans,* 2 vols. (Westport, CT: Greenwood, 1975, 1983), 2: 242; C. Peter Ripley et al., eds., *The Black Abolitionist Papers,* 5 vols. (Chapel Hill: University of North Carolina Press, 1991), 3: 302–3n; *The Liberator,* 15 April 1842.

5. Letter from Michel Castor, A. Lambert, B. Duplessy, D. G. Cerci, and Jean L. Chabert to Monsieur [Pierre Toussaint], 19 November 1839, Pierre Toussaint Papers, Manuscripts Division, NYPL; Ellen Tarry, *The Other Toussaint: A Modern Biography of Pierre Toussaint, a Post-Revolutionary Black* (Boston: Daughters of St. Paul, 1981), 334; Keletso E. Atkins, in her study of Natal, looked to the African tradition of men uniting to answer community concerns to explain migratory workers' ability to apply their ethic to the rapidly changing political and economic environment of nineteenth-century South Africa. Some skilled workers in men's occupations with traditional counterparts were able to organize trade guilds to effectively protect their economic interests. "Kitchen associations," informal evening assemblies along kinship and village networks, allowed other migrant workers in Natal to impose principles of mutual obligation and mutual dependence by sharing meals, accommodations, aid, and information about employers, and by organizing to set labor prices. Kitchen associations operated on principles similar to African societies. Keletso E. Atkins, *The Moon Is Dead! Give Us Our Money! The Cultural Origins of an African Work Ethic, Natal, South Africa, 1843–1900* (Portsmouth, NH: Heinemann, 1993), 106–7, 111–14, 122–29.

6. Downing was responding to Henry Highland Garnet's public embrace of emigration. Thomas Hamilton was democratic enough to give Garnet's views a fair public hearing. Frederick Douglass dealt with the rivalry and disagreement by simply ignoring Garnet's work inside or outside the United States. See Joel Schor, *Henry Highland Garnet: A Voice of Black Radicalism in the Nineteenth Century* (Westport, CT: Greenwood, 1977), 58, 152; *Weekly Anglo-African,* 26 January 1861, 23 February 1861, 9 March 1861.

7. *The Liberator,* 12 February 1831; 2 July 1831. Since there is no existing roll for the Woolman Society, it is unclear if Pennington and Hogarth were members; however, in 1830, both helped the Reverend Benjamin Croger, Woolman's first president, found the Brooklyn Temperance Association. On the rise and influence of the ACS, see P. J. Staudenraus, *The African Colonization Movement, 1816–1865* (New York: Columbia University Press, 1961).

8. James McCune Smith, M.D., "Introduction" to Rev. Henry Highland Garnet,

A Memorial Discourse; by Rev. Henry Highland Garnet, Delivered in the Hall of the House of Representatives, Washington City, D.C. on Sabbath, February 12, 1865 (Philadelphia: Joseph M. Wilson, 1865), 24; W. E. B. Du Bois, *The World and Africa: An Inquiry into the Part Which Africa Has Played in World History* (1946; New York: International Publishers, 1990), 265.

9. *The Liberator*, 1 February 1839, 11 May 1849.

10. [American Colonization Society], *Memorial of the Semi-Centennial Anniversary of the American Colonization Society, Celebrated at Washington, January 15, 1867* (Washington, DC: Colonization Society, 1867), 190; *African Repository and Colonial Journal*, Vol. 6 (April 1830), 61; William M. Brewer, "John B. Russwurm," *Journal of Negro History*, Vol. 13, No. 4 (October 1928), 416–22; Smith, "Introduction" to Garnet, *Memorial Discourse*, 23–24; *New York Age*, 3 August 1905.

11. *The Liberator*, 12 February 1831.

12. Three years later, Williams was serving on the American Antislavery Society's first board of managers. Rhoda Golden Freeman, *The Free Negro in New York City in the Era before the Civil War* (New York: Garland, 1994), 24–25; Leonard P. Curry, *The Free Black in Urban America, 1800–1850: The Shadow of the Dream* (Chicago: University of Chicago Press, 1981), 224.

13. *Minutes and Proceedings of the First Annual Convention of the People of Colour, Held by Adjournments in the City of Philadelphia, from the Sixth to the Eleventh of June, Inclusive, 1831* (Philadelphia, 1831), in Howard Holman Bell, ed., *Minutes of the Proceedings of the National Negro Conventions, 1830–1864* (New York: Arno, 1969), 1–16; George G. Williams, *History of the Negro Race in America, from 1619 to 1880*, 2 vols. (New York: G. P. Putnam's Sons, 1883), 2: 61–65.

14. Williams, *History of the Negro Race in America*, 68–78. The difficulty of black people's struggle was succinctly captured in the following statement: "the *phenomenon* of an *oppressed people*, deprived of the rights of citizenship, in the midst of an enlightened nation, devising plans and measures for their personal and mental elevation, by *moral suasion alone*." *Minutes and Proceedings of the Second Annual Convention, for the Improvement of the People of Color in These United States, Held by Adjournments in the City of Philadelphia, from the 4th to the 13th of June Inclusive, 1832* (Philadelphia, 1832), in Bell, ed., *Minutes of the Proceedings*.

15. *Minutes and Proceedings of the Third Annual Convention, for the Improvement of the Free People of Color in These United States, Held by Adjournments in the City of Philadelphia, From the 3d to the 13th of June Inclusive, 1833* (Philadelphia, 1833), in Bell, ed., *Minutes of the Proceedings*.

16. Bracey Jr. et al., *Black Nationalism in America*, 51; *The Liberator*, April 12, 1834.

17. William Hamilton Sr., president of the Conventional Board, *Address to the Fourth Annual Convention of the Free People of Color of the United States, Delivered at the Opening of Their Session in the City of New-York, June 2, 1834* (New

York: S. S. Benedict and Co., 1834), 3–6, Schomburg Collection, NYPL; *American Anti-Slavery Reporter*, Vol. 1, No. 1 (January 1834), 7; *African Repository and Colonial Journal*, Vol. 9 (July 1833), 158, Vol. 10 (July 1834), 149; *Minutes of the Fourth Annual Convention, for the Improvement of the Free People of Colour, in the United States, Held by Adjournments in the Asbury Church, New-York, From the 2d to the 12th of June Inclusive, 1834* (New York, 1834), in Bell, ed., *Minutes of the Proceedings*.

18. Hamilton, *Address to the Fourth Annual Convention*, 6–7.

19. *Minutes of the Fourth Annual Convention*, 8–32.

20. Ibid.

21. Howard Holman Bell, "A Survey of the Negro Convention Movement, 1830–1861" (Ph.D. dissertation, Northwestern University, 1953), 15, 19, 35, 43, 66.

In February 1837 a convention of Manhattan's people of color at Phoenix Hall addressed statewide threats to their freedom. Philip Bell and Edward V. Clark of the NYASMR were secretaries, and three petitions were forwarded to Albany calling for "the repeal of laws authorizing the holding of a person to service as a slave in the State," the granting of "a *trial by jury* for their liberty to persons of color within this State arrested and claimed as fugitive slaves," and "an alteration of the Constitution, so as to give the right of voting to all the male citizens of the State on the same terms without distinction of color." Attendees to the convention volunteered to man tables at Phoenix from 3:00 to 9:00 P.M. for several days so that each of Manhattan's black residents would have a chance to sign the petitions. Six hundred twenty men of color signed for the right to vote. *Weekly Advocate*, 22 February 1837; Curry, *Free Black in Urban America*, 222.

In 1841 the New York County Committee of the State Convention, whose members included six African Society for Mutual Relief initiates with John J. Zuille as chair, called for a local meeting to coordinate their suffrage struggle. (At the same time, Alexander Crummell was leading the suffrage struggle in Providence, Rhode Island, where he headed Christ Church.) "A strong repugnance to transmit such a baneful legacy to our children, and a desire that they at least may enjoy the fruits of the arduous toil of their forefathers, calls loudly upon us for earnest and united action, to remove from our State Constitution its last vestige of oppression," asserted the committee. *Colored American*, 2 October 1841; Robert J. Cottrol, *The Afro-Yankees: Providence's Black Community in the Antebellum Era* (Westport, CT: Greenwood, 1982), 73.

In 1840 McCune Smith opposed attempts to hold a segregated national convention, placing himself at odds with Charles B. Ray and other members of the NYASMR. A convention distinguished by the color of its participants' skins would only encourage prejudice, reinforce the divisive logic of race, waste money that could be better used, and eliminate white allies who were equally committed to the principles that the convention purported to champion, he argued: "I am not at all opposed to all action on the part of the colored people, but am opposed to action based upon complexional distinction; believing that whilst a movement based on principle will effect our enfranchisement, that, on the other hand, a movement based on the complexion of the skin, will end in riveting still more firmly the chains which bind us." But, among New York City's black men, Smith's was a losing position. See James McCune Smith to Charles B. Ray, 12 August 1840, in Ripley et al., eds., *Black Abolitionist Papers*, 3: 345–46.

By 1845 many black men were looking to the Liberty party as a vehicle for equal suffrage that avoided the sectional and ideological opposition of the Whigs and Democrats. Henry Highland Garnet was an early supporter. John Zuille and Charles Ray, both of whom eventually served as presidents of the NYASMR, were on the party's Nominating Committee. In June 1845 Zuille joined seven other black men—including three fellow Mutual Relief members and two leading Prince Hall Masons—in penning a letter to the Liberty party asking that they make public their opinion on strategies to equate black voters. See Schor, *Henry Highland Garnet*, 32–34; Ransom F. Wake, John Peterson, Alexander Crummell, Henry Williams, Daniel J. Elston, George Montgomery, Benjamin Stanly, and John J. Zuille to Gerrit Smith, 13 June 1845, in Ripley et al., eds., *Black Abolitionist Papers*, 3: 468–70.

22. David Ruggles, "Kidnapping in the City of New York," *The Liberator*, 6 August 1836; Wilbur H. Siebert, *The Underground Railroad from Slavery to Freedom* (New York: Macmillan, 1898), 35; *The First Annual Report of the New York Committee of Vigilance, for the Year 1837* (New York: 1837), in Herbert Aptheker, ed., *A Documentary History of the Negro People in the United States* (1951; New York: Citadel, 1969), 161–63.

23. Carter G. Woodson, *The History of the Negro Church* (1921; Washington, DC: Associated Publishers, 1945), 152; *Age*, 26 July 1906; Siebert, *Underground Railroad*, 415, 434–39; Freeman, *Free Negro in New York City*, 24–30; *Cleveland Gazette*, 17 November 1894; Charles H. Wesley, "The Negroes of New York in the Emancipation Movement," *Journal of Negro History*, Vol. 24, No. 1 (January 1939), 78–79; Mary White Ovington, *Half a Man: The Status of the Negro in New York* (1911; New York: Schocken, 1969), 24.

24. *The Colored American*, 30 October 1841. By 1841 Zuille was particularly active in Brooklyn and Williamsburg. Three years later, Zuille served as secretary of a meeting called at Manhattan's Philomathean Hall to respond to Secretary of State John C. Calhoun's insults against people of color. James McCune Smith read the call and objectives, and a Committee of Nine was elected to draft a rebuttal. Brooklyn and Williamsburg were invited to the future meetings. *The Liberator*, 10 May 1844. On Zuille's work for suffrage and civil rights in Brooklyn and Williamsburg, see *The Colored American*, 3 July 1841, 29 August 1841. Willis Augustus Hodges, *Free Man of Color: The Autobiography of Willis Augustus Hodges*, edited with an introduction by Willard B. Gatewood Jr. (Knoxville: University of Tennessee Press, 1982), 49–50; [Abyssinian Baptist Church], *The Arti-*

cles of Faith, Church Discipline, and By-Laws of the Abyssinian Baptist Church in the City of New York, April 3, 1833 (New York: J. Post, 1833), 11.

25. Stuckey, *Slave* Culture, 187; see *Walker's Appeal, with a Brief Sketch of His Life. By Henry Highland Garnet. And Also Garnet's Address to the Slaves of the United States of America* (New York: Privately printed, 1848), vi; *Minutes of the National Convention of Colored Citizens: Held at Buffalo, on the 15th, 16th, 17th, 18th, and 19th of August 1843* (New York: Piercy and Reed, 1843), in Bell, ed., *Minutes of the Proceedings*, 12–13, 18.

26. Ibid.; Henry Highland Garnet, *An Address to the Slaves of the United States of America* ([published with David Walker, *Walker's Appeal in Four Articles*], 1848; New York: Arno, 1969), 89; J. N. Gloucester to Captain Brown, 9 March 1858, in Benjamin Quarles, ed., *Blacks on John Brown* (Urbana: University of Illinois Press, 1972), 4–5.

27. Stuckey, *Slave Culture*, 184–87.

28. Garnet, *Address to the Slaves*, 90, 93, 96.

29. Ibid., 90–91.

30. Ibid., 91, 94, 96; *Minutes of the National Convention of 1843*, 18–19.

31. Garnet, *Address to the Slaves*, 92–93.

32. Ibid., 94–96.

33. Ibid.

34. *Minutes of the National Convention of 1843*, 24.

35. Letter from Henry Highland Garnet to Mrs. Maria W. Chapman, 17 November 1843; *The Liberator*, 8 December 1843.

36. Schor, *Henry Highland Garnet*, 58–61; W. M. Brewer, "Henry Highland Garnet," *Journal of Negro History*, Vol. 13, No. I (January 1928), 48; W. E. Burghardt Du Bois, *John Brown* (1909; New York: International Publishers, 1987), 75, 100, 180; Stephen B. Oates, *To Purge This Land with Blood: A Biography of John Brown* (New York: Harper and Row, 1970), 61.

37. Maritcha Remond Lyons, "Memories of Yesterdays, All of Which I Saw and Part of Which I Was: An Autobiography" (unpublished manuscript, ca. 1924), 23, in Williams [Lyons] Family Papers, Schomburg Collection, NYPL; Martin R. Delany, *The Condition, Elevation, Emigration and Destiny of the Colored People of the United States* (1852; Baltimore: Black Classic, 1993), 34; *The Liberator*, 14 May 1852.

38. Phillip Foner, *Essays in Afro-American History* (Philadelphia: Temple University Press, 1978), 88–97; Harriet A. Jacobs, *Incidents in the Life of a Slave Girl, Written by Herself* (1861; Cambridge, MA: Harvard University Press, 1987), 190–91; Freeman, *Free Negro in New York City*, 61–62; *The Liberator*, 18 October 1850, 25 October 1850.

39. Ibid.

40. Foner, *Essays in Afro-American History*, 98–99; R. J. M. Blackett, *Building an Antislavery Wall: Black Americans in the Atlantic Abolitionist Movement, 1830–*

1860 (1983; Ithaca, NY: Cornell University Press, 1989), 169; *The Liberator*, 7 February 1851, 20 June 1856; Lyons, "Memories of Yesterdays," 3.

41. Bracey Jr. et al., *Black Nationalism in America*, 51; African Civilization Society, "Constitution," in Brotz, ed., *Negro Social and Political Thought*, 191–96.

42. *Weekly Anglo-African*, 5 January 1860; *The Liberator*, 27 April 1860, 4 May 1860.

43. Ibid.; George T. Downing to Rev. Alexander Crummell, 12 April 1860, in Letters, Alexander Crummell Papers, Schomburg Collection, NYPL.

44. *Weekly Anglo-African*, 12 January 1861.

45. Ibid., 19 January 1861.

46. Garnet, *Memorial Discourse*, 65–67, 69–91; Hon. Jas. Matthews, "Oration, on the Life and Character of Hon. Henry Highland Garnet, Delivered at Albany, NY, April 17, 1882," in Misc. Manuscripts, John E. Bruce Collection, Schomburg Collection, NYPL.

47. Garnet, *Memorial Discourse*, 65–91.

48. Ibid.

49. Ibid.

NOTES TO CHAPTER 9

1. Russell Duncan, ed., *Blue-Eyed Child of Fortune: The Civil War Letters of Colonel Robert Gould Shaw* (Athens: University of Georgia Press, 1992), 320n, 325; Luis F. Emilio, *A Brave Black Regiment: History of the Fifty-Fourth Regiment of Massachusetts Volunteer Infantry, 1863–1865* (Boston: Boston Book Company, 1894), 57–58, 330; Joseph Mason Andrew Cox, *Great Black Men of Masonry, 1723–1982* (Bronx, NY: Blue Diamond Press, 1982), 187. Vogelsang first joined the African Society in 1849. It was common practice for the association to exempt soldiers from dues. He rejoined the NYASMR after the war.

2. *The Liberator*, 30 August 1861, 18 October 1861.

3. *Weekly Anglo-African*, 4 May 1861.

4. *The Liberator*, 18 October 1861; Phillip Foner, *Essays in Afro-American History* (Philadelphia: Temple University Press, 1978), 98–99; Maritcha Remond Lyons, "Memories of Yesterdays, All of Which I Saw and Part of Which I Was: An Autobiography" (unpublished manuscript, ca. 1924), 3, in Williams [Lyons] Family Papers, Schomburg Collection, NYPL; C. Peter Ripley et al., eds., *The Black Abolitionist Papers*, 5 vols. (Chapel Hill: University of North Carolina Press, 1991), 3: 303n.

5. In the following months, George Downing, who preceded Peterson as grand master of the Odd Fellows, was corresponding with federal and state officials to assure that black troops would receive equal pay, equipment, and protection. *The Liberator*, 16 January 1863, 15 May 1863, 26 December 1863.

6. Sterling Stuckey, *Slave Culture: Nationalist Theory and the Foundations of*

Black America (New York: Oxford University Press, 1987), 185; *The Liberator*, 24 July 1863.

7. Letter from Wm. P. Powell, New Bedford, to Friend [William Lloyd] Garrison, 18 July 1863, in *The Liberator*, 24 July 1863. A year later Powell was back in business. He wrote Garrison from the Colored Sailor's Home to defend the role of abolitionists: "The question is now settled beyond the shadow of a doubt, that Slavery was the sole cause of the war, and not instigated by the so-called ravings of a handful of non-resisting abolitionists." He went on to note that Garrison, other abolitionists, and he had many opportunities to disagree during the years of struggle, but "honest differences of opinion never should alienate friends." Ibid., 30 September 1864.

8. Lyons, "Memories of Yesterdays," 8–10.

9. Ibid.

10. Ibid., *The Liberator*, 24 July 1863; "Report of the Board of Supervisors," 2 February 1864, 150, in Williams Family Papers.

11. James McCune Smith, M.D., "Introduction" to Rev. Henry Highland Garnet, *A Memorial Discourse; by Rev. Henry Highland Garnet, Delivered in the Hall of the House of Representatives, Washington City, D.C. on Sabbath, February 12, 1865* (Philadelphia: Joseph M. Wilson, 1865), 59–62.

12. James Walker Rutledge, of Brooklyn, chaired the board for a quarter of a century. Robert L. Swan, a Brooklynite, spent four decades as chaplain to the NYASMR. Brooklyn's Walter B. Warren, the great-grandson of James Varick and a member of the Boyer Masonic lodge, replaced Rutledge as chair. By 1900 the president, vice president, and secretary were all Brooklynites, as were three of the five board members. Brooklyn contributed at least a third of the members of every major committee, and, in the following years, most board and committee meetings were being held at Brooklyn's Carlton YMCA. Eato provided one of the few examples of NYASMR political action when he served on the New York Civil Rights Committee. William Powell, abolitionist and Mutual Relief member, was chair. Neither participated as members of the African Society. Herbert Aptheker, ed., *A Documentary History of the Negro People in the United States* (1951; New York: Citadel, 1969), 1: 624–25.

13. On the transition from a political to a financial association, see Craig Steven Wilder, "'The Guardian Angel of Africa': A Financial History of the New York African Society for Mutual Relief, 1808–1945," *Afro-Americans in New York Life and History* (forthcoming).

14. Rebecca J. Scott, *Slave Emancipation in Cuba: The Transition to Free Labor, 1860–1899* (Princeton, NJ: Princeton University Press, 1985), 267–71.

15. E. Franklin Frazier, *Black Bourgeoisie* (New York: Free Press, 1957), 195–203; Harry A. Williamson, "Folks in Old New York and Brooklyn" (Bronx, NY: Unpublished manuscript, July 1953), 11, Williams Family Papers, Schomburg Collection, NYPL; Irma Watkins-Owens, *Blood Relations: Caribbean Immigrants and the*

Harlem Community, 1900–1930 (Bloomington: Indiana University Press, 1996), 65; Kevin K. Gaines, *Uplifting the Race: Black Leadership, Politics, and Culture in the Twentieth Century* (Chapel Hill: University of North Carolina Press, 1996), 1–5, 34–37, passim.

16. *Minute Book, 1867–1875*, 9 March 1874; *Minute Book, September 1886– June 1901*, 14 February 1887, 13 October 1890, 16, 106; *Minute Book, 1901–1909*, 13 April 1908, 201, in the NYASMR Papers, Long Island University, Brooklyn. Caribbean men fared better in Masonry. See, for instance, the application of Robert Francis of St. Thomas, WI, "To the Worshipful Master, Wardens and brethren of Covenant Lodge 17 [New York City]—of Free & Accepted Masons," undated, in Misc. Manuscripts, John E. Bruce Collection, Schomburg Collection, NYPL.

17. *Minute Book, September 1886–June 1901*, ? December 1888, 69, NYASMR Papers.

18. *Minute Book, No. 2, March 8, 1909 to May 11, 1914*, special meeting of February 1910, 43, NYASMR Papers; C. Eric Lincoln and Lawrence H. Mamiya, *The Black Church in the African American Experience* (Durham, NC: Duke University Press, 1990), 60.

19. *Minute Book, No. 2, March 8, 1909 to May 11, 1914*, 14 March 1910, 46–49, NYASMR Papers.

20. The following resolution was passed in honor of Ray:

Whereas the Great Ruler of the universe, in his infinite wisdom, has removed from our midst one of the most preeminent of our co-workers, a man whose long and faithful membership having during that time been entrusted for a period with the responsibility of the highest office in the gift of its members, all making it fitting that we record our appreciation of his worth, therefore—

Resolved, That in the demise of Rev. Charles B. Ray this Society condoles with the family of the deceased and their bereavement, and sincerely unite in appreciation of his worth as an honorable citizen, a kind and affectionate parent, the endeared companion, and as an exemplary Christian Minister, whose life and good deeds are remembered by all who knew him—whose influence and labor strengthened the cord of humanity, and promoted the cause of universal liberty.

Resolved, That a copy of this Preamble and resolutions herein contained be spread upon the minutes of this meeting, and that a copy of the same signed by our President and Recording Secretary be tendered to the family of the deceased.

Minute Book, September 1886–June 1901, 13 December 1886, 11–12, NYASMR Papers. This type of eulogistic tribute was a holdover from the antebellum days. Thomas Jennings's passing (11 February 1859) was remembered with a lengthy resolution of praise and loss that was written during the regular meeting and published in the local press. The statement wore the signatures of Peter Vogelsang, president, pro. tem., and John J. Zuille, secretary. See "The Worthy Dead— Tribute of Respect," *Anglo-African Magazine*, Vol. 1, No. 4 (April 1859). Vogelsang received the most passionate of the NYASMR's eulogies:

In Memoriam

Whereas, in the dealings of Divine Providence, it has transpired that time has brought with it the summons for the demise of our esteemed brother and faithful worker[,] our former Secretary Peter Vogelsang, Esq. and

Whereas, not only custom, but the high character our brother bore as a citizen and a soldier of the Republic makes it commendable that an expression of our regards be set forth therefore Resolved, That in consequence of the death of the late Peter Vogelsang, this society places upon record its deep regret for its own loss—its high regard for the memory of the deceased—not only for the devoted life to duty and honor which our beloved brother always sustained, the halo of social purity which characterized him, but also for his devotion to duty, justice and right.

Resolved, That as a volunteer soldier in the late war, our brother followed the instincts of his own nature in a sacrifice for his country's unity, for the liberty of the oppressed, and was in every way worthy of the promotions conferred upon him, having been raised from the ranks to a Lieutenancy and Quartermaster of his regiment.

Resolved, That we condole with the family of the deceased in every expression of sorrow, and record our sympathy with them in every token of respect.

Resolved, That a copy of the Preamble and resolutions herein submitted be entered upon the minutes of the society and that a duplicate of the same be tendered to the family signed by the President and recording Secretary.

Respectfully Submitted
Wm. H. Anthony
John J. Zuille

Minute Book, September 1886–June 1901, 13 June 1887, 31, NYASMR Papers.

21. *Record (Minute Book), No. 3, June 8, 1914–May 12, 1920*, 254; *Minute Book, No. 4, June 14, 1920–February 4, 1926*, 10 December 1923, 196; *Record (Minute Book), No. 5, March 8, 1926–January 13, 1930*, 10 June 1929, 296–98, NYASMR Papers; Bishop R. R. Wright, Jr., *The Bishops of the African Methodist Episcopal Church* (Nashville, TN: A.M.E. Sunday School Union, 1963), 388.

22. *Minute Book, September 1886–June 1901*, 13 November 1893, 192; *Minute Book, 1901–1909*, 13 May 1907, 170; "Annual Report of the Board of Directors for the Fiscal Year Ending, September 30, 1938," in Binder 1, Box 4, NYASMR Papers.

23. The allegation was apparently made by the twentieth-century members and historicized by Arthur Schomburg; see "Jupiter Hammon before the New York African Society," *New York Amsterdam News*, 22 January 1930.

24. The research was funded from the treasury, and Zuille delivered regular reports on the status of the manuscript. *Minute Book, September 1886–June 1901*, 11 April 1887, 23; 11 May 1891, 116; 9 January 1893, 167; 13 November 1893, 192; 9 April 1894, 204. The printing was later expanded to 350 copies. *Minutes of the Board of Trustees, 15 September 1886–5 October 1915*, 7 September 1893, 118, NYASMR Papers. Quoted in John J. Zuille, *Historical Sketch of the New York African Society for Mutual Relief* (New York: Privately printed, 1893), 36. The most consistent moral voice in the postbellum era now gone, the members captured Zuille's lofty presence in a paragraph of their memorial message:

> Resolved, That in his life we can present *one who by his devotion to the cause of freedom did yeoman service in the antislavery cause*; his many years as a teacher in the Public Schools of this City aided the intellectual growth of our people; the responsible positions of trust which he had occupied[;] his strict integrity, his devotion to family, are characteristics . . . which present themselves to us not only of the present but for the future generations to copy, and his good name we shall cherish and preserve as a priceless legacy.

The whole memorial resolution was published in the *New York Age* and a copy was delivered to Zuille's family. *Minute Book, September 1886–June 1901*, 9 April 1894, 203–4, NYASMR Papers.

25. For instance, in 1917 James Williams was appointed historian only after Frederic Davis reminded the members that they were supposed to have one. *The Annual Report of the New York African Society for Mutual Relief for the Year Ending October 1st, 1902; Record (Minute Book), No. 3, June 8, 1914–May 12, 1920*, 10 December 1917, 206; *Record (Minute Book), No. 5, March 8, 1926–January 13, 1930*, 12 September 1927, 12 November 1928, 152, 250, NYASMR Papers; on the Masonic connection, see Harry A. Williamson, "Arthur A. Schomburg, The Freemason" (unpublished lecture delivered in New York), Schomburg Collection, NYPL. Schomburg's letter follows:

December 17th, 1928.

My Dear Mr. Beekman:

Agreeable to our interview of Saturday, I am pleased to state [that] I will be willing to engage, gather, collect, inspect, peruse, study and verify all material available in the various institutions where I know and believe [that] they can be had, books, papers and documents relating to the New York African Society for mutual relief. To write a succinct history of the above mentioned society, to contain not less than 10,000 words (or a book of 300 pages,) represented in three sections. (A) Historical comprising the

Africans in the City of New York previous to 1770 and about the time the said Society was established and the notable incidents that have occurred during that period down to 1825. (B) The organizingation [*sic*] itself, its social and benevolent activities and whatever else it has done within its own sphere and reflected in the community in so far, as the people of color are concerned. (C) A bibliographical section containing a brief life sketch of every member with their distinguished attainment. (D) An Addenda with three excellent pamphlets, the work of members of the Society which did much good in those days.

The number of illustrations will be regulated by what is available of the early members and founders. The picture of the present members can be grouped. The Society will determine on this matter and will provide the sketches from the living members with their respective portrait.

The work will include photographic and photostatic copies of rare pictures of persons and buildings where the Society first started, if such buildings are still erected, and if not, to make diligent search for such historical material[.] To copy rare documents in historical institutions, visit Washington Congressional Library to delve in the newspaper files of early New York days, Philadelphia, Penna; Worcester, Mass. and Boston, Mass. in quest of data in those library warehouses. To present to the Society or its agents the work ready for the printer carefully edited, to supervise the printing of the same, making arrangements for the lowest bid. To circularize the Libraries of the United States (10,000) on the book of the oldest social society of the African Race. To affix the price of the printed volume.

The time required for the completion of this work is not less than six calendar months, to report to whomever the Society may designate, from time to time, the progress of the work, to assist with documents, data, papers, etc. which may be needed in the accurate prosecution of this work, and to give a receipt for same.

The honorarium of the compiler for the work will be fifteen hundred dollars, payable two hundred and fifty dollars on acceptance of the conditions of the work; two hundred and fifty dollars first quarter thereafter, and the balance when the work as been presented and accepted by the Society or its representatives.

Trusting the foregoing meets with your views,
Believe me, sincerely yours,
(Signed) Arthur A. Schomburg.

From a reprinted letter in Box 5, NYASMR Papers.

26. In November 1898 President Eato had the members approve a letter of congratulations to the pastor of the Abyssinian Baptist Church on its ninetieth anniversary, an anniversary that it shared with the African Society, which was

delivered by messenger that day. *Minute Book, September 1886–June 1901*, 14 November 1898, 324. The new spirit was deeper than image. In 1898, when the widow of James E. Stotes wrote the members for help, a serious internal debate occurred. Twelve years earlier, Stotes had defrauded the society and was subsequently arrested on the order of the trustees. In 1895 Stotes applied for readmission to the NYASMR, recalling that he had repaid the stolen funds and "that some credit be given me for my age, my long residence in this community, and my identification with the society in days when the farthers [*sic*] of our younger men were the control[l]ing spirits of this organization." "I have suffered much from . . . feelings within for the misfortune which led to the loss of my membership in your society," Stotes admitted. The most painful part of the separation was finding himself at the end of "an honorable life outside the brotherhood for Mutual relief, whose principle you labored for years to carry out in harmony with the intentions of those who establish[ed] the society." In spite of Stotes's eloquent and contrite appeal, the African Society not only refused to discuss his case, they voted against even receiving his letter. Nevertheless, three years later, the members voluntarily taxed themselves to support Stotes's widow after agreeing that she was ineligible for regular relief. Ibid., 1 August 1895, 10 October 1898, 298, 321, NYASMR Papers.

27. *The Annual Report of the New York African Society for Mutual Relief for the Year Ending October 1st, 1905* (New York: Privately printed, 1905); *Minute Book, 1901–1909*, 9 October 1905, 111, NYASMR Papers; Samuel Scottron, "New York African Society for Mutual Relief—Ninety-Seventh Anniversary," *Colored American Magazine* (December 1905), 687.

28. Booker T. Washington, *The Story of the Negro Race: The Rise of the Race from Slavery*, 2 vols. (1909; New York: Negro Universities Press, 1969), 1: 212–13. Each member was charged five dollars to underwrite the costs. *Minute Book, 1901–1909*, 11 March 1907, 162; 9 December 1907, 189; 5 March 1908, 196–97; 11 May 1908, 204–5, NYASMR Papers; *New York Age*, 18 June 1908. Some members actually contributed more than the required amounts in exchange for extra tickets or to help meet the obligations. See *Minutes of the Board of Trustees, November 1905–November 1917*, 4 June 1908, 42, NYASMR Papers. At the turn of the century the young George Frazier Miller was rejected by the NYASMR. On the philanthropic style of the local black fraternities and sororities, see the society section of the *New York Age*, especially during the 1930s.

29. *Minute Book, 1901–1909*, 12 October 1903, 9 November 1903, 56–58, 60; *Minute Book, No. 2, March 8, 1909 to May 11, 1914*, 14 November 1910, 10 June 1912, 86, 219; *Record (Minute Book), No. 3, June 8, 1914–May 12, 1920*, 8 April 1918, 10 June 1918, 222, 230, NYASMR Papers; *New York Age*, 13 April 1918; *Minute Book, No. 4, June 14, 1920–February 4, 1926*, 10 September 1923, 180, NYASMR Papers; Letter from John W. Dias, President to the Society, 13 April 1936 in "Minutes of the Board of Directors & Misc.," Box 3. Ceremony was intended to motivate the mem-

bers to commit to the association. In 1911 President Linwood noted that there was no constitutional "authority for this annual presidential talk, either in the Articles of Incorporation or in our Constitution and By-laws, but the custom is manifestly a wise one, that I not only follow it without hesitation, but I found real pleasure in its preparation." Mutual Relief's members did gain a sense of purpose from such ceremony. Secretary James Williams described the 1922 collation: "Under the personal supervision of Mr. J. Hoffman Woods, a sumptuous and palatable repast was served and thoroughly enjoyed by all.

> When the table had been cleared of the debris, the President rapped for order and following a few remarks in which he expressed his appreciation for the work of the committee in arranging an affair so enjoyable, he called on Mr. Charles T. Smith, who read a brief history of the Society and its connections with the affairs of old New York a century and more ago. This was followed by Mr. M. P. Saunders, who at the request of the President, related some reminiscences of his earlier life and experiences as an oil merchant prior to the period when night life was made lighter and brighter by the introduction of gas and[,] later on, electricity.

Record (Minute Book), No. 3, June 8, 1914–May 12, 1920, 9 October 1916, 142; *Minute Book, June 14, 1920–February 4, 1926,* 9 November 1922, 131, 10 December 1922, 139; *Minute Book, No. 2, March 8, 1909–May 11, 1914,* 9 October 1911, 153, NYASMR Papers.

30. *Age,* 2 August 1917, 9 August 1917; Herbert Aptheker, *A Documentary History of the Negro People in the United States, 1910–1932* (Secaucus, NJ: Citadel, 1972), 181–83.

31. Ibid., *Age,* 2 August 1917, 9 August 1917.

32. Gilbert Osofsky, *Harlem: The Making of a Ghetto, Negro New York, 1890–1930,* 2nd ed. (New York: Harper Torchbooks, 1971), 116–18; *Record (Minute Book), No. 3, June 8, 1914–May 12, 1920,* special meeting, 8 May 1916, 118–19; Minutes of a regular meeting on 9 June 1932 in "Minutes, 1932–1935," in Box 2, File 2, NYASMR Papers. For decades after the Civil War, Mutual Relief's social agenda was either limited to local apolitical issues or the result of individual members' benevolence. A special tax supported the 1926 Fraternal Night at St. Augustine's P. E. Church in Brooklyn, and all the absent members were contacted to insure their attendance. Before he died in 1928, James Williams left his eight hundred dollar death benefit to the Brooklyn Home for Aged Colored People.

Three years later, Dr. Walter Beekman implored the society to support the petition of the colored citizens of Brooklyn for representation on the boards of the public hospitals so that they could improve the care and treatment of black patients. The members authorized the president to sign the draft on behalf of the NYASMR. In 1935 the members again taxed themselves at a regular meeting to support the budget-balancing campaign of the Carlton Young Men's Christian

Association in Bedford-Stuyvesant, Brooklyn. While the thirteen-dollar gift was not its largest, the tax was evidence of the organization's new commitment to fulfilling some civic responsibilities.

In 1928 the members voted to order the Board of Trustees to open an account in the name of the NYASMR at the Dunbar National Bank in Harlem as a gesture of their support for that institution. Several months later, on 20 May 1929, the president and the trustees visited Dunbar Bank at the invitation of its management. Bank president Joseph D. Higgins met the guests and took them on a tour of the institution while explaining the intents of its backers and how it hoped to impact on the Harlem community. *Record (Minute Book), No. 5, March 8, 1926–January 13, 1930,* 11 October 1926, 10 June 1929, 73, 300; WHRS, *Minutes 1921–1937,* 20 February 1928, 100; Letter from Carleton Avenue Branch YMCA to NYASMR February 20, 1935, and receipt, in Box 5. *Record (Minute Book), No. 5, March 8, 1926–January 13, 1930,* 10 September 1928, 10 June 1929, 231, 297–98, NYASMR Papers.

33. Bertram L. Baker, "Masonic Notes," *Age,* 11 June 1932. Quote from a draft on letterhead in the NYASMR Papers.

34. Diaz and Ince lived at 394 and 395 Hancock Street, respectively. Clyde G. Atwell, *The Paragon Story (1939–1969)* (Brooklyn: Privately printed, ca. 1975), 13, 21–22, 29–30, 62, 86, passim.

35. Ibid.

36. See Wilder, "'The Guardian Angel of Africa.'"

37. *New York Amsterdam News,* 5 April 1969; William J. Walls, *The African Methodist Episcopal Zion Church: Reality of the Black Church* (Charlotte, NC: A.M.E. Zion Publishing House, 1974), 90.

NOTES TO CHAPTER 10

1. Loretta J. Williams, *Black Freemasonry and Middle-Class Realities* (Columbia: University of Missouri Press, 1980), passim; William Alan Muraskin, "Black Masons: The Role of Fraternal Orders in the Creation of a Middle-Class Black Community" (Ph.D. dissertation, University of California, Berkeley, 1970), 6–8, 48–49, 63–64, 183; E. Franklin Frazier, *The Negro in the United States* (New York: Macmillan, 1949), 385–86.

2. Gunnar Myrdal et al., *An American Dilemma: The Negro Problem and Modern Democracy* (1944; New York: Harper and Row, 1962), 639; Charles W. Ferguson, *Fifty Million Brothers: A Panorama of American Lodges and Clubs* (New York: Farrar and Rinehart, 1937), 184–202; *The Ram's Horn,* 5 November 1847.

3. Mark C. Carnes, *Secret Ritual and Manhood in Victorian America* (New Haven, CT: Yale University Press, 1989), 3, 14, 23–29. In contrast, contemporaneous voluntary societies in London were largely thrift associations. See Charles Booth, *Labour and Life of the People: East London,* Vol. 1 (London: Williams and Norgate, 1891), 106–12.

4. Hilda Kupler and Selma Kaplan, "Voluntary Associations in an Urban Township," *African Studies*, Vol. 3, No. 4 (December 1944), 178–86; Bishop R. R. Wright Jr., *The Bishops of the African Methodist Episcopal Church* (Nashville, TN: A.M.E. Sunday School Union, 1963), 378; W[illia]m. Wells Brown, M.D., *My Southern Home: Or, The South and Its People* (1880; New York: Negro Universities Press, 1969), 194.

5. Frazier, *Negro in the United States*, 371–72; Moses Dickson, *A Manual of the Knights of Tabor, and Daughters of the Tabernacle, Including the Ceremonies of the Order, Constitutions, Installations, Dedications, and Funerals, with Forms, and the Taborian Drill and Tactics* (St. Louis: G. I. Jones, 1879), 5–6, passim.

6. Iver Bernstein, *The New York City Draft Riots: Their Significance for American Society and Politics in the Age of the Civil War* (New York: Oxford University Press, 1990), 29; "Coachmen's Union League Society, Inc." *The Messenger* (September 1925), 320–21.

7. Ibid.

8. George Edmund Haynes, *The Negro at Work in New York City: A Study in Economic Progress* (1912; New York: AMS Press, 1968), 68–69, 97.

9. E. A. Williams, S. W. Green, and Jos. L. Jones, *History and Manual of the Colored Knights of Pythias* (Nashville, TN: National Baptist Publication Board, 1917), 13–18.

10. Frazier, *Negro in the United States*, 372–73; William Patrick Burrell, *Twenty-Five Years' History of the Grand Fountain of the United Order of True Reformers, 1881–1905* (Richmond, VA: GF UOTR, 1909), 17, 35–44; *New York Age*, 19 July 1906, 21 February 1907.

11. Herbert Aptheker, ed., *A Documentary History of the Negro People in the United States* (1951; New York: Citadel, 1969), I: 765, 774–75.

12. Charles Harris Wesley, *History of the Improved Benevolent and Protective Order of Elks of the World, 1898–1954* (Washington, DC: Association for the Study of Negro Life and History, 1955), 27–30, 34, 39–46.

13. Cyril V. Briggs, "The African Blood Brotherhood," in William L. Van Deburg, ed., *Modern Black Nationalism: From Marcus Garvey to Louis Farrakhan* (New York: New York University Press, 1997), 34–36; Winston James, *Holding Aloft the Banner of Ethiopia: Caribbean Radicalism in Early Twentieth-Century America* (New York: Verso, 1998), 155–63.

14. E. Franklin Frazier, *Black Bourgeoisie* (1957; New York: Free Press, 1965), 91–92; Myrdal, *An American Dilemma*, 316–17. Also see Kilolo Kijakazi, *African-American Economic Development and Small Business Ownership* (New York: Garland, 1997).

15. *Age*, 26 July 1906; Muraskin, "Black Masons," 140–50.

16. The association was named for Hiram Abif, the master stoneworker whom Solomon called to help in the building of the Temple and whose story provides much of Freemasonry's tradition. See 1 Kings 7:13–40. Muraskin, "Black

Masons," 137–38. *Constitution and Laws of the Hiram Masonic Relief Association, of the State of New York. Revised May 31st, 1898. Incorporated under the Law of New York* (New York: Keystone Printing, 1898), 1–6; *Annual Report of the Hiram Masonic Relief Association of the State of New York, 1893–4*, passim; *Annual Report of the Secretary-Treasurer of the Hiram Masonic Relief Association, from May 23, 1900 to May 22, 1901*, passim, all in the Harry A. Williamson Collection of Negro Masonry, Schomburg Collection, NYPL.

17. *Age*, 20 April 1905, 10 January 1907; *Amsterdam News*, 7 October 1925; Harry A. Williamson, "Folks in Old New York and Brooklyn" (Bronx, NY: Unpublished manuscript, July 1953), 11, Williams Family Papers, Schomburg Collection, NYPL; Irma Watkins-Owens, *Blood Relations: Caribbean Immigrants and the Harlem Community, 1900–1930* (Bloomington: Indiana University Press, 1996), 56–74; Harry A. Williamson, "Prince Hall Masonry in New York State," unpublished typescript, Vol. 5, 81, Harry A. Williamson Collection, Writings, Box 1 (1), Schomburg Collection, NYPL; Bertram L. Baker, "Masonic Notes," *Age*, 13 February 1932. One scholar has found a diverse range of benevolent associations among recent Caribbean immigrants in Toronto. See Frances Henry, *The Caribbean Diaspora in Toronto: Learning to Live with Racism* (Toronto: University of Toronto Press, 1994), 235–40. For an interesting glimpse at Jewish benevolent associations in twentieth-century Brooklyn, see Alter F. Landesman, *Brownsville: The Birth, Development and Passing of a Jewish Community in New York*, 2nd ed. (1969; New York: Bloch, 1971), 266–86.

18. Muraskin, "Black Masons," 12–15, 82; Frazier, *Negro in the United States*, 378–81.

19. *Age*, 9 July 1908; Williamson, "Folks in Old New York and Brooklyn," 11, 17. On Harry A. Williamson, see Bertram L. Baker, "Masonic Notes," *Age*, 5 December 1931.

20. Frazier, *Negro in the United States*, 381–85; see Deborah Gray White, *Too Heavy a Load: Black Women in Defense of Themselves, 1894–1994* (New York: Norton, 1999), 157–59.

21. S. R. Scottron, "Masonic Department," *Colored American Magazine* (December 1905), 728–29; Harry A. Williamson, *The Story of the Carthaginian Lodge, No. 47, F. & A. M.* (Brooklyn: Carthaginian Study Club, 1949), 5–9.

22. Scottron, "Masonic Department," 731.

23. After the war, Rolston entered into real estate in Brooklyn "from which he receives a very remunerative income." W. Preston Moore, "The Elks' Convention in Brooklyn Continued," *CAM* (November 1906), 343–45, 347; *New York Times*, 16 August 1928; *Age*, 9 August 1906; 30 January 1932, 6 August 1932.

24. John Purroy Mitchel, Mayor of New York City, "The Public Schools of New York," in *The Crisis: A Record of the Darker Races*, July 1917, 132; Gilbert Osofsky, *Harlem: The Making of a Ghetto: Negro New York, 1890–1930*, 2nd ed. (New York: Harper and Row, 1971), 5; Harold X. Connolly, *A Ghetto Grows in Brooklyn*

(New York: New York University Press, 1977), 24; Nicholas Marlow, "Bedford-Stuyvesant Place-Names" (Master's thesis, Brooklyn College, 1963), 8; Mary Manoni, *Bedford-Stuyvesant: The Anatomy of a Central City Community* (New York: Quadrangle, 1973), 2.

25. Osofsky, *Harlem*, 118; Jervis Anderson, *This Was Harlem, 1900–1950* (1981; New York: Noonday, 1991), 15; *Age*, 12 July 1906; Muraskin, "Black Masons," 17–22, 39; Carter G. Woodson, "Comments on Negro Education," *Age*, 19 September 1931.

26. Wright, Jr., *Bishops of the African Methodist Episcopal Church*, passim.

27. Williamson, "Prince Hall Masonry in New York State," Vol. 3, 7–18, passim.

28. Aptheker, ed., *Documentary History of the Negro People*, 1: 765. The Crummell Club was apparently organized by John E. Bruce. Crummell Historical Club, "Rules," in Misc. Manuscripts, John E. Bruce Collection, Schomburg Collection, NYPL. Crummell's address was delivered on December 5, 1892, and later published. Alex[ander]. Crummell, *Charitable Institutions in Colored Churches* (Washington, DC, 1892?), passim, Schomburg Collection, NYPL. In 1872 St. Mary's established a society for "church aid." See Alexander Crummell's minutes of the 12 September 1877 vestry meeting for St. Mary's P.E. Church, Washington, DC, in Letters, Alexander Crummell Papers, Schomburg Collection, NYPL.

29. At the end of 1881, Garnet left Shiloh to minister in Liberia and died there that spring. W. M. Brewer, "Henry Highland Garnet," *Journal of Negro History*, Vol. 13, No. 1 (January 1928), 50–51; see advertisement for the "Complimentary Entertainment for the Benefit of Rev. Henry Highland Garnet, D.D." held at Shiloh Presbyterian on 17 January 1872, in Misc. Manuscripts, John E. Bruce Collection; *Age*, 20 July 1905; Harry A. Williamson, "The Brooklyn Literary Union," Williams Family Papers, Schomburg Collection, NYPL.

30. Anne Meis Knupfer, *Toward a Tenderer Humanity and a Nobler Womanhood: African American Women's Clubs in Turn-of-the-Century Chicago* (New York: New York University Press, 1996), 1, passim; Rev. J. Francis Robinson, D.D., "The Importance of Women's Influence in All Religious and Benevolent Societies," *National Baptist Magazine* (November and December 1899), 118; C. Eric Lincoln and Lawrence H. Mamiya, *The Black Church in the African American Experience* (Durham, NC: Duke University Press, 1990), 275.

31. C. C. Adams and Marshall A. Talley, *Negro Baptists and Foreign Missions* (Philadelphia: National Baptist Convention, 1944), 31–48; Evelyn Brooks Higginbotham, *Righteous Discontent: The Women's Movement in the Black Baptist Church, 1880–1920* (Cambridge, MA: Harvard University Press, 1993), 150–58; Bettye Collier-Thomas, *Daughters of Thunder: Black Women Preachers and Their Sermons, 1850–1979* (San Francisco: Jossey-Bass, 1998), 101–47; Tullia Brown Hamilton, "The National Association of Colored Women, 1896–1920" (Ph.D. dissertation, Emory University, 1978), 151; Idonia Elizabeth Rogerson, comp., *Historical Synopsis of the Woman's Home and Foreign Missionary Society, African Methodist Episcopal Zion Church* (Charlotte, NC: A.M.E. Zion Publishing House,

1967), passim. The white Woman's Congress of Missions offered an authority on missionary work for Negroes who accepted that "as a race the [black] people are ignorant, superstitious, immoral, and often 'vicious.'" Miss Mary G. Burdette, "Woman and the American Negro: Woman's Work for the American Negro," in Rev. E. M. Wherry, D.D., comp., *Woman in Missions: Papers and Addresses Presented at the Woman's Congress of Missions, October 2–4, 1893, in the Hall of Columbus, Chicago* (New York: American Tract Society, 1894), 127.

32. Maritcha Remond Lyons, "Memories of Yesterdays, All of Which I Saw and Part of Which I Was: An Autobiography" (unpublished manuscript, ca. 1924), 4–5, 12, 55, Williamson Family Papers.

33. Ibid., 4–5, 16, 30–36.

34. Ibid., 32–33; White, *Too Heavy a Load*, 27; Higginbotham, *Righteous Discontent*, 17, 58–59, 67–68; Hamilton, "National Association of Colored Women," 12–21; "Official Programme, First Annual Meeting of the Afro-American Council, at the Metropolitan Baptist Church, R Street between 12th and 13 Streets N.W., Washington, D.C.," 1, and "Constitution and By-Laws of the National Afro-American Council, Organized at Rochester, New York, September 15th, 1898" (New York: Edgar Printing, 1898), passim, all in the Daniel A. P. Murray Collection, Library of Congress.

35. Frances Blascoer, *Colored School Children in New York* (1915; New York: Negro Universities Press, 1970), 175; Hamilton, "National Association of Colored Women," 74; *Age*, 26 July 1906; Osofsky, *Harlem*, 56–57. Matthews used the theme of black women's historic suffering and benevolence for a short story. See Victoria Earle, *Aunt Lindy: A Story Founded on Real Life* (New York: J. J. Little, 1893).

36. Rosalyn Terborg-Penn, *African American Women in the Struggle for the Vote, 1850–1920* (Bloomington: Indiana University Press, 1998), 87, 94–95, passim; Hamilton, "National Association of Colored Women," 146–52; Dorothy Sterling, ed., *We Are Your Sisters: Black Women in the Nineteenth Century* (New York: Norton, 1984), 440–43; William Seraile, "Susan McKinney Steward: New York State's First African-American Woman Physician," *Afro-Americans in New York Life and History* (July 1985), 27–40; *Age*, 30 April 1908.

37. *Age*, 9 July 1908, 3 September 1908.

38. Judith Weisenfeld, *African American Women and Christian Activism: New York's Black YWCA, 1905–1945* (Cambridge, MA: Harvard University Press, 1997), 37–43; Cynthia Neverdon-Morton, *Afro-American Women of the South and the Advancement of the Race, 1895–1925* (Knoxville: University of Tennessee Press, 1989), 207–15; *Age*, 20 August 1908.

39. Maude K. Griffin, "The Negro Church and Its Social Work—St. Mark's," in the Survey, *The Negro in the Cities of the North* (New York: Charity Organization Society, 1905), 75–76.

40. Hamilton, "National Association of Colored Women," 74, 149–50.

41. Blascoer, *Colored School Children in New York*, 49–50, 146; Watkins-

Owens, *Blood Relations*, 57–58; A. Clayton Powell Sr., *Against the Tide: An Autobiography* (New York: Richard R. Smith, 1938), 45–46, 154–59.

42. Higginbotham, *Righteous Discontent*, 1.

43. Aptheker, ed., *Documentary History of the Negro People*, 1: 623.

44. W. E. B. Du Bois, ed., "The Negro Church: Report of a Social Study Made under the Direction of Atlanta University together with the Proceedings of the Eighth Conference for the Study of the Negro Problems, Held at Atlanta University, May 26th, 1903," 5, in Vol. 2 of W. E. B. Du Bois, ed., *Atlanta University Publications* (New York: Octagon, 1968).

Bibliography

MANUSCRIPT COLLECTIONS

The Association for the Benefit of Colored Orphans Records, New-York Historical Society.
John E. Bruce Collection, Schomburg Collection, NYPL.
Alexander Crummell Papers, Schomburg Collection, NYPL.
Dorcas Society Misc. Mss., New-York Historical Society.
Historic American Buildings Survey (NPS), Library of Congress.
Jay Family Papers, New-York Historical Society.
John Jay Papers, Columbia University.
John Street Church Records, Manuscripts Division, New York Public Library.
Ladies Benevolent (Dorcas) Society Records, St. Mark's Church, New-York Historical Society.
Daniel A. P. Murray Collection, Library of Congress.
New York African Society for Mutual Relief Papers, Long Island University, Brooklyn Campus.
New York Manumission Society Records, New-York Historical Society.
Pierre Toussaint Papers, Manuscripts Division, New York Public Library.
Rutherfurd Papers, New-York Historical Society.
The Society for the Prevention of Pauperism Records, New-York Historical Society.
The Society for the Relief of Poor Widows with Small Children Records, New-York Historical Society.
The Society of Mechanics and Workingmen Records, New York City, New-York Historical Society.
Williams [Lyons] Family Papers, Schomburg Collection, NYPL.
Harry A. Williamson Collection of Negro Masonry, Schomburg Collection, NYPL.

PERIODICALS

African Repository and Colonial Journal
American Anti-Slavery Reporter
The Anti-Slavery Examiner
The Boston News-Letter
The Cleveland Gazette
The Colored American
The Colored American Magazine
Ebony

The Elevator
Freedom's Journal
The Liberator
The Messenger
The National Baptist Magazine
The New York Age
The New York Amsterdam News
The New-York Evening Post

The New York Genealogical and Biographical Record
The New York Herald
The New York Times
The Ram's Horn
The Weekly Advocate
The Weekly Anglo-African

GOVERNMENT PUBLICATIONS

The Colonial Laws of New York from the Year 1664 to the Revolution, Including the Charters to the Duke of York, the Commissions and Instructions to Colonial Governors, the Duke's Laws, the Laws of the Dongan and Leisler Assemblies, the Charters of Albany and New York and the Acts of the Colonial Legislatures from 1691 to 1775 Inclusive. Albany: State Printer, 1894.

Journal of the Legislative Council of the Colony of New-York. Began the 9th Day of April, 1691; and Ended the 27 of September, 1743. Albany: Weed, Parsons and Co., 1861.

Laws of the State of New York. Albany, 1812–1845.

Minutes of the Common Council of the City of New York, 1675–1776, 8 vols. New York: Dodd, Mead and Company, 1905.

Minutes of the Common Council of the City of New York, 1784–1831, 18 vols. New York: Published by the City of New York, 1917.

New York State Library, *Calendar of Council Minutes, 1668–1783.* Albany: State University of New York, March 1902.

O'Callaghan, E. B., M.D., *The Documentary History of the State of New-York; Arranged under the Direction of the Hon. Christopher Morgan, Secretary of State,* 4 vols. Albany: Weed, Parsons and Co., 1849.

———, ed., *Documents Relative to the Colonial History of the State of New-York; Procured in Holland, England and France by John Romeyn Brodhead, Esq., Agent.* Albany: Weed, Parsons and Co., 1855.

———, comp., *Laws and Ordinances of New Netherland, 1638–1674.* Albany: Weed, Parsons and Company, 1868.

Return of the Whole Number of Persons within the Several Districts of the United States, According to "An Act Providing for the Enumeration of the Inhabitants of the United States," *Passed March the First, One Thousand Seven Hundred and Ninety-One.* Philadelphia: Childs and Swaine, 1791.

BOOKS, ARTICLES, AND MANUSCRIPTS

[Abyssinian Baptist Church], *The Articles of Faith, Church Discipline, and By-Laws of the Abyssinian Baptist Church in the City of New York, April 3, 1833.* New York: J. Post, 1833.

[Abyssinian Benevolent Daughters of Esther], *Constitution and By-Laws of the Abyssinian Benevolent Daughters of Esther Association, of the City of New York,* Adopted April 19th, 1839. New York: Zuille and Leonard, 1853.

Adams, C. C., and Marshall A. Talley, *Negro Baptists and Foreign Missions.* Philadelphia: National Baptist Convention, 1944.

[African Education and Civilization Society], *Report of the Formation of the African Education and Civilization Society, Containing the Preamble and Resolutions Passed at Their First Meetings, the Constitution and Officers of the Society, Together with a Statement of the Objects of the Society by the Executive Committee.* New York: Privately printed, 1845. Collection of the New-York Historical Society.

[African Marine Fund], *Constitution of the African Marine Fund, for the Relief of the Distressed Orphans, and Poor Members of This Fund.* New York: John C. Totten, 1810. Collection of the New-York Historical Society.

[American Bible Society], *Third Report of the American Bible Society, Presented May 13, 1819, with an Appendix, Containing Extracts of Correspondence.* New-York: Printed for the Society, 1819.

[American Colonization Society], *Memorial of the Semi-Centennial Anniversary of the American Colonization Society, Celebrated at Washington, January 15, 1867.* Washington, DC: Colonization Society, 1867.

[The American Convention . . .], *The American Convention for Promoting the Abolition of Slavery and Improving the Condition of the African Race: Minutes, Constitution, Addresses, Memorials, Resolutions, Reports, Committees and Anti-Slavery Tracts,* 3 vols. New York: Bergman Publishers, 1969.

Alexander, Arthur J., "Federal Officeholder in New York State as Slaveholders, 1789–1805," *Journal of Negro History,* Vol. 28, No. 3 (July 1943).

Alexander, William, comp., *Memoir of Captain Paul Cuffee, a Man of Colour: To Which Is Subjoined "The Epistle of the Society of Sierra Leone, in Africa, & c."* London: W. Alexander, 1811.

Allen, Bishop Richard, *The Life, Experience and Gospel Labors of the Rt. Rev. Richard Allen.* Privately printed, 1833.

Anderson, Jervis, *This Was Harlem, 1900–1950.* 1981; New York: Noonday, 1991.

Aptheker, Herbert, "Maroons within the Present Limits of the United States," *Journal of Negro History,* Vol. 24, No. 2 (April, 1939).

———, *American Negro Slave Revolts.* 1943; New York: International Publishers, 1987.

———, ed., *A Documentary History of the Negro People in the United States.* 1951; New York: Citadel, 1969.

Armstrong, Lebbeus, *William Morgan Abducted and Murdered by Masons, in Conformity with Masonic Obligations; and Masonic Measures, to Conceal That*

Outrage against the Laws; a Practical Comment on the Sin of Cain. Illustrated and Proved in a Sermon, Delivered in Edinburgh, Saratoga County, Sept. 12, 1831. New York: L. D. Dewey, 1831.

Arnett, Rev. Benjamin W., P.G.M., *Biennial Oration before the Second B.M.C. of the Grand United Order of Odd Fellows.* Dayton, OH: Christian Publishing House, 1884.

Arua, Emea O., "Yam Ceremonies and the Values of Ohafia Culture," *Africa*, Vol. 51, No. 2 (1981).

Atkins, Keletso E., *The Moon is Dead! Give Us Our Money! The Cultural Origins of an African Work Ethic, Natal, South Africa, 1843–1900.* Portsmouth, NH: Heinemann, 1993.

Atwell, Clyde G., *The Paragon Story (1939–1969).* Brooklyn: Privately printed, ca. 1975.

Babchuck, Nicholas, and Ralph V. Thompson, "The Voluntary Associations of Negroes," *American Sociological Review* (October 1962).

Bailyn, Bernard, ed., *The Apologia of Robert Keayne: The Self-Portrait of a Puritan Merchant.* New York: Harper Torchbooks, 1965.

Baker, George Claude, Jr., *An Introduction to the History of Early New England Methodism, 1789–1839.* 1941; New York: AMS, 1969.

Baldwin, Lewis V., *"Invisible" Strands in African Methodism: A History of the African Union Methodist Protestant and Union Methodist Episcopal Churches, 1805–1980.* Metuchen, NJ: Scarecrow Press, 1983.

Barnes, Gilbert Hobbs, *The Antislavery Impulse, 1830–1844.* New York: Appleton-Century, 1933.

Bastide, Roger, *The African Religions of Brazil: Toward a Sociology of the Interpenetration of Civilizations*, translated by Helen Sebba. 1960; Baltimore: Johns Hopkins University Press, 1978.

Bayley, Rev. J. R., *A Brief Sketch of the Early History of the Catholic Church on the Island of New York.* New York: Catholic Publication Society, 1870.

Bayor, Ronald H., and Timothy J. Meagher, eds., *The New York Irish.* Baltimore: Johns Hopkins University Press, 1996.

Beattie, J. H. M., "The Blood Pact in Bunyoro," *African Studies*, Vol. 17, No. 4 (1958).

Bederman, Gail, *Manliness and Civilization: A Cultural History of Gender and Race in the United States, 1880–1917.* Chicago: University of Chicago Press, 1995.

Beidelman, T. O., "The Blood Covenant and the Concept of Blood in Ukaguru," *Africa*, Vol. 33, No. 4 (October 1963).

Bell, Howard Holman, "A Survey of the Negro Convention Movement, 1830–1861." Ph.D. dissertation, Northwestern University, 1953.

———, ed., *Minutes of the Proceedings of the National Negro Conventions, 1830–1864.* New York: Arno, 1969.

Bernstein, Iver, *The New York City Draft Riots: Their Significance for American Society and Politics in the Age of the Civil War.* New York: Oxford University Press, 1990.

Bethel, Elizabeth Rauh, *The Roots of African-American Identity: Memory and History in Free Antebellum Communities.* New York: St. Martin's, 1997.

Blackett, R. J. M., *Building an Antislavery Wall: Black Americans in the Atlantic Abolitionist Movement, 1830–1860.* 1983; Ithaca, NY: Cornell University Press, 1989.

Blascoer, Frances, *Colored School Children in New York.* 1915; New York: Negro Universities Press, 1970.

Bangs, Mrs. [Charlotte Rebecca] Bleecker, *Reminiscences of Old New Utrecht and Gowanus.* Brooklyn, NY: 1912.

Blight, David W., "In Search of Learning, Liberty, and Self Definition: James McCune Smith and the Ordeal of the Antebellum Black Intellectual," *Afro-Americans in New York Life and History* (July 1985).

[Boston African Society], *Laws of the African Society; Instituted at Boston, Anno Domini, 1796.* Boston: Printed for the Society, 1802. Collection of the New-York Historical Society.

Bowser, Frederick P., *The African Slave in Colonial Peru, 1524–1650.* Stanford, CA: Stanford University Press, 1974.

Boyd, James Robert, ed., *The Task, Table Talk, and Other Poems of William Cowper, with Critical Observations of Various Authors on His Genius and Character, and Notes, Critical and Illustrative.* New York: A. S. Barnes and Co., 1853.

Bracey, Jr., John H., August Meier, and Elliot Rudwick, *Black Nationalism in America.* Indianapolis, IN: Bobbs-Merrill, 1970.

Brewer, William M., "Henry Highland Garnet," *Journal of Negro History*, Vol. 13, No. 1 (January 1928).

———, "John B. Russwurm," *Journal of Negro History*, Vol. 13, No. 4 (October 1928).

[Brooklyn African Woolman Benevolent Society], *Constitution of the Brooklyn African Woolman Benevolent Society*, Adopted March 16, 1810. Brooklyn, NY: E. Worthington, 1820. Collection of the New-York Historical Society.

Brooks, George E., *Landlords and Strangers: Ecology, Society, and Trade in Western Africa, 1000–1630.* Boulder, CO: Westview Press, 1993.

Brotz, Howard, ed., *Negro Social and Political Thought, 1850–1920.* New York: Basic Books, 1966.

Brown, William Wells, *The Black Man, His Antecedents, His Genius, and His Achievements.* New York: Thomas Hamilton, 1863.

———, *The Rising Son; or, The Antecedents and Advancement of the Colored Race.* Boston: A. G. Brown, 1874.

———, *My Southern Home: Or, The South and Its People.* 1880; New York: Negro Universities Press, 1969.

Browning, James B., "The Beginnings of Insurance Enterprise among Negroes," *Journal of Negro History* (October 1937).

Bullock, Steven C., *Revolutionary Brotherhood: Freemasonry and the Transformation of the American Social Order, 1730–1840*. Chapel Hill: University of North Carolina Press, 1996.

Burrell, William Patrick, *Twenty-five Years' History of the Grand Fountain of the United Order of True Reformers, 1881–1905*. Richmond, VA: GF UOTR, 1909.

Burrows, Edwin G., and Mike Wallace, *Gotham: A History of New York City to 1898*. New York: Oxford University Press, 1999.

Butchart, Ronald E., "'We Best Can Instruct Our Own People': New York African Americans in the Freedmen's Schools, 1861–1875," *Afro-Americans in New York Life and History* (January 1988).

Butt-Thompson, Captain F. W., *West African Secret Societies: Their Organisations, Officials, and Teaching*. 1929; Westport, CT: Negro Universities Press, 1970.

Campbell, Dugald, *In the Heart of Bantuland: A Record of Twenty-nine Years' Pioneering in Central Africa among the Bantu Peoples, with a Description of Their Habits, Customs, Secret Societies and Languages*. 1922; New York: Negro Universities Press, 1969.

Campbell, James T., *Songs of Zion: The African Methodist Episcopal Church in the United States and South Africa*. New York: Oxford University Press, 1995.

Campbell, Mavis C., *The Maroons of Jamaica, 1655–1796: A History of Resistance, Collaboration and Betrayal*. Granby, MA: Bergin and Garvey, 1988.

Cardozo, Manoel S., "The Lay Brotherhoods of Colonial Bahia," *Catholic Historical Review* (April 1947).

Carnes, Mark C., *Secret Ritual and Manhood in Victorian America*. New Haven: Yale University Press, 1989.

Chauncey, George, *Gay New York: Gender, Urban Culture, and the Making of the Gay Male World, 1890–1940*. New York: Basic Books, 1994.

Chesneaux, Jean, *Secret Societies in China in the Nineteenth and Twentieth Centuries*, translated by Gillian Nettle. Ann Arbor: University of Michigan Press, 1971.

———, ed., *Popular Movements and Secret Societies in China, 1840–1950*. Stanford, CA: Stanford University Press, 1972.

Clarkson, Rev. T[homas]., M.A., *An Essay on the Impolicy of the African Slave Trade, in Two Parts*. 1788; Freeport, NY: Books for Libraries Press, 1971.

———, *The History of the Rise, Progress, and Accomplishment of the Abolition of the African Slave-trade, by the British Parliament*. Philadelphia: James P. Parke, 1808.

Clawson, Mary Ann, *Constructing Brotherhood: Class, Gender, and Fraternalism*. Princeton, NJ: Princeton University Press, 1989.

Clute, J. J., *Annals of Staten Island: From Its Discovery to the Present Time*. New York: Chas. Vogt, 1877.

Collier-Thomas, Bettye, *Daughters of Thunder: Black Women Preachers and Their Sermons, 1850–1979.* San Francisco: Jossey-Bass, 1998.

Comhaire, Jean, "Sociétiès Secrètes et Mouvements Prophétiques au Congo Belge," *Africa,* Vol. 25, No. 1 (January 1955).

Connolly, Harold X., *A Ghetto Grows in Brooklyn.* New York: New York University Press, 1977.

Conway, Moncure Daniel, ed., *The Writings of Thomas Paine,* 4 vols. New York: Putnam's Sons, 1894.

Cooper-Lewter, Nicholas C., and Henry H. Mitchell, *Soul Theology: The Heart of American Black Culture.* San Francisco: Harper and Row, 1986.

Cottrol, Robert J., *The Afro-Yankees: Providence's Black Community in the Antebellum Era.* Westport, CT: Greenwood, 1982.

Countryman, Edward, *A People in Revolution: The American Revolution and Political Society in New York, 1760–1790.* Baltimore: Johns Hopkins University Press, 1981.

Couve de Murville, M. N. L., Archbishop of Birmingham, England, *Slave from Haiti: A Saint for New York? A Life of Pierre Toussaint.* London: Catholic Truth Society, 1995.

Cox, Joseph Mason Andrew, *Great Black Men of Masonry, 1723–1982.* Bronx, NY: Blue Diamond Press, 1982.

Crawford, George W., *Prince Hall and His Followers: Being a Monograph on the Legitimacy of Negro Masonry.* New York: The Crisis, 1914.

Creel, Margaret Washington, *"A Peculiar People": Slave Religion and Community-Culture among the Gullah.* New York: New York University Press, 1988.

Cronin, Anne, "The Struggle for Freedom and a Proper Burial," *New York Times,* 28 February 1993.

Cross, Whitney R., *The Burned-over District: The Social and Intellectual History of Enthusiastic Religion in Western New York, 1800–1850.* Ithaca, NY: Cornell University Press, 1950.

Crummell, Alexander, *The Future of Africa, Being Addresses, Sermons, Etc., Etc., Delivered in the Republic of Liberia.* 1862; New York: Negro Universities Press, 1969.

———, *Charitable Institutions in Colored Churches.* Washington, DC, ca. 1892.

———, *Destiny and Race: Selected Writings, 1840–1898,* edited by Wilson Jeremiah Moses. Amherst: University of Massachusetts Press, 1992.

Crummey, Donald, ed., *Banditry, Rebellion and Social Protest in Africa.* Portsmouth, NH: Heinemann, 1986.

Cruse, Harold, *The Crisis of the Negro Intellectual.* New York: Morrow, 1967.

Cugoano, Quobna Ottobah, a native of Africa, *Thoughts and Sentiments on the Evil and Wicked Traffic of the Slavery and Commerce of the Human Species, Humbly Submitted to the Inhabitants of Great-Britain,* edited by Vincent Carretta. 1787; New York: Penguin, 1999.

Curry, Leonard P., *The Free Black in Urban America, 1800–1850: The Shadow of the Dream*. Chicago: University of Chicago Press, 1981.

Dallas, R. C., *The History of the Maroons*, 2 vols. 1803; London: Frank Cass, 1968.

Daniels, Douglas Henry, *Pioneer Urbanites: A Social and Cultural History of Black San Francisco*. Berkeley: University of California Press, 1990.

Daniels, John, *In Freedom's Birthplace*. 1914; New York: Arno, 1969.

Dann, Martin E., ed., *The Black Press, 1827–1890: The Quest for National Identity*. New York: Putnam's Sons, 1971.

Davis, David Brion, *The Problem of Slavery in Western Culture*. Ithaca, NY: Cornell University Press, 1966.

———, *The Problem of Slavery in the Age of Revolution, 1770–1823*. Ithaca, NY: Cornell University Press, 1975.

Davis, Fei-Ling, *Primitive Revolutionaries of China: A Study of Secret Societies in the Late Nineteenth Century*. 1971; Honolulu: University of Hawaii Press, 1977.

Davis, H. P., *Black Democracy: The Story of Haiti*. New York: Dial, 1928.

Davis, Susan G., *Parades and Power: Street Theatre in Nineteenth-Century Philadelphia*. Philadelphia: Temple University Press, 1986.

Davis, Thomas J., "The New York Slave Conspiracy of 1741 as Black Protest," *Journal of Negro History*, Vol. 56, No. 1 (January 1971).

———, *A Rumor of Revolt: The "Great Negro Plot" in Colonial New York*. New York: Free Press, 1985.

Delany, Martin R., *The Condition, Elevation, Emigration and Destiny of the Colored People of the United States*. 1852; Baltimore: Black Classic Press, 1993.

Dickson, Moses, *A Manual of the Knights of Tabor, and Daughters of the Tabernacle, Including the Ceremonies of the Order, Constitutions, Installations, Dedications, and Funerals, with Forms, and the Taborian Drill and Tactics*. St. Louis: G. I. Jones, 1879.

Diouf, Sylviane A., *Servants of Allah: African Muslims Enslaved in the Americas*. New York: New York University Press, 1998.

Douglass, Frederick, *My Bondage and My Freedom*. 1855; New York: Dover, 1969.

Douglass, Rev. W[illia]m., *Annals of the First African Church, the United States of America, Now Styled the African Episcopal Church of St. Thomas, Philadelphia*. Philadelphia: King and Baird, 1862.

Du Bois, William Edward Burghardt, *The Autobiography of W. E. B. Du Bois: A Soliloquy on Viewing My Life from the Last Decade of Its First Century*. New York: International Publishers, 1968.

———, *John Brown*. 1909; New York: International Publishers, 1987.

———, *The World and Africa: An Inquiry into the Part Which Africa Has Played in World History*. 1946; New York: International Publishers, 1990.

———, ed., "The Negro Church: Report of a Social Study Made under the Direction of Atlanta University together with the Proceedings of the Eighth Conference for the Study of the Negro Problems, Held at Atlanta University, May

26th, 1903," Vol. 2 of W. E. B. Du Bois, ed., *Atlanta University Publications.* New York: Octagon, 1968.

———, ed., *Economic Co-operation among Negro Americans.* Atlanta: Atlanta University Press, 1907.

Ducille, Ann, "Blues Notes on Black Sexuality: Sex and the Texts of Jessie Fauset and Nella Larson," *Journal of the History of Sexuality,* Vol. 3, No. 3 (1993).

Earle, Victoria, *Aunt Lindy: A Story Founded on Real Life.* New York: J. J. Little, 1893.

Ellis, Edward Robb, *The Epic of New York City.* New York: Coward-McCann, 1966.

Emilio, Luis F., *A Brave Black Regiment: History of the Fifty-Fourth Regiment of Massachusetts Volunteer Infantry, 1863–1865.* Boston: Boston Book Company, 1894.

Equiano, Olaudah, *The Interesting Narrative of the Life of Olaudah Equiano, Written by Himself,* edited by Robert J. Allison. 1791; Boston: Bedford, 1995.

Evans-Pritchard, E. E., "Zande Blood-Brotherhood," *Africa,* Vol. 6, No. 4 (October 1933).

Fausset, Hugh I'Anson, *William Cowper.* New York: Harcourt, Brace, 1928.

Fay, Bernard, *Revolution and Freemasonry, 1680–1800.* Boston: Little, Brown, 1935.

Fergus, Howard A., "The Early Laws of Montserrat (1668–1680): The Legal Schema of a Slave Society," *Caribbean Quarterly,* Vol. 24, Nos. 1–2 (March–June 1978).

Ferguson, Charles W., *Fifty Million Brothers: A Panorama of American Lodges and Clubs.* New York: Farrar and Rinehart, 1937.

Finney, Rev. C. G., *The Character, Claims, and Practical Workings of Freemasonry.* Cincinnati: Western Tract and Book Society, 1869.

Fitts, Robert K., *Inventing New England's Slave Paradise: Master/Slave Relations in Eighteenth-Century Narragansett, Rhode Island.* New York: Garland, 1998.

Foner, Eric, *Tom Paine and Revolutionary America.* New York: Oxford University Press, 1976.

Foner, Philip S., *History of Black Americans: From Africa to the Emergence of the Cotton Kingdom.* Westport, CT: Greenwood, 1975.

———, *Essays in Afro-American History.* Philadelphia: Temple University Press, 1978.

———, *History of Black Americans: From the Emergence of the Cotton Kingdom to the Eve of the Compromise of 1850.* Westport, CT: Greenwood, 1983.

———, ed., *The Life and Writings of Frederick Douglass,* 5 vols. New York: International Publishers, 1975.

Foner, Philip S., and George E. Walker, eds., *Proceedings of the Black National and State Conventions, 1865–1900.* Philadelphia: Temple University Press, 1986.

Fox, George, *A Collection of Many Select and Christian Epistles, Letters and Testimonies, Written on Sundry Occasions, by That Ancient, Eminent, Faithful Friend, and Minister of Christ Jesus,* 2 vols. Philadelphia: Marcus T. Gould, 1831.

Frazier, E. Franklin, *The Negro in the United States.* New York: Macmillan, 1949.
————, *Black Bourgeoisie.* 1957; New York: Free Press, 1965.
Freeman, Rhoda Golden, *The Free Negro in New York City in the Era before the Civil War.* New York: Garland, 1994.
Frey, Sylvia R., *Water from the Rock: Black Resistance in a Revolutionary Age.* Princeton, NJ: Princeton University Press, 1991.
Frey, Sylvia R., and Betty Wood, *Come Shouting to Zion: African American Protestantism in the American South and British Caribbean to 1830.* Chapel Hill: University of North Carolina Press, 1998.
Furman, Gabriel, *Antiquities of Long Island.* 1874; Port Washington, NY: Ira J. Friedman, 1968.
Gaines, Kevin K., *Uplifting the Race: Black Leadership, Politics, and Culture in the Twentieth Century.* Chapel Hill: University of North Carolina Press, 1996.
Gara, Larry, *The Liberty Line: The Legend of the Underground Railroad.* Lexington: University of Kentucky Press, 1961.
Garnet, Henry Highland, *An Address to the Slaves of the United States of America.* Published with David Walker, *Walker's Appeal in Four Articles.* 1848; New York: Arno, 1969.
————, *A Memorial Discourse; by Rev. Henry Highland Garnet, Delivered in the Hall of the House of Representatives, Washington City, D.C. on Sabbath, February 12, 1865, with an Introduction, by James McCune Smith, M.D.* Philadelphia: Joseph M. Wilson, 1865.
Garrison, William Lloyd, *Thoughts on African Colonization.* 1832; New York: Arno, 1968.
Genovese, Eugene D., *Roll, Jordan, Roll: The World the Slaves Made.* 1972; New York: Vintage, 1976.
Gilje, Paul A., *The Road to Mobocracy: Popular Disorder in New York City, 1763–1834.* Chapel Hill: University of North Carolina Press, 1987.
Gilje, Paul A., and Howard B. Rock, eds., *Keepers of the Revolution: New Yorkers at Work in the Early Republic.* Ithaca, NY: Cornell University Press, 1992.
Gist, Noel P., *Secret Societies: A Cultural Study of Fraternalism in the United States.* Columbia: University of Missouri Press, 1940.
Gomez, Michael A., *Exchanging Our Country Marks: The Transformation of African Identities in the Colonial and Antebellum South.* Chapel Hill: University of North Carolina Press, 1998.
Goodfriend, Joyce D., *Before the Melting Pot: Society and Culture in Colonial New York City, 1664–1730.* Princeton, NJ: Princeton University Press, 1992.
Gould's History of Freemasonry throughout the World, 6 vols. Revised by Dudley Wright. New York: Scribner's Sons, 1936.
Greenberg, Douglas, *Crime and Law Enforcement in the Colony of New York, 1691–1776.* 1974; Ithaca, NY: Cornell University Press, 1976.
Griffith, Henry Thomas, ed., *Cowper,* 2 vols. Oxford: Clarendon, 1874–75.

Grimshawe, Rev. T. S., A.M., F.S.A., M.R.S.L., ed., *The Works of William Cowper: His Life, Letters, and Poems*. New York: Robert Carter and Brothers, 1851.

Hamilton, Tullia Brown, "The National Association of Colored Women, 1896–1920." Ph.D. dissertation, Emory University, 1978.

Hamilton, William, *Address to the New York African Society, for Mutual Relief, Delivered in the Universalist Church, January 2, 1809*. New York: Privately printed, 1809. Schomburg Collection, NYPL.

———, Sr., President of the Conventional Board, *Address to the Fourth Annual Convention of the Free People of Color of the United States, Delivered at the Opening of Their Session in the City of New-York, June 2, 1834*. New York: S. S. Benedict, 1834. Schomburg Collection, NYPL.

Hammon, Jupiter, "An Address to Miss Phillis Wheatly, Ethiopian Poetess, in Boston, who came from Africa at eight years of age, and soon became acquainted with the gospel of Jesus Christ," in "Six Broadsides Relating to Phillis Wheatley (Phillis Peters)." Schomburg Collection, NYPL.

Hansell, George H., *Reminiscences of Baptist Churches and Baptist Leaders in New York City and Vicinity, from 1835–1898*. Philadelphia: American Baptist Publication Society, 1899.

Hardie, James, A.M., *An Account of the Malignant Fever, Lately [sic] Prevalent in the City of New-York*. New York: Hurtin and McFarlane, 1799.

Hardman, Keith J., "Charles G. Finney, the Benevolent Empire, and the Free Church Movement in New York City," *New York History*, Vol. 67, No. 4 (October 1986).

Harris, Robert L., Jr., "Early Black Benevolent Societies, 1780–1830," *Massachusetts Review* (Fall 1979).

———, "Charleston's Free Afro-American Elite: The Brown Fellowship Society and the Humane Brotherhood," *South Carolina Historical Magazine*, Vol. 82, No. 4 (October 1981).

Hastings, Hugh, ed., *Ecclesiastical Records of the State of New York*, 8 vols. Albany, NY: James B. Lyon, 1901–5.

Hausknecht, Murray, *The Joiners: A Sociological Description of Voluntary Association Membership in the United States*. New York: Bedminster, 1962.

Hay, Samuel A., *African American Theatre: A Historical and Critical Analysis*. Cambridge, UK: Cambridge University Press, 1994.

Haynes, George Edmund, *The Negro at Work in New York City: A Study in Economic Progress*. 1912; New York: AMS Press, 1968.

Heale, M. J., "Patterns of Benevolence: Associated Philanthropy in the Cities of New York, 1830–1860," *New York History* (January 1976).

Heckethorn, Charles William, *The Secret Societies of All Ages and Countries: A Comprehensive Account of Upwards of One Hundred and Sixty Secret Organisations—Religious, Political, and Social—from the Most Remote Ages Down to the Present Time*, 2 vols. New York: New Amsterdam Book Company, 1897.

Henry, Frances, *The Caribbean Diaspora in Toronto: Learning to Live with Racism.* Toronto: University of Toronto Press, 1994.

Herlehy, Thomas J., "Ties That Bind: Palm Wine and Blood-Brotherhood at the Kenya Coast during the 19th Century," *International Journal of African Historical Studies*, Vol. 17, No. 2 (1984).

Hershberg, Theodore, "Free Blacks in Antebellum Philadelphia: A Study of Ex-Slaves, Freeborn, and Socioeconomic Decline," *Journal of Social History* (Winter 1971–72).

Herskovits, Melville J., *The Myth of the Negro Past.* 1941; Boston: Beacon Press, 1990.

Herskovits, Melville J., and Frances S. Herskovits, *Rebel Destiny.* 1934; Freeport, NY: Books for Libraries Press, 1971.

Higginbotham, Evelyn Brooks, *Righteous Discontent: The Women's Movement in the Black Baptist Church, 1880–1920.* Cambridge, MA: Harvard University Press, 1993.

Hill, Christopher, *The World Turned Upside Down: Radical Ideas during the English Revolution.* 1972; London: Penguin, 1991.

Hill, Errol, *Shakespeare in Sable: A History of Black Shakespearean Actors.* Amherst: University of Massachusetts Press, 1984.

Hine, Darlene Clark, and Earnestine Jenkins, eds., *A Question of Manhood: A Reader in U.S. Black Men's History and Masculinity.* Bloomington: Indiana University Press, 1999.

[Hiram Masonic Relief Association], *Annual Report[s] of the Hiram Masonic Relief Association of the State of New York [1893–1901].* Schomburg Collection, NYPL.

———, *Constitution and Laws of the Hiram Masonic Relief Association, of the State of New York. Revised May 31st, 1898. Incorporated under the Law of New York.* New York: Keystone Printing, 1898. Schomburg Collection, NYPL.

Hirsch, Leo H., Jr., "The Negro and New York, 1783 to 1865," *Journal of Negro History*, Vol. 16, No. 4 (October 1931).

[Historical Records Survey, WPA], *Inventory of the Church Archives of New York City: The Methodist Church.* New York: Historical Records Survey, 1940.

Hobsbawm, E. J., *Primitive Rebels: Studies in Archaic Forms of Social Movement in the 19th and 20th Centuries.* New York: Norton, 1959.

———, *Bandits.* New York: Delacorte, 1969.

Hodges, Graham Russell, "Black Revolt in New York City and the Neutral Zone: 1775–83," in Paul A. Gilje and William Pencak, eds., *New York in the Age of the Constitution, 1775–1800.* Rutherford, NJ: Fairleigh Dickinson University Press and the Associated University Presses, 1992.

———, *Root and Branch: African Americans in New York and East Jersey, 1613–1863.* Chapel Hill: University of North Carolina Press, 1999.

Hodges, Willis Augustus, *Free Man of Color: The Autobiography of Willis Augustus*

Hodges, edited with an introduction by Willard B. Gatewood Jr. Knoxville: University of Tennessee Press, 1982.

Holland Society of New York, *New York Historical Manuscripts: Dutch*, Vols. GG, HH, and II. Baltimore: Genealogical Publishing, 1980.

Holt, Thomas C., "Slavery and Freedom in the Atlantic World: Reflections on the Diasporan Framework," in Darlene Clark Hine and Jacqueline McLeod, eds., *Crossing Boundaries: Comparative History of Black People in Diaspora*. Bloomington: Indiana University Press, 1999.

Hood, Bishop J[ames]. W[alker]., D.D., LL.D., *One Hundred Years of the African Methodist Episcopal Zion Church; or, the Centennial of African Methodism*. New York: A.M.E. Zion Book Concern, 1895.

Horsmanden, Daniel, *The New-York Conspiracy, or a History of the Negro Plot, with the Journal of the Proceedings against the Conspirators at New-York in the Years 1741–2*. 1810; New York: Negro Universities Press, 1969.

Horton, James Oliver, *Free People of Color: Inside the African American Community*. Washington, DC: Smithsonian Institution Press, 1993.

Horton, James Oliver, and Lois E. Horton, "Violence, Protest, and Identity: Black Manhood in Antebellum America," in Darlene Clark Hine and Earnestine Jenkins, eds., *A Question of Manhood: A Reader in U.S. Black Men's History and Masculinity*. Bloomington: Indiana University Press, 1999.

Hughes, Langston, and Milton Meltzer, *Black Magic: A Pictorial History of the Negro in American Entertainment*. Englewood Cliffs, NJ: Prentice Hall, 1967.

Hurd, John Cadman, *The Law of Freedom and Bondage in the United States*, 2 vols. 1858; New York: Negro Universities Press, 1968.

Ignatiev, Noel, *How the Irish Became White*. New York: Routledge, 1995.

Irving, Washington, *Diedrich Knickerbocker's A History of New-York*. 1854; Tarrytown, NY: Sleepy Hollow Press, 1981.

Isaac, Rhys, "Evangelical Revolt: The Nature of the Baptists' Challenge to the Traditional Order in Virginia, 1765 to 1775," *William and Mary Quarterly*, Vol. 31, No. 3 (July 1974).

Jacobs, Harriet A., *Incidents in the Life of a Slave Girl, Written by Herself*. 1861; Cambridge, MA: Harvard University Press, 1987.

James, C. L. R., *The Black Jacobins: Toussaint L'Ouverture and the San Domingo Revolution*. 1938; 2nd rev. ed., New York: Vintage, 1963.

James, Winston, *Holding Aloft the Banner of Ethiopia: Caribbean Radicalism in Early Twentieth-Century America*. New York: Verso, 1998.

Jedrej, M. C., "Medicine, Fetish and Secret Society in a West African Culture," *Africa*, Vol. 46, No. 3 (1976).

Jeffreys, M. D. W., "The Nyama Society of the Ibibio Women," *African Studies*, Vol. 15, No. 1 (1956).

Johnson, Kirk A., "The History in 'Dem Bones,'" *Heart and Soul* (February–March 1996).

Johnson, Paul E., *A Shopkeeper's Millennium: Society and Revivals in Rochester, New York, 1815–1837*. New York: Hill and Wang, 1978.

Johnson, James Weldon, *Black Manhattan*. 1930; Salem, NH: Ayer, 1990.

Jones, Thomas, *History of New York during the Revolutionary War, and of the Leading Events in the Other Colonies at That Period*, 2 vols., edited by Edward Floyd de Lancey. New York: For the New-York Historical Society, 1879.

Jordan, Winthrop D., *White over Black: American Attitudes toward the Negro, 1550–1812*. 1968; New York: Norton, 1977.

Joyce, Donald Franklin, *Gatekeepers of Black Culture: Black-Owned Book Publishing in the United States, 1817–1981*. Westport, CT: Greenwood, 1983.

Karasch, Mary C., *Slave Life in Rio de Janeiro, 1808–1850*. Princeton, NJ: Princeton University Press, 1987.

Kent, R. K., "Palmares: An African State in Brazil," *Journal of African History*, Vol. 6, No. 2 (1965).

Kijakazi, Kilolo, *African-American Economic Development and Small Business Ownership*. New York: Garland, 1997.

Knupfer, Anne Meis, *Toward a Tenderer Humanity and a Nobler Womanhood: African American Women's Clubs in Turn-of-the-Century Chicago*. New York: New York University Press, 1996.

Kolchin, Peter, *American Slavery, 1619–1877*. New York: Hill and Wang, 1993.

Kopytoff, Barbara, "The Development of Jamaican Maroon Ethnicity," *Caribbean Quarterly*, Vol. 22, Nos. 2–3 (June–September 1976).

Kuper, Hilda, and Selma Kaplan, "Voluntary Associations in an Urban Township," *African Studies*, Vol. 3, No. 4 (December 1944).

Kupperman, Karen Ordahl, *Providence Island, 1630–1641: The Other Puritan Colony*. New York: Cambridge University Press, 1993.

Laguerre, Michel S., *American Odyssey: Haitians in New York City*. Ithaca, NY: Cornell University Press, 1984.

Lan, David, *Guns and Rain: Guerrillas and Spirit Mediums in Zimbabwe*. Berkeley: University of California Press, 1985.

Landesman, Alter F., *Brownsville: The Birth, Development and Passing of a Jewish Community in New York*. 2nd ed., 1969; New York: Bloch, 1971.

Laurence, K. O., "The Tobago Slave Conspiracy of 1801," *Caribbean Quarterly*, Vol. 28, No. 3 (September 1982).

Lennhoff, Eugen, *The Freemasons: The History, Nature, Development and Secret of the Royal Art*, translated by Einar Frame. New York: Oxford University Press, 1934.

Lincoln, C. Eric, and Lawrence H. Mamiya, *The Black Church in the African American Experience*. Durham, NC: Duke University Press, 1990.

Lindsay, Arnett G., "The Economic Condition of the Negroes of New York Prior to 1861," *Journal of Negro History*, Vol. 6, No. 2 (April 1921).

Little, K[enneth]. L., "The Poro Society as an Arbiter of Culture," *African Studies*, Vol. 7, No. 1 (March 1948).

————, "The Political Function of the Poro" (Part I), *Africa*, Vol. 35, No. 4 (October 1965).

————, "The Political Function of the Poro" (Part II), *Africa*, Vol. 36, No. 1 (January 1966).

Litwack, Leon F., *North of Slavery: The Negro in the Free States, 1790–1860*. Chicago: University of Chicago Press, 1961.

Logan, Rayford W., *Haiti and the Dominican Republic*. New York: Oxford University Press, 1968.

Logan, Rayford W., and Michael R. Winston, eds., *Dictionary of American Negro Biography*. New York: Norton, 1982.

Lyons, Maritcha Remond, "Memories of Yesterdays, All of Which I Saw and Part of Which I Was: An Autobiography." Brooklyn, NY: Unpublished manuscript, ca. 1924. Williams [Lyons] Family Papers, Schomburg Collection, NYPL.

McNaughton, Patrick R., *The Mande Blacksmiths: Knowledge, Power, and Art in West Africa*. Bloomington: Indiana University Press, 1988.

McWilliams, Wilson Carey, *The Idea of Fraternity in America*. Berkeley: University of California Press, 1973.

Magid, Alvin, "Political Traditionalism in Nigeria: A Case-Study of Secret Societies and Dance Groups in Local Government," *Africa*, Vol. 42, No. 4 (October 1972).

Manoni, Mary, *Bedford-Stuyvesant: The Anatomy of a Central City Community*. New York: Quadrangle, 1973.

Marlow, Nicholas, "Bedford-Stuyvesant Place-Names." M.A. thesis, Brooklyn College, 1963.

Marshall, Bernard, "Slave Resistance and White Reaction in the British Windward Islands, 1763–1833," *Caribbean Quarterly*, Vol. 28, No. 3 (September 1982).

Marshall, Herbert, and Mildred Stock, *Ira Aldridge: The Negro Tragedian*. 1958; Washington, DC: Howard University Press, 1993.

Marshall, Paule, *Brown Girl, Brownstones*. 1959; New York: Feminist Press, 1981.

Marx, Karl, and Frederick Engels, *Karl Marx and Frederick Engels: Collected Works*. New York: International Publishers, 1975.

Mather, Cotton, *Bonifacius: An Essay upon the Good, That Is to Be Devised and Designed by Those Who Desire to Answer the Great End of Life, and to Do Good While They Live*. Boston: B. Green, 1710.

————, "Rules for the Society of Negroes, 1693," in Thomas James Holmes, *Cotton Mather: A Bibliography of His Works*, 3 vols. Cambridge, MA: Harvard University Press, 1940.

Mathews, Donald G., *Slavery and Methodism: A Chapter in American Morality, 1780–1845*. Princeton, NJ: Princeton University Press, 1965.

Matthews, Donald H., *Honoring the Ancestors: An African Cultural Interpretation of Black Religion and Literature.* New York: Oxford University Press, 1998.

Miller, Perry, *The New England Mind: The Seventeenth Century.* 1939; Cambridge, MA: Harvard University Press, 1982.

Mintz, Sidney W., and Richard Price, *The Birth of African-American Culture: An Anthropological Perspective.* 1976; Boston: Beacon, 1992.

Mitchel, John Purroy, Mayor of New York City, "The Public Schools of New York," in *The Crisis: A Record of the Darker Races* (July 1917).

Morgan, Edmund S., *The Puritan Dilemma: The Story of John Winthrop.* Boston: Little, Brown, 1958.

———, *Visible Saints: The History of a Puritan Idea.* 1963; Ithaca, NY: Cornell University Press, 1965.

———, ed., *The Diary of Michael Wigglesworth, 1653–1657.* New York: Harper Torchbooks, 1946.

Morris, Ira K., *Morris's Memorial History of Staten Island, New York.* 2 vols. West New Brighton, Staten Island, NY: Privately printed, 1900.

Moses, Wilson Jeremiah, *The Golden Age of Black Nationalism, 1850–1925.* New York: Oxford University Press, 1978.

———, *Alexander Crummell: A Study of Civilization and Discontent.* Amherst: University of Massachusetts Press, 1992.

Moss, Richard Shannon, *Slavery on Long Island: A Study of Local Institutional and Early African-American Communal Life.* New York: Garland, 1993.

Mullin, Michael, *Africa in America: Slave Acculturation and Resistance in the American South and the British Caribbean, 1736–1831.* Urbana: University of Illinois Press, 1992.

Muraskin, William Alan, "Black Masons: The Role of Fraternal Orders in the Creation of a Middle-Class Black Community." Ph.D. dissertation, University of California, Berkeley, 1970.

———, *Middle-Class Blacks in a White Society: Prince Hall Freemasonry in America.* Berkeley: University of California Press, 1975.

Murphy, William P., "Secret Knowledge as Property and Power in Kpelle Society: Elders versus Youth," *Africa,* Vol. 50, No. 2 (1980).

Murphy, William P., and Caroline H. Bledsoe, "Kinship and Territory in the History of a Kpelle Chiefdom (Liberia)," in Igor Kopytoff, ed., *The African Frontier: The Reproduction of Traditional African Societies.* Bloomington: Indiana University Press, 1987.

Musambachime, Mwelwa C., "The Ubutwa Society in Eastern Shaba and Northeast Zambia to 1920," *International Journal of African Historical Studies,* Vol. 27, No. 1 (1994).

Myrdal, Gunnar, et al., *An American Dilemma: The Negro Problem and Modern Democracy.* 1944; New York: Harper and Row, 1962.

Nash, Gary B., *Race, Class, and Politics: Essays on Colonial and Revolutionary Society.* Urbana: University of Illinois Press, 1986.

Nell, William C., *The Colored Patriots of the American Revolution.* New York: Arno, 1968.

Neverdon-Morton, Cynthia, *Afro-American Women of the South and the Advancement of the Race, 1895–1925.* Knoxville: University of Tennessee Press, 1989.

Newton, Rev. John, *Letters and Conversational Remarks, by the Late Reverend John Newton, Rector of St. Mary Woolnoth, Lombard Street, London,* edited by John Campbell. New York: S. Whiting, 1811.

———, *The Journal of a Slave Trader, 1750–1754, with Newton's Thoughts upon the African Slave Trade,* edited by Bernard Martin and Mark Spurrell. London: Epworth, 1962.

Newton, Rev. John, and Rev. Richard Cecil, *The Life of the Reverend John Newton, Rector of St. Mary Woolnoth, London. Written by Himself to* A.D. *1763, and Continued to His Death in 1807, by Rev. Richard Cecil, Minister of St. John's Chapel, London.* New York: American Tract Society, ca. 1850.

Newton, Joseph Fort, *The Builders: A Story and Study of Freemasonry.* New York: Macoy Publishing and Masonic Supply, 1930.

Nicholson, Norman, *William Cowper.* London: Longmans, 1960.

Niebuhr, H. Richard, *The Kingdom of God in America.* Hamden, CT: Shoe String Press, 1956.

Oates, Stephen B., *To Purge This Land with Blood: A Biography of John Brown.* New York: Harper and Row, 1970.

Officer, Debbie, "Last Rites," *African Voices* (March 1994).

Olson, Edwin, "The Slave Code in Colonial New York," *Journal of Negro History,* Vol. 29, No. 2 (April 1944).

O'Neale, Sondra A., *Jupiter Hammon and the Biblical Beginnings of African-American Literature.* Metuchen, NJ: American Theological Library Association and the Scarecrow Press, 1993.

Osofsky, Gilbert, *Harlem: The Making of a Ghetto: Negro New York, 1890–1930,* 2nd ed. New York: Harper Torchbooks, 1971.

Outler, Albert C., ed., *John Wesley.* New York: Oxford University Press, 1964.

Ovington, Mary White, *Half A Man: The Status of the Negro in New York.* 1911; New York: Schocken Books, 1969.

———, *The Walls Came Tumbling Down.* 1947; New York: Arno, 1969.

Odum, Howard W., *Social and Mental Traits of the Negro.* New York: Columbia University Press, 1910.

Owens, Leslie Howard, *This Species of Property: Slave Life and Culture in the Old South.* New York: Oxford University Press, 1976.

Ownby, David, *Brotherhoods and Secret Societies in Early and Mid-Qing China: The Formation of a Tradition.* Stanford, CA: Stanford University Press, 1996.

Ownby, David, et al., eds., *"Secret Societies" Reconsidered: Perspectives on the Social History of Modern South China and Southeast Asia.* Armonk, NY: M. E. Sharpe, 1993.

Parker, Percy Livingstone, ed., *The Heart of John Wesley's Journal.* New York: Fleming H. Revell, 1903.

Parrinder, Geoffrey, *West African Religion: A Study of the Beliefs and Practices of Akan, Ewe, Yoruba, Ibo, and Kindred Peoples.* 1949; New York: Barnes and Noble, 1969.

Patterson, Orlando, *The Sociology of Slavery: An Analysis of the Origins, Development and Structure of Negro Slave Society in Jamaica.* London: Macgibbon and Kee, 1967.

Payne, Daniel A., *History of the African Methodist Episcopal Church*, edited by Rev. C. S. Smith. 1891; New York: Arno, 1969.

Perlman, Daniel, "Organizations of the Free Negro in New York City, 1800–1860," *Journal of Negro History*, Vol. 56 (1971).

Perry, Lewis, *Radical Abolitionism: Anarchy and the Government of God in Antislavery Thought.* Ithaca, NY: Cornell University Press, 1973.

Phillips, Christopher, *Freedom's Port: The African American Community of Baltimore, 1790–1860.* Urbana: University of Illinois Press, 1997.

Phillips, Ruth B., "Masking in Mende and Sande Society Initiation Rituals," *Africa*, Vol. 48, No. 3 (1978).

Piersen, William D., *Black Yankees: The Development of an Afro-American Subculture in Eighteenth-Century New England.* Amherst: University of Massachusetts Press, 1988.

———, *Black Legacy: America's Hidden Heritage.* Amherst: University of Massachusetts Press, 1993.

Pointer, Richard W., *Protestant Pluralism and the New York Experience: A Study of Eighteenth-Century Religious Diversity.* Bloomington: Indiana University Press, 1988.

Pomerantz, Sidney I., *New York: An American City, 1783–1803.* New York: Columbia University Press, 1938.

Porter, Dorothy B., "David Ruggles, an Apostle of Human Rights," *Journal of Negro History*, Vol. 28, No. 1 (January 1943).

Powell, A. Clayton, Sr., *Against the Tide: An Autobiography.* New York: Richard R. Smith, 1938.

Powell, J. H., *Bring Out Your Dead: The Great Plague of Yellow Fever in Philadelphia in 1793.* 1949; New York: Time Reading Program, 1965.

Priestman, Martin, *Cowper's Task: Structure and Influence.* Cambridge, UK: Cambridge University Press, 1983.

Quarles, Benjamin, *The Negro in the American Revolution.* Chapel Hill: University of North Carolina Press, 1961.

———, ed., *Blacks on John Brown.* Urbana: University of Illinois Press, 1972.

Raboteau, Albert J., *Slave Religion: The "Invisible Institution" in the Antebellum South*. 1978; New York: Oxford University Press, 1980.

———, *A Fire in the Bones: Reflections on African-American Religious History*. Boston: Beacon, 1995.

Reis, João José, *Slave Rebellion in Brazil: The Muslim Uprising of 1835 in Bahia*, translated by Arthur Brakel. 1986; Baltimore: Johns Hopkins University Press, 1993.

Richardson, Marilyn, ed., *Maria W. Stewart: America's First Black Woman Political Writer*. Bloomington: Indiana University Press, 1987.

Riddell, William Renwick, "The Slave in Early New York," *Journal of Negro History*, Vol. 13, No. 1 (January 1928).

Riker, James Jr., *The Annals of Newtown, in Queens County, New-York: Containing Its History from Its Earliest Settlement, Together with Many Interesting Facts Concerning the Adjacent Towns; Also, A Particular Account of Numerous Long Island Families Now Spread over This and Various Other States of the Union*. New York: D. Fanshaw, 1852.

Ripley, C. Peter et al., eds., *The Black Abolitionist Papers*, 5 vols. Chapel Hill: University of North Carolina Press, 1991.

Roberts, J. M., *The Mythology of Secret Societies*. New York: Charles Scribner's Sons, 1972.

Robinson, Carey, *The Fighting Maroons of Jamaica*. Jamaica: William Collins and Sangster, 1969.

Rock, Howard B., ed., *The New York City Artisan, 1789–1825: A Documentary History*. Albany: State University of New York Press, 1989.

Roff, Sandra Shoiock, "The Brooklyn African Woolman Benevolent Society Rediscovered," *Afro-Americans in New York Life and History*, Vol. 10, No. 2 (July 1986).

Rogerson, Idonia Elizabeth, comp., *Historical Synopsis of the Woman's Home and Foreign Missionary Society, African Methodist Episcopal Zion Church*. Charlotte, NC: A.M.E. Zion Publishing House, 1967.

Rosenzweig, Roy, and Elizabeth Blackmar, *The Park and the People: A History of Central Park*. 1992; New York: Henry Holt, 1994.

Rotundo, E. Anthony, *American Manhood: Transformations in Masculinity from the Revolution to the Modern Era*. New York: Basic Books, 1993.

Rudolph, L. C., *Francis Asbury*. Nashville, TN: Abingdon Press, 1966.

Rury, John L., "Philanthropy, Self Help, and Social Control: The New York Manumission Society and Free Blacks, 1785–1810," *Phylon: The Atlanta University Review of Race and Culture*, Vol. 46, No. 3 (1985).

Rush, Christopher (with George Collins), *A Short Account of the Rise and Progress of the African Methodist Episcopal Church in America*. New York: Privately printed, 1843.

Russell-Wood, A. J. R., "Black and Mulatto Brotherhoods in Colonial Brazil: A

Study in Collective Behavior," *Hispanic American Historical Review* (November 1974).

Schor, Joel, *Henry Highland Garnet: A Voice of Black Radicalism in the Nineteenth Century*. Westport, CT: Greenwood, 1977.

Schutte, A. G., "Thapelo Ya Sephiri: A Study of Secret Prayer Groups in Soweto," *African Studies*, Vol. 31, No. 4 (1972).

Scott, Kenneth, "The Slave Insurrection in New York in 1712," *New-York Historical Society Quarterly* (January 1961).

Scott, Rebecca J., *Slave Emancipation in Cuba: The Transition to Free Labor, 1860–1899*. Princeton, NJ: Princeton University Press, 1985.

Seabury, Samuel, *A Discourse Delivered in St. James' Church, in New-London, on Tuesday the 23d of December, 1794: Before an Assembly of Free and Accepted Masons, Convened for the Purpose of Installing a Lodge in That City*. New London, CT: Brother Samuel Green, 1795.

Seaman, Samuel A., A.M., *Annals of New York Methodism: Being a History of the Methodist Episcopal Church in the City of New York from A.D. 1766 to A.D. 1890*. New York: Hunt and Eaton, 1892.

Selyns, Henricus, *Records of Domine Henricus Selyns of New York, 1686–7, with Notes and Remarks by Garret Abeel Written a Century Later, 1791–2*. New York: Holland Society of New York, 1916.

Semmel, Bernard, *The Methodist Revolution*. New York: Basic Books, 1973.

Shields, John C., ed., *The Collected Works of Phillis Wheatley*. New York: Oxford University Press, 1988.

Siebert, Wilbur H., *The Underground Railroad from Slavery to Freedom*. New York: Macmillan, 1898.

[Simmel, Georg], *The Sociology of Georg Simmel*, translated, edited, and with an introduction by Kurt H. Wolff. New York: Free Press, 1950.

Simmons, Rev. William J., D.D., *Men of Mark: Eminent, Progressive and Rising*. 1887; New York: Arno, 1968.

Simms, Rev. James M., *The First Colored Baptist Church in North America, Constituted at Savannah, Georgia, January 20, A.D. 1788, with Biographical Sketches of the Pastors*. 1888; New York: Negro Universities Press, 1969.

Sipkins, Henry, a descendant of Africa, *An Oration on the Abolition of the Slave Trade, Delivered in the African Church in the City of New-York, January 2, 1809*. Schomburg Collection, NYPL.

Smith, Edward D., *Climbing Jacob's Ladder: The Rise of Black Churches in Eastern American Cities, 1740–1877*. Washington, DC: Smithsonian Institution Press, 1988.

Smith, James McCune, M.A., M.D., "Toussaint L'Ouverture and the Haytian Revolutions," in Alice Moore Dunbar, ed., *Masterpieces of Negro Eloquence: The Best Speeches Delivered by the Negro from the Days of Slavery to the Present Time*. New York: Bookery Publishing Company, 1914.

Sobel, Mechal, *The World They Made Together: Black and White Values in Eighteenth-Century Virginia*. Princeton, NJ: Princeton University Press, 1987.

[Society for Mitigating and Gradually Abolishing the State of Slavery throughout the British Dominions], *Substance of the Debate in the House of Commons, on the 15th May, 1823, on a Motion for the Mitigation and Gradual Abolition of Slavery throughout the British Dominions*. 1823; New York: Negro Universities Press, 1969.

Soderlund, Jean R., *Quakers and Slavery: A Divided Spirit*. Princeton, NJ: Princeton University Press, 1985.

Stanfield, James Field, Late a Mariner in the African Slave Trade, *Observations on a Guinea Voyage. In a Series of Letters Addressed to the Rev. Thomas Clarkson*. London: James Phillips, 1788.

Staudenraus, P. J., *The African Colonization Movement, 1816–1865*. New York: Columbia University Press, 1961.

Sterling, Dorothy, ed., *We Are Your Sisters: Black Women in the Nineteenth Century*. New York: Norton, 1984.

Stevens, Abel, *The History of the Religious Movement of the Eighteenth Century, Called Methodism, Considered in Its Different Denominational Forms, and Its Relations to British and American Protestantism*, 3 vols. New York: Carlton and Porter, 1858–61.

Stevenson, David, *The Origins of Freemasonry: Scotland's Century, 1590–1710*. Cambridge, UK: Cambridge University Press, 1988.

Stiles, Henry R., *A History of the City of Brooklyn, Including the Old Town and Village of Brooklyn, the Town of Bushwick, and the Village and City of Williamsburgh*, 3 vols. Brooklyn, NY: Privately printed, 1867–70.

Stott, Richard B., *Workers in the Metropolis: Class, Ethnicity, and Youth in Antebellum New York City*. Ithaca, NY: Cornell University Press, 1990.

Stuckey, Sterling, *Slave Culture: Nationalist Theory and the Foundations of Black America*. New York: Oxford University Press, 1987.

Sudbury, Julia, *"Other Kinds of Dreams": Black Women's Organizations and the Politics of Transformation*. London: Routledge, 1998.

The Survey, *The Negro in the Cities of the North*. New York: Charity Organization Society, 1905.

Sutphen, Rev. David S., *Historical Discourse, Delivered on the 18th of October, 1877, at the Celebration of the Two Hundredth Anniversary of the Dutch Reformed Church of New Utrecht, L.I., and an Historical Address, by Hon. Teunis G. Bergen*. Brooklyn, NY: Privately published, 1877.

Suttles, William C., Jr., "African Religious Survivals as Factors in American Slave Revolts," *Journal of Negro History*, Vol. 56, No. 2 (April 1971).

Swan, Robert J., "John Teasman: African-American Educator and the Emergence of Community in Early Black New York City, 1787–1815," *Journal of the Early Republic* (Fall 1992).

Sweet, William Warren, *Methodism in American History*. New York: Abingdon, 1933.

Tarry, Ellen, *The Other Toussaint: A Modern Biography of Pierre Toussaint, a Post-Revolutionary Black*. Boston: Daughters of St. Paul, 1981.

Taylor, Clarence, *The Black Churches of Brooklyn*. New York: Columbia University Press, 1994.

Teasman, John, *An Address Delivered in the African Episcopal Church, on the 25th March, 1811. Before the New York African Society, for Mutual Relief; Being the First Anniversary of Its Incorporation*. New York: J. Low, 1811. Schomburg Collection, NYPL.

Teborg-Penn, Rosalyn, *African American Women in the Struggle for the Vote, 1850–1920*. Bloomington: Indiana University Press, 1998.

Thompson, E. P., *The Making of the English Working Class*. 1963; New York: Vintage, 1966.

Thornton, John, *Africa and Africans in the Making of the Atlantic World, 1400–1800*. 1992; Cambridge, UK: Cambridge University Press, 1998.

Truth, Sojourner, *Narrative of Sojourner Truth; A Bondwoman of Olden Time, with a History of Her Labors and Correspondence Drawn from Her "Book of Life."* 1850; New York: Oxford University Press, 1991.

Turner, Howard H., *Turner's History of the Independent Order of Good Samaritans and Daughters of Samaria, Together with a Concise History of the Ancient Samarians as Spoken of in the Bible*. Washington, DC: R. A. Waters, 1881.

Tyson, John R., ed., *Charles Wesley: A Reader*. New York: Oxford University Press, 1989.

Upham, Dr. Francis Bourne, Pastor, *The Story of the Old John Street Methodist Episcopal Church, 1766–1932*. New York: Privately printed, 1932.

[Van Cleef, Frank L.], "Marriage Fees; Deaths; Members and Other Miscellaneous Matter Culled from the Records of the Reformed Protestant Dutch Church of the Town of Flatbush, Kings Co., New York," translated by Frank L. Van Cleef. Unpublished typescript, Brooklyn, 1915.

Van Deburg, William L., ed., *Modern Black Nationalism: From Marcus Garvey to Louis Farrakhan*. New York: New York University Press, 1997.

[Vogelsang, Peter], a Member, *An Address Delivered before the New-York African Society for Mutual Relief, in the African Zion Church, 23d March, 1815, Being the Fifth Anniversary of Their Incorporation*. New York: Printed for the Society, 1815. Collection of the New-York Historical Society.

Von Eschen, Penny M., *Race against Empire: Black Americans and Anticolonialism, 1937–1957*. Ithaca, NY: Cornell University Press, 1997.

Voorhis, Harold Van Buren, *Negro Masonry in the United States*. New York: Henry Emmerson, 1949.

Wakeley, Rev. J. B., *Lost Chapters Recovered from the Early History of American Methodism*. New York: Privately printed, 1858.

Walker, David, *David Walker's Appeal, in Four Articles; Together with a Preamble, to the Coloured Citizens of the World, but in Particular, and Very Expressly, to Those of the United States of America*, edited with an introduction by Charles M. Wiltse. 1829; New York: Hill and Wang, 1965.

Walker, George E., *The Afro-American in New York City, 1827–1860*. New York: Garland, 1993.

Wallace, Anthony F. C., *Rockdale: The Growth of an American Village in the Early Industrial Revolution*. 1972; New York: Norton, 1980.

Waller, Henry D., *History of the Town of Flushing, Long Island, New York*. Flushing, NY: J. H. Ridenour, 1899.

Walls, William J., *The African Methodist Episcopal Zion Church: Reality of the Black Church*. Charlotte, NC: A.M.E. Zion Publishing House, 1974.

Ward, Samuel Ringgold, *Autobiography of a Fugitive Negro: His Anti-Slavery Labours in the United States, Canada, and England*. London: John Snow, 1855.

Warriner, Rev. Edwin, *Old Sands Street Methodist Episcopal Church, of Brooklyn, N.Y., an Illustrated Centennial Record, Historical and Biographical*. New York: Phillips and Hunt, 1885.

Washington, Booker T., *The Story of the Negro Race: The Rise of the Race from Slavery*, 2 vols. 1909; New York: Negro Universities Press, 1969.

Washington, Joseph R., Jr., *Black Religion: The Negro and Christianity in the United States*. Boston: Beacon, 1964.

———, *Black Sects and Cults*. Garden City, NY: Doubleday, 1972.

Watkins-Owens, Irma, *Blood Relations: Caribbean Immigrants and the Harlem Community, 1900–1930*. Bloomington: Indiana University Press, 1996.

Weber, Max, *The Protestant Ethic and the Spirit of Capitalism*. 1930; New York: Routledge, 1992.

Webster, Nesta H., *Secret Societies and Subversive Movements*, 2nd ed. London: Boswell Printing, 1924.

Weisenfeld, Judith, *African American Women and Christian Activism: New York's Black YWCA, 1905–1945*. Cambridge, MA: Harvard University Press, 1997.

Welch, Herbert, ed., *Selections from the Writings of the Rev. John Wesley, M.A.* New York: Abingdon, 1918.

Wesley, Charles H., "The Negroes of New York in the Emancipation Movement," *Journal of Negro History*, Vol. 24, No. 1 (January 1939).

———, *History of the Improved Benevolent and Protective Order of Elks of the World, 1898–1954*. Washington, DC: Association for the Study of Negro Life and History, 1955.

Wesley, John, A.M., *Thoughts upon Slavery*, in *A Collection of Religious Tracts*. Philadelphia: Joseph Crukshank, 1773.

Wherry, Rev. E. M., D.D., comp., *Woman in Missions: Papers and Addresses Presented at the Woman's Congress of Missions, October 2–4, 1893, in the Hall of Columbus, Chicago*. New York: American Tract Society, 1894.

White, Deborah Gray, *Too Heavy a Load: Black Women in Defense of Themselves, 1894–1994*. New York: Norton, 1999.

White, Shane, *Somewhat More Independent: The End of Slavery in New York City, 1770–1810*. Athens: University of Georgia Press, 1991.

Wiggins, Rosaline Cobb, ed., *Captain Paul Cuffe's Logs and Letters, 1808–1817: A Black Quaker's "Voice from within the Veil."* Washington, DC: Howard University Press, 1996.

Wilder, Craig Steven, "A Covenant with Color: Race and the History of Brooklyn, New York." Ph.D. dissertation, Columbia University, 1994.

———, "The Rise and Influence of the New York African Society for Mutual Relief, 1808–1865," *Afro-Americans in New York Life and History* (July 1998).

———, "'The Guardian Angel of Africa': A Financial History of the New York African Society for Mutual Relief, 1808–1945," *Afro-Americans in New York Life and History* (forthcoming).

Wilken, Robert L., *The Christians as the Romans Saw Them*. New Haven, CT: Yale University Press, 1984.

Williams, E. A., S. W. Green, and Jos. L. Jones, *History and Manual of the Colored Knights of Pythias*. Nashville, TN: National Baptist Publication Board, 1917.

Williams, George G., *History of the Negro Race in America, from 1619 to 1880*, 2 vols. New York: G. P. Putnam's Sons, 1883.

———, "The Religious Background of the Idea of a Loyal Opposition: A Protestant Contribution to the Theory and Practice of Ecumenical Dialogue," in D. B. Robertson, ed., *Voluntary Associations: A Study of Groups in Free Societies: Essays in Honor of James Luther Adams*. Richmond, VA: John Knox Press, 1966.

Williams, Loretta J., *Black Freemasonry and Middle-Class Realities*. Columbia: University of Missouri Press, 1980.

Williams, Peter Jr., *An Oration on the Abolition of the Slave Trade; Delivered in the African Church in the City of New York, January 1, 1808*. New York: Samuel Wood, 1808. Schomburg Collection, NYPL.

———, *Discourse Delivered on the Death of Capt. Paul Cuffe, before the New-York African Institution, in the African Methodist Episcopal Zion Church, October 21, 1817*. New York: African Institution, 1817. Schomburg Collection, NYPL.

Williams, T. Desmond, ed., *Secret Societies in Ireland*. New York: Barnes and Noble, 1973.

Williams-Myers, A. J., "The African Presence in the Hudson River Valley: The Defining of Relationships between the Masters and the Slaves," *Afro-Americans in New York Life and History*, Vol. 12, No. 1 (January 1988).

Williamson, Harry A., "A History of Freemasonry among the American Negroes." New York: Unpublished manuscript, 1929. Schomburg Collection, NYPL.

———, *The Story of the Carthaginian Lodge, No. 47, F. & A. M.* Brooklyn, NY: Carthaginian Study Club, 1949.

————, "Folks in Old New York and Brooklyn." Bronx, NY: Unpublished manuscript, July 1953. Schomburg Collection, NYPL.

————, "Arthur A. Schomburg, the Freemason." New York: Unpublished lecture, undated. Schomburg Collection, NYPL.

Wills, David W., and Richard Newman, eds., *Black Apostles at Home and Abroad: Afro-Americans and the Christian Mission from the Revolution to Reconstruction*. Boston: G. K. Hall, 1982.

Wilson, Charles B., *The Official Manual and History of the Grand United Order of Odd Fellows in America. Authorized by the Third B.M.C., and Approved and Published by the Sub-Committee of Management*. Philadelphia: George F. Lasher, 1894.

Wilson, Joseph T., *The Black Phalanx: A History of the Negro Soldiers of the United States in the Wars of 1775–1812, 1861–'65*. 1890; New York: Arno, 1968.

Winch, Julie, *Philadelphia's Black Elite: Activism, Accommodation, and the Struggle for Autonomy, 1787–1848*. Philadelphia: Temple University Press, 1988.

Wood, Forrest G., *The Arrogance of Faith: Christianity and Race in America from the Colonial Era to the Twentieth Century*. New York: Knopf, 1990.

Woodson, Carter G., *The History of the Negro Church*. 1921; Washington, DC: Associated Publishers, 1945.

————, *The Negro in Our History*. 1922; Washington, DC: Associated Publishers, 1941.

————, *The Negro Professional Man and the Community, with Special Emphasis on the Physician and the Lawyer*. 1934; New York: Negro Universities Press, 1969.

————, *The African Background Outlined, or Handbook for the Study of the Negro*. 1936; New York: Negro Universities Press, 1968.

————, ed., *The Mind of the Negro as Reflected in Letters Written during the Crisis 1800–1860*. Washington, DC: Association for the Study of Negro Life and History, 1926.

Woolman, John, *The Journal of John Woolman*. Boston: Houghton Mifflin, 1871.

Worrall, Arthur J., *Quakers in the Colonial Northeast*. Hanover, NH: University Press of New England, 1980.

Wright, Philip, "War and Peace with the Maroons, 1730–1739," *Caribbean Quarterly*, Vol. 16, No. 1 (March 1970).

Wright, Bishop R. R. Jr., *The Bishops of the African Methodist Episcopal Church*. Nashville, TN: A.M.E. Sunday School Union, 1963.

Yoshpe, Harry B., "Record of Slave Manumissions in New York During the Colonial and Early National Periods," *Journal of Negro History*, Vol. 26, No. 1 (January 1941).

Zamora, Emilio, *The World of the Mexican Worker in Texas*. College Station: Texas A & M University Press, 1993.

Zuille, John J., *Historical Sketch of the New York African Society for Mutual Relief*. New York: Privately printed, 1893.

Index

Abolitionists, 56, 88, 91, 93, 94, 96, 106, 107, 126, 136, 143, 145, 146, 148, 150, 153, 164, 166, 167–71, 173, 201, 263–65n; Civil War-era activities of, 182–83, 271n

Abyssinian Baptist Church (Manhattan), 48–49, 132, 166, 194, 209, 211, 275n; woman dominance in, 48–49; women's Highway and Hedges Society, 217

Abyssinian Benevolent Daughters of Esther Association, 75, 87

Africa, 3, 9, 30, 57, 60–61, 63, 76, 80, 132, 182, 265n; in African American ideology, 73, 76–78, 89–92, 96, 156, 157–59, 160–64, 168, 173, 177, 186, 187–89, 240–41n; Central, 13, 226n; compared to Greece and Rome, 90; Gold Coast, 19; religions of, 25, 26, 30–31, 65, 226n; West, 12, 16, 20–21, 22, 23, 25, 26, 27, 30–31, 33, 62, 65, 70, 76, 86, 116, 123, 199, 200–201, 217, 221n; in white thought, 144

African Americans, 36, 54, 62; attacks upon, 181, 183–85; celebrations and parades among, 89, 105, 111, 120–23, 126, 132, 164, 182–83, 254n; charity among, 80, 87–88, 103–4, 108, 111, 124–29, 201, 205; community, 2, 4, 24, 29–30, 40, 52–53, 63–64, 81, 86, 87, 97, 101–5, 112, 116, 118, 121, 124, 125, 129, 133, 149, 151–52, 158, 194, 207, 209; descriptions of, 145; high society among, 187; ideologies of, 24–25, 41, 54–55, 64, 65, 68, 73, 76–80, 81–83, 86–87, 89–97, 109–10, 121–24, 129, 131, 133, 147, 155–66, 167–71, 176–78, 187, 197, 200, 263n; immigrant communities among, 76, 87, 187, 205; institutions among, 4, 36, 53, 73, 76, 87, 88–89, 93, 95, 103, 118–19,

123, 125, 128–29, 131, 136, 138–40, 154–55, 183–86, 186, 192, 199, 209, 215; protests by, 77, 110, 119, 157–61, 165–67, 172, 186, 206; in South, 177; women's social work among, 212–17; youth, 66, 69, 81, 87, 120–21, 123–26, 128–29, 130, 131, 138, 142, 149, 150, 151, 164, 183, 184, 195, 208, 212, 216, 217

African Baptist Church (Nantucket), 37

African Benevolent Society (Newport), 53

African Bethel Church (Baltimore), 37

African Bible Society of New York, 113, 129

African Blood Brotherhood, 2, 204–5

African Burial Ground (Manhattan), 33, 228–29n

African Civilization Society (Manhattan), 173–74, 176

African Diaspora, 3, 22, 25, 27–29, 30–31, 32, 38, 83, 110–11, 116, 123, 155–56, 168, 232n

African Dorcas Association (Manhattan), 127, 128, 135

African Education and Civilization Society, 144

African Female Bible Society of New York, 129

African Free Meeting Methodist Society. *See* Union Society (Manhattan)

African Greys (Providence), 121

African Improvement Society (New Haven), 235n

Africanisms, 9–12, 23, 24–25, 167, 199, 220–21n; in burial and funerary rituals, 32–34, 36, 65, 229n; defined, 3, 9; in religious culture, 23, 25, 30–31, 32–34, 36, 38–40, 65, 217, 232n; in South Carolina Sea Islands, 13, 37–38

African Meeting House (Boston), 37, 113, 116

Black church *(continued)*
toward, 49; women's clubs in, 214;
women's dominance in, 45, 48–49, 129,
232n; women's dominance in postbellum mission work, 212–17
Blackett, R. J. M., 146
Black nationalism, 70, 76–78, 82, 87, 88, 89,
103, 131, 154, 157–59, 170–71, 177, 201,
204, 240–41n; decline of African symbolism in, 157–59, 162–63; defined, 73,
155–56; masculinity and, 168; and the
National Colored Conventions, 161–65,
167–71; the NYASMR's post–Civil War
rejection of, 187–89; and political radi-
calism, 166
"Black Revolt," 30
Blood oaths, 18, 19, 20, 23, 26, 27, 28, 224n
Blue, Moses, 254n
Boston, 115, 116, 121, 128, 134–35, 148,
149, 214; and National Colored Conven-
tions, 165
Boston African Society, 37, 53, 113, 116
Boston Female Antislavery Society, 170
Boston Massacre, 116
Boston News-Letter, 17
Boston Philomathean Society, 130
Boukman (Haitian high priest), 28
Boulé, 207, 210
Bounty hunters. *See* Slave catchers
Bowdoin College, 135, 140
Bowles, Eva, 216
Boyer, Jean Pierre, 113
Boyer Grand Lodge of New York State
(Masonic), 113–15; dependence on
NYASMR, 114–15; lodges warranted
under, 114; relationship to the black
church, 210–11
Boyer Lodge No. 1 in the City of New York
(Masonic), 74, 111–16, 117, 132, 139; de-
pendence on NYASMR, 114; relationship
to the black church, 210–11
Boyer Masonic Hall (Manhattan), 114, 156;
lodge room, 149, 157
Bracey, John, Jr., 73, 155, 162
Brazil, 19, 28–29, 83; African confraternities and black Catholic brotherhoods of,
14, 32–33, 38, 83, 123; Angolan brotherhood of Our Lady of Belem, 33; Bahia,
28; Congolese brotherhood of St. Philip
and St. James, 33; *maltas*, 28; maroons

in, 28; Mina, 83; Nazaré, 28; Palmares,
16, 20; Rio de Janeiro, 28, 33, 38, 123;
War for Independence, 28
Bridge Street A.W.M.E. Church (Brook-
lyn), 37, 182, 193, 203, 215
Briggs, Cyril, 204
British Committee for the Abolition of the
Slave Trade, 105
Broadway Tabernacle (Manhattan), 107,
137, 139, 145, 265n
Bronx, the, 216
Brooklyn (Kings County), 1, 14, 15, 23, 34,
59, 88, 121, 127, 151, 158, 172, 177, 182,
188, 191, 192, 194, 196–97, 203, 205, 206,
207, 208–9, 213, 268n; Bedford-
Stuyvesant, 102, 196; black neighbor-
hoods in, 102; black women's clubs in,
213–16; Carleton YMCA, 271n,
277–78n; "Crow Hill," 102; Crown
Heights, 102; during and after Draft
Riots, 181, 183, 186; evangelicalism in,
41; first black churches in, 49–50, 51;
Irish benevolent societies in, 108; Jewish
benevolent societies in, 280n; maroons
in, 16; settlement houses, 215;
Sheepshead Bay, 207; Underground Rail-
road in, 166
Brooklyn African Tompkins Association,
75, 86, 93, 162
Brooklyn African Woolman Benevolent
Society, 37, 74, 87, 88, 93, 102, 122, 131,
265n; and Brooklyn's black schools, 127,
208–9; and the founding of Bridge Street
Church, 49–50; influence of the
NYASMR, 245n; meeting hall, 158; polit-
ical actions of, 158, 162, 166–67
Brooklyn Board of Education, 140, 208–9
Brooklyn College of Pharmacy, 140
Brooklyn Home for Aged Colored People,
277n
Brooklyn Literary Union, 81, 212, 214
Brooklyn Lodge, No. 32, B.P.O.E., 208
Brooklyn Temperance Association, 88, 265n
Brotz, Howard, 155
Brown, Abraham, 162
Brown, Charles, 84
Brown, Henry, 162
Brown, Reverend James, 211
Brown, Dr. John (black activist), 139, 148,
243n

Mayor's Housing Committee (New York), 195

M'Caine, Reverend Alexander, 50

McEwen, James, 83

McKinney, Reverend William, 191

McMurray, Reverend George W., 197

Medford, Clarence, 197

Meier, August, 73, 155, 162

Memphis, 214

Memphis Riots, 194

Men's Aid Society, No. 1, Sheepshead Bay, Brooklyn, 207

Methodist Antislavery Society (Manhattan), 45

Methodist Episcopal church, 32, 34, 37, 40, 46, 47, 49, 52, 55, 85, 132; and antislavery, 41–42, 45, 56–59, 62; British, 40, 106; in Brooklyn, 49–50; in the Caribbean, 232n; development of the system, 40; divisions over slavery, 107; impact on labor, 55–59; in Manhattan, 41, 44, 45, 49; Northern, 45; overrepresentation of black people in New York and Brooklyn churches, 45, 49–50; racism within the, 45–46, 47, 49–50; rise of the black denominations, 50–51, 59; Southern, 41, 45; woman dominance in black Methodism, 45, 49; woman dominance in black missions, 213

Metropolitan Hall (Manhattan), 172

Mexico City, slave revolts, 27

Miller, Emma, 84, 243n

Miller, Reverend George Frazier, 191, 192, 194, 276n

Miller, Perry, 72

Miller, Reverend Thomas, 86, 129, 232n; and the founding of Mother Zion, 45, 46, 47

Miller, Bishop William, 85, 126, 129, 132, 161, 254n; and the founding of the A.M.E.Z. denomination, 50–51; and the founding of Mother Zion, 45; and the founding of the New York African Society for Mutual Relief, 83; and the founding of the Wilberforce Philanthropic Association, 86; and Freemasonry, 113; houses Manhattan's African Chapel, 46, 47; and the rise of the Asbury Church, 49

Ministers' Mutual Assistance Society (Manhattan), 85

Mintz, Sidney, 11

Mirror of Liberty, 148

Missionaries, 31, 35, 52, 106, 136, 144, 160, 165, 171, 173, 175–76, 282n; blamed for insurrection in Jamaica, 42; women's dominance of black missions, 212–17

Mississippi, 203

Mitchell, Henry H., 30

Monitor League (San Juan Hill, Manhattan), 209

Monroe, James, 93

Montreal, 137

Montserrat Benevolent Association (New York City), 194

Montserrat Progressive Society (New York City), 206

Moore, Fred, 194

Moore, George, 134; and the founding of Mother Zion, 45

Moralism, 80–82; and black elitism, 79, 81–82, 86, 199; and black masculinity, 121–22, 123–25, 129, 133; of black voluntary associations, 80–83, 84, 86–87, 88, 97, 204, 208; declines in the NYASMR, 191; in English working-class associations, 242n; equated with whiteness, 78–79, 81

Moral reform, 79–80, 82–83, 96, 103, 104, 109–10, 113, 147, 161, 163, 164, 177, 266n; defined, 79–80; evidence of, 89, 92, 133, 151–52, 157, 168; internationalization of, 147; Sojourner Truth on, 128

Moravian church, 34

Morgan, Edmund S., 71

Morgan, William, 112

Moses, Wilson Jeremiah, 155

Mother Bethel Methodist Church (Philadelphia), 37

Mother Zion Church (African Methodist Episcopal Zion Church of Manhattan), 38, 40, 49, 59, 87, 88, 89, 91, 94, 101–2, 123, 172–73, 197; burial ground, 47, 101, 228n; founding of, 45–48, 52, 59, 84–85, 233n; and *Freedom's Journal*, 148; guarantees black male governance, 48; inspiration from the biblical account of the City of Zion, 47, 252n; relationship to Masonry, 113–16, 211; relationship to the Methodist Episcopal Church of New York, 48, 50–51; schisms within, 49,

Mother Zion Church *(continued)*
246–47n; white hostility towards, 49;
white interference limited in, 48
Mulattos, 21, 34–35, 83, 141, 186
Mullin, Michael, 19
Muraskin, William Alan, 78–79, 111, 116,
198
Murray, Rufus, 197
Murray, Simon, 51
Muslims, 10, 28, 83, 208; Hausa, 28
Mutual Aid Society of St. Mark's Church
(New York City), 216
Mutual Relief Association of New York,
189
Myrdal, Gunnar, 199, 205

Nail, John B., 194, 209
Nail, John E., 194–95, 209
Nail and Parker Realty (Harlem), 195
Nash, Gary, 10, 41, 103
Natal, 265n
National Afro-American Council, 214
National Association for the Advancement
of Colored People, 194, 215
National Association of Colored Women,
214–15, 216
National Baptist Convention, Woman's
Auxiliary of the, 213
National Colored Conventions, 130, 153,
155, 157, 161–65 166, 167–69; ideologi-
cal differences between the Manhattan,
Philadelphia, and Boston delegations at,
164–65, 167–69; New York African soci-
eties' influence on, 161–65, 167–69
National Federation of Afro-American
Women, 214
National League of Colored Women, 214
National Watchman (Albany-Troy), 148
Native Americans, 17, 21, 22, 34, 35, 90, 97,
232n; religious missions to, 39
Natural rights philosophy, 56–57, 58, 59,
62, 89, 94
Neau, Elias, 34
Negro Board of Trade (Harlem), 195
Negro Burial Ground. *See* African Burial
Ground (Manhattan)
Negro History Association of New York
City, 197
Nell, William C., 130
New Amsterdam, 15

Newark, 161
New Bedford, Massachusetts, 135
Newburgh, New York, 84
New England, 23, 30, 32, 63, 65, 69, 72, 115,
128, 153, 185, 223n, 236n
New England Anti-Slavery Society,
264–65n
New Era (Washington, D.C.), 133, 217
New Haven, 51
New Haven ferry, 184
New Jersey, 24, 30, 63, 115, 125, 137, 138,
161, 190
New Netherland, 13–15, 34, 150, 156
Newport African Union Society (Rhode
Island), 37
Newspapers, 132, 133; antislavery, 130, 135,
164; black (or opposition), 130, 132, 133,
135, 137, 143, 147–50, 152–53, 160, 164,
165; and proslavery violence, 145–46;
white, 149; workers', 149
Newton, Reverend John, 60, 62–63
New Town, Queens County, 17, 137
New Utrecht, Kings County, 34
New York Academy of Medicine, 140
New York African Clarkson Association,
74, 81, 93, 122, 127
New York African Institution, 80
New York African Marine Fund, 47, 74, 87,
127
New York African Society (NYAS), 2, 42,
53, 64, 74, 83, 88, 103; relationship to
black church, 38, 47, 52, 73
New York African Society for Mutual Relief
(NYASMR), 47, 59, 74, 77, 78, 79, 81,
83–87, 88, 89, 91, 93, 94, 95–96, 125–26,
129–37, 138–40, 145, 160, 173, 213,
254n, 264–65n, 267–68n, 272–73n;
African Society Hall and other meetings
houses of, 105–6, 114, 122, 130, 152, 156,
193, 196; Civil War–era activities, 183;
constitution of, 84, 86, 105, 119, 202,
245n; defrauding of, 276n; Draft Riot attacks on members of, 183–86; dues exemption for soldiers, 270n; effect of
Draft Riots on, 186, 271n; enslaved and
emancipated members of, 84–86, 243n,
249n; folding of, 197; founding and incorporation of, 103–6, 154–55; and the
founding of Boyer Masonic Lodge,
111–15; foreign-born men in, 187–88,

Parker, Henry C., 195
Parker, John, 203
Patriarchy, 121, 123, 129
Patterson, Orlando, 30, 32
Paul, Reverend Thomas, 48
Pauw, Michael, 150
Payne, William Oscar, 208
Pennington, Reverend J. W. C., 135, 137,
146, 148, 158, 173, 265n; in Under-
ground Railroad, 166
Pennsylvania, 24, 115, 116, 138
People's Press (Troy) 148–49
Perlman, Daniel, 78
Perry, Lewis, 68
Peru, 19–20
Petersburg, 201
Peterson, Reverend John, 117, 131, 134,
139, 147, 160, 183, 185, 270n
Peyton, Redmond, 197
Phi Beta Sigma, 207, 210
Philadelphia, 51, 62, 122, 130, 136, 199,
214, 242n, 253n; benevolent societies in,
36, 37, 53, 87, 103, 117; Cedar Ward, 103;
and the National Colored Conventions,
161–65
Philadelphia Library Company and Debat-
ing Society, 117
Philippines, 208
Philips, Dr. George, 140
Phillips, Wendell, 263n
Philomathean Hall (Manhattan), 117, 130,
156, 268n
Philomathean Literary Society (Manhat-
tan), 117–18, 129–30, 138–39, 147
Philomathean Lodge, No. 646, New York
City, 75, 117
Phoenix Hall (Manhattan), 130, 156, 267n
Phoenix Literary Society (Manhattan), 74,
124–25, 130, 135, 136, 138, 144, 148, 162
Piersen, William D., 4, 30
Pietist, 55
Pirrson, William, 125–26
Pittsburgh, 130
"Plutarch," 127
Pontier, Samuel, 46
Poro society, 13, 21, 37, 123
Portugal, 16, 28; customs of, 38
Portugis, Anthony (enslaved African appel-
lant of 1644), 13–14
Potter, James, 53

Powell, Reverend Adam Clayton, Jr., 209
Powell, Reverend Adam Clayton, Sr., 194,
211
Powell, William, 119, 131, 146, 153, 156,
159, 263n, 271n; biography of, 264–65n;
civil rights work, 271n; Draft Riot at-
tacks upon, 183–85; emigration of,
171–73; returns to United States, 182
Powell, William, Jr., 182
Preachers' Mutual Benefit Society of the
African Methodist Episcopal (Zion)
Church in America, 85, 243n. *See also*
African Methodist Episcopal Zion de-
nomination; Rush, Bishop Christopher
Presbyterian church, 34, 132, 209, 247n
Price, Henry, 115
Price, Richard, 11
Prince (enslaved leader of the 1741 conspiracy), 24
Prince Hall Grand Lodge (Massachusetts),
135; origins, 115; warrants New York
City's first four lodges, 113
Prince Hall Masonry, 78–79, 80, 93, 119,
134, 135–36, 138, 139, 174, 191, 193, 195,
198–99, 204, 206, 207–8, 209; African
Lodge, No. 459, 115, 148; among
Caribbeans in New York, 206; in antebellum civil rights, 268n; and antislavery,
113–14, 119, 146; entrance into Manhattan and Brooklyn, 111–16; involvement
in banking and insurance, 205; military
lodge, 182; relationship to the black
church, 113–17, 210–11
Protestant ethic, 55–56; antislavery implications of, 56–59, 62, 67; and the "calling," 55, 56; defined, 55–56; impact on
labor, 55–59, 236n
Protestantism, 11, 23, 34, 35, 40, 55, 64, 68,
71, 174, 208; and Antimasonry, 112; and
antislavery, 56, 58, 60–61, 87; civil versus
sacred authority in, 68; dissent tradition
within, 71–72; and fanaticism, 71, 106;
labor imagery in, 55–59, 62, 67,
235–36n; Karl Marx on, 64; and separatism, 71; and witch hunts, 71
Providence, Rhode Island, 136, 213, 267n
Providence Island, 20
Providence Temperance Society, 246n
Provident Society (Manhattan), 109
Public sphere, 103, 104, 119, 121–22, 123;

Voluntary associations, 1–5, 12, 78, 82, 87, 200–201, 265n; black state associations among migrants, 206; in Caribbean and South America, 83, 123, 186; and the creation of black neighborhoods, 101–3; defined, 1–2; English, 110, 278n; functions of, 1–2, 40–41, 47, 53, 78–79, 81–82, 83, 89, 95–96, 97, 103, 110, 117, 121, 123, 125, 141, 161, 197, 202–4, 206, 207, 209, 211–17, 265n; illegal functions of, 103, 110, 118, 119; labor, 109, 110; mulatto, 141, 186; mutualism and other values of, 77, 79–83, 86–87, 88, 103, 123, 133, 154–57; national associations among black immigrants, 206; origins of insurance in, 205; Roman, 110; secrecy within, 83, 88, 103, 108, 110, 111, 122, 201; spiritual and benevolent societies among black people in the United States, 36–38, 64, 73–81, 88, 140–41, 194, 201–5; unisex, 87, 88; white, 106–8; women's, 2, 5, 87, 88, 93, 97, 103, 118, 123, 212–17
Voodoo, 28

Wake, Ransom, 139, 160, 174
Wakeley, Reverend J. B., 43
Walker, Madame C. J., 194
Walker, David, 148; *Appeal to the Coloured Citizens*, 167–68, 170–71
Wall Street, 133
Walls, Bishop William, 39, 45–46, 52, 113, 116, 197
Walters, Bishop Alexander, 192
Ward, Philip, 86
Ward, Reverend Samuel Ringgold, 134, 136–37, 141, 142–43, 156; journalism of, 148
War of 1812, 128, 256n
Warren, Walter B., 271n
Washington, Booker T., on the NYASMR, 192
Washington, D.C., 131, 135, 136, 176, 211, 214
Washington, General George, 29, 122, 169, 221n
Washington, Joseph R., Jr., 10, 31, 44, 52, 110
Watkins-Owens, Irma, 206
Webb, Thomas, 42, 44, 63, 85

Weber, Max, 55
Webster, D. Macon, 193
Weekly Advocate, 138; renamed the *Colored American*, 148
Weekly Anglo-African, 148, 152
Weeks, James, 102
Weeksville (Brooklyn), 102; during Draft Riots, 185
Weisenfeld, Judith, 216
Wells, Ida B., 214
Wesley, Reverend Charles, 39–40, 41, 56
Wesley, Reverend John, 39–40, 41, 42; antislavery arguments of, 56–59, 62; on independence of American church, 44; influence of, 45, 60, 85, 90, 92; *Thoughts upon Slavery*, 56–58, 72
Wesleyan Church (Philadelphia), 51
Wesleyan College, 134
Westchester County, 18, 30
West Indian Federation (New York City), 206
West Indian Forum (New York City), 206, 216
West Indians, 23, 76, 77, 132, 188, 194, 196, 216, 280n; benevolent associations and fraternities in New York, 194, 206, 272n
West Indies, 23, 27, 52, 132, 174, 175–76, 188, 272n
Wheatley, Phillis, 72, 238n; "On Being Brought from Africa to America," 65
Wheeler, Noyes, 183
Whigs, 268n
White, Deborah Gray, 214
White, George: and the founding of Mother Zion, 45; relationship to Richard Allen, 51
White, Dr. Philip A., 140, 208, 213
White, Reverend Sampson, 131, 132, 173
White, Shane, 77, 103
White, William, 53
Whitefield, Reverend George, 42
Whitehead, Elizabeth, 101
Whitehead, John, 101
White House, the, 194
White people, 63, 92–93, 95, 97, 103, 137; attacks upon colonial, 16–20, 22–25, 27–30; colonial, 14, 25, 31, 32, 34–35, 65; described and judged, 89, 94, 161, 168, 170–71, 173, 189, 263n, 267–68n; and Freemasonry, 112–13; hostilities of, 89,

White people *(continued)*
101–2, 104, 105, 122, 136, 158; interference of, 81, 159, 165; at the National Colored Conventions, 165; philanthropy and concerns of, 42–43, 59, 79, 105, 124, 185–86; racism of, 44–50, 88, 101–3, 121–22, 134, 136, 142–46, 149, 156–57, 162–63, 181, 183–85, 199, 248n, 282n; reform among, 88, 106–8; scholarly and other privileging of, 2–3, 10–11, 31–32, 78–79, 81, 111, 121, 155–56, 170–71, 187, 198–200, 219n; servants, 21, 232n
White Rose Association (Manhattan), 214–15; Clarksville, Tennessee, home 215
Wibecan, George, 192
Wigglesworth, Reverend Michael, 71
Wilberforce, William, 93
Wilberforce College, 215
Wilberforce Philanthropic Association (Manhattan), 48, 74, 86, 93, 121, 122, 126
Wilentz, Sean, 103
Wiley, Alice, 215
William of Orange, 108
Williams, Andrew, 101, 102
Williams, George H., 71
Williams, Henry, 243n
Williams, James S., 189, 274n, 277n
Williams, Julia, 247n
Williams, Mary, 85
Williams, Oliver, 209
Williams, Reverend Peter, Jr., 42, 76, 80, 85–86, 89–91, 94, 104, 125, 126, 131, 132, 134, 136, 143–44, 146, 147, 149, 161, 191, 213; and the American Anti-Slavery Society, 266n; and the NYASMR, 244n
Williams, Peter, Sr., 42–44, 85, 144, 232n; and the founding of Mother Zion, 45, 46, 47; and the independent A.M.E.Z. denomination, 50
Williams, Robert F., 129
Williams, T. Desmond, 108
Williams, William, 86
Williamsburg (Brooklyn), 88, 128, 140, 151, 166–67, 172, 268n
Williamsburg ferry, 185
Williamsburg Union Temperance Benevolent Society, 88, 166–67
Williamson, Henry "Harry" Albro, 101, 114, 134, 207

Wilson, Lloyd, 197
Wilson, William J., 176, 178; "Ethiop," 153
Wilson, Woodrow, 194
Woman's Home and Foreign Missionary Society (Methodist), 213
Women, 2, 13–14, 46, 57, 58, 120, 127, 145, 151, 160, 182, 186, 206, 207, 282n; black women's club movement, 212–17; black working-class, 175, 215, 216; dominance in black churches of New York, 45, 48–49, 129, 212–17; dominance in black Christian domestic and foreign missions, 212–17; Draft Riot attacks upon black, 183, 184, 185; role in moral reform movements, 124, 148, 257n; in societies, 20–21, 87, 97, 118, 123, 127–29, 206, 207, 212, 247n, 257n; and spread of evangelicalism in the Caribbean, 58, 232n
Women's Baptist Home Mission Society, 215
Women's Loyal Union of New York and Brooklyn, 214, 215
Wood, Betty, 31, 40, 58
Wood, Fernando, 176
Wood, Forrest G., 11, 33–34, 47
Woodhull, Caleb S., 172
Woods, George, 158
Woods, J. Hoffman, 277n
Woodson, Carter G., 10, 12, 31–32, 209
Woolman, Reverend John, 58, 93
Wright, Reverend Theodore S., 94, 128, 144, 165, 166, 167, 170, 171

Young, Bishop George Benjamin, 201
Young Men's Christian Association, 195
Young Women's Christian Association, 216, 217

Zambia, 13
Zamora, Emilio, 82, 103
Zimbabwe, 226n
Zion Baptist Church (Manhattan), 171, 233n
Zuille, John J., 139, 171, 174, 267–68n, 273n; attempts to save the NYASMR, 191; death of, 191, 274n; influence in Brooklyn, 166; as publisher, 148, 149, 268n; in Underground Railroad, 166, 171

About the Author

Craig Steven Wilder is associate professor of History and chair of African-American Studies at Williams College. He is the author of *A Covenant with Color: Race and Social Power in Brooklyn* (2000).